Praise for Ma

Above all, MacGibbon celebrates her resilience and her willingness to keep laughing. She goes in swinging, and from the first vivid scene, it's clear that she is a natural comedian and a wonderful storyteller. As she tackles her difficult adolescence and young adulthood, she seems to ask, "What else ya got?"

—*Foreword Clarion Reviews* ★★★★★

Being a huge fan of Marti MacGibbon's first memoir, *Never Give in to Fear*, I am happy to say that the prequel, *Fierce, Funny and Female*, does not disappoint! It hits the ground running and never stops. Understanding where Marti came from is intense but her journey is so inspiring, with humor in exactly the right places so that you can't put the book down. The spirit of this book offers hope and encouragement to anyone who feels lost in the system...a story for anyone who wants equality for themselves, their daughters, wives or mothers.

—*Karen Rontowski, comic,*
David Letterman and Comedy Central

Marti's story is so strong and personal that it is impossible not to be enthralled. As she speaks and entertains, she moves around the room utilizing humor and reality in the perfect balance. Marti has the incredible ability to make both urban 9th graders and their mid-50s teachers laugh involuntarily and then moments later, think deeply about what is important for their respective future moving forward...she delivered a message that will not be forgotten.

—*Brian W. Moore, Social Studies Teacher,*
Holmes High School, Covington, KY

Marti MacGibbon is a dynamic, motivating, and effective facilitator. She provides great insight, and her personality definitely is an asset and her energy resounds...Ms. MacGibbon has a unique ability to be entertaining, professional, humorous, motivational, and informative all in the same presentation.

—Jenny Felt,
Department of Human Services, State of Iowa

Thank you for sharing your experiences and your humor with us. The entire room roared with laughter at some of your antics. You are such an enjoyable speaker. I do not believe I have ever seen our crowd give a standing ovation to anyone, yet at the end of your presentation, all were on their feet! I believe you could have had their attention for another hour!

—Donna Henry, RN, BSN,
Senior Vice President of Residential and Clinical Services,
Four County Counseling Center, Logansport, IN

Our goal was for staff to feel inspired, rejuvenated, to laugh a lot and enjoy the day. Marti was able to produce those results with her energy and humor. The audience was laughing out loud and even crying with laughter at times. Not only was she funny, but her story of how she overcame barriers in her life was inspirational.

—Shelly Todd, Staff Services Analyst,
Health and Human Services Agency, Napa, California

Ms. MacGibbon provides exactly what she advertises, and does so with great authenticity and enthusiasm. I would highly recommend Marti MacGibbon as keynote speaker for other audiences of mental health professionals.

—Brittany Yates, MSN, APRN, FPMHNP-BC,
American Psychiatric Nurses Association – Kentucky

The presentation you gave was articulate, impassioned, well informed, and humorous but real world—it was an incredible testimony of hope and life...Rarely does our speaker get a standing ovation, which you were given spontaneously for several minutes!

—*James Lemons, M.D., Professor of Pediatrics,*
Indiana University School of Medicine

The audience hung on her every word, both because her story was clearly so authentic, and also because she told it with such expert care. I would make this recommendation based on Marti's storytelling ability alone. But perhaps most importantly, her story and the way she tells it is one of empowerment.

—*Luke Blocher, Director of National Strategic Initiatives,*
National Underground Railroad Freedom Center

Thanks again Marti for your presentation and the work that you do. You are an inspiration of strength and courage. Shame and blame can easily take over one's life and create a rock solid barrier to overcome, but with the work you do, others can see a way to break the trauma barriers.

—*Peggy Surbey, MSW, Director/Regional Manager,*
Indiana Department of Child Services Marion County

Marti MacGibbon's presentation deeply touched everyone on my staff: clinicians, disease intervention specialists, and support personnel at all levels. The combination of humor and tragedy motivated all of us to a higher awareness and a dedication to those entrapped in a world wrapped in pain.

—*Janet N. Arno, M.D.,*
Associate Professor of Clinical Medicine,
Indiana University School of Medicine,
Director: Bell Flower Clinic

Marti MacGibbon is a speaker like no other! Her amazing story of hurtling great obstacles and moving into a life of prosperity and success is what makes Marti someone worth listening to. She uses humor (she is also a standup comic) and emotion to show others how they can change their professional and personal lives for the better. Your group will laugh, cry and make those positive changes in their lives.

—Pam Lontos, Consultant,
Author of "I See Your Name Everywhere",
Pam Lontos Consulting, Orlando, Florida

Marti MacGibbon was one of the most fascinating guests we've ever had on the show...Even though we're a sports talk station, I'm always looking for guests who are interesting—Marti is certainly that! Her stories are captivating; her delivery keeps the audience listening; and her positivity is nothing short of amazing. She's an interview that will be remembered by our listeners for a long, long time!

—Marc Hochman,
Host of "Hochman and Zaslow Morning Show"
AM 790 and FM 104.3 The Ticket
(ESPN Radio Affiliate), Miami

FIERCE, FUNNY, AND FEMALE

A JOURNEY THROUGH MIDDLE AMERICA, THE TEXAS OIL FIELD, AND STANDUP COMEDY

Marti MacGibbon

Copyright © 2017, Marti MacGibbon

ISBN: 978-0-9860067-3-9

Library of Congress Control Number: 2015906299

Printed in the United States of America.

CONTENTS

ACKNOWLEDGMENTS

Infinite thanks to my husband, Chris Fitzhugh: you are the love of my life, you've got the heart of a lion, and you've stood by me since we met in 1987. Thank you Yvonne Dauphin, for your insightful editing, and your wonderful sense of humor. Deepest respect and gratitude to all those who get back up when they get knocked down, rise to meet each challenge and setback, laugh in the face of adversity, and never, ever give up. You're my kind of people!

Photos of me during the time I worked in the Texas oil patch.

PROLOGUE

THE WRONG SIDE OF THE FENCE

I hit the dirt, facedown in the grassy pasture, bullets buzzing over-head. *Whoa! Now I know what it feels like to be shot at...*I turned my head to the left, a few yards downhill all five of my coworkers lay prone, heads down. Hearing even more ammo zinging by, I lifted my head just enough to catch a glimpse of two redneck farmers in the distance, silhouetted by the late afternoon sun, shouldering their rifles and taking aim.

"Marti, GIT YER HEAD DOWN AN' KEEP IT DOWN!" Scott hollered. "These RANCHERS think we're ESCAPED CONVICTS!"

Wow. We ARE pretty close to Huntsville. Scott'd told me about the Penitentiary. His brother was doing five-to-ten for possession.

Roger, the crew's leader, weighed in, his hoarse bark emphatic. "JIMMY JOE, grab your GODDAM WALKIN' STICK an' TIE some flaggin' on it AN' WAVE THE SUMBITCH AROUND as high as you can without gettin' y' HAND blown off, so they can see we're with the COMP'NY! We're on the wrong side o' the fence, remember?"

Jimmy Joe moved lightning-quick, like a cobra—amazing con-sidering how stoned he was. Earlier that afternoon in the woods, he'd fashioned the walking stick from a tree branch in order to keep from staggering. In milliseconds, the fluorescent orange flagging was waving in the air like a neon Cheetos-brand flag of truce, and the rustic snipers momentarily ceased fire.

Suddenly, I tore off my baseball cap, shook out my long blond hair and jumped up, waving the cap frantically at the paused shooters.

I threw off my jacket for good measure, hoping that, even though I was dressed in a work shirt, just like the guys, the hayseed infantry might recognize my female form and hesitate before gunning me down.

The ranchers shouldered their rifles and broke into a run, rapidly closing the distance between us, one of them shrieking at the top of his lungs, "IS THAT A GUUUURRRRLLLL?" When the yokel militia jogged within earshot, Roger stepped up and introduced himself as our crew chief.

The leathery gun-toters snorted derisively. Both wore Bull Durham ball caps, Wrangler jeans, western shirts, and denim jackets. The one with the beer belly spat tobacco juice on the ground and barked, "Don' y'all know yer s'pose to stay on the other side o' the fence? Y'all damn near gotcherselves killed, y'know that? We get a bounty fer every escaped convict—dead or alive, it don' matter! Heh. Heh..."

"Yep. That's raht. Good thing we seen you had a gal along. We shoot first an' ask questions later," growled the other rancher, the leaner and more menacing of the two. He turned, jabbed a gnarled finger in my direction and rasped, "Hey there MISSY, what're YOU doin' way out here?"

I met his jaundiced gaze with what I hoped was a steady, stone-cold stare, but inwardly, I wavered. *Yeah...Come to think of it, what AM I doin' out here?*

Of course, it only took a second to remember what I was doing way out there in the sticks: working in the Texas oil field, one of the last bastions of male supremacy. Thanks to this new career I now earned a decent wage—a man-sized paycheck. And I had some deeper, more personal reasons, too, in that I was driven by a broken heart, but I pushed my emotions down and consciously toughened up my vibe. I was in for the long haul. I'd need plenty of money to hire an attorney for the fight of my life. Remembering steeled my resolve and sharpened my focus.

CHAPTER 1

BUGS BUNNY, THE CORN BELT, AND THE YELLOW BRICK ROAD OF ADOLESCENCE

DEEP DOWN, I'VE ALWAYS BEEN FIERCE, BUT DIDN'T COME TO grips with that till later on. Funny's different. My earliest memories revolve around funny stuff: laughing at funny stuff and getting in trouble for laughing too much. By the time I was six, I knew for sure I wanted to be a comedian. I knew I was funny, and since I was a rebel even back then, I never let the Dominican nuns at elementary school cramp my style. Whenever possible, I watched standup comics on television, especially the very few females in the comedy prime time scene. I checked out joke books from the library and studied them intently. Soon I began producing original material, comedic monologues or parodies of commercials that I performed first for my parents, then for my friends and their parents—and the cool thing is, I actually got laughs. The laughs hooked me. I wrote a sitcom script in second grade, and tried to get Sister Mary Elizabeth to greenlight my production. I planned on producing, directing, casting, and playing a major role, but she killed it right outta the gate...she said the family depicted in my script was not a good Catholic family. Hell, I modeled it after the Honeymooners and Bugs Bunny cartoons, with lots of sarcasm and conflict—that's the way I viewed life, even at that tender age. But it didn't play with the convent crowd.

Finally convinced that the nuns were simply too square to get my humor, I focused all my energy on the neighborhood, cultivating the loyal following I'd built up around the cul de sacs and carports in my little corner of the suburban Corn Belt. I grew up in Middle America, far from the bright lights and glamour of New York and L.A., but oh, how I longed to get to one of those two show biz Meccas. Looking back now, it's revealing to recall my determination, my hunger and thirst to get in front of an audience and throw out some punchlines. Funny is fierce; it's badass, a force to be reckoned with. Standup comedy is martial, you can tell by the lexicon of the trade—terms like "punchline," for instance. Backstage, after a set, comics comment on their performances with, "I killed," "I bombed," "I crushed," "I died," "killer set," "I blew the roof off." It's a certain kind of badassery.

Along with Marilyn, another funny kid who lived in the neighborhood, I co-wrote, co-produced, co-directed, and starred in a one-hour sketch comedy show. Marilyn and I cast our friends in some of the sketches, and we created props and scenery. None of this shit was Golden Globes caliber, or even Peoples' Choice level, but for second graders it rocked. We packed the house—well, it was a carport, and the audience sat in folding chairs in the driveway, but still. The show killed! And we made some money. Tickets were fifty cents, and we sold refreshments (popcorn and cookies our moms made) at intermission. Fucking amazing.

I was always fierce, but focused on funny. About two weeks into first grade at St. Agnes School, the Dominican sisters began the process of squelching my nascent ferocity by suspending me from school for a day. Like many a prison movie, the riot had broken out in the yard, so to speak. I was out on the playground at recess, swinging on the swing set. Behind me I heard screams, so I jumped off, tucked, rolled, and rose to a crouch in my shiny patent leather shoes. Whirling toward the shrill cacophony of my female classmates, I saw dozens of girls stampeding, thundering across the playground in adrenaline-fueled panic. I grabbed one of them by the arm as they sped past. "Hey! Why are you running?"

She stopped, gasping for breath, and looked back over her shoulder. "The boys! They're chasing us—if they catch you, they knock you down and pull up your dress and then, um, they PULL YOUR UNDERWEAR DOWN!!" She bolted away, gibbering in terror.

I couldn't figure out why they were running. There were almost twice as many girls as boys in our class. We had them outnumbered! I shouted at the top of my lungs, hoping to rally the troops for a counterattack. "HEY! ALL YOU GIRLS!! WE DON'T HAVE TO STAND FOR THIS! C'MON, FOLLOW ME!" I spun, turned to face the pack of boys. Three of them had knocked down a pigtailed girl in a plaid dress with a lacy white collar. She was crying, I could see her face turning redder and redder. Furious, and pumped with adrenaline, I charged, hollering a spontaneous battle cry. "BOMBS AWAAAYYY!"

Running full-speed into the fray, I instinctively zeroed in on the biggest kid, the ringleader, a dentist's son with red hair and freckles. I slammed into him head-on, knocked him onto his back, then jumped on his chest. Sitting astride him I pounded my fists on his face, chest, and shoulders. At that point, two nuns appeared out of nowhere, pulled me off, and dragged me away. Punishment proved swift. They called my mom and sent me home. But when I told my folks my side of the story, they laughed it off and told me not to do it again.

To the nuns who steered me through the primary grades, I was probably a challenge, if not an outright pain in the ass. I talked too fast, laughed too loud, and asked troublesome questions. "Why don't they let women be priests?" They hated that one. The first time I asked that one, good ol' Sister Mary Elizabeth practically foamed at the mouth.

She fixed me with a disapproving stare. "Shame on you, little one! ALL of the WARS in the WORLD were caused by WOMEN WHO DIDN'T KNOW THEIR PLACE! See that you know yours. Pray to God, that he may SHOW you your PLACE!!!" She shook her finger at me several times for emphasis.

No way could I buy the questionable bill of goods Sister Mary Elizabeth was slinging. But I wondered at her rabid fury at my question. So I brought it up at the dinner table that night. My parents looked at each other and tried to stifle their laughter. My father, a professor, used the opportunity to present a sort of Cliff Notes, G-rated version of what caused WWI, WWII, and the ongoing Cold War. I was relieved to know that my instincts had been correct: Sister Mary Elizabeth's worldview was skewed.

Dad was totally cool. He always gave me the straight stuff, but on my level. My mom assured me that someday women would be astronauts, senators, maybe even presidents. But she couldn't guarantee me that they'd get to be priests. Then both of my parents, possibly as an afterthought, rolled out the respect-the-nuns-and-pay-attention-in-class-you-get-a-better-education-in-parochial-school theme. They encouraged me to keep on taking the nuns' cray-cray comments with a grain of salt.

I mulled it over a moment. "Okay. I wanna be in show business, anyway. Comedy. Or an archaeologist. Or an astronaut." Astronaut was my third choice, since the Space Program, in its infancy at the time, didn't seem all that promising.

Toward Christmas of second grade, I took one last run at cracking the Catholic school show biz circuit. Our class was slated to do the Nativity Play, and the third graders would be attending. Sister Mary Elizabeth cast a petite brunette named Mary Jane Hays as the Blessed Virgin—a docile, ponytailed girl who apparently knew her place in the world—and a handsome blond boy named Jim Jasper as the long-suffering Joseph. Okay, when Mary Jane landed the coveted Madonna part, hopes for the Best Actress Oscar took wing and departed my young soul, but still, I champed at the thespian bit.

And I was tenacious, stayed the course. I tried out for angel, but Sister Mary Elizabeth was only auditioning kids who could sing for that slot. *Dang!* I took a swing at shepherd, even though it was a traditional male role, but struck out. Crestfallen, I slogged home through the snow after school, racking my brain for an answer, for a way to slake my thirst for the stage. Applause, bright lights, Broadway hits, rave reviews, all of that and more danced in my brain, a vision that drove me.

I knew Sister Mary Elizabeth regarded me with suspicion. I wrote left-handed, and she'd tried to break me of that during the first week of school that year. "My child, you MUST learn to write right-handed before it's TOO LATE! Left-handed people turn out to be THIEVES!!!" I resisted her, bearing in mind the bat-shit opinions of the convent crowd, but she continued to nag me relentlessly. Finally, my parents intervened, and now my relationship with the obviously disturbed, medievally-oriented nun was an uneasy one, at best.

That night, I talked it over with my folks. My mom spoke up first. "Why don't you think about creating a role for yourself?"

My dad set down his coffee cup. "Yes! Let's have a look at the script."

The Nativity Play didn't really have a script; all I had to work with was the song lyrics. The whole thing was set to music. The Virgin Mary, Joseph, the shepherds and even the angels would be pantomiming or standing around like statues while the chorus sang narrative and dialogue. Anybody who didn't have a costumed role would be used as mere cannon fodder; we'd either be singing the chorus or sitting in the audience. And no way would I settle for sitting in the audience—not with my talent. During the first rehearsal, as we ran through the songs and their lyrics, I discovered a role for myself—as the ox. According to the play's lyrics, Mary and Joseph can't find a room at the inn, they're wandering in the cold, and there's a part where the ox calls out to them to come into the stable with the sheep and the rest of the posse. Of all the animals in this Nativity scene, the ox was the only character endowed with the power of speech—this wasn't ideal, not a glam role...but I definitely could work with it.

I took the initiative and created an ox costume that night. Mom gave me a piece of oil cloth that she used for a table cover when she worked on art projects. It was the color of the ox in our nativity set at home. And I constructed a paper mache' ox mask, complete with curving horns, which I painted with tempera paints. The next morning I hauled the completed ox getup to school. When I pitched my idea to Sister Mary Elizabeth, she reluctantly agreed.

I was a little kid, so of course it didn't occur to me to say, "Fuck it, it's show biz." But even though I hadn't acquired the vocabulary, "fuck it" was still pretty much my attitude. I did the ox thing and made a big entrance, working off-script at the last minute. As ox, during my seven-line chorus I exited the stable area and escorted the Holy Family to the manger, as if the ox had helpfully informed Mother Mary which of the barn furnishings might be the most comfortable for the Baby Jesus to sleep in. Sister Mary Elizabeth was annoyed, but I counted it as a win, since I'd played my role with style and poise. Besides, even if it'd bombed, the third graders wouldn't have been able to kick my ass on the playground later—the ox mask concealed my identity.

Seventh grade rocked—finally I'd made it to public school. Back then they put seventh, eighth, and ninth grade together and called it junior high. Placed in accelerated classes with all the smart kids, I hung out after school with the wilder kids who got lower grades but were regarded as "in crowd." Some of the eighth graders, the cool ones, accepted me as one of the pretty girls. I'd never thought of myself as pretty, but now I aspired to be cool. And in the daunting, vicious, kill-or-be-killed Serengeti atmosphere of early adolescence, pretty was cool.

Funny and cool began to wrestle for dominance as I stumbled through the grades, weird but well-liked. In ninth grade, I produced, wrote, directed, and performed in another comedy show. It was a satire of the Courtship of Miles Standish, an onerous, totally yawnsworthy 1858 poem by Henry Wadsworth Longfellow, involving a love triangle between some moldy old pilgrims in the sucktastic era of the Mayflower. The faculty approved the project for a Thanksgiving convocation, since it was based on a poem from curriculum. This sounds like a tough sell for my audience, but surprisingly, it killed. In one scene, I actually got a standing ovation.

We capped off the program with a pitch to save the turkeys— yes, I was ahead of my time with the animal rights there...any of my cast members who shared my shameless thirst for laughs joined me in the closer. We dressed up like turkeys, in costumes we made ourselves, consisting of scuba flippers spray-painted orange, football jerseys stitched with feathers made of crepe paper, and cardboard tail feathers. Oh yeah, and you know that thing dangling down from a turkey's beak? It's called a snood. Anyway, we wore cardboard beaks, and suspended red-painted rubber gloves from the beaks. As a sort of curtain call, we donned the crazy-ass poultry outfits, formed a chorus line, came out with some Rockettes-type high kicks, and sang a song whose lyrics pled for leniency on execution day. Believe it or not, it worked. Well, we didn't get slammed in lockers afterward, anyway. A popular jock, who was also very funny, was one of the dancing turkeys, and I was kinda badass too, so nobody fucked with us.

Okay, on with the coming of age story. Not all of it's funny, but that's okay...I'm not gonna sugarcoat it. My childhood went pretty smoothly, growing up on the prairie and all, but my adolescence turned out to be a far cry from Norman Rockwell-esque. All my aspirations, my dreams of being a comedian, blew out the window in the summer before my sophomore year. Strangely, I became obsessed with growing up fast, as fast as possible so I could move to California or New York and be part of the Age of Aquarius, or whatever. And my folks were not happy with that vision. At that point, as my childhood idol Bugs Bunny used to say, "I musta taken a wrong toin at Albuquoique." Things went to hell. My resulting stormy adolescence led to the events that broke my heart into a zillion tiny little bits.

And later, as an adult woman working in a badass man's job out there in the oil field, my heartbreak lay coiled like a rattlesnake in my subconscious mind, poised to strike at any moment of carelessness, any gap in my painstaking vigilance. Looking back now, I realize that my angst...wait a minute, let's be real here—my PTSD— kicked off with traumatic events during adolescence, some involving authority figures.

SUMMER OF 1969. I WAS NOW FIFTEEN YEARS OLD. STILL judging myself too young—or rather, lacking the rage—to shake off parental restraints and strike out for one of the coasts, I'd resigned myself to finding whatever experience of the cultural revolution that I could in the quiet Midwest town I called home. I yearned to be as high and wild and beautiful as the college students I saw in the news and read about in my parents' issues of Time Magazine.

Since 1964, mainstream radio'd been bringing me the Beatles, the Rolling Stones, and R & B greats like Aretha Franklin, Wilson Pickett, Marvin Gaye and Sam Cook. During the summer of

'69, the music of acid rock greats like the Doors, Jimi Hendrix, Cream, and Jefferson Airplane enthralled me. My hometown was so far buried in the backwater of Mid-America that my frustration at being a year or so behind the newest trends was palpable. Bobbi Ann, the girl who lived next door, turned me on to the local rock stars—our small town scene consisted of two garage bands whose front men, good looking guys with long hair, made us teenyboppers swoon, sigh, and yearn to join the beautiful Sixties counterculture.

Taking Bobbi Ann's lead, I began doing what she referred to as, "following the bands." She'd invite me over to spend the night, and we'd sneak out the window of her bedroom, go wherever either of the two main garage bands were playing, and join a bevy of very young girls, fellow fans who shared our obsession with these dudes. Nobody ever carded us or asked us our ages. No one seemed to notice or care; a failing on the part of adults that made me feel luxuriously hip, grownup, and sexy.

Bobbi and I also listened to rock albums together. She turned me on to Iron Butterfly, a band that has been called the first heavy metal band in American rock history. I bought a copy of their album, In-A-Gadda-Da-Vida, and listened to it in awe. The title song, "In-A-Gadda-Da-Vida," took up an entire side of the vinyl, a whopping seventeen-plus minutes in duration. Raised in an era when Top Forty hits averaged three minutes in length, the testosterone-laden opus, recorded in Paris, entranced me. When my folks weren't home, I'd play it on their stereo and crank up the volume, then stand in front of the speakers so I could feel the music vibrating through my body. I didn't realize it at the time, but I'd begun hurtling down a rocky descent into a fiery volcano of emotional and physical chaos—also known simply as adolescence. My hormones were racing, and I struggled to find an identity, any identity other than my child self.

One of the bands Bobbi and I sneaked out to see was a crew that called themselves, "Sorcery." These guys impressed us. They played mostly original songs and few covers, and their style, with a heavy bass line, a light show, wah-wah pedals, and synthesizer, reminded me of Iron Butterfly. Looking back now, I'm sure their music sucked big time, mostly wannabe and wah-wah. And Roddy Mack, the lead singer from Sorcery, wore black leather pants, and a black leather vest with no shirt underneath. Sleazebag—yeah, I know. But at fifteen, I thought he looked hardcore, dangerously hot, and badass. We live, we learn.

Bobbi Ann introduced me to her friend Tanya, who was older, drove a car, and changed her hair color often. Tanya and I started to talk on the phone, and soon I was hanging out with her and meeting some of her friends, who were older, faster, and wilder than Bobbi. One afternoon, at Bobbi's house, Tanya brought up the topic of Free Love. Bobbi squealed, bounced up and down on her bed, grabbed a framed photo of Jim Morrison, kissed it passionately and, with special care, set it back on her nightstand. "Oooh, it's groovy! I'm so glad I turned on."

Turned on? I thought turning on was dropping acid. WTF? I expressed my misgivings aloud. "Yeah? If you mean sex, I don't know if I'm ready for that." I felt myself blushing, and tried to save face. "Er, but I'd love to try LSD! For REAL!"

Bobbi's eyes widened. "Whaat?? You mean you haven't tried SEX yet?"

"No, uh, well, if you mean, 'Have I gone all the way,' well...no." I was starting to feel silly and immature—I'd kissed boys, but never let them touch my boobs, or put a hand past my knee. Strictly first base stuff.

Bobbi shot me a look. "It's a beautiful thing, man. When two people get it on."

"What about getting pregnant? That'd be the worst thing EVER!"

At this point, Tanya, designated woman of the world, possessor of a driver's license and big hoop earrings, weighed in. "You don't have to worry about getting pregnant if you pick the right guy. You gotta get it on with one who knows what he's doing."

Bobbi nodded, grinned at Tanya first, then me, then turned back to face Tanya, jerking a thumb in my direction. "Tell her, Tanya! Help her. She CAN'T stay like this, a VIRGIN?! She's FIF-TEEN already, for Chrissakes!!!!" Bobbi appeared to equate being a fifteen-year-old virgin with contracting small pox, leprosy, or bubonic plague.

Tanya twisted a strand of her hair around a finger and looked thoughtful. "Yes, we need to do something about this. I mean, you GOTTA get started, girl! Everybody's doing it."

"Really?"

Tanya burst out laughing. "Well...yeah!!! Whaddya think all the rock songs are saying in the lyrics? When Jim Morrison sings, 'C'mon baby, light my fire,' he's not inviting some dumbass Girl Scout to rub two sticks together and toast marshmallows with him!" She snorted, and Bobbi Ann lapsed into apoplectic giggles. Tanya turned her laser-like gaze on me again, her expression somber. "Sex is the MAIN THING! Even before drugs." She put her hands on her hips. "I'm gonna set you up with Roddy from Sorcery. I had my first time with him, and so did Bobbi, and plenty of other girls. He knows what he's doing, and nobody's gotten pregnant yet."

Bobbi nodded, wide-eyed. "Okay then. It's settled. Marti, we're gonna get you laid."

---

*L-L-LAID? OKAY. I GUESS...*IT TOOK ME A WHILE TO GET ADJUSTED to the idea. A sharp little warning, a stab of panic, rose up within me. Embarrassed at being such a scaredy-cat, I hurried home to drown my unease in rock music, and listened to Steppenwolf sing, "Why doncha come with me Little Girl...on a Magic Carpet Ride?" They seemed to be talking to me and other young chicks, I figured. *Are they talking to us, to...little girls? Hmph.* I sneaked into my big sister's room, snatched up her Ten Years After album, and closed my eyes while listening to Alvin Lee sing, "Good Morning Little Schoolgirl." *Schoolgirls...Little girl. Yep, guess I've been missin' out on the whole scene. Time to catch up with the Magical Mystery Tour and find out what everybody's talkin' about. And better to learn from an experienced adult than to fumble around in the back of a car and get pregnant...Right?*

I soon found out that Roddy Mack led a double life: Reigning local rock star by night, emerging high school teacher by day. Roddy was working at Tanya's high school that summer, teaching Science classes to the recalcitrant, lackluster audience comprised of kids mandated to make up time for failing grades or days lost to truancy. He wasn't a student teacher anymore, but was not yet fully certified and ready for full-time employment in education. "He's our Participant," Tanya told me. That was the term for it, "Participant." Well, Mr. Mack was participating in a hell of lot more than classes. By today's standards he was a full-fledged, balls out, serial child molester. But in the oblivious haze of the late Sixties, he managed to float under the radar, and as far as I know, he never got caught...at least, not in our town. I never turned him in, and neither did Tanya, Bobbi Ann, or any of the others I learned about later.

"You've got to ASK him," Tanya whispered. "THAT'S the deal." We walked briskly down the linoleum-tiled corridor of her school, late Friday afternoon sun filtering in through the open doorways on opposite ends of the building. Tanya stopped outside a classroom door. The bell had already rung, and a few stragglers slouched out of the room and meandered disconsolately down the hall toward the exit. Tanya signaled for me to wait; she seemed to be counting to ten, or a hundred—with my heart hammering in my chest, I lost track of time. Tanya gave my left shoulder a little squeeze, then a push forward. I drew a deep breath and strode into the room, shoulders back, head high. *I am in control...* Roddy was standing around in front of the desk, ruffling papers, obviously killing time. He looked up and saw me. Our eyes met, and I saw a flash of recognition in his eyes. *He's seen me in the audience, he's noticed me before.* I cleared my throat. "Um, um. I-I'm a virgin, and I don't want to be that way anymore. Tanya told me you should be the—the one."

I looked down at the floor, then back at him. At fifteen, I was only an inch shy of six feet tall, so I easily matched his stare, and saw a glint of—greed, anticipation, or...something I couldn't identify. He shot a furtive glance out into the hallway, rubbed his hands together, then released them to hang at his sides. "Uh, yeah, okay. Tell Tanya to bring you over—tonight. She knows what to do. Now, go on, before anybody sees you." He waved me away and turned to fidget around on his desk. *So...that's IT?* My rational mind began tossing objections at me, but the irrational, teenage, wanna-grow-up-wanna-grow-up-now-no-matter-what-it-takes impulse squelched every argument. I was cut loose, in the wind, flying blind, feeling panic mingled with cheap thrills, the kind I'd felt on carny rides like The Zipper, or The Mad Mouse roller coaster at the County Fair every summer leading up to this one. But THIS summer, I didn't care about carnival rides. I was wading in deep! *Maybe Roddy Mack will drop acid with me, too. After all, he's a rock musician. Who knows? Now, what story can I tell my parents on short notice?*

———

TANYA'S RED 1964 DODGE DART SHIMMIED AT 55 MPH, SO SHE took back roads to Roddy's—not one of the two-lane highways that, like the Yellow Brick Road of Oz, ultimately led out of our town to bigger, brighter, and shinier dreams. In the town where I grew up, our Emerald City was Chicago. I'd never been there, but now, seated in the red-and-white-vinyl-upholstered bucket seat of Tanya's Dart, I fantasized about running away and experiencing the excitement of the big city. Mom didn't like Tanya, so I'd fought valiantly to convince her to let me spend the night at her house. I'd finally told her Tanya and I would be babysitting her little brother, and that sewed it up. Tanya brought her nine-year-old bro along in the front seat when she picked me up at my house, sort of as a prop for my mom, who peered anxiously out the window—then we dropped him off at Tanya's. Her dad was home and only looked up from the television screen for a nanosecond when Tanya told him we'd be home late. He nodded, chugged the remainder of a Schlitz beer, then reached for the backup bottle he'd set up on the coffee table.

And that was all it took to unlock the gate to what was, by my naive young estimate, a nearly unlimited freedom. *Wow. I've got a date with a rock musician.* I stuck my hand out the open window into the sweet, hot, summer night air, felt the rushing wind caress my fingertips. "Hey Tanya, how old is Roddy? Like, twenty or twenty-one?" *Twenty-one's only six years older than me. Almost my age, even.*

"Roddy's twenty-six!" Tanya laughed softly, reached out, turned up the radio, then placed both hands on the steering wheel. Tonight, she'd painted her fingernails dark purple. Mine were just plain, no polish. I felt a flash of regret at not asking Tanya to do mine, but remembered my mom would have noticed, and that it was safer this way. *Twenty-SIX! Eleven years older...* I sat up straighter, tried to concentrate on older, more sophisticated topics to talk about with him when I got there.

Back then, I was a smart kid who'd been sheltered so that I lacked street smarts or any kind of Spidey sense about people. Completely devoid of even a hint of self-protective skill, I waltzed into his ramshackle double wide trailer home with breathless, youthful glee. Yes, Roddy Mack lived in a trailer on the outskirts of town. He shared the dump with three roommates around his age: a member of his band and two roadies. This leather-clad perp actually drove a windowless white Ford Econoline van, a conveyance now widely recognized as a creepmobile. Oh sure, he and the roommates shared the vehicle and used it to haul amps and other equipment to gigs, but puh-lease, can it get any more cliche? Later, I learned that one of Roddy Mack's nicknames was, "Captain Schoolyard." Sadly, my young self was oblivious to the many red flags.

––––––––––

Tanya entered the trailer without knocking, and I followed her in. Roddy Mack stood up from the rickety stainless steel dinette set, rubbing his hands together, his leer almost comical, and looked me up and down. He whirled around to address his roommates, who slouched on a saggy couch and a duct-taped Lazy-boy recliner. "Oooh! In a coupla minutes, THAT'S gonna be MINE!" He laughed, and the other men laughed, and he spun to face me again. "Yeah! C'mon, sit down."

I felt myself getting flustered, fought to keep my composure, took a step backward. Tanya spoke up. "Give her a break, Roddy." She sauntered toward the kitchen, opened one of the cabinets, pulled out two heavy glass A & W Root Beer mugs, hopped over to the freezer, and started filling the mugs with ice cubes. Then she motioned me to sit down beside her at the table and handed one of the mugs to me. Roddy approached, a bottle of Ripple wine in each hand, and began pouring. Tanya leaned in close. "Drink plenty of that, it'll help you relax." Then she put her mouth next to my ear and whispered, "Get drunk, and it'll make you nice and...it won't hurt a bit." Ripple was an el-cheapo wine, akin to Thunderbird, and not as well-known as the Boone's Farm of legend. I'd never heard of any of those brands till that night. In spite of Tanya's admonition, I only drank a few sips. I was too nervous, and too busy trying to disguise my nervousness with false bravado.

After a few minutes, a shirtless Roddy led me into his bedroom, which was adjacent to the kitchen. He pushed me up against the wall and unbuttoned my best white crepe blouse—I'd chosen it with care for this special occasion. His hands pawed at my bra. "Is that all you, girl, or is that padding?" I took off the blouse and folded it carefully, looking for a place to hang it up. He snorted, moved behind me, unfastened my bra, tossed it away, grabbed both breasts and squeezed. "Get outta those jeans before I rip 'em off ya." My face felt hot as I complied. He dropped his jeans—it was the first time I'd ever seen an erection. He entered me without foreplay, affection, lubrication, or protection. It hurt, and I felt ashamed. The walls in the trailer were paper thin, I could hear his roommates making rude comments about me from the kitchen. At one point, he stopped thrusting, turned his head toward the kitchen, and yelled, "Shut the fuck up!" through the rickety wall. His assault, my intended initiation to Flower Power—De-Flower-Power, rather—continued, briefly. Then a grunt, and he rolled off me.

"I use early withdrawal as birth control," Roddy'd announced prior to penetration. "I'll come on your stomach, then give you a towel to wipe it off." Now that he'd finished, he tossed me a dingy white towel. "Don't get any of that near your pussy." He groped my thigh. "Oooh. You are niiice. I can teach you some tricks...you could pull in twenty dollars a throw. Come see me next week and I'll give you another lesson." He stood up, flipped off the light, and walked out.

I wiped off my stomach, in shock, trying to comprehend the combination of feelings seeping in: emotional numbing, physical pain between my legs, and frantic feelings of rejection, disgust, insult. And rage, very real, but buried far too deeply for me to access to my advantage in the moment. *Is this all there is to it? So...is THIS sex? This is what they're all talking about?* I fought the urge to run, felt desperate to be cool, to salvage some kind of deluded perception that I was in control. *I've done it—done IT, now I am a grown woman. I need to act mature.* I hesitated, embarrassed to walk out into the kitchen, where I could hear muffled conversation, low chuckles. My breath caught in my chest, a choking sensation. I shivered, grabbed the sheet and wrapped it around me.

Footsteps...the door opened, the silhouette of a naked man filled the threshold. He entered the dark room. I hoped he would say something nice, do something kind, show me to the shower. I covered my face with my hands and lay face down on the bed, trying to gain my equilibrium. Some part of me still clutched at the childish hope that he'd see I was upset, and he'd try to cheer me up, be nicer. I squeezed my eyes shut as he mounted me, then forced himself inside me—a casual, dispassionate act. The pain in my genitals escalated from aching to searing. When it was over he got up and turned on the light, and I realized that this was not Roddy Mack. It was a guy named Chico, another member of the band who was the same size and build, and had the same color and length of hair as Roddy. In the darkness, backlit, I'd mistaken him for my "date." At that moment, my self-esteem withered, but I rallied and told myself I could come back from this.

"Hey Girl," Chico strutted back to the bed, sat down, and smoothed my hair away from my face. "Don't worry, I pulled out in time, came on your back. You're pretty—you really got me sexed up." He smiled, stood up, and left the room.

I wrapped a sheet around me, leaned out the bedroom door, took a step into the kitchen. Tanya was sitting stark naked at that crappy kitchen table with all of the guys, who were buck naked, except for Chico who'd donned a tiny pair of black bikini panties and was brandishing a hash pipe. He inhaled, and his crotch bulged out of the girlie undies. He noticed me standing there and leaned forward. "Hey Little Girl, wanna suck on my...pipe? He smirked, and everyone, including Tanya, hooted with laughter. "Naw, hey, I'm jus' playin' around, Honey. C'mon, drop that sheet an' siddown with us, an' get high." Roddy smiled and waved a hand my way, as if echoing his bandmate's invite, then stared drunkenly into space. My stomach lurched.

I kept the sheet on, sat down and took my first hit ever from a hash pipe, figuring I might as well get to experience some drugs, now that the sex and the rock n' roll'd failed me. I held in the smoke as long as I could stand it, but didn't feel even a hint of a buzz. *Bummer.* One of the roadies, a guy they called "Wolf," refilled the pipe and held a Zippo lighter over the bowl, coaxing the tiny nugget of dope to ignition, then filling his lungs. His hairy chest and back made him look ursine, a grizzly. Exhaling the hit, he knit his unibrow over the jutting occipital ridge that served as his forehead, as if struggling to prepare a snappy comment. "Y'all don' think I'm a ladies' man." He slammed a hammy fist on the table—it shivered under the impact. He grimaced at Roddy. "But yer DEAD WRONG! I got THREE illiterate chuldren back in Florida...from diff'runt wimmin!" He sat back, seeming satisfied, as if he'd established his cred as a lothario and passed the pipe to Sam, the other roadie.

I started to laugh, then stifled it, unsure whether or not Wolf was joking. "Er, you, uh, uhmm—you mean you've got three illegitimate children, right? Out of wedlock?"

The hirsute roadie curled his lips into a snarl. "That's WHUT I SAID, DAMMIT!"

"Uh, yeah, right...that's what you said..." I drummed my fingers on the table, distracted by the fleeting realization that Wolf had spoken truth. Of course his offspring would be illiterate—a dominant gene in his lineage. The kids' legitimacy was a moot point. If they were lucky, they'd never find out who'd sired them, and ignorance would indeed be bliss. If they were luckier still, they wouldn't inherit his unibrow, protruding forehead, and runaway body hair. Sarcasm boiled up in me, and with it, the urge to say something caustic, but I clamped a lid on it.

I might've been a naive, sheltered fifteen-year-old, but I knew better than to sit around that table for long. Still tightly clutching the sheet, I got up and walked away from what I didn't realize at the time was likely an orgy-in-progress. I found the shower, washed, and shampooed my hair with the dregs of a bottle of Prell that I found on the floor of the shower stall. I managed to find a clean towel to dry off with, and got dressed. Walking briskly into what passed for a living room in that dingy double-wide, I sat down on the couch and waited for Tanya. She was in Roddy's room for a short time, then came out fully dressed, jangling her car keys in her hand. "C'mon, Chick." She breezed past me, impersonal now, distancing herself from me in front of the men, acting like she barely knew me. And, true...she barely did.

On the way home, Tanya warmed up and engaged in some one-sided girl talk. "Well, naturally we swapped, right? I mean, they're close friends, and they look so much alike, Rod an' Chic, I mean..." (She pronounced it, "Cheek." Chico was Cheek, for short.) "They've got different styles in bed, of course." And blah, blah, blah. She was trying to get me to say whether I had a good time or not. Anxious to maintain my dimming bravura, I came up with something to say.

"Yeah, uh...yeah, it was fun," I lied, valiantly battling to believe my own words in hopes of preserving some concept of self. Tanya seemed energized, elated. I felt numb, and began to wonder if there might be something wrong with me, like I wasn't grownup enough to appreciate an adult party. "Yeah, it was COOL." I sat on my hands to keep from fidgeting.

She turned away from the road, faced me for a second, smirking. "Man, Marti...you came in wrapped up in that sheet! What were you doing?" She fixed her eyes on the road again, and we drove on in silence. Strangely, I didn't feel angry with Tanya. I felt nothing, abso-fucking-lutely nothing, so I determined to pump up my natural-born, fierce exuberance, and power on through. I started joking around, making Tanya laugh, and hearing the laughter I felt better. That's how I survived the night—by being funny.

My mother had warned me to be home before noon or I'd get grounded, so she looked visibly relieved when I walked in, carrying my little overnight case. I ran upstairs and unpacked, then collapsed on my bed. My sister was gone for the day and Dad had taken my little brothers out somewhere, leaving the house blessedly quiet. I wouldn't be forced to put on a show of normalcy—at least not till dinnertime, when the family'd assemble, so I figured I'd better hunker down and take a nap. Much needed sleep proved impossible due to the pain between my legs. I fended off worries that I'd gotten pregnant, but still felt tense as hell, and panicked when my mom called from downstairs. *She knows! I'm dead! Hey! How could she know??*

I crept down the staircase, stopped halfway, sat down on one of the stairs, peered into the living room, and hoped my mother couldn't see how sore and achy and shaken I felt. "You called me, Mom?"

She smiled at me. "Well, I've got a surprise. Let's go shopping. The Sidewalk Sales are on, and a couple of other places are having specials. We'll find you something new and fun for school."

The woman who was talking seemed distant, as if I'd never really seen her before. Sure, she was my mother, but now, things were different. She seemed alien, or maybe it was me. Emotional numbness set in again, and I smiled. "Sounds great! Thanks, Mom." And off we went to the store.

Looking back now, I think my mother sensed that something was wrong, she intuitively sensed my pain, and wanted to make it better by taking me shopping. My parents were very careful with money; my mother didn't often take us shopping. Mom made lots of our clothes growing up, and she was so talented that people thought they were store-bought. My sister and I learned to sew, too, and were able to augment our wardrobes with cool stuff that never looked homemade.

My shame and discomfort forgotten for a while, I found a nice summer dress for a low, low price. In the dressing room I fought the jittery sense of unease and managed to stop my hands from shaking when I stepped outside the fitting area to show her. "It's perfect!" Mom said, smiling, and for some reason I felt nervous, suspicious. Usually she was shushing me for joking around too much or laughing too loud. *Something's wrong. Yep, something's wrong, and...and it's me.* When we got home, she asked me to try the dress on again. "Put it on and wear it, Honey. Sometimes it's nice to get dressed up, just for fun." She sat down in an armchair, folded her hands in her lap.

"Alright, I'll put it on." My voice sounded husky, I looked away, ran upstairs, changed into the dress and a pair of sandals. I walked back down and sat in a chair across from my mother, wincing at a twinge of pain, a reminder of the sexual battering my body'd sustained. Carefully, I willed my face to remain neutral. She'd picked up a book to read, but seeing me, closed it and set it on the coffee table.

We sat in silence...friendly silence that tore at me, broke my heart, confused me. I felt her love, and a part of me burned to tell her what'd happened to me, to ask for comfort and help and strength and answers. But in that moment, my fear won out. I convinced myself I could never let her know because it would kill her, and it would kill my father as well. No, I had to protect them. I had crossed an invisible line, and now I was one of the bad girls, bad because something bad had happened to me, but bad nevertheless. The only choice I had was to keep it secret and be charming, and happy, and smart and funny, and fight off all the other stuff, the dark stuff that would ruin their lives forever. I would never let anyone find out.

I didn't know that the invisible line I'd crossed was a line within my adolescent brain, a series of neuronal and synaptic changes that followed the sexual assault and abuse. Adolescents are inherently valiant, and I was no exception. I steeled myself to carry the burden. *I'm an adult now, I have done adult things, and there is no turning back.* Of course it wasn't true, I was only fifteen. And my anger knew the truth. My teenage rage awakened, and grew stronger each day, under the surface, waiting...

CHAPTER 2

A TICKET ON THE PHARMACEUTICAL EXPRESS

"Can-O-Matic!!!" I rasped it this time, idly noticing how dry my mouth'd become, and basked in the resulting gale of raucous laughter from my companions. "Can-O-Matic..." My right hand shot out in front of me again, gyrating. "Can-O-Matic...I...am SO...WIRED!" The dexedrine and benzedrine had kicked in hard a few hours ago, and we'd been walking around the quiet streets adjacent to the university campus. Tanya'd become a mentor, a guide to all things wild and weird in my world, and tonight she'd introduced me to speed, along with some of her friends, older kids who did drugs and stayed out as late as they wanted to. One guy, Seth, had even been to Haight Ashbury with his older brother—had actually tripped on not only one, but two hits of Owsley acid.

"My bro and I, we're goin' back out there in the spring, an' we're gonna bring back a load of it, an' I'll give you some; we'll take a trip, man." Seth looked directly at me, dilated eyes shining, and shook his head back and forth several times, as if he couldn't believe the good news himself. He licked his lips and smoothed his shoulder-length hair back from his face. On some level I realized Seth had a crush on me, and so did other guys in our group. But I didn't want to focus on pretty and popular. These guys, although older than me, were still high school age—too young for me, I figured. After what'd happened with Roddy Mack and his side-kick

Chico, youthful flirtations didn't interest me. I didn't want to lead anybody on, had completely lost the taste for those things.

But I'd acquired a ravenous appetite for emotional oblivion—drugs, thrill-seeking, anything to numb the pain and confusion that roiled and writhed deep inside me. Following the night at Roddy's trailer, and what I now had compartmentalized in my mind as my initiation into the wild world of Sixties Counter Culture, I'd wrestled with shame, outrage, and terror of becoming pregnant. But today I'd started my period, and the relief I felt intoxicated me almost as much as the speed and Boone's Farm wine coursing through my veins.

Now I'd taken four hits of speed, dexedrine in the form of diet pills, even though the college dude I got them from said to take one. The pharmaceutical amphetamine packed a wallop—my first time on stimulants. I'd started getting off on the stuff, and felt breathlessly joyous, free of any cares. The buzz kept on building, my heart pounding, thoughts zooming, and after about a half hour, my right hand'd begun churning like one of the beaters on an electric mixer. The whole thing was involuntary, totally beyond my control, and would've been weird, sad, and embarrassing if I hadn't covered it by clowning around and creating the Can-O-Matic routine. I was riffing on an electric can opener that lots of our moms had in their kitchens; the name just popped into my hopped-up head and provided me with a way to turn the disadvantage of having to contend with the freaky spasms that plagued my hand at intervals.

Fortunately, I didn't have to go home. I'd gained permission to spend the night with Tanya, an opportunity to experience the cheap thrills of any drugs I could lay hands on without facing consequences from my folks. I knew Tanya wanted to go to hear Sorcery play at the Shindig, a rock music club situated on the freeway north of town. We knew how to fix our makeup, and dress and act college age or older, and so far the bouncers had never carded us. Now that my hand was going crazy, they probably would, though. But I didn't give a fuck about that. I didn't want to go...didn't want to go backstage with Tanya, where Roddy or Chico—or both—would put their hands on me with brash, calculated aggression, confident that I'd been marked as their property. That'd been part of it, of the initiation, that I was now one of their girls, expected to be available anytime, anywhere.

And I didn't want to be one of their girls. No, I knew what I wanted. I wanted to run! Far away, anywhere, anyhow—and forever...away from this town, my parents, my life, and myself. And the drugs helped me to feel as if somehow, that dream—or nightmare, depending on how I looked at it—was within my reach. Strong impulses, self-destructive urges, welled up in me, but I stubbornly chalked them up to a thirst for adventure. *Yeah, that's it, I'm looking for some fun, some fuckin' excitement. And what's wrong with that? Nothing. I will ride the Pharmaceutical Express, ride that motherfucker all the way to the end of the line. And when I get there, it's gotta be better than this.*

Suddenly, my arm stiffened up, and my hand began another mini-seizure, that jerky spin cycle attack. I turned to the others, shot them a winning smile, barked it loud, out of the side of my mouth this time, for extra emphasis. "CAN-O-MATIC!" And the laughter followed. I loved making them laugh...

———

Oh no. He REALLY DOES have a glass eye! I resisted the urge to whirl around, vault over the rickety porch railing and catapult down the weed-choked concrete path to the street, gibbering in terror. But I steeled myself. *This is the only way...*I cleared my throat. "Uhm, um, D-Doctor LaVigne? Can I, uh, make an appointment?"

Danny, the college guy Tanya and I got our diet pills from, had briefed me on the small town legends surrounding Dr. LaVigne, along with the old quack's address downtown. And Brian, a friend of Tanya's, a twenty-something dealer who got me high on killer hash that day for free in exchange for me taking a ride in his car, had regaled me with more of the local lore surrounding the infamous doc—chilling tales of mayhem—while driving me past the crumbling old Victorian and pointing out the peely-painted wooden sign in the front yard, emblazoned with, "Bernard J. LaVigne, M.D."

"Yep, there." Brian stuck a thumb out the window, jerked it in the direction of the spooky old house, downshifted, sped past. "Yeah, Dr. LaVigne's the guy that does all the back alley abortions, an' he moves a lotta pills—downers, uppers, you name it. Gives the stuff away to the college girls, especially when they look like you. Be sure an' say yer in college." He raked his gaze over me, lingered a moment on my mini-skirted thighs, then returned his focus to the road ahead. "You can get anything from the ol' perve if you bat your eyelashes at him." He smirked. "Oh shit, eyes! Hey! I forgot to tell ya, Marti, he's only got one eye, the other's glass, an' if ya look close y'can see the old burn scars from the sulphuric acid. See, the word on the street is, the Doc killed his wife, back in fuckin' 1933 or somethin'—cuz he's reeeaaal OLD, y'know?"

I nodded encouragement as Brian warmed to his story. "Okay, so he ran 'er through with this big ol' antique sword he kept hung up over the mantelpiece, then to get ridda the body without a trace he dissolved it—in ACID, in the bathtub, one o' those old claw-foot tubs, an' when he was pourin' alla that acid into the tub to COVER THE CORPSE, some o' the acid SPLASHED in his EYE an' burned it CLEAR OUTTA HIS HEAD!!" He caressed the steering wheel then, and leaned back. His glee in recounting the tale was obvious and apparently scintillating to him. I wondered if he were getting an erection, and covertly grasped the door handle. In a few weeks' time, I'd become hyper-aware of men's hunger for young chicks...at least the kind of men like Tanya hung out with...as it'd turned out, I seemed to be hanging out with them, too—but figured it was necessary, to get the drugs I needed, to keep my ticket on the Pharmaceutical Express and escape from all of it. That's why I now clutched the door handle, so I could bail out of the vehicle if this guy made a move on me.

But he didn't, he kept going with the story. "Well, he WAS a DOCTOR, so he flushed the acid outta the socket before it ate its way into his brain, but he had this big gaping hole where the eye'd been, an' he closed down his office fer weeks, musta sent for a mail-order glass eye, y'know, prob'ly from a medical catalog or whatever, an' after a while, he showed up around town, re-opened his doctor biz, told everybody he'd had an accident in his lab. Some say he even filed a missing person report on his wife, but I like the story where he goes around cryin' and sobbin', boo-hoo-hoo, sayin' his wife ran off with a traveling salesman. The cops suspected, and they never could prove it, but they tried. This one time, they broke down the door o' his house, with a search warrant, an' the way I heard it, ol' Doctor LaVampire comes barrelin' down the stairs, grabs that same ol' sword, it was Civil War era, or maybe even from the Revolutionary War or somethin', reeaaallll old an' everything, and he BRANDISHED the sword and started screamin' at the pigs—it was a standoff, he's like, 'YOU'LL NOT TAKE ME ALIIIIIVE!!' and the cops had to use teargas on him, and they beat the shit outta the ol' fuck and threw 'im in jail, but he got out. Insufficient evidence, that's what they call it."

Ooookay. "Hey Brian, thank you for the ride, and the hash. But you better take me back to school now. I've got a test in English today, can't miss this one."

"Uh, yeah. Right. Gotcha covered, Chick." He straightened in his seat, headed for the high school. Classes had only begun a few weeks before, and I thought I was doing okay, that no one could tell there'd been a fundamental change in my existence. For the first time in my life, I'd been skipping classes. My high school was huge, crammed with students, and situated downtown, but within walking distance of the university campus. I felt invisible, anonymous in that huge school, and figured I wouldn't even be missed. I'd never felt like that before, but I'd never disconnected myself from everyone my own age before, either. Now I was isolated, angry, bewildered, but pushed the intense emotions down until all that remained was an aching. And I'd started dieting, constantly regarding my slender, shapely body as too fat, so I chalked the ache up to hunger and pushed that down, too. I realize now that I was attempting to control the trauma not only with drug seeking, but with anorexia, that this is fairly common behavior for a teen with post-traumatic stress, but then I only knew I was running, as fast as I could, to keep ahead of some unknown, inexorable destruction.

I'd learned how to shoplift, and frequently skipped school to hit the head shop near the college, a place called the Kaleidoscope, where they sold incense, hippie jewelry, mini dresses, jeans and paraphernalia. The guys that worked there thought I was cute and funny, and I used my fast-talking skills and quick wit to get them laughing while I went into the dressing room and tried stuff on. I figured they just thought of me as a potential lay, another piece, didn't see me as a threat. I always left the place with enough stuff to trade for dope or sell for cash to buy some.

Fortunately, the hash buzz'd worn off when I took the English test. I sat through Biology—finished the school day, then headed straight for Dr. LaVigne's. Tanya'd been sharing her mom's Librium and Valium with me, so I owed her. But I wasn't going to try to get any downers. Or uppers, for that matter. Birth control pills, that's what I wanted. A prescription for birth control pills, for security, so that if a guy my age came along, and I liked him, I wouldn't have to worry about getting pregnant. Or if some creep in a car jumped on me, raped me...

Now Dr. LaVigne, infamous pill-pusher, purported wife-skewerer and corpse-dissolver, stood in his front doorway. I sneaked a look past him, and to my amazement, caught a clear view of an ornate fireplace, with an antique sword hung over the mantel. *Damn!* "I take walk-ins," he offered, smiling ever so slightly. He was tall, and carried an air of refinement with overtones of sleaze and maybe a touch of self-deprecatory wit. The vibe I was picking up suggested he knew he was a quack and a local monster myth, but reveled in it.

"Uuuh, yeah, okay...well, I, um, I need a prescription for birth control pills, Dr. LaVigne. I'm a student at the university, and my fiance and I, well, we—" I gulped in a lungful of air, glanced up at the ol' doc, prepared to launch into what I figured'd be an Academy Awards-worthy performance, hitting him with a sob story: my fiance was diagnosed with cancer, we had no time to wait for our wedding day, something like that.

But the old devil cut in. "Follow me, Miss." He stepped over the threshold, smiling sardonically, crossed the decrepit front porch, and led me down a narrow flagstone path at the left side of the crumbling Victorian till we reached what appeared to be an office in the back, complete with a tattered green awning. The ancient wooden door shuddered on its hinges as he jarred it open. The renegade medico motioned me inside, I stepped in, heard the door snick shut behind me, and stifled a gasp. A creepy, antiquated gynecological exam table crouched menacingly, nearly filling the tiny office, its rusty-looking stirrups protruding out the end of the apparatus like talons, hungry for prey. My horrified gaze slid down the expanse of cracked and worn-out mahogany-colored leather upholstery that clung to the table like a mange-ravaged hide. *What. The. Fuck. Does he really do abortions here? On THIS?*

Dr. LaVigne coughed slightly, then cleared his throat. "Er, Miss?" I wrenched my focus away from the exam table, blocked the cavalcade of racing thoughts that threatened to gallop away with my composure. A stealthy gleam crept into the old sawbones' solitary blue eye. He gestured toward the exam table. "Sit if you like."

"No, thank you, I..."

He chuckled, a brittle sound, like dry leaves skittering down a sidewalk, turned, rummaged in a small wooden cupboard a moment, whipped out a prescription tablet, and scribbled something indecipherable. He peeled off the page and handed it to me, pointing out the printed address on the bottom of the page. "Here you go," he wheezed, "be sure to fill it at this pharmacy." He wheezed again, and it struck me that he was actually stifling a laugh. The old asshat was fucking with my mind—and enjoying every minute of it.

The pharmacy seemed like a front for the Mafia, circa Al Capone's era. Creaky floors, dusty shelves, and a scowling pharmacist behind the counter. But they filled that scrip without a second glance.

———

THE WAY I FIGURED IT, NOW THAT I'D TOTALLY FUCKED UP, my life might be extinguished before I'd even gotten a chance to leave town. How could I have let somebody fuck me over like that? I'd arrived at school that morning to another big cop thing—metal detectors, dogs, lockdowns, provoked by fear of race riots—1969 was a breakthrough year for lots of social change and civil rights progress, which in turn caused backlash. The police made me take my cool silvery chain belt off my red hip hugger mini skirt to go through the metal detector. But a couple of hours later, I took advantage of the campus chaos and skipped classes.

I met Dusty at the Kaleidoscope, right after I ditched school that day, and didn't feel threatened by him, probably because he was middle-aged, frumpy, and paunched. He drove a fluorescent pink Jeep convertible with a striped ragtop. I got in his goofy car when he promised to get me high, and now I hated myself. After the debacle, I learned he owned a nightclub in a nearby city, and everybody told me the club was a front for an LSD lab. Whether he owned a lab or not, Dusty had no trouble getting dope that day, and when we got to his place—a little ranch style brick house in a neighboring town, he gave me hits of speed, with Seven Up to wash them down, and there must've been something else in the Seven Up, something that made me trip like crazy, to the point where I completely lost it. I never figured out what that extra something was, and still could only recall bits and pieces of that day, but I'd done something terrible under the influence...not sex, Dusty was too fat to get a hard-on, but a new low in my fucked up young life: after he'd wheedled and begged for what seemed like hours, I'd agreed to pose for nude photos. The porcine predator had lights, a big camera and all the equipment for a full-fledged photography studio.

Dusty'd promised he wouldn't show the photos to anyone, and assured me that I could have the negatives, even said he was gay, probably so I'd be in no fear of him hitting on me. At that point, I'd been so wasted that I didn't care, only wanted to get it over with. Dusty'd definitely been turned on—breathing heavily, red in the face, gasping for air like a corpulent landed codfish the whole time he snapped pictures of me. Afterward, the pig'd dropped me off on a corner near the campus. Walking back to my house, I lost my way several times, threw up once or twice, and got so dizzy I saw stars. When I finally made it home, I told my mom I had the flu and went up to bed.

The next morning, I woke up freaked out about the events of the day before. I called Dusty and asked him for the negatives. Dusty snarled, called me a stupid little bitch, and threatened to show the pictures to everybody in town, including my parents, if I ever breathed a word. And now I had to worry about those pictures floating around, who might see them…a reality that caused me panic whenever I thought of it. Later, I asked around about Dusty on the street, and learned he kept photos of naked chicks in his night club. I skipped school again. Whenever I thought about that pudgy old slob Dusty and his sweaty old freak friends, drooling over naked pictures of me hanging on the walls in his bar, I freaked out, started crying and couldn't stop.

I called Tanya and spilled the story to her, embarrassing myself by crying some more. "Marti, you're having a nervous breakdown!! I've got an appointment with my shrink today, you should come along. I'll pick you up." It seemed like a good idea. The guy seemed cool; he let me cry in his office, didn't boss me around, only listened, and handed me a lot of Kleenex. Afterward, I toughened myself up to go home, but at first glimpse of my folks and their worried faces, my bravado burst like a dam and I broke down all over again. I told Mom and Dad about Dr. Katsaros and asked them if I could go back to see him. My main motivation was fear of being insane. Yes, it never occurred to me that my innocence had been sheared away, and that the loss of it was traumatic. I thought the reason my life had derailed was that I was crazy. My parents somehow scraped together the money to pay for some counseling sessions.

My first appointment with the child psychologist proved disappointing. He didn't write me a prescription for meds, for one thing—and on some deep level he seemed cloyingly invasive. I never talked with Dr. Katsaros about Dusty and the photos, didn't trust him enough to unburden myself. I could have reported Dusty to the police for crimes against a minor, but I didn't think of myself as a minor; my brief engagement in the drug scene had already taught me never to snitch, never to trust the cops. I was a teenaged girl desperately trying to live like an adult, and I saw myself as solely responsible for the consequences of my actions. I wondered if I could live it down, wrestled with thoughts of suicide, then decided against it. Instead, I focused on revenge and the steely resolve to never give that fat fuckwad the satisfaction of driving me to self-destruction. No matter what, I was still smart, pretty, tough and funny. I determined not to think about the pictures and to move on. Of course, in my traumatized mind, moving on meant doing drugs and carving out a plan to run away from home, although there was nothing at home to run from. I still loved my parents...but I figured I'd simply screwed up my life so profoundly that I'd need to leave town before they discovered the horrible truth about me.

———

POP-BANG! THE LIGHT BULB'S GLARE SEARED THROUGH THE bloodshot haze over my eyes and into my addled consciousness. "You wanna be a HIPPIE? Is THAT it?!" The cop's face was bright red—*Or maybe it's only that bloodshot haze? Oops, wrong color haze, man! It's PUR-PLE-HAZE-ALL-IN-MY-BRAIN! S'cuse me, while I KISS THE SKY!!!—Aaaawww, but no, that cop is MAD!!!* And the officer was, indeed, bright red, he was very pissed off, I could see that now. He scowled in icy outrage, and big veins protruded out of his neck, his very red neck...*REDNECK!! Oh, yeah, HE IS A RED-NECK, of COURSE he is!* I struggled to gain some metaphysical traction, but a considerable portion of my hallucinating brain resisted traction, instead it flowed like a shimmering alpine stream over the sharp stones of present circumstance, babbling giddily. That part of my mind simply did not give a flying fuck whether I'd fallen into the clutches of the police state—it wanted to play. I hurled myself back into the paranoid portion—at least there I could get some kind of grip on survival. *PIG! I TELL YOU NOTHING!!!* I straightened myself in the chair they'd sat me down in and glowered back at the Sheriff's Deputy, willing myself to sepulchral silence. *Pig, I tell you...NOTHING!*

Suddenly another cop's face loomed into view, thrust out of the dim expanse of nothingness that surrounded the lightbulb's aura. This cop still wore his hat, in fact, he reached up and touched the brim, as though that minute adjustment gave his authority all the more weight and substance. "Whut was you THINKIN' anyhow?" He snickered, looked over his shoulder, as if to get a rousing, 'Amen!' from a chorus of other lawmen who no doubt waited in the wings, eager to take their shot at interrogating me. "Hmph. Betcha you wuz thinkin' yer pretty smart. Runnin' off inta the creek! An' we had to wade in there an' GETCHA. Mah pant legs're SOAKED THROUGH!!"

Another deputy leaned in, his face a rictus of stony disapproval that signaled his resolve—I understood he would take no sass from my kind, give no quarter to runaway kids who refused to cooperate, who dilly-dallied with longhairs, pot smokers, draft dodgers, communist sympathizers, flag burners and any of the other guitar-toting, raggedy-assed no-goods and ne'er do wells that littered the landscape. "Girl, I've seen COCK-A-ROACHES in dark corners that looked a helluvalot better than those scumbuckets in that trailer! Whadidja think you were DOIN' with the likes of them?? Didja think they were FLOWER CHILDREN? THEY'RE SCUM! Get that through your head!" He spat the words out, grimaced, and receded.

My resistance adamantine, I offered no reply. *PIG!!! I'M NO SNITCH.* They'd never break me...

My adolescent rage and deep sense of the dramatic, combined with a pharmaceutically induced, semi-psychedelic fog, wreaked havoc on my perception of this moment and the events leading up to it. A few days before, when I'd skittered in late for dinner, my parents'd confronted me, furious at news from my school that I'd been missing tons of classes. A couple of teachers'd said they suspected me of taking drugs. Severe punishment loomed, imminent. But, lucky for me, my mom and dad had invited a lot of their friends over for a bridge party and it was too late to cancel, so they couldn't bring the parental hammer down immediately. Instead, they announced I was grounded for a month and sent me up to my room to await the more serious reckoning after their guests left.

The party gave me the edge I needed. Downstairs, in the living room, my folks played cards with their social circle, and the music and laughter disguised whatever noise I made as I feverishly began fashioning a makeshift rappel line. Half-giggling, half-sobbing, I twisted my sheets and pillow cases into cords and tied the ends together, then pushed my bed up against the window and fastened the line to one of its legs. My getaway'd been swift and secretive. My sister was out with a study group, my brothers were eating popcorn and watching TV downstairs in the family room. No material witnesses. I took off running as soon as my feet touched ground.

Once clear of the house and the neighborhood, I'd headed down toward the campus, looking for someone to give me a ride to Chicago. I knew absolutely nothing about the Windy City, except that it was relatively close to my little prairie hometown and that all kinds of excitement awaited me there, bright lights, big city, blah, blah, blah. It'd do.

I polled the creeps who skulked around the college, asking if anybody was headed to Chi-town. No one offered, but I did manage to get my hands on two black beauties, enough to keep me awake till I could figure out what to do. I ended up walking around town, diving into the shadows whenever a police car rolled by and shivering in the autumn night. At one point, a guy who looked about twenty-one or so told me I could sleep on the couch in his little apartment, but after about half an hour, thinking I was asleep, he'd slinked in and started dry-humping me. I gritted my teeth and played possum till a shudder announced his climax, then extricated myself and ran.

Additional, decidedly sordid scenarios presented themselves over the next few days—and nights—and they were bad enough that I figured I might as well head for the sleazy trailer on the outskirts of town, the abode of Rocky and Chico, to seek asylum. Or maybe...I still hoped, maybe a ride to Chicago. On the way, I'd taken some Romilar cough medicine, a lot of it, and although I vomited most of it up, it packed a punch. And somebody had given me a hit of what they said was belladonna. Whatever it was, it knocked me cross-eyed, sideways, and senseless. The only thing that kept me on my feet was the two black beauties. And yeah, when I got to the infamous trailer, Wolf and another slimy dude named Skeeter were pounding down Southern Comfort and smoking a joint. Wolf squinted blearily at me, then unzipped his pants, exposing an erect crooked penis. "Hey lil' girl, you wanna gimme a handjob? C'mon!" When Chico intervened and led me into his room, I'd almost felt a sense of gratitude. Almost.

Then the cops had shown up, knocked, pounded, hammered on the door, and the rickety trailer'd shimmied as if an earthquake'd hit. Somehow, Chico and Roddy'd seen them ahead of time, because they'd slapped me awake, hustled me across the threadbare carpet, and tossed me out a flimsy little side door into the darkness. Adrenaline took over from there. I heard a pack of dogs barking and howling—and instantly knew they'd brought bloodhounds after me! Hell, the yowling pack of mongrels most likely lived in that crummy trailer park and, even if they'd want to, couldn't have passed the necessary drug screens for K-9 work due to secondhand weed smoke from their owners—to sum it up in a few words, I was trippin'. But in that moment, the Code Red signal to my agitated grey matter was that the hounds were hot on my trail!! *Oh fuck-oh-fuck-oh fuck!!!!!* I bolted for the woods, crashed through branches and thick underbrush, ran up against a barb wire fence, tore the leg of my jeans, and felt a stinging sensation where the barb wire'd slashed my right thigh. *Damn! I'll have to get a tetanus shot...*I heard water rushing, and it dawned on me I'd reached a creek. *Thank you God!!!* I knew from watching Westerns on TV that running water would totally fuck up the bloodhounds' sense of smell! I charged over the fence, straight into the water, and waded downstream till the oinkers took me down.

They hauled me out of the creek and dragged me to the roadside, handed me over to a plainclothes juvie officer, a creepy old bald guy with a bulging gut. "He's gonna give you a ride to the station," one of the cops announced, then pointed a finger at me. "We'll see you there."

The creepy juvie guy ushered me into the car, told me to sit in the front seat, and started driving down the deserted country road. I sat upright, far as I could from his cigar smell, muscles rigid from stress, belladonna, and the dregs of Romilar. After a few minutes, he leaned over and squeezed my leg with his fat paw, saying, "Y'know, honey, there's more'n one way to skin a cat. I'll pull into that motel up ahead, and if you be nice, I can fix everything for ya... you'll never even have to look at that ol' jail."

I batted his hand away, crushed myself against the passenger side door, and then screamed, threatened, and verbally assailed him with every single insult or curse I could conjure. I guess I sufficiently intimidated the old toad, because he snapped his mouth shut, grabbed the wheel with both hands, and drove in silence back to the cop shop, where he'd delivered me into the custody of these very angry and indignant peace officers.

They grilled me some more, then locked me up. I spent the rest of the night in a cell with a couple of barfing drunks, but I felt a sense of satisfaction. I had harnessed my teenage rage and fashioned it into a weapon that enabled me to both fend off the corrupt juvie guy and successfully make it through police interrogation without saying one word, all this accomplished despite being devastatingly impaired by illegal substances. *Pretty good for my first run-in with Johnny Law...*

Somehow, Derek's top hat managed to cling to his head as he danced, bobbed and jumped, his harmonica his only accompaniment as he belted out extemporaneous blues lines. A crowd of onlookers and listeners had formed, some dancing, some clapping and urging him on. Wearing my red dress, I stood tall just to his right, my approving gaze an endorsement. I'd met Derek during the first week at my new high school adjacent to the university. My father's connections, combined with high test scores and grades, had earned me admission into a progressive program for gifted students. The school was totally cool, and they'd set me up to audit college English courses for high school credit. The day we met, Derek'd been panhandling outside the Student Center on the college campus, his top hat upended to collect change. His dark hair hung below his shoulders, and he'd grinned lopsidedly at me, hazel eyes twinkling, wire rimmed, hippie-style glasses slightly askew. He was raising money for bail, he'd told me, bail for a friend of his who'd gotten busted with pounds of weed. I'd sneaked a peek into the hat. "How much've you got so far?"

"Almost five bucks."

"Hold on, I'll help you out." I turned on all my charm and energy, flirting with guys, engaging girls by spinning a dramatic tale of heroic weed crusaders pitted against the Establishment, and in an hour or so, Derek and I'd raised over half of his friend's bond. He'd invited me to come to his house for dinner, and to my surprise, my folks had let me go, lifting the "grounded" status I'd been under since jail. Derek was seventeen, two years older than me, and lived in a neighboring town, about a half hour's drive from my house and school. His folks seemed rich to me—his dad was a psychiatrist, and they lived in a big Victorian furnished with antiques and cool stuff. His parents owned multiple cars for their kids, and let Derek drive a burgundy Gran Torino to and from school.

Tonight was our third date. We'd come to see a Battle of the Bands in Derek's hometown, and on the break, he'd jumped up and started playing, and attracted an audience of not only kids our age, but people in their twenties, too. My boyfriend was audacious, and I liked that—I was no shrinkin' violet, either. Derek's friends were in their twenties; he was dealing weed and hash with three of them—that impressed me. So far, we'd only kissed, but tonight we were going to drop some acid, Orange Sunshine, from Derek's dad's stash—according to my boyfriend, his father'd done LSD with Timothy Leary as part of a clinical workshop—and spend the night together, taking advantage of the fact his parents were away on vacation in Cozumel all weekend. I'd lied to my parents, telling them I was spending the night with Tanya.

Derek finished his riffs, took a bow, basked in the applause. The group scattered as the break ended and the next band mounted the stage, began tuning up. He put an arm around my waist. "Ready, Meshuggener?" Derek'd picked up that bit of slang from a Lenny Bruce album. He'd played it for me the first night we'd met, and I'd loved it. Lenny Bruce was amazing, his comedy eclipsed anything I'd heard Bill Cosby do, totally kicked ass; he was making fun of religion, the government, everything...he was dangerously funny. Derek loaned me the record so I could bring it home and listen, but my mom'd been horrified, she'd made me take it back and warned me never to bring any more "filth" into the house again. But tonight, we'd listen to Lenny and laugh, and listen to Hendrix, the Doors, Captain Beefheart. And we'd be tripping.

"Yep. Ready as I'll ever be."

———

We were peaking on the acid when Derek's sister opened the door a crack and stuck her head in. "Mom and Dad are home." The door closed. Adrenaline surged through my system, but I took care not to panic. This was my first trip, but not Derek's. He'd told me when he met me that he'd done acid a thousand times. So for him, this was trip one-thousand-and-one. *He'll know what to do, right?* It's not like we'd actually been caught in flagrante delicto. We were naked and we'd been trying...the colors and patterns whirling in my brain'd taken the shape of a dragon with rainbow scales, distracting me, but I knew Derek was on top of me. He'd been fumbling around in an attempt to put himself inside me, but so far nothing had happened. *Maybe he saw the dragon, too...looks like acid, at least at the peak, is not famous for its aphrodisiac properties.*

Our movements jerky, marionette-like, we yanked our clothes on, descended the stairs, and braced ourselves for confrontation. Focusing all my concentration and energy on not allowing my thoughts to stray into the treacherous, oh-my-god-I-am-flipping-out territory where I might ponder how my parents were going to kill me for all of...this, I slapped a smile on my face and remembered to address Derek's folks as, "Ma'am," and, "Sir."

The upshot of the whole thing was that his mom and dad were scared I was pregnant. To my surprise, they never asked if we were high, none of that. Never asked me if my parents knew where I was. Derek began talking first. "Um, Mom, Dad, Marti is on the pill, she can't get pregnant. And, uh, we, uh...we're going steady, in fact, we're in LOVE." He shot me a sidelong glance.

"Uh, yeah! Yeah, we're going steady, and...we ARE in love." I smiled now, warming to the topic, luxuriating in the kind of glow one experiences only when talking about love while peaking on a hit of pure, pharmaceutical-grade Orange Sunshine.

Derek's mom's face registered dismay and confusion, but his dad smiled benevolently and began to hold forth on the virtues of young romance. "Well, love can be a very blissful experience, it's a big part of growing up and finding one's path in life..." The middle-aged, bearded psychiatrist folded his hands behind his neck and leaned back into the sofa cushions. *Is he...HIGH? Oh, well...*

We talked about love, life, and dreams with Derek's dad for the next few hours, and his mom sat mostly silent, petting her three toy poodles, but occasionally tossing in an encouraging comment. I fell in love with both Derek and his parents that night. His folks were so enlightened and understanding and...cool, and they didn't seem to be afraid of anything. Maybe it was the acid, but I desperately wanted to be a part of their family, dreaded going home to my own people. When Derek's dad asked me about my birth control pills, I showed them to him—I carried them around in my purse all the time. "Just a minute." He handed the packet back to me, stood up, and left the room, then returned with several sample packs, pressing them into my hand. "When you're finished with what's left of your pills this month, switch to these. They're much more effective, much safer."

At dawn, the acid began receding, and Derek gave me a ride back to my town. I called Tanya, and she helped me out, dropping me off at my house so my parents wouldn't know I'd been with Derek all night. Later, up in my room, I hid the birth control pills Derek's father'd given me, trusting in his assurance that they were safer and more effective, and took a moment to savor the milestones I'd reached on my progression toward twenty-one years of age. *So what if I'm fifteen on paper? I'm wise beyond my years, a woman of the world now. I've tripped on LSD, I KNOW things. And I control my destiny.*

————

"Oooh! Wow, Man! Thanks!!!" Don Van Vliet, aka Captain Beefheart, grabbed Derek's hand and shook it exuberantly, eyes wide with astonished appreciation. "You MADE this?"

Derek nodded, smiling blissfully. "Yeah! In art class, man." My boyfriend was beyond thrilled. We'd traveled all the way to Cincinnati to see Captain Beefheart and His Magic Band, and Iggy and the Stooges, at Ludlow's Garage, so Derek could present Beefheart with the trout mask he'd made. The mask, a mixed media project, was an homage to Captain Beefheart's third album, Trout Mask Replica, released in 1969 and produced by Frank Zappa. Beefheart introduced us to Zoothorn Rollo, his bass player. Other members of the Magic Band were Winged Eel Fingerling and Mascara Snake, but we didn't get to meet them. After presenting the Captain with his replica-of-a-trout-mask-replica, we actually made it home within my parents' curfew.

On another date, we went to Cincinnati again, this time on Sunday afternoon, to see Jefferson Airplane, and Derek got together with his cousin, Jarvis, who'd lived with the Airplane family in San Francisco. Jarvis, a heroin addict, had brought some along, and Derek snorted a line but refused to shoot up. "It's not that I haven't tried it," he told me later, on the drive home. "Yeah, I've shot things—LSD, mostly, but I've shot heroin, too. Thing is, you gotta be really careful about SHOOTING heroin...it's REAL easy to get strung out, man."

I listened, made no comment. Jarvis hadn't offered me any heroin, and I hadn't asked for fear my parents would be able to detect it when I got home. I'd only taken a few hits on a joint. But I couldn't help feeling admiration for Derek. He'd experienced life in a way that I'd never had a chance to; he'd done all kinds of drugs, seen so many bands, hell, he'd even been to Woodstock Festival. And now Derek'd opened the door, held it wide open, and on the other side lay the world, waiting for me to walk through and set it ablaze. Longing for adventure, for independence, I champed at the bit, yearning to whisk away the years and be twenty-one, legal age, free. Time slogged by at a frustratingly glacial pace. I wasn't even sixteen yet! But at least I was on my way, I was on the train, on the Pharmaceutical Express, and the ride was getting smoother. I knew for sure I was in love—with a boyfriend who liked drugs, too, knew all about drugs, drove a big, fast car—and I knew he was in love with me. Derek turned up the stereo, it was Led Zeppelin's "Ramble On." I settled into my seat, looked out the window at the passing scenery, and in my head I sang along with the lyrics. *Ramble on, and now's the time, the time is now, sing my song...*

CHAPTER 3

A SUITE AT SEIZURE'S PALACE, A THREE-RING CIRCUS, AND THE BIG QUESTION

A FLASH OF CONSCIOUSNESS CRACKED THE ABYSMAL DARKNESS, like a lightning strike, brief yet blindingly brilliant. I awoke, tried to look around me but somehow could not find my eyes. Blackness pressed in, enshrouded me; I could feel the overwhelming depth of it. Next, my body registered the pain of penetration, and anger exploded in my brain along with an outraged recognition of my own helplessness. In my mind I began to struggle, to claw my way upward and outward, fighting to gain control of my faculties and muscles so I could strike back, kill my assailant—strangle the motherfucker with my bare hands. I could feel those invading fingers, inflicting more and more pain as they thrust deeper, insistent, probing in vicious, arrogant disregard for my human dignity. I screamed—but no sound came out. Then suddenly, I emerged into the light, finally got enough control to find my eyelids. I blinked once, heard a male voice, hushed and urgent, inches from my ear. "Oh! Hey! She's wakin' up! Better shoot 'er down again."

A second male voice, behind me. "Yeah. Got it."

I felt the needle pierce my right hip. My muscles locked in reflexive resistance to a searing pinch of pain, then that awful darkness descended again, engulfing me in a leaden wave of oblivion.

The cycle continued for days. Loss of consciousness precipitated by injection, then a brief struggle toward the surface, followed by another needle full of poison. A few times I awoke alone, and during those moments began to take stock of my surroundings. I lay on the floor of a locked room, on a bare mattress, clad in one of those hospital gowns that tie at the neck and stay open in back. I had nothing to cover myself with, nothing to protect me from the two male voices and their acts of penetration. After a few moments of consciousness, they'd inject me with the drugs and I would drown again in a wave of stygian blackness.

At a certain point, I managed to fully regain my awareness and sit up. Sunlight streamed in from an open window. I could see a patch of blue sky, reckoned the room must be several stories up. A white bird flew past, and my mind registered it as a dove, a sign of peace. Hey, I know now it must've been a pigeon, but a dove seemed right at the time. See, during the worst of it I'd thought God was punishing me, so when I caught a glimpse of what I took to be a dove—symbol of peace—through psych-med-hazed eyes, hope of forgiveness washed over me.

A woman in surgical scrubs entered the room, saw me, and dashed back out again. She returned with a second woman, and this one wore a white nurse's uniform. They tried to get me to talk and gave me some water, a good thing since my mouth was so dry that my lips cracked open when I sipped it. Then I felt fear, and my neck and shoulders began to convulse. I was having another seizure and started to scream. This time sound came out, but my words didn't make any sense. The woman in scrubs began to prepare a syringe. "She's a catatonic schizophrenic, had a grand mal seizure. We've gotta keep her sedated till she stops having these episodes." They knocked me out again.

When I finally wrested myself from the seizure, I began trying to put all the pieces back together, and it wasn't easy, probably because of all the crazy-ass psych meds they'd bludgeoned my bloodstream with. I remembered a blindingly bright light that triggered a seizure, and I'd been paralyzed, helpless while I waited for someone to come to my aid. Then seventeen years old, I'd been working a part time job as a teaching assistant in a rural elementary school, acting as an interpreter for Spanish-speaking migrant workers' children. I'd obtained the job through the State Employment Commission. It was my second day at work. The kids had left and I was doing some filing in one of the offices in the school building. I'd gone down the hall to a supply closet to get paper, when a blazingly brilliant light had frozen me in my tracks. At least I'd perceived it as a light.

I lay twisted on the floor, in the throes of the seizure, my entire body convulsing, totally conscious but unable to speak, and at one point, I'd actually left my body—hovered high above it, looking down. A part of me wanted to split the scene—it registered more as an urge than a thought, but then I took a second glance at my body far below. Then—*I'd give anything to get back there!*—a moment later, I was back. Did the out-of-body experience translate as a near-death experience? Maybe.

Months later, I would learn that I'd become extremely malnourished and dehydrated, partly as a result of anorexia, and that's what caused the seizure. It was physiological in origin. But, it being 1971, once they found me in the linoleum-floored hallway, the school's faculty chalked it up to LSD, totally freaked out, and called the cops.

When the County Sheriff's Deputy arrived, he stood over me, leaned in, and with pudgy fingers pushed my eyelids back, whistled low, then barked, "Call a meat wagon!" Finally the ambulance arrived, they loaded me onto a stretcher and took me to the ER. They pumped my stomach, thinking I was a drug casualty or OD. After determining I was chemical-free, an asshole child psychiatrist, Dr. Yardley, banished me to the psych ward upstairs, prescribing colossal doses of Phenobarbital, Thorazine, and who knows what else. The nightmare unfolded and continued to unfold. I'd been labeled a catatonic schizophrenic, drugged into a stupor, tossed onto a bare mattress on the floor, and sexually molested.

The two male orderlies who'd alternately violated and drugged me were working on the ward—I recognized them by their voices. One was white, one black; agents of malice—lurking in the hallways, smirking and/or scowling at patients. I never reported them to the psychiatrist or any of the staff, figuring no one would believe me. My parents began regular visits, and I could tell they were scared and worried out of their minds, so I never mentioned the orderlies to my folks, never told them what happened.

I spent the next few months locked up in there, fighting the system at the outset—hunger strikes, refusal to answer any questions—but after weeks of resistance, I realized that in order to gain even a shred of a hope of being released, I'd need to cooperate with Dr. Yardley, the dickwad child psychiatrist. I hated that guy, despised his sneering condescension and air of entitlement. He had me so heavily doped up that when I started moving around the ward, I could barely slide my nut-house-issue, sock-clad feet across the floor. The other patients called it, "The Thorazine Shuffle." My arms hung stiff at my sides—I couldn't lift them. And the muscles in my face seemed paralyzed, so that even basic self-expression—power of speech or ability to smile, for instance, had been chemically hog-tied.

I must've been allergic to one or all of those meds, because my skin broke out in big red blisters. When I asked that pig to lower my dosage, he said I still needed chemical restraint. After a month or so, I saw our family practitioner, Dr. Bergman, in the ward visiting some other patient. I grabbed the opportunity to show him the welts on my skin, and he looked horrified. A few days later, they changed my medication, and the rash stopped. But I couldn't shake that Thorazine Shuffle...yet. Later, I learned how to hold the pills under my tongue, fake-swallow them with the little Dixie Cup of water the nurses gave me to wash down my dose. After that, I'd spit out the meds, flush them down the toilet, and revel in my act of defiance.

The ward was co-ed, populated by men and women from various backgrounds, all walks of life. Many of the patients professed devout religious faith; in fact, several seemed outright fanatical, which didn't surprise me. I knew from experience with LSD that people invest some of their deepest fears around God or sex.

I was one of two teens on the ward, both of us female. I guess no boys'd wigged out that season. The other girl, Gina, told me she was only passing through. "Marti, I've been in state hospitals for three years. You do NOT want to end up there! I got in trouble with my dad, he's a doctor, and he sent me to the psych ward. I gave them a run for their money, for sure...fucked with their minds, stuff like that. Then they transferred me to the state hospital. I tried being a badass in there, but they're not fuckin' around! They made me scrub toilets and mop the hallway where the violent patients are. They try to pull you through the bars!" She shuddered, then reached for a deck of cards. "I don't wanna talk about any of that now, though. I'm goin' home. Hey, wanna play Go Fish?"

The rest of the patients were adults. One woman, Sherry, rolled into the ward in a wheelchair, her neck wrapped in gauze bandages and adhesive tape. She told me she'd slit her throat from ear to ear after binging on downers and Bacardi 151. "What prob'ly caused me to snap was, I married a dude during a blackout, and woke up in his motel room, diamond ring on my finger, the whole schlemiel— so I started screaming, 'WHO the FUCK are YOU? WHERE THE FUCK ARE WE?'" He says, 'I'm your Prince Charming...Bitch,' and then, 'We're at the HEARTBREAK HOTEL!! Don't move or I'll wring your neck!' Then I jumped up, and I yelled, 'FUCK YOU!' It was like, an impulse, see...when I drew the knife blade across my throat. I mean, that WAS craaazy, right? Can't remember where that knife came from, though..."

Another woman, Charlene, told me she was a high school music teacher on a leave of absence from her career. "I'm not going back to work until I'm better," she'd tell Sherry and me at breakfast. Charlene had undergone a series of shock treatments, all of them voluntary. "The shock treatments are helping me to forget." Charlene shook her head slowly, looked at her hands, then took a sip of orange juice. "And when I've gotten rid of all the toxic memories, I won't be depressed anymore." After breakfast, Charlene would leave for another shock treatment, and would return later, prone, unconscious, wheeled in on a gurney, the skin of her face looking red, slick, and shiny, blistered almost, as if it'd been burned.

Another patient, Lloyd, a professional welterweight boxer, was okay to be around. He'd do push-ups, sit-ups, and other stuff to stay in shape, knew all kinds of cool ways to accomplish a full-body workout using only a chair. Sometimes, when my folks visited, Dad and Lloyd would talk. Lloyd helped me out one day, shared some valuable insight with me as we sat in the common room. I'd been half-assed complying with the hospital and Dr. Dickface, but wasn't doing enough to get them to cut me loose—and I was still acting out my defiance. The staff'd been rounding up volunteers to go bowling; they had a van ready and everything. Mike, one of the medical interns, tried to convince me to go on the trip, but I stubbornly refused. "No, Mike, I don't wanna go." Mike walked away. Lloyd filled me in on the danger of playing chicken with the psychiatric status quo.

"Not goin' bowlin' with 'em, huh?"

"Uh...No."

"Listen, Marti. I know a lot about the world we're in. I've been in and out of psych wards and mental hospitals for years now, got sent to state hospital for being combative. You know, I'm a boxer, so I can do combat, right?" He chuckled. "But I learned some stuff the hard way, and I can save you a whole lot of trouble if you take my advice.

"Um, okay. So?"

"Kid, you've been in here a long time now. Your dad's prob'ly got good insurance benefits, but by this long, the benefits're prob'ly running out. When that happens, if you're not compliant, the shrink can remand you to a state hospital, and if you go there, you never know when you'll get out. I know, I lived it. So here's the thing I learned in there—the REAL truth is that you're the only one responsible for your life, your mind, and your own happiness. Nobody can do it for you. You gotta look out for yourself, be smart. Mike and the other staff, they're taking people out there on that bowling trip to see how they do on the outside. You need to go along, play along, show them you can function, see? If you don't go, then they'll write it up. If you go, it shows progress. Get it?"

I sat still for a minute. "Lloyd, how come you're not gonna go bowling?"

"I'm gonna be released in about an hour, that's why, and I am never comin' back. Remember what I said. And good luck."

I jumped up. "Good luck, Lloyd."

So, I went bowling. When I got back, Lloyd was gone.

––––––––––

THE STOUT NURSE AIDE APPROACHED ME, HANDS ON HIPS. "Marti, you've got a visitor."

"Really? Who?" I'd been cooperating with Dr. Dickweed's orders. He'd told me that when I gained twenty-five pounds he'd let me out. My weight at admission to the ER was something like 110 pounds, cadaverously thin at five-eleven. I'd gained about twenty so far, and I went along on all the bowling trips. My capitulation reaped a few small perks—non-family member visits, and day passes to see my parents...privileges that didn't exactly inspire paroxysms of joy or an urge to turn cartwheels.

My visitor, a cute chick around my age, smiled at me and squeezed my hand. I pulled back. "Who are you?"

"Hey, uhmm." She shot me a conspiratorial look, tossed her thick black hair. "Marti, I'm Crystal. Derek sent me. He wants you to know he still loves you, and that he's changed. He's downstairs, in the lobby. Wanna see him?"

"Huh?" After my extended stay on the ward, with the psychopharmaceutical blitzkrieg my brain'd endured, and the sexual abuse, witty repartee escaped me. "Oh, well...let me think about this for a minute..."

A lot'd happened since I'd met Derek in 1969, at fifteen years old, and this moment, at seventeen, in the psychiatric ward on the seventh floor of my hometown's only hospital. Jimi Hendrix, Janis Joplin, and Jim Morrison had died of overdoses; we mourned their passing, along with millions of other fans. The war in Viet Nam dragged on and the Draft Lottery required all men to register at eighteen years of age. Derek had reached nineteen now, and was, according to Uncle Sam, eligible for combat in the jungles of Viet Nam.

During our first year and a half as boyfriend and girlfriend, we'd taken to smoking daily bong loads of weed or hash, and all that THC'd made me apathetic. My grades dropped. Still, I managed to complete all of my homework assignments, and also my boyfriend's. Derek and I were having sex on a regular basis, and his dad kept on giving me those birth control pill samples. Derek skipped school a lot more than I did; in fact, he missed so many classes they ended up expelling him. This was his third high school. The first one kicked him to the curb for refusing to cut his hair, the second one—a fancy prep school—tossed him out after he dosed his fellow cross country teammates with LSD and got into a fist fight with the coach.

Hellion though he was, Derek's parents always supported him, no matter what. His expulsion from school increased the worry of Derek getting drafted if his folks couldn't get him safely tucked into college. Still, Derek convinced his folks to pay rent on an apartment for him in Denver, and to help him out with putting together and promoting a rock band. At the time of his expulsion, Derek was playing bass in a band on weekends. The drummer, Billy, and the lead guitar, Jack, were serious about going on the road full-time, so when Derek got ousted, the trio discussed the possibility of moving to Denver and making it happen.

Derek studied for the GED, and when he passed it, his folks agreed to bankroll a move to the Rockies. And with all of these plans in play, they mistakenly figured their son would be safer if his cousin Jarvis went along, too. I never could figure out if Derek's folks knew Jarvis was a junkie, but I couldn't see how they could not have noticed since the guy was really scrawny, had been treated for hepatitis multiple times, and, from what Derek told me, had OD'd a few times, too. I worried that if Derek were hanging out with his cousin all the time, he might get strung out on heroin. I warned him to be careful.

Derek promised me he wouldn't do junk, and I promised him I'd be faithful to him till I graduated high school and could join him in Colorado...or wherever he might be by then. Derek's dad gave me a whole bunch of birth control pill samples so I wouldn't run out. My boyfriend assured me he'd be returning to visit soon, that he loved me and couldn't live without me. And then Derek, Billy, Jack, and Jarvis headed west to seek their rock n' roll fortune.

With Derek gone, I quit doing weed and my grades skyrocketed. I devoted myself to my classes and focused on being thin, on eating as little as possible. I felt more in control, more serene, when my stomach was empty, and I loved being thin. I didn't socialize with any other kids at school. I felt as though I couldn't relate to anybody. I realize now that the trauma of earlier sexual abuse, combined with the damaging effects of what I now know was a very dangerous type of birth control pill during my formative years, drove me to anorexia in an attempt to manage all the stress and anxiety. My menstrual cycle shut down and didn't come back, but I kept taking the pills in anticipation of a conjugal visit from my wannabe rock star boyfriend.

Derek and I wrote letters back and forth, professing undying love for each other. He called me on the phone once a week. Before he left, we'd been dabbling in metaphysics, trying to discover some kind of higher consciousness, and we encouraged each other in the pursuit of enlightenment. On our third phone call, Derek announced he'd arrived at a new level of consciousness. "The heroin has enlightened me, man, it really takes you there!! The rush is like thunder! And the band, yeah. We're doin' mescaline, too, and we're gettin' loads of songs written. Wait'll you hear us, we're gonna be huge, like Zeppelin!"

"Oh. Yeah, cool!" I wasn't doing any dope and didn't like the idea of needing dope to arrive at enlightenment. "Hey Derek, didn't we begin the Fourth Way so we could be high without drugs?"

"Yeeaah, but...I'm not in school anymore. You better not be doing anything, though. Well, maybe smoke a joint, but that's all."

"Derek, I'm not getting high, and I like it. My mind is clear."

"Yeah? Well, uh, great. Hey, I gotta go now. Miss you, Lover."

Prior to his departure, Derek and I'd been reading books by a couple of Russian mystics, guys named Gurdjief and Ouspensky. They taught a sort of philosophy called "The Fourth Way." The whole thing revolved around achieving what they called "Cosmic

Consciousness." They talked about the body and mind being a machine, stuff like that. Now that Derek'd left, with my brain THC-free, I focused heavily on achieving a higher consciousness. I worked really hard on that crazy shit, because I didn't want to be left behind. I mean, Derek was achieving enlightenment, right? I needed to keep up.

One afternoon, on a visit to the university's art gallery, I bumped into a guy I'd known at my former high school, the one my father'd helped me transfer from. This guy, Mark Avila, was older, he'd been a classmate of my sister's and captain of the debate team. I remembered him sneering and calling me, "Teenybopper." In fact, he'd always behaved like a supreme dick. But now, he was smiling, really sweet, giving off good vibes...a complete reversal of his former style.

"Mark, you, uh, you seem so..."

"Nice? Different?" He threw back his head and laughed. "My life is transformed, and I'm happy now. I discovered the secret of—EVERYTHING."

"Oh yeah? Know anything about Cosmic Consciousness?"

He waved a hand. "No, things like that are of the MIND. I've found something better. Really. It's Jesus. I mean, I'm a Christian, but not in any way you've ever heard of. This is real. It's a new revelation, and the secret is to let your mind die so you can accept the truth and have peace."

"Whaaat?"

"No, really. Got time to walk with me? You can meet some good friends of mine, Larry and Leah."

And I went, partly to argue, partly out of curiosity. I figured Mark was probably hitting on me but reckoned I could fend off his advances. By the time we got to Larry and Leah's, I'd begun to warm up to the idea of listening to him, meeting those friends of his. Sure, he'd been captain of the debate team, no doubt possessed powers of persuasion. But something else drew me. He seemed...joyful.

We arrived at a coffeehouse, and joined Larry and Leah at their table. Leah's long, wavy, blond locks glistened. Larry's wavy long hair, the same color, shone like a halo. The two of them exuded an air of subdued thrill, a sort of exuberant vibe similar to Mark's. Larry turned to Mark and solemnly intoned, "Today I addressed the carnal mind and told it to keep still." *What the fuck??*

And Mark nodded, crossed his arms over his chest and said, "Amen...Amen." Really weird, nonsensical stuff. Then Larry and Leah started spouting off about their upcoming trip. They were packing, they said, and heading for California, and then when the time was right, on to British Guyana with a really spiritual group of people.

Leah locked her blue-eyed gaze on me. "Their leader, the Reverend Jim Jones, is a visionary; he's establishing a temple for all people. At the People's Temple, nobody even needs money, because we all share everything. It's just like the early Christian church. It's reeeaally beeeaauuutiful."

Mark mentioned something about "Wings of Deliverance." When Larry and Leah got up to leave I walked with Mark as far as the edge of campus, then walked home, thinking about some of the things he'd told me. *Wow. That was kinda weird...but they look so...happy...*

Okay, I didn't join up with the People's Temple and the infamous Jim Jones. But I did end up getting sucked into what I think of now as a Rapture Vortex, where I got brainwashed, terrorized, and exploited by cultish, fanatical, Bible-thumping, prophesy-pumping, speaking-in-tongues-ing evangelical Christian extremists known as Jesus People, or Jesus Freaks, in the jargon of the day. I also survived a brief foray into the congregation of a renegade wing of the Pentecostal Holiness Church, where they scared the shit out of me with their talk of hell, eternal damnation, and punishment of sin. The subconscious baggage of guilt, fear, and shame from Catholic elementary school, combined with my trauma history, somehow rendered me ripe for swallowing their entire con game hook, line, and sinker.

I'd been reading the Bible—Yep, King James Version, the light and breezy translation—and since both the Old and New Testament are chock full of stern references to "whores," "harlots," and "adulterous women," and passages about sin coming into the world through Eve, and blah, blah, I began to view my entire short life as a constant stream of sin, evil, and lust—crimes of the flesh punishable by eternal damnation. When Derek came back to the Midwest in June, I told him I was through with premarital sex and we broke up. I quit the birth control pills and tried to sneak all the remaining sample packets out to the garbage can, but my mom busted me with them and grounded me indefinitely. I stayed in my room or the yard through July and August, reading the Bible, praying, consuming as little food and water as I could in penance. *Yeah, I WAS a little crazy for a while there.* The job in the rural elementary school soon followed, and the grand mal seizure. All of it took place over the summer of my seventeenth year.

———

And now Derek had come here to the hospital, seeking a reconciliation. He loved me and wanted me back. *But...What do I want?*

"Hey, uhhmmm, MARTI? Um, HEY!! Are you listening to me? Hey, Derek's IN LOVE with you! Don't you wanna see him? I can go get him now."

I slapped on a smile, tried to sound perky. "Oh, yeah, sure! Go get him, Crystal. Tell him I can't wait!"

"When we broke up, I cried, Marti." Derek looked down at his hands, then shook his head. "Thing is, I was really torn up—but then I realized I couldn't've lost ya to a better man." He chuckled.

"Jesus, I mean. And then I started thinking about how you're right not to get high, not to...sin. I went to the woods and sat out there, listening to the wind in the trees, and I felt my grandfather's presence. He was a preacher, you know."

"Right, I remember you told me that on his deathbed, his last words were, 'Don't let the kids date Catholics.'"

"Yeah." Another chuckle. "But...I was close to him growing up. Anyway, I had a moment, where I felt the presence of, of—God, you know? And I came here to tell you I've changed. I quit getting high. Weed, acid, everything. But I can't quit you. I tried, believe me. But...I love you." He exhaled slowly. "And I want you to marry me. I'll wait while you make up your mind, I know you need time." He took my hands in his. "I...there's something else I wanna tell you. There's this guy Jimmy, he's a man of God, and he lives out by the drag race track. He's taught me a lot about God. He says there's no hell or damnation or anything, and that God is only pure love. I go hang out there, there's a whole crowd of regulars at Jimmy's place. He plays guitar, and I jam with him sometimes. If you want to get hold of me, you can call me there. Hold on, I've got the number."

Derek reached into the pocket of his fringe jacket, drew out a business card, and gently pressed it into my hand. Then he stood up and exited, leaving me alone in the nuthouse. I turned the card over, noticed a few lines of plain black text. It read, "In the deepest night, there shines a light, that binds the power of darkness. A hand to hold, a love to share, a promise that's eternal." Then on the other side, a phone number.

I welcomed that card and its inscription, murmuring those words, repeating them to myself, over and over, till I had it memorized, hoping it'd give me strength. All that day, before Derek's appearance, I'd been wrestling with the stress of returning to my high school in the morning. Even though I pantomimed gulping down the meds whenever possible, I couldn't manage to get away with that every time, so I was still heavily impaired. I dreaded showing up over there, even though I'd been socially disconnected for the past year or so. Worse, I'd be forced to return to the hospital after school! Dr. Crudball's orders. But I needed to cooperate, no matter how tough the situation, because once I'd knuckled under and fulfilled the demands of the child psychiatrist, sweet freedom awaited me out on that wild, un-medicated frontier, beyond Crazy Town City Limits. I yearned to reach that milestone.

———

"Happy Birthday to me. Eighteen years today! And Happy Wedding Day to me, too!" I said it out loud, a celebratory statement of fact, then stepped out of bed onto the icy-cold hardwood floor of my bedroom. January weather in the Midwest can get positively polar. But the sun shone brightly. I reached for my James Taylor album, Sweet Baby James, and carefully set the record player needle down on my favorite song, "Fire and Rain." These days, I listened to a lot of laid back music, no more twangy, loud, electric guitar riffs. I sang along with the lyrics as I laid out my simple wedding dress and prepared to head for the shower. "Oooh, I've seen fire and I've seen rain, I've seen sunny days that I thought would never end, seen lonely times when I could not find a friend—when James Taylor got to the "...could not find..." part, I always lost track of the tune. *Reality check. Tin ear. Oh well...*

Looking back now, I think the lion's share of my exultation that day issued from the knowledge that my parents were furious, especially my mom. My mother and father had protested my marriage to Derek, but I defied them by marrying him on my eighteenth birthday, the very first moment when parental consent was no longer legally required. Reveling in delicious rebellion, I'd bought my wedding dress with my very own paycheck from Kresge's, the five-and-dime store downtown, one of a chain of department stores that would soon evolve into the Kmart corporation. And I'd planned on baking my own wedding cake, but my friend Beth Ann, one of the girls who hung out at Jimmy's Place, had volunteered to bake the cake, and she and her mom'd promised to provide the flowers for the ceremony. My parents had refused to support the venture in any fashion, probably hoping I'd back down, but that didn't stop me. I printed up flyers that said something like, "Open House Wedding, Bride is Baking Her Own Cake, blah, blah, blah," and then gave the address of Jimmy's Place, the house by the drag race track where it would happen. One mercy for my parents was that the event would take place in Derek's town, about a half hour drive from our town. This would no doubt save them, especially my mother, some embarrassment.

I was putting on the dress when my mom walked to the foot of the stairs and called me. "Honey!" She paused long enough for an eloquent sigh, then soldiered on. "Honey, are you ready? Your dad's warming up the car." At the last moment, they'd insisted on driving me over there. Maybe they thought it'd be bad luck if the groom picked me up in his sister's Vega as we'd planned. My Aunt Julie and Uncle Jack had come up from Louisiana, most likely to help my mom survive the ordeal.

When we got there, the place was jammed, standing room only. Hordes of Jesus freaks, local musicians, plain old freaks, and some dyed in the wool rednecks I figured must be denizens of the neighboring drag strip jostled for space in the living room. I had to push my way into a back room to put on my veil and the wreath of flowers that held it in place. One of the musicians'd brought a keyboard, but all of a sudden, it dawned on the guy that we'd need to play the bridal march. "I don't know that one!!" He ran his hands through his long red hair, then shot out into the crowd, yelling, "Anybody know how to play the bridal march on a Fender Rhodes??"

One guy volunteered to play, "96 Tears," but the bystanders shouted him down, snorting in derision. "Okay then, how about some Procol Harum? I can do the lead-in for 'Whiter Shade of Pale!!"

Sequestered in the back room, I stepped to the doorway and yelled my approval at the top of my lungs. "I LOVE THAT SONG!"

The music sounded fantastic, the keyboard player showed real skill. The traveling preacher Jimmy'd collared to do the ceremony turned out to be more of a boxcar-hopping hobo, and he kept calling Derek, "Durbin," all the way through the vows and everything, but he did possess a valid license to marry people in our state. My mom nearly fainted, but Dad and Aunt Julie held her up. All those people brought wedding gifts, or even cash. At the end of the day, we ran for "Durbin's" sister's Vega. He tossed our suitcases in, slammed down the trunk. We jumped in the car, eager to set off on our honeymoon, a weekend stay in Derek's folks' cabin in the Ozarks. My groom's face glowed with blissful anticipation. We'd been celibate since the breakup in June. Then his face fell and he clapped a hand to his forehead. "Oh NO!! I—I—LOCKED the KEYS in the TRUNK!!!"

———————

DOUG AND BRANDON WOBBLED INTO THE KITCHEN, FACES greenish-tinged. "Still throwing up, huh?" I handed Doug the box of Arm & Hammer baking soda...again. *Eeew. I wonder why he thinks it's gonna help him?*

Doug managed a feeble smile, nodding his thanks. "We did everything according to Scripture!" He bit his lower lip, then gulped the bicarbonate mixture. "Just like John the Baptist!"

Brandon leaned in, open Bible in hand, index finger stabbing the page in frustrated emphasis. "Yeah, that's right! It's right here in Matthew 3:4: 'Now John himself had a garment of camel's hair and a leather belt around his waist; and his food was locusts and wild honey.' There. End of story." He snapped his Bible shut and smacked the cover with the flat of his hand.

"Uummm. It talks about a camel hair garment and a leather belt."

Brandon and Doug moved in unison, vehemently, lifting their Billabong and Vans surfer shirts just high enough to show me their leather belts without revealing bare skin.

"Oookaay. Camel's hair?"

Doug shot out of the kitchen, pounded across the living room and charged up the stairs, two at a time. He galloped back down in a heartbeat, waving a wire hanger with a sport coat draped on it. "Camel hair sport coat! Hundred percent camel hair. Check out the tag. We are of the Word, man. Didn't say he WORE the garment. Just said he HAD it." He stared, triumphant, hands on hips. Then his face looked greener all of a sudden and he lurched for the door. His buddy Brandon ran after him, probably to hold Doug's hair back while he hurled. Both guys were surfers, far from California, their home turf.

I shouted after him. "Okay, okay, you're scripturally accurate. But this is your third day. Don't you think God will reward your fast after three days? I think you guys can quit now, that's all I'm saying." I went back in the kitchen, washed my hands carefully, then prepared to punch down my bread dough. It was the summer of the seventeen-year locust plague, and here in Springfield, Missouri, locusts peppered the hot humid air, studded the landscape, and swarmed over every inch of vegetation. They chirped and chittered all night long, assassinating slumber for all but the most narcoleptic of the population. There seemed to be no escape. I walked back to the doorway, hollered to the surfer boys. "Three days is PLENTY! And the health food store is OUTTA WILD HONEY, so y'can't ask for ANY of MINE! I need it for whole wheat bread. HEY—just THROW in the TOWEL, will ya?"

Helen Harlan shuffled into the kitchen, poured herself a cup of coffee. "Mah Staahs, it's easeh to see whahy thehy think this locusts-and-wild-honey fast is divahnely inspiahed. Whah, Ah declayah, everwheah you look, LOOCUUSTS!" She sipped, smacked her lips ever so slightly. "Ah'm so verreh tiahd, honeh, will you be a deah an' fetch me the sugah? Ah was up till all houahs last naht. James, an' George, and Samuel and I, we weh on ouah faces befoah the Loahd, in prayuh, houah aftah houah. Prayuh warriahs!" I nodded, passed her the sugar bowl and a spoon.

Helen, an elegant, fortyish divorcee from Macon, Georgia who wore her honey blonde hair in a chignon, held the position of housemother. Here, in the boys' dormitory of the Academy of the Overcomer, she reigned as queen. As assistant cook and mere minion, I put up with her bullshit day in and day out, and worse, was subject to her crazy menu planning—along with the unfortunate male Bible students in residence. Even the sight of her signature dish, Baloney-and-Cheese Casserole, a culinary phantasm containing chunks of the traditional jailhouse lunchmeat plus a mix of aerosol cheddar and Velveeta, hurled my stomach into free fall. Each and every Wednesday, when she served it, I prayed feverishly that a famished raccoon with an iron stomach would scratch at the back door, so I could toss the varmint my uneaten portion. No divine intervention so far, though. Doug and Brandon'd been living at the dorm for a good five months now, so it came as no surprise they'd initiated the locust fast. *What'd they have to lose?*

Helen cocked her head and raised an eyebrow. "Wheah's Derek?"

"In our room, I guess."

"He must be in prayuh. Or studyin' the Loahd's Wuhd."

"Uhh. Yeah. Probably."

"Well, Sistah Mahthah, I wanted to ask y'huusband to taaghten the screws on the laaght switch covah here in the kitchen, but if he's deep in prayuh, well…Ah know he's vereh devoted to holiness in the Loahd."

I hated it when she started in about Derek. I knew what he was doing—sleeping till dusk, or strumming his guitar. He played with the amp unplugged most of the time, but sometimes he jammed with Zechariah, the youngest and newest addition to the dorm and the son of a traveling evangelist and faith healer from Tennessee. The guys called him Zeke. It seemed to me Zeke yearned to take a walk on the wild side—to get a little taste of what his dad and the other holiness ministers so vehemently eschewed. But he'd been deposited here, by his folks, to study the Good Book and piously follow in his daddy's footsteps. The closest Zeke could get to Sin City was to learn the chords to "Light My Fire," by the Doors. Zeke justified playing a satanic acid rock song in the dorm living room by changing the word, "Baby," to "Jesus."

A few strangled notes reached my ears. They were evidently engaged in a spirited jam session now. "Come-on-Jesus-light-my-fire." Strum. Strum. "Try-to-set-the-night-on—FY-AAAHH!" A torrent of mangled notes formed a quasi-instrumental bridge, then: "Yeah…Come-on-Jesus-light-my—OH, MAN! I goofed it up, Derek. Let's start again…" Fumbling noises.

No. Not again, fellas! Fuck, no. I intervened. "Hey, umm, Derek?"

"Yeah, Sugar Beet?" He laid his guitar across his knees and smiled up at me.

"Yeah, Derek, Helen needs you to do some maintenance work. Tighten the screws on the light switch in the kitchen."

"Oh yeah…well, okay." He put his guitar in its case, shut the lid, rummaged in his toolbox for a Phillips screwdriver, and sauntered into the kitchen.

We'd landed here at the Academy of the Overcomer only a few weeks before—a slow- moving train wreck for me, but a lucky break for my husband. At Jerry's place, a traveling Jesus freak'd given Derek a flyer that advertised the school, and my spouse had been really stoked about going there to check it out. I'm not sure why it appealed to him; maybe it was the part in the flyer where they mentioned, "gathering the Sons of God into the Army of the Lord." Derek's number was inching up the draft lottery list and the way I figured it, if he wanted to join an army, he could stay put and wait for induction by Uncle Sam. Then three guys from Jerry's— Duane, Brent, and Gordy, offered to pitch in gas money. That'd cinched the deal. We'd piled into the little Volkswagen Derek's Dad'd given him and headed for Springfield, Missouri. When we rolled into town and located the Academy of the Overcomer and the church attached to it, the car overheated, we ran out of gas, and our total cash holdings amounted to about ten bucks—instant, involuntary relocation.

We called it a win when Brother Mike Manchester, the preacher who ran the Academy, took pity on us, offering both Derek and me a working scholarship. Brother Mike told us he needed a married couple to live in the boys' dormitory and provide support for the housemother. My duties included cooking meals for twenty-three people and cleaning the living room and common areas, and Derek's job was to provide security and do the basic handyman chores. Easy Peazy—seemed like a terrific deal to me at the time. Sure, I didn't really want to go to Bible school and yeah, it totally sucked that they made me throw away my "apparel of a man." There's a verse in the Old Testament that forbids women to wear the apparel of a man, and the Academy of the Overcomer interpretation of that verse included banning females from wearing jeans, shorts, or slacks. Turned out I had to spend our last ten bucks at the local Goodwill store, buying a couple of skirts long enough to fit the church's dress code.

Our jobs didn't come with wages. No paycheck. We worked for room and board. Oh yeah, and of course we got free "tuition," since the job required each of us to attend every class at the Academy of the Overcomer. I engaged in fleeting contemplation of getting an annulment and returning to live at my folks' house—I missed my dad. But then I remembered how my mom'd said I'd be back in no time, begging to come home, and the memory stiffened my resolve. *Sink or swim, I'll never admit failure.* I hunkered down and worked my ass off, rolling out biscuits for breakfast every morning at 5:30 a.m., standing at the sink washing dishes, and peeling potatoes for Baloney-n-Cheese Casserole or whatever gastronomic waterboarding mechanism Helen might've contrived for the evening meal. Mizz Helen pumped potatoes, spam, or baloney into the menu every chance she got.

"Sistah Mahthah! SISTAH MAAAHTHAAAH!!" Helen's voice waxed uber-shrill when she shouted. "Come on in heeah!!! It's TAAHM to fix DINNAH!!"

I hustled into the kitchen, began the dreaded task of prepping fresh okra. When you cut into raw okra, a sort of slimy gel oozes out and gets all over your fingers. And Helen's recipe called for rolling the okra slices in cornmeal, a process resulting in corn-dog-like digits on both hands. Helen loved okra, but only if it was breaded in cornmeal and deep fat fried. Weather simmering at ninety-seven degrees with ninety-nine percent humidity for five consecutive days couldn't dissuade Mizz Helen from whipping up a big batch. *No stopping her. Gotta power on through...I gotta make biscuits next.* During the first few days at the Academy, I'd become painfully aware of the fact that my husband got the better deal. He seldom left our room—only for meals and classes. Today's request for Derek to tighten a light switch was the second time in nearly a month's residency that he'd been called on to play handyman. And security? Well, these guys were glassy-eyed, cultish types, sworn to serve the Lord...no need to break up any fist fights in this joint.

But the real payoff for Derek in all of this was that he now had a bona fide draft deferment: studying for the ministry. Derek's dad had assisted him in filling out the necessary forms—as a psychiatrist with anti-war sentiments, he'd helped others who'd been called up, so it'd been no trouble helping his son obtain asylum from possible deployment. What blew me away was that the feds recognized the Academy of the Overcomer as legitimate, a seminary of sorts.

I recognized resentment rising up in me, began wrestling with it. I'd been immersed in theology for several weeks now, what with studying both Testaments of the Bible, a lot of it had rubbed off on me. My conscience worked overtime, weeding out sin and evil from my thoughts. Maybe if I'd allowed myself to get really pissed off, I'd have mustered the gumption to hitch a ride on a boxcar— I lacked the cash for even a humble handful of Greyhound—and split that town…left my husband and all the rattlesnake-handlers behind, moved to Vegas or Chicago or Miami. But I didn't.

Instead, I stuck it out, stood there in that sweltering kitchen. I've never acquired the art of the poker face, and my transparency back then was no doubt glaring. Perhaps that's the reason Sister Helen lunged into my personal space just then, kicking in the door of my inner thought life like a lunatic-fringe-evangelical SWAT team. "Sistah Maahthah, we must pray!" *Oohh, MAN!* I pretended not to hear her, focused on the slippery wedges of okra, reached for additional cornmeal. Helen coughed loudly. Then: "SISS-tah MAAHthah, the Loahd spoke to me just now. He wants us to bend ouah heads in prayuh." She held out a cornmeal-coated hand, squeezed her eyes shut, and inclined her head toward heaven. I took a deep breath, exhaled, then joined hands in "prayuh," hoping this session'd be mercifully brief. At the Academy, prayer was often a marathon, seldom a sprint.

I didn't close my eyes. "Yes, um, thank you, uh, thank you for uh, for this…food." *Yeah, and please show the locusts where the okra crops are growing, okay, God? How about a short term okra short-age? Not a famine, just a break in the okra action, Amen.* "And, and... Bless Helen."

Helen clenched my hand tighter in hers, and globs of corn-meal breading fell to the linoleum. "Yeesss, Loahd! Bless Sistah Mahtah, and bless this woahk we do. Please keep us huumbllle, and puuuah. And help us to be SUBMISSIVE WAHVES to ouah husbands..."

Whaaat? What. The. F—Oh, no she didn't say that! Fury boiled up in me. *This bitch doesn't even have a husband, she's divorced!! She's talkin' to ME! Submissive wives...where's my biscuit cutter and how long would take to convert it into a shank? I'll cut you, Helen... Hey, wait a minute, we're praying here...*I struggled with my outrage, finally subdued the urge for bloody vengeance.

Sistah Helen continued, working herself into a frothy religious rapture. "Ooh yeesss, Loahd, do help us to be TRULY submissive, and to have the meek and quahet spirit that becometh a woman of the Loahd, and to know that SIN entahed into the woahld through woman, but God delivahs us from sin, if we ah willin' to be cleansed. And may the marriage bed be always holy, and puuah, and—" I in-terrupted the housemother's hysterics by wrenching my hand away.

"Yes, and—praise the Lord. Amen." I lunged for the sink, turned on the hot water tap, began washing my hands. "Great prayer ses-sion, now back to work." *Crazy-ass woman!*

That was a typical workday at the Academy of the Overcomer's boys' dormitory. A few weeks later, Derek and I traveled to Ar-kansas for a week-long tent revival with Brother Manchester and a bunch of other students at the Academy, which was cool, because it afforded me a reprieve from Helen's prayer sessions, the okra, the baloney, etc. But I didn't outrun my biscuit ministry. It seemed that my biscuits were highly esteemed in the Overcomer community; the Sons of God who lived in the boys' dorm bragged so avidly about my skills with dough that the women of the cook tent pressed me into service. And since tents don't have light switch covers, Derek was free to do whatever he wanted with his time.

The tent revival is a hearty hunk of Americana, a long-cherished tradition in the rural regions. This particular one was deep in the heart of the Ozark Mountains, far from civilization, with a plethora of tents involved—a kind of tent revival convention. There was the cook tent and the tents where we camped—these were communal, and segregated by gender. All of us lowly women, by whom, according to some, sin had entered the world, slept in one or two big tents; all of the men, who were, according to some, made in the image of God and to whom we women must be submissive, slept in the other. And presiding in splendor over all other pavilions in this pageant was the actual revival tent itself, the big top, where the three-ring circus of holy rolling signs and wonders unfolded each day and every night.

From my seat on a folding chair under the canopy of the revival tent, I heard from preachers, evangelists, and faith healers of every stripe but never saw an exorcism or a rising from the dead—though it was rumored that such miracles had been worked the previous year. Brother Mike had warned us, on the trip to the event, about charlatans and exploiters. "Wolves in sheep's clothing," he'd called them. Apparently, the holiness movement was rife with sexual predation, incest, larceny, and fraud.

The craziest thing I saw that week was on Saturday night during a faith healer's pitch. The healer guy had the crowd mesmerized. His preaching lathered them up into delirium, and at the apex of the turmoil he challenged them to demonstrate their faith with deeds. A guy in the back heaved a crutch in the direction of the altar; it pinwheeled end over end, landing just to the left of the preacher's spit-shined brogans. Then everybody hollered, "Hallelujah!"

Another dude ran up the aisle, stopped a few feet from the altar, tore his bifocals off his face, threw them into the sawdust-strewn aisle and stomped on them. More spectacle-wearers followed suit. A cane shot down the aisle, and the man who flung it tried to run after it, but fell down hard, tucked and rolled, barely avoiding the pounding feet of an obese redneck who tossed his toupee in the air, yelling, "Glory!"

A blood-curdling "Praise be!" rent the sultry night air, and we all turned to see a dude jerk a truss out of his khakis and wave it around in a circle over his head before hurling it skyward, where it caught on a string of lights and stuck there. Then, as the shouts and applause of the faithful reached a deafening crescendo, an elderly gent tottered halfway down the aisle, then stopped stock still, and swaying only slightly, reached into his mouth with trembling fingers, pulled out an entire set of false teeth, slow-pitched them toward the altar, and as the dentures skittered down the aisle, cavorted and cackled with glee.

After the faith healer passed the hat, we filed out of the revival tent. I crashed out quickly, as soon as my head touched the pillow, but was up at 4:30 a.m. with the other cook staff. The morning mist lay thick on the landscape, making it difficult to see more than a yard or two in front of my face on my way to the cook tent, and I goofed up, blundering into the revival tent instead. That's when I saw him— the octogenarian who'd capered so merrily the night before after casting off his choppers to the roar of the throng. Sadder but wiser, he'd returned to the scene at dawn, in search of that set of false ivories. Sometimes the miracle of modern dentistry is miracle enough. At first sight of the old duffer, I felt a strong urge to help him look, but thought better of it. He probably wanted to keep it on the down low. Anyway, the Lord helps those who help themselves, right?

―――――――――

WE RETURNED TO THE ACADEMY FROM THE TENT MEETING, and found all hell had broken loose in the boys' dorm. Helen Harlan had caused a scandal. Helen, the fortyish housemother, and Samuel, nineteen years old and one of the dorm's residents—one of the "prayuh warriahs" that Helen mentioned often—had gone to the elders, requesting to be married. They told the church officials they were already "married in the eyes of God," and that they needed to live together as man and wife, in Helen's room in the dormitory. The church people, horrified, began to question the dorm's residents about whether they'd noticed any unchaste conduct. That's when James and George broke down and confessed that Helen the housemother was a Jezebel who'd led them astray, into fornication, and two more "prayuh warriahs" bit the dust. Upon that disclosure, the elders jettisoned Helen, permanently banning her from the church and the school for eternity and beyond. The students were put on probation.

At that point, Derek and I accepted an offer to work with another cluster of nutbags, in a Christian communal setting on the outskirts of Cushing, Oklahoma. Our foray into a communal corner of Rapture City didn't last more than six months. From there, we took up with a radical remnant of religious fanatics in Canada and Norway, and trekked to Scandinavia for a summer of crazy-ass camp meetings with a horde of rabidly right wing evangelicals from Switzerland, England, Germany, Denmark, Sweden, Norway, Finland, and the Netherlands. To my amazement, a contingent from Poland arrived at one point, having somehow cadged visas from the Soviet Union to attend for a few days. How they managed to break through the Iron Curtain during the height of the Cold War to sing hallelujahs remains a mystery.

This particular group's dogma prohibited the use of any birth control whatsoever, including the rhythm method, due to their literal interpretation of a verse in Genesis, "Be fruitful and multiply," which the male leaders insisted was the first commandment to proceed from the mouth of the Creator. They preached that women be entirely submissive to their husbands in even the tiniest details of life. The church elders imposed draconian dress codes for women, condemning females to drab colors, long, dowdy dresses, and the kind of shoes only worn by prison guards, postal workers, or the stereotypical little old ladies Boy Scouts help to walk across the street. But lumpen garments and clompy shoes weren't enough to impose modesty and meekness among the females of their sect. The holiness of the males might be threatened by feminine hairstyles. "Lead us not into temptation" was a mandate given to women and girls, and they carried it out by pulling their hair back in a braid and clipping it tight behind their heads, ensuring that not one come-hither-tendril could escape and frame one face, not one hint of style could exude from any feminine form or feature. And even a trace of makeup was considered beyond demonic. Any painted Jezebel was clearly a minion of Satan!

I didn't wear makeup anyway, so that regulation didn't matter, but I hated the idea I could never wear my jeans and boots again for the rest of my life. And I hated wearing my hair that way. It seemed as though the dress code was created to constrict female freedom of movement and to stamp out any creative expression. But the Scandinavian women set out to convert me—chicks my own age! And I can testify that the Viking blood running in their veins makes them fierce opponents in a debate. They battered me like a British monastery under attack from a battalion of berserkers, and eventually I caved to the pressure, donning a long skirt and primly stuffing my hair up in a bun. Back then I didn't consider myself an adolescent, but current science suggests that the brain is still in development till twenty-three or even twenty-five years of age. Trauma affects development...maybe that's how a badass like me could be subdued, even repressed. Religion, like a tidal wave, is a powerful force. Blind to its destructiveness, I tried to paddle out, catch it, and ride it to safety, but it crushed me...temporarily.

Under the dress code, men didn't exactly prance around in sartorial splendor. They wore white shirts and black pants, Mormonish haircuts, and ratty old wool sweaters or sport coats. But they enjoyed the privileges that males in repressive societies do, and females in the same social order do not: freedom of speech and expression, the possibility of achieving recognition within the group, and the chance of obtaining positions of responsibility and prestige in the outside world through their employment.

According to this church's ideology, women were strictly forbidden to work outside the home. If any woman wasn't chosen by a man to be his wife, or if a woman had been divorced, or was widowed, she would be employed as a helper, governess, or housekeeper in the home of one of the "fruitful" families who'd spawned a dozen or more offspring. I never found out if these dictates amounted to life sentences for the unmarried females, but the lifetime imprisonment of the mothers of double-digit broods of kids was both glaringly obvious and terrifying to witness. I talked with women who held advanced degrees in engineering, psychology, and law, but'd surrendered their successful careers to trudge a treadmill—an uninterrupted cycle of pregnancy, nursing, childcare, and household drudgery—and whose ultimate release came only in the form of menopause or death.

Why did they do it? Religious zeal, brainwashing...yeah, maybe. But the chilling possibility, the bogey man of a notion that crept into my mind daily was that maybe those women did it out of love for their husbands, or out of loyalty to their marriage vows; they followed their spouses into the cult and disappeared. Vibrant personalities, lives swallowed whole or, at best, dismembered by zeal, by dogma, by rigid statutes of piety. Sure, a lot of them must've been born into it. Either way, it sucked to be a woman in that scene!

The fundamentalism appealed to Derek. Both his grandfathers had been evangelists, so it may have seemed familiar, even comforting to him. Me? I was running from my trauma, trying to create a new identity, a sense of self proceeding from the evangelical concept of being born again, washing away the sexual abuse that dogged me, howling, and the shame and fear that followed close on its tail.

After a couple of months of tent living near the fjords and brainwashing among the fanatics, Derek and I returned to the U.S. We settled down in a little house situated only a few miles from his parents' place. The traveling carnival of religious extremism we'd run off with had carried us across the Atlantic and back again, then dumped us out onto the American prairie I'd been so desperate to flee in the first place. Cycle completed. The Scandinavian sect, wielding their wacko tenets like Thor's hammer, had successfully programmed us so that we clung to the bizarre beliefs. We'd made friends with other young convert couples from around the U.S. and Europe and stayed in touch via mail. Our peer group urged us to start a "fellowship" in our hometown area.

My enthusiasm lagged, but Derek was on fire. He began to talk about having children. He'd admired the cult patriarchs—and patriarchal power, maybe—and their siring of dozens of children. I wasn't on birth control of any kind. A few weeks after my nineteenth birthday, I'd made an appointment with a crotchety old doctor, an OB/GYN, to find out if my periods would come back, and I told him how I'd taken birth control pills into my seventeenth year and had ceased to menstruate during my sixteenth year. He examined me, pursed his lips in disdain, and pronounced me irreversibly sterile. "Your uterus is underdeveloped, and so is everything else." He snapped off his plastic examination gloves, crossed his arms over his chest, and glared at me. "It's called infantile uterus. And it's from those pills. You had to go out and have yourself a good time, didn't you, Miss? Well, now you're paying the price for premarital sex."

I'd glared back at him, stifling the urge to scream expletives and lunge for his throat. I repented of the urge, left the old pig's office, and went back home, which, at the time, was the screwball commune in Oklahoma, attempting to contain the MMA cage-fighting match between white hot rage and Christian code of conduct as applies to hurling invectives. *Infantile uterus! Fuuuuck HIM. Mother FUCKER!!! Er, sorry, uhm, Lord. Uhm, I...repent...*

Now two months shy of my twentieth birthday, back in the Midwestern state of my origins, I secretly felt relieved to be sterile. At least I wouldn't have to risk bearing and raising nine, eleven, or who-knows-how-many children.

In a strange twist of fate, Darla and Pete, a couple we knew from Jimmy's Place, had been sucked into the Nordic cult, the cyclone of berserker Bible-thumping that'd blown all rational thought out of our brains. Darla and Pete had joined up with a Canadian splinter of the Viking Christian Crazy Town that summer. Darla now wore those long, creepy skirts and the old lady shoes, and she and Pete'd evangelized another couple in the Midwest as soon as they'd hit town. That couple snagged another couple, and another, and soon we had a core group, a fellowship, a flock. Some already had babies, one chick was pregnant with her first.

The guys began vying for leadership. Fanatical religion can act like a drug, rendering people high out of their minds on the mere whisper of a chance to take power over others. The fertility mandate of the church implied that only a man with sons could lead. Derek wanted to be a leader, felt called to preach. He prayed over me, beseeching, begging for a miracle healing, began referring to me as "barren" and tried to draw comparisons between himself and Abraham, remarking that Abraham's wife, Sarah, was "also barren." Our freakshow lifestyle demanded meekness and submissive behavior from us loooowly women, so I resisted the urge to backhand my spouse; only asked that he apply for divine intervention in private.

The batshit crazy Nordic nutfest didn't believe in doctors. The elders—the faithful looked upon them as modern day Apostles—traveled around the U.S. and Canada, so on one of their visits, Derek asked them for help with my "barren womb," instigating an annoying volley of naturopathic medicinal recommendations. The nature doctor treatment plan required me to ingest herbal concoctions that stank, tasted nasty, or caused nausea. But it was the headaches, lower back pain, and anxiety attacks that drove me to seek legitimate medical care.

I made an appointment with Dr. Dooley, a general practitioner whose office was located within walking distance of my house. This second medico was younger, kinder, and had a good sense of humor. I told him about the birth control pills I'd taken during my teens, told him the brand, but left out the part about how the man who was now my father-in-law had supplied them.

The doc delivered his diagnosis in a brisk, let's-get-down-to-business tone, his attitude upbeat. "You've experienced a very rare event known as 'secondary uterine failure.' Your ovaries have shut down, too; they're atrophic." He added that in his opinion, the birth control pills had definitely caused the whole thing. Dr. Dooley paced the length of the examination room, then turned to face me. "Hmmm. Let's see...you started taking them at fifteen...yep, that'd do it." He crossed his arms over his chest. "Y'know, those Ovulen pills, the early ones, had all kinds of serious side effects. Seizures, blood clots, strokes...there was a case where Ovulen caused a psychotic episode. The estrogen levels were way too high—WAY too high. Where'd you get those pills, anyway? Some quack, right? Nobody else would prescribe those to a teenager. Or to anyone."

My face felt hot, my body shaky and weird. I wanted to leap off the exam table and run out of there. "Um, yeah. Some quack. They...they were sample packs, not a prescription, really. Um, it was a bad mistake. I was young and wild—I don't wanna talk about it."

In that moment, flustered, I told myself that what I felt was shame over having engaged in premarital sex. Or guilt about birth control. Both were taboo under my adopted religious coda. But looking back now, I think it was something deeper, a ferocity that'd been repressed, denied, buried for years. What I really felt that day was rage against my father-in-law who'd shelled out those poison contraceptives to me all those years, the guy who'd interrupted my young body's development, who'd put it in harm's way. I reflexively and instantaneously covered for him, gave him a pass, allowed him to remain anonymous, even in my own mind. Back then I nearly worshipped Derek's parents.

Doctor Dooley shrugged. "Well, I don't think it'll stop us from getting you fixed up. All you need is a couple of rounds of birth control pills—low estrogen, low impact—to kick this thing in the ass and get your hormones going. Everything will go back to normal." He scribbled on a notepad, tore off the page, handed it to me. "Here y'go. Start these tonight, take it with a light snack. I'll see you once a month or so, to monitor the process. Call if you need anything in between."

"Okay, but I'm not so sure about this, Doctor Dooley. Birth control pills caused the trouble, and—well, it's…"

"It's a safe regimen, and it'll be beneficial. I'm confident it can restore your reproductive system, and as you heal, you'll feel a whole lot better. The hormones'll help you from the neck up, too."

Okay, so I started taking the pills, and for the next seven months, the hormones raced around my body, surging through my brain, wreaking havoc on my central nervous system. An oddly familiar, born-again puberty stalked my emotional well-being like a pack of howling wolves. On the estrogen-progesterone roller coaster I felt jittery, skittery, depressed, then devoid of any feeling, and finally, overcome by emotion—sobbing. Abdominal cramps, lower back pain, headache, nausea. And then one day, like a prodigal daughter, my period returned. A week or so later, I went in for my monthly exam and the doctor informed me my ovaries were back in business. "Now that you're fertile, you'd better decide what kind of contraceptive you'd like to use. Talk it over with your husband and let me know." He exited, closed the door behind him.

Two weeks later, when the morning sickness began, I went back for a pregnancy test, and the results floored me. Dr. Dooley's nurse beamed and shook my hand. "Congratulations! You're pregnant!!" Apparently, when I'd come in for that last visit, I'd already conceived, but it was too early to show up in an examination.

"Oh my gosh I can't believe it!" I felt like I'd won the lottery—ecstatic, exuberant, giddy with the news. I also felt apprehensive as a flock of questions, born of self-doubt, began winging their way across my cerebral cortex. *What kind of a mom will I be? Am I strong enough? What about money—will I be able to provide enough for my child? Will my baby be healthy?* My legs felt wobbly, my chest tightened, and I felt my heart pounding. *What if I die in childbirth? STOP IT! Do. Not. Think. That. Thought. DO NOT!!!* I felt silly, emotional, and dorky...and yes, kinda freaked out.

I ran-walked-ran home from the doctor's office, leaning into the chilly March wind, lost in thought. *This child wants to be born, and he or she is going to be exceptional, brilliant, a miracle. This IS a MIRACLE! ARE YOU KIDDING ME? Only a few months ago, I was sterile. And today, I stand at the threshold, poised to welcome a new person into this realm, into the human race...Please, God, let me—just please let me be a good mother...*

Derek was thrilled—so were his parents. My baby would be their first grandchild. My folks offered congratulations, but their pinched faces showed me how worried they were for me. And no wonder: my three years and three months of marriage had so isolated me from them that we'd seldom seen each other.

Except for the unrelenting nausea, pregnancy agreed with me. Since my time in the psych ward at seventeen and crazy-ass "religious conversion," the fierce and funny aspects of my personality'd gone underground. I'd suppressed my real nature, attempted to fit the profile of—sainthood? Fuck, who knows? Anyway, it wasn't me. But when my child began to grow within me, I got re-connected with my genuine self. I began to think deeply about the events of my life so far. Slowly, carefully, I began to untangle the snarls of religious programming, examining them, looking for answers; and my questions weren't easy ones—God questions never are. Life questions, love questions, both are perplexing. Right and wrong, complicated! But I worked relentlessly on all of them.

I was trying to find a way out, to give myself permission to leave the toxic, three-ring circus of fanaticism I thought of as, "The Fellowship." I'd been conflicted, wrestling with it all along, fighting tooth and nail against the terror of God and Hell that the nuns'd instilled in me from the first minute I'd set foot in Kindergarten class at St. Agnes school. The fear awaited me, icy cold, pitch black, and deeper than the Arctic Ocean. As an expectant mother, I began to question the cult edicts. *What if my child is a girl? She'll be doomed to growing up in a culture that universally downgrades females, relegates us to the back of the bus. How can I do that to her? Hey—come to think of it, how can I do this to MYSELF?*

Throughout all of this soul-searching, another fear rose up within me, born of adverse experience and armed with the Big Question, "Am I Crazy?" That ominous doubt roamed the wilds of my unconscious mind, provoking panic and recollections of the psych ward, and the orderlies, and the medications that gave me welts and blistered my skin, and the possibility of being committed, confined to such a place for life.

During my nine months of expectancy, I didn't win the death match with the Crazy question, and I didn't arrive at any definitive answers to my questions about life, love, God, and right/wrong. But the stronger-better-faster-smarter-funnier-fiercer-fighter part of me tossed me a life line. The one Big Answer I did come up with was that although I didn't have any idea who God was, I knew what love was. I loved my yet-to-be-born baby. And I would cherish and nurture my child.

CHAPTER 4

HEADING OUT AND BREAKING AWAY

Derek stood in the kitchen of our tiny house, heating up a Swanson Frozen TV Dinner. I walked around the bedroom between contractions, mindful of my breathing, keeping my muscles as relaxed as possible. We'd been prepping for this together—attending Lamaze natural childbirth classes and practicing all of the strategies as a team. I lay down on the bed to rest, but moments later my water broke. "Derek! It's time."

On the drive to the hospital, I looked up at the starry sky, saw a full moon ascending. A light blanket of snow covered the landscape—perfect scenery for the Christmas season. The labor went smoothly with no complications. I'd been training for nine months, working out every day to be in top physical shape so I could be awake when the baby came. Eventually the labor grew so intense that it seemed to me I was rafting on a river of pain, but floating above it somehow—and at a certain point I felt the presence of both death and life, as if navigating between the two realms. That's when I felt my child's spirit approaching the threshold of this world as the realm of death rolled away, leaving only a celebration of life. I heard Dr. Dooley say, "Okay, it's time, the baby's coming."

Giving birth was like charging into battle and emerging victorious. My first glimpse of my newborn daughter filled me with bliss. I heard healthy squalls as they swaddled her body and handed her to me. I cradled her in my arms, and looked into her eyes. She looked back at me, reached out a tiny hand as if to touch my face, and the love I experienced is beyond description.

Derek and I were still following the cult and "abstaining from worldly pursuits," so we didn't keep up with the current trends in rock n' roll—but we did occasionally listen to FM radio in the stores or on long road trips to stay awake. Back then, there was a band called, "Heart," featuring two badass chicks who played amazing guitar. "Dreamboat Annie" was the title song of their debut album, and the first two lines of the lyrics were, "Heading out this morning, into the sun. Riding on the diamond waves, little darlin' one." I named my daughter Anne Marie, Annie for short, inspired by that song.

I devoted myself to being a loving mother, and could no longer see any point in grappling with facing a future shaped by the Fellowship's demands. I knew I couldn't handle living without some form of birth control—wanted to focus on effectively providing for and nurturing this one child. Soon, I put my foot down, broke away from the cult—and Derek came along with me. For a couple of months, everything seemed perfect.

Then the postpartum depression crept in, predatory, cold, silent—and dug in its claws. I fought back against its inexorable stranglehold, stayed busy reading and studying when the baby slept, still searching for answers to the God questions. I exercised to lift my spirits, kept telling myself I'd be all right as soon as spring returned bringing sunshine and flowers. I didn't tell anyone how down I felt, hoping if I didn't talk about it, it'd go away. Back in those days, the term "postpartum depression" wasn't part of the popular lexicon. Even if I'd wanted to talk about it, I might not have found the words.

Before and during my pregnancy I'd been working nights at my in-laws' psychiatric clinic, cleaning the offices until the third trimester when I'd quit for the sake of the baby. Derek worked for his dad's clinic too, as a maintenance man. Good thing his folks paid him a salary—Derek liked to sleep past noon, so his work performance tended to be spotty.

When Annie was about three months old I went back to work, cleaning the offices at night; took her along with me, since I was still nursing. Derek would sometimes accompany me, but would sit in his mother's house while I worked, drinking coffee and visiting. Occasionally, they would watch the baby for me.

I worried about money constantly, but my husband seemed immune to financial anxiety. Any time he needed a bailout or money for a treat, he'd turn to his folks, and they'd kick down some cash, and on the rare occasions when they didn't, he'd use a credit card. Derek's parents paid his way through a vocational school, where he studied carpentry, and when he completed his training, credit card offers came flooding in. He signed us up for joint credit with Sears, where he purchased lots of tools, and J. C. Penney and other retail stores. He also set us up with several gas credit cards. Derek spent money the way he'd seen his parents do it, never pausing to think about how he didn't earn enough income to pay the account balances. The mounting credit card debt fueled my depression.

During my pregnancy, Derek's family had begun to experience financial pressure from the IRS and Blue Cross/Blue Shield. Derek told me the IRS fined his dad a quarter of a million dollars and Blue Cross demanded some hefty retribution. Apparently charges against my then father-in-law were that his clinic had been billing hours for therapy—and collecting for them—using fictitious client files. There were several therapists working at the clinic, and Derek's dad was also practicing on site. Derek also told me his father'd been investigated for over-medicating patients and ethical violations, but I found that difficult to believe. Derek's father's corporate attorneys immediately set to work defending him. The legal fees must've been expensive. About a month after I'd gone back to work there, the clinic underwent major budget cutbacks, and they laid off the therapists. Derek got laid off too, and my job sailed out the window along with his.

Anne Marie was a little over four months old and I was still nursing her. Reluctant to sever the bond between us, I didn't look for another job right away. Besides, Derek wanted me to stay at home with the baby. Insisting that the man should bring home the bacon, Derek assured me he'd land a job in construction. Eventually he found one, and celebrated getting hired by stopping at the Sears store and charging some new tools. He arrived home with news that he'd begin the new job in the morning. That new career lasted only a couple of weeks before they let him go.

Relegated to the sidelines, I watched in frustration as my spouse burned through job after job, consistently showing up late to work, or knocking off early with lame excuses until they fired him. Finally, he managed to hold a position with a custom home builder. After collecting his second paycheck, Derek called in, faking sick, for three days in a row, and when he showed up on the fourth day, the boss tossed his ass off the construction site. Arriving home that night, Derek gave me the news that he'd charged a new oven range at Sears and had been fired, all in the same breath. "You need a new stove to cook on, Sweetie. It'll cheer you up."

Sweetie? Really? If I didn't have breast milk, our baby would starve. I stared at him, hands on hips. "Wait a minute...we've got ZERO dollars to buy food, and you go shopping for new KITCHEN APPLIANCES? What were you thinking?"

"NO! You NEED a new stove. I'M THE MAN OF THE HOUSE, and I say what stays and what goes, NOT YOU!" He turned his back and marched out, slamming the door behind him. We owned one car, which he took because he'd designated himself breadwinner.

For the next week, Derek spent his days at his mother's house, and left me home with Annie and an empty refrigerator. He'd done this so often I'd become accustomed to it. When he returned, I told him I couldn't take any more. "Something has got to change, Derek." I stepped into the nursery, glanced at the baby, reassured myself she was still sleeping peacefully. I stalked back into the kitchen. "There's no food, and no money, and if you won't go to work, I will!"

"It's not your place to work outside the family. The man is the head of the home."

"Oh yeah? We left the Fellowship, so get over it. Either you get a job and keep it, or I'm leaving."

Derek stood staring, slack-jawed. My assertiveness stunned him. He'd grown accustomed to my cult-imposed submissive role earlier in our marriage, never realizing the tremendous effort it'd taken for me to adapt to him, his family, his attitudes and wishes. And after the baby came, the depression had taken all the fight out of me. But that night I stood my ground.

After a mini-tantrum, he stomped out, slamming the door behind him. In a moment or two, I heard the car engine rev and tires squealing. Annie woke up and started to cry, so I hurried into the nursery, picked her up and held her in my arms. I spent the next hour pacing the house with the baby on my shoulder or sitting in the rocking chair with her in my lap. She fell back to sleep, and I gently laid her on her back in the crib. Exhausted, I shuffled back into the living room, sat down in the rocking chair and tried to clear my thoughts.

Derek returned after a bit, wild-eyed and panicky, waving a plastic prescription bottle. He slumped onto the couch, gripping the pill bottle in his fist, then swiveled his head my way. "Okay, I'm going to tell you something, but I want you to stay calm."

A fresh wave of exhaustion washed over me. I exhaled loudly. "What is it?"

He lurched forward, thrusting the pill bottle in my face. "Dad says you need to take this." He paused, as if for emphasis, inhaled sharply, waved the pill bottle around some more, then continued. "It's Lithium. Dad says you're manic depressive, and that's the reason we have financial problems, and marriage problems, and everything else. Dad says so."

As the immensity of this betrayal began to dawn on me, I felt outraged. But strangely, my mind became perfectly clear, tranquil, even. Then outrage gave way to numbness. "Oh, so he sent you over here to relay the DIAGNOSIS? Just like that?" I snapped my fingers.

Derek looked at me, blinked twice, and continued speaking. He was yammering really fast, nearly auctioneer speed; maybe he felt disappointed that I wasn't freaking out. Who knows? "Hey, I had no IDEA Dad was gonna give me news like this! I mean, I went over there, to Mom n' Dad's...and—and I was so upset because my marriage is falling apart, I mean, you said you're gonna LEAVE!—and I went to him, and I asked him for help, to see what I could do about our PROBLEMS. And DAD said that I don't have any problems, it's YOU that's the problem, and that MY problems are external, and that's okay, it's NORMAL—but YOUR problems are internal, and that's what's CAUSING THE TROUBLE!!" Derek stopped to catch his breath, then jumped up, began pacing, and went on barking out his Dad's manifesto. "At first, when Dad told me you were MANIC DEPRESSIVE, I thought, like, that you're a MANIAC, like MANIACAL, like Jekyll and Hyde, like, like, INSANE! And I told that to Dad, and he said, 'No, son, tell her it's a disease of genius,' that's what he said, see? See, it's a DISEASE OF GENIUS, and really smart people get it, and all you gotta do is TAKE THE LITHIUM, but first, you gotta wean the baby, like, right away, and I gotta bring you over to Mom n' Dad's house tomorrow and Dad'll give us more instructions for the things YOU NEED TO DO!" My husband finished his speech, stood stock still, waved the pills around again, and stared down at me.

I didn't reply, but felt the numbness draining away and recognized anger replacing it. I jumped up, snatched the pill bottle out of Derek's hand. "Give me the car keys."

Derek glared angrily at me, seemed to consider his options a moment or two, then dropped his gaze, forked over the keys, and headed back to the couch. "Where are you going?"

"I'm going to have a talk with your father." I turned to the door. "You look after Annie. Don't worry, she's fast asleep. I'll be back right away." I stumbled out to the car. Derek's parents lived only fifteen minutes away from our house. I slid into the driver's seat, started the engine, and backed out of the driveway. I figured I'd drive over there, confront my father-in-law, throw the Lithium in his face, tell him, "Thanks but no thanks," and get back home to my baby within forty-five minutes. *How could he do this to me? I thought he loved me like a daughter...*

By the time I reached my in-laws' place, I was trembling, breathing hard, trying to contain my emotions but not succeeding. I knocked on their door and heard my father-in-law's voice. "C'mon in," he called out. I stepped inside, saw him sitting in an armchair. He wore a robe over pajamas, and slippers on his feet. I didn't see my mother-in-law, figured she was already asleep or hiding in the bedroom to avoid facing me.

On the way over there, I'd hoped to describe to Derek's dad the hurt and sense of betrayal I felt, but when I got there, the only thing I succeeded in conveying was rage. I held out the prescription bottle. "You have no right...how dare you send me a...message like that—from a distance!" I clenched my hands into fists, felt my knees lock, fought to maintain composure.

He started talking softly, his tone cajoling, wheedling, manipulative. "You see, Marti, I'm doing you a favor. If I have you hospitalized—and I can do that—it'll be difficult and embarrassing for you. From what Derek's told me it's very plain to see you're manic depressive. With the disease of manic depression, your mind works fifteen times faster than the normal mind, you have flights of thoughts, mood swings...the Lithium will straighten you out. And I'll give you some Haldol, too. It's best we keep this in the family, you see?" He offered a tentative smile that looked phony and infuriated me.

"No, I don't see! What has Derek told you? Why didn't you ever talk to me about all this?"

"Your behavior right now can be interpreted as unbalanced. If I recommend you be sent to the psychiatric ward, they'll keep you there as long as I want them to. If you're not cooperative with the hospital, you could be detained indefinitely. Why not take the Lithium and the Haldol and save yourself the trouble?"

I stood still, trying to think of an argument that would convince my father-in-law I wasn't...well, crazy. But then I realized that according to the law he could easily have me committed to a mental hospital for life. At best, he'd send me to the local psych ward for a couple of months. I'd been in that same psych ward as a teenager, and no way would I willingly return.

So I began to think that the only route to self-preservation would be to capitulate...to take the Lithium. He'd crushed me, quickly and concisely. Exhausted and outgunned, I picked up the bottle of pills and headed for the door. My father-in-law stood up. "Good girl. Remember now, you don't take the Lithium until you've weaned my granddaughter. I'll give you the details tomorrow. Hey—better take these, too!" I turned. He handed me a couple of Valium. "These'll calm you down so you can sleep."

"Oh. Okay." I slogged off to the car, headed back home, and when I got there, tiptoed into my baby's room. For a moment, I watched her sleeping sweetly. Then I broke down and cried. I didn't take the Valium that night—Derek did.

The next day I bathed and dressed Anne Marie, loaded up her stroller, and got into the car with Derek. We drove to my in-laws' place, where Derek's father issued his mandate. He'd prescribed both Lithium and Haldol for me, with several refills. He expected me to wean the baby in three days or less, so I could get started on the medication. And he expected me to take the medication for the rest of my life. Derek's mother sat beside him, nodding in agreement with everything her spouse said. A part of me wanted to tell them to mind their own business, to go to hell, in fact, but I knew that kind of resistance would be useless. They held all the cards.

I did try to argue for leniency. Through nursing my child, I'd formed a strong bond with her, and I'd read that weaning should be gradual so as not to put unnecessary stress on the baby or create physical pain for the mother. If the weaning is forced, the milk backs up and there's a real risk of developing an infection in the breast. I explained all of this to Derek's parents, but they dismissed me, glibly waving away my concerns. I knew that my mother-in-law had never nursed any of her children, so I wasn't surprised that she didn't get it. I did expect my father-in-law, as a physician and psychiatrist, to listen to me. *Didn't he take the Hippocratic Oath? "First do no harm," right?*

I took another stab at it. "Look, I'm not resisting your, um, diagnosis. I just want to be allowed some extra time to complete the weaning process."

My father-in-law exchanged glances with Derek and pointed a finger in my direction. "I can't allow that. We've got to get you started on the Lithium right away. You can use icepacks on your breasts to manage any discomfort."

Boy, did I need those icepacks! However, the physical pain paled in comparison with the emotional anguish I experienced during those three days. The baby cried a lot, didn't sleep much, didn't understand what was going on, didn't seem to like the rubber nipple and the taste of the baby formula. I walked the floor with her, trying to soothe her, holding her close to my swollen, aching breasts, abstaining from sleep tending to her. Eventually, she took the bottle. All weekend, Derek lay on the couch or on our bed, making disparaging comments. At one point, when I asked him if he would go to the store for me, he only stared. "I'm so depressed I can't do anything! I'm completely destroyed by this whole thing, I mean, it's like...you have a flaw. You have a FLAW!"

I started taking the Lithium, struggled to adjust to it. My hands shook, I felt very tired and weak, experienced eye pain, and my limbs felt numb. (Later, my skin broke out in a rash, and I gained weight.) Even though I experienced these unpleasant side effects, my father-in-law assured me that such reactions could be expected, that they were normal. And he pushed the Haldol, a drug prescribed for acute psychosis, schizophrenia, and Tourette's syndrome that carries some nasty side effects. Looking back on this now, I think the man was punishing me on behalf of his son, assaulting my personality with his chemical arsenal, corralling me within high walls built of psych meds.

Over the next several months, my marriage to Derek began to crumble. His parents offered to pay his way through college, but he procrastinated registering for classes and refused to look for steady work, insisting we could live on credit cards till he got into school. Finally, one frigid night in January, with our mortgage three months behind and the bank announcing foreclosure, with our utility bills three months in arrears and disconnect notices in the mailbox, I picked another fight with my mate. The baby was sound asleep so we argued about money in hushed tones. I don't recall what I said, or what he said, but I remember he slammed me up against the wall, wrapped his hands around my throat and started choking me. I felt the airway close off, the grip of fear as I grew dizzy and my vision darkened. And then, for no apparent reason, I started laughing—well, laughing as much as is humanly possible while being strangled, anyway. The whole situation was so ridiculously miserable.

Derek pulled his hands from my neck, pushed me away, and headed for the door. Once again, he retreated to Mommy and Daddy's—took the car and stayed there. I felt anger, defiance, and elation as the divorce proceeded. Since I applied as a pauper, I got what I paid for. Derek's father's corporate attorney represented him. Looking back now, I figure they must've bought my lawyer. The judge ruled that because I was living in the house, it constituted assets, even though the house was in foreclosure and the utilities would soon be disconnected. They only required minimal child support from Derek, around twenty-five dollars a month. He never made any of those payments, but I didn't report it to the court. I was too busy working to support myself and my child.

I didn't allow the lack of a vehicle to prevent me from looking for work as soon as I filed the divorce papers. My next-door neighbors' sixteen-year-old daughter watched the baby for me while I went out job hunting on foot—in the snow. I applied at gas stations, department stores, restaurants, a convenience store, anywhere they'd let me fill out an application. I also stopped at the utility companies and negotiated with them to give me some more time to find work before they cut off the water, heat, and lights. And I pleaded with the bank for some time to pay off the mortgage. I didn't get work immediately, but I did convince the bank and utilities to delay the foreclosure and the disconnects for a few weeks. My daughter and I stayed warm, with a roof over our heads, at least temporarily. And when my father bought me a battered old Volkswagen Hatchback, I expanded my job search, combing through all the ads in the local newspaper.

When I finally landed a job as a cocktail waitress I wasn't exactly thrilled, but managed to be optimistic. The ad was for a place called "The Island," and when I called to inquire, they hired me over the phone and told me I could start immediately that same day on the four-to-eleven shift. That should've been a red flag for me, but I had no clue—I visualized The Island as a place with a tropical theme: Hawaiian shirts, Mai Tais, Jimmy Buffett music. Fun in January. It was a Friday, so the neighbor's sixteen-year-old daughter was available to babysit till midnight.

When I arrived and parked my car, I realized how The Island had earned its name. A ramshackle three-story wooden building, complete with peeling paint and a neon sign, squatted on the concrete island between two stretches of highway. The only remotely tropical thing here was the magenta and mango colors in its blinking neon sign. Across one freeway from the Island, a meatpacking plant belched fetid smoke, and on the other, a sheet metal fabrication plant stood, lights on, its shreddings, grindings and gougings audible from the curb.

I fortified my will, squared my shoulders, and headed into the bar, promising myself there'd be cash tips to take home after my shift. I'd worn my very best dress, a hilarious detail considering the clientele and working conditions. The walls inside the Island looked sooty, as though they'd absorbed the greasy exhaust from the meatpacking plant's smokestack over several generations. The wooden tables and chairs'd been carved with nicknames, dates, and the occasional phallic symbol.

The female denizens of this joint were brassy barflies—their hairdos defying gravity with multiple layers of reinforcement from Aqua Net Hair Spray. The male revelers were craggy, hardened types in jeans and flannel shirts. The slow pace disappointed me, until an earsplitting shriek came from the meatpacking plant across the way, blotting out the jukebox and triggering a flurry of activity at the bar. The bartender, a stout dude named Butch, turned to me, waved a hand toward the entrance and hollered, "Theeeeere's the break whistle! Better git ready, Girl!"

I got ready. The door swung wide and a rush of meatpacking plant workers, clad in blood-drenched aprons and gore-spattered smocks, stampeded into the lounge. They crowded around the tables and bellied up to the bar, clamoring for Schlitz, Budweiser, Pabst Blue Ribbon, and Carling Black Label. I worked feverishly to slake their collective thirst. The burly butchers shot appreciative glances at me and my dress, the best one in my closet and intended to impress, but a glaringly wrong choice under the circumstances. I wondered if a dry cleaner could remove the beer stains and blood specks. I noticed a slim, dark-haired man in denim, sitting in the corner, went to take his order. "Bud. Say Miss, are you in this for the money or the social contacts?" He flashed a hint of a smile.

I laughed. "The money."

"The Westway Inn's looking for a cocktail waitress, and the money's good. Ask for Tanya. Tell her Jeb sent ya."

"I'll do that. Thanks, Jeb."

After that one beer, the meatpackers dispersed as suddenly as they'd arrived. "Break time's over," one heavily muscled dude informed me as he made for the exit. Butch and I bustled around, clearing away empty longneck beer bottles, wiping table tops, and straightening chairs. Suddenly another deafening siren blew, from the direction of the sheet metal works.

Butch raised an eyebrow. "Ready?" I nodded. A throng of sheet metal fabricators mobbed the place, each one howling for his favorite brand of beer. At 11 p.m., the factories' whistles pierced eardrums for miles, and a smaller wave of workers visited the bar. I ran a marathon that night, but when I counted my tips at the end, it only amounted to ten dollars and thirty-five cents, most of it in change.

I stepped up to the bar. "Butch, I'm sorry, this is all I made tonight. Can you give me a five and five ones? I'll give you a dollar-thirty-five, that's more than ten percent of my tips."

"Ten bucks? That's more'n any of the other waitresses here have EVER MADE in a night!! You did good."

REALLY? I'm-in-it-for-the-money- I'm-in-it-for-the-money-please, please, let there be money. Not someday. NOW! "Uhmm, thank you. Okay, G'night then!"

The Westway Inn was one of those Midwestern motel/restaurants, one with a smorgasbord buffet on weekends. I worked in the El Cid Lounge. The El Cid was furnished with red vinyl-upholstered booths and round tables with red vinyl-upholstered captain's chairs. Spectacularly cheesy mock medieval weapons adorned the walls and swag lamps provided dim lighting. Each afternoon around three, I'd begin my shift by lighting the red glass votive candles on the tables and booths. Bridget, the bar manager and my boss, trained me as a bartender and a waitress, so that I could help to supply drinks for the waitresses that served the smorgasbord customers. I learned how to mix all the drinks, and how to set up and break down the bar.

Tall, blonde, attractive, organized and energetic, with the gift of gab, I began making good tips right away, and soon averaged about fifty bucks cash per shift. I found a dependable babysitter, Caroline, a woman with a daycare center in her home, who had three kids of her own. Caroline agreed to keep Annie overnight if I paid double the price of daytime care. I would take the baby to Caroline's in the afternoon, before reporting to work at 4:00 p.m. My shift ended at last call. Immediately after work, I'd head home, catch a few hours' sleep, get up at 6:00 a.m., drive to Caroline's, and pick up the baby before her kids got up for school. Each day, on the way to work, I'd stop at the bank, then at the utility companies, and distribute my tips among them in order to stave off foreclosure and disconnection. I sustained this routine, put the house on the market, caught up with the payments, and held off the credit card companies for a year while awaiting sale. I gave it all I had, fought hard to make a way for myself and Annie.

When the house sold, Derek showed up, acting friendly now that the equity would pay off his credit card debt. He knew how to push my buttons, and succeeded in provoking the maternal guilt in me. He lamented the fact our baby was "growing up without both parents," and suggested we reconcile and live together. This from a guy who hadn't paid the minimal child support—not one payment—for an entire year, and who'd scarcely visited the baby during all that time. But his arguments unsettled me, and I was tired. *Maybe it would be better for Anne Marie to have both parents...* I told him I'd think about it. Meanwhile, I found a house to rent and Annie and I moved in by ourselves.

I continued to take the Lithium regularly, the original prescriptions from my former father-in-law. The side effects never went away like he'd said they would. But I was too intimidated by his threats to stop taking the stuff, even though I was now separated from Derek. A number of awful things occurred as I continued my sleep deprived, overworked schedule. I got raped after work one night. The attacker, a massive guy with freakishly pale skin, a jagged scar on his forehead, and huge hands, intercepted me in the parking lot as I walked to my car. He coerced me into driving to another location, where he held me for hours. The rapist, who was talking to me in different voices, obviously deranged, raped me more than once, slapped me around, and finally dumped me out of my car onto the street. In shock, crying, I ran to a service station, asked the attendant to call the police. A kindly older man with white hair, who'd been standing at the pump, overheard me asking for help and offered to drive me to the police station. "I'm a retired police chief," he said, "I've got daughters your age. I'm so sorry this happened to you."

The retired police chief dropped me off in front of the station, where I reported the crime to the local police, and they began filling out the report, asking me questions. "Name?" The cop sat across a desk from me, a look of concern on his face. I gave him my name. "Occupation?" I told him I was a cocktail waitress, and gave him the name of the restaurant. The cop set down his pen and smirked at me. "Cocktail waitress? You can't press charges for rape, lady. You just picked up the wrong john."

I demanded to see a female officer, and after a long wait with the smirking cop, a middle-aged woman entered, looked at my summer skirt and halter top, and said, "Is that what you were wearing?" I had to pay for my own rape kit, and received absolutely no support from the three cops. Convinced the guy was dangerous, and that he'd likely hurt someone else, I insisted on filing the report. I wanted them to act on my leads and description, but they refused. One of the cops told me that unless I had at least an inch-and-a-half deep stab wound, or at least one broken bone, my rape charge would never hold up in court, so they saw no sense in pursuing it. (Months later, my assailant got arrested thousands of miles away, and the feds contacted me as a witness. They flew me to Washington, where I testified against him, along with dozens of his other victims. The feds convicted the rapist and sentenced him to life without parole. When I told the federal officers about the disrespect the local police force had shown me, they encouraged me to sue. But I feared what might happen to me in my small town if I filed suit.)

Returning to work immediately after the assault, I felt apprehensive. My boss told me the cops had come around the Westway Inn "asking what kind of girl I was." The attacker had taken my beat-up VW, but had later abandoned it on the interstate outside town, so the police found it pretty quickly. At least I didn't have to buy another car, but I felt really nervous that the rapist could so easily identify it, and might be able to follow me to my house. I had trouble sleeping. After my shift ended at work, I dreaded going out to the parking lot, and felt ashamed whenever I asked security to walk me to my car. Then one night, Lady Luck smiled on me.

While I was working a double shift at the Westway, the VW met its Waterloo. An eighteen-wheeler parked in the neighboring lot had rolled downslope, bumped into my car, and crushed it, flat as a pancake against the delivery truck parked on the other side. The driver of the semi claimed he set the emergency brake, but it didn't engage. My screams of joy and gratitude drowned out the trucker's profuse apologies.

With my battered vehicle blessedly totaled, I collected the Blue Book value and perused the newspaper ads for used cars. I found one for a 1972 Dodge Charger, a hot rod, the kind with a blower on the hood and a herd of horse power—for only 700 bucks, a steal. The muscle car's owner, a Pentecostal preacher, signed the papers and thanked me for taking it off his hands. "My son bought that car a few months back, an' the boy ran wild behind the wheel, seemed he was demon possessed. He's come back to the fold now, an' we couldn't wait to get rid of it. You'll be in my prayers, Miss."

All the equity from the sale of the house had gone to pay off Derek's credit card debt. Derek came around my place to visit from time to time, and Anne Marie was always happy to see him. He'd been employed at a General Motors factory for a short time, earning good wages, but during those months he'd never paid any support money. One day, he dropped by and convinced me to let him stay with us. "I'm laid off from the factory, so I can babysit while you're at work. You can save money on child care."

That time, it seemed like a good idea. With a man in the house, I might be able to forget about the rapist coming back. Maybe I'd sleep better. I told him I didn't want to have sex with him, but would accept the rest of the arrangement on a trial basis. I went to work that night, and when I came home, I found Derek in my bed with a woman. She got up and exited the house, and I threw him out.

But I forgot to make him give back his key. From time to time, he'd stop by the house and steal specific things. For some weird reason, he ripped off my favorite books, The Riverside Shakespeare and an entire collection of history volumes by Will and Ariel Durant. Nerdy? Guilty as charged—but they were leather bound copies, and they reassured me I was intelligent even though I served drinks for a living. I figured Derek was doing heroin again. He'd mentioned it, but I reckoned that since I was drinking after work when the baby was overnight with the sitter, I was in no position to judge.

I kept working, sometimes seven nights a week, hoping to obtain a daytime job outside the hospitality industry. Finally, I landed a position in the security department at a big discount chain store—at last I would be working the day shift and not serving alcohol. On my final night as a waitress, I stayed after work to party with friends. We barhopped, and at this one dive bar, a couple of guys, friends of friends, joined us. I knew I needed to get going, and wondered if I could drive. I addressed the cluster of drunks sitting in our booth: "Hey, I gotta get on the road. Anybody got something to stay awake with?" One guy, a blond with curly hair, pulled a plastic baggie out of his leather jacket and held it up to the light. The bag contained a hodgepodge of brightly-colored pills, widely variant in size and shape. After a moment of scrutiny, he pulled out a jelly-bean-like, forest-green capsule and handed it to me. For a nano-second, I hesitated, thinking I'd never seen an upper that looked like that, then changed tack and rationalized. *Yeah, it looks weird, but you've been taking that crappy Lithium and Haldol...what difference will one pill make?*

In a stunning stroke of idiocy, I shrugged, closed my eyes, gulped down the pill, stood up, and headed for the car. Everything went black. The next thing I remember is waking up with that blond, curly-haired guy on top of me. I'd passed out, and he'd mounted me and begun raping me while I was unconscious. I'd awakened suddenly, in the midst of being violated. I struggled, pushed him off, and jumped to my feet, screaming, "WHAT IS GOING ON?"

"H-h-hey girl, it's okay." He jumped up, started pulling his pants on. "See, you got so wasted you weren't safe to drive, so I took the keys...did you a FAVOR...yeah, I brought you here to a friend's house. One thing led to another and..." He stopped talking, shrugged, as if that explained everything, as if he weren't a predator, not really, simply a nice guy, a Boy Scout who walked old ladies across the street, but since the old ladies weren't out this late, he'd opened his big heart (and his fly) and stepped up to escort me, a damsel in distress, and since one thing led to another, well...

One thing led to another...a FAVOR? One thing led to another? Fury bubbled up within me. The sexual abuse at fourteen, fifteen and sixteen, the marriage, the "diagnosis" by my father-in-law, the hideous psych meds, the abrupt weaning of my baby, the divorce, my ex's behavior, the sexual harassment on the job as a waitress, the rape, now this outrage, this...second rape. *I have got to...get home...to my baby. I have got to start a new life. Away from...this!* My adrenalin levels soared. I was now wide awake. I looked around in the darkened room and saw my purse, tossed onto the ratty carpet, its contents spilling out, and amidst the mess, my spare car keys. I dove to the floor, grabbed the keys, scooped up all of my crap, stuffed it into the purse and slung it over my shoulder. "Where is my coat? MY COAT?"

I left without my coat. Curly Blond followed me, in a frenzied attempt at persuasion. "Hey Girl, you gotta take it easy, you gotta stay, you, uh, you can't drive! That was a jelly-belly I gave you, it wasn't an upper! It was a Placidyl!"

I snorted in disdain. I had no idea what a Placidyl was, and nothing could stop me from escaping this creep. I marched forward in the darkness, feeling my way toward the exit. My right hand found a door knob, and to my satisfaction, the door wasn't latched. I swung it open, ran down the sidewalk, and immediately caught a glimpse of my Dodge Charger parked sideways. I jumped in and sped off into the night.

I had no idea where the creep had taken me, but I somehow found my way to the freeway and headed toward my place. I knew the drive would take about a half hour. I rolled down the windows, turned off the heater, and figured the late November cold would keep me alert enough to stay awake for the duration. I was wrong. I nodded off at the wheel, and woke up just in time to see myself in the left lane of a deserted freeway, zooming straight toward another set of headlights. A glance at the speedometer told me I was going 70 mph.

I jerked the wheel toward the correct lane, the right side of the freeway. My car went into a high-speed spin. The opposing headlights never swerved, but sped on past, oblivious. The spin continued, and my vehicle careened across the right lane, plowed through the guard rail, thudded against something big, bounced off, swerving wildly, crashing and bumping. Time seemed to slow to a glacial pace, and I could only stare, stupefied, as the big Dodge spiraled on, across the freeway again, headed straight for a brick building in what appeared to be a strip mall. Everything blurred. Strangely, on instinct, I released my seat belt, slid out from under the wheel and down to the floorboards, preparing for impact, hoping to spare my face from hitting the windshield. I closed my eyes, tried to relax. Then I heard a crash.

The collision must've knocked me out, but only for a few minutes. I awoke, in darkness and eerie silence. I jumped out of the Charger, looked, and saw a bunch of liter-sized Coca-Cola bottles scattered across the hood of my ride. I panicked, got back in behind the wheel. The key was still in the ignition, so I turned it, cranked the engine, and backed the car up. As I backed out of the store, I looked up, saw a neon sign, its lurid scarlet text screaming out, "KARATE! TAE-KWONDO!" I backed up far enough to take in a horrified glimpse of a demolished 7-Eleven store, adjacent to a martial arts academy, then maneuvered my shattered machine back onto the freeway, and resumed driving. (That was back when 7-Eleven stores were actually open from 7:00 a.m. to 11:00 p.m., so no employees were inside. Good thing, or somebody might've been hurt.)

Of course I was reacting from shock, didn't grasp the extent of the damage my one-car Demolition Derby'd incurred. When I pressed my foot down on the accelerator, it didn't have quite the same effect as usual. For some reason, I just couldn't get any traction. The road seemed terribly bumpy, but I told myself to press on, that soon I'd be at my place, and a few minor repairs'd be all I'd need to patch things up. *Yeah, that's right, a little body work and no one'll be the wiser...*

Suddenly, I noticed the windshield. Reality set in. The glass looked like an intricate mosaic containing thousands of pieces, and worse, it seemed to be imploding—sagging, crumpling, melting inward! And no, I was not hallucinating—the shatterproof auto safety glass was giving up the ghost, literally caving in on me. I steered the car onto the shoulder, put it in park, and lunged for safety. I collected myself, took a deep breath, then walked around the car, surveying the destruction: twisted metal, four flat tires hanging in shreds from rims so bent they seemed to scream in agony. It struck me that I hadn't been driving on a bumpy road, no, I'd been ker-bumping along on those tortured, collapsed rims! *Wow! This. Is. Bad.*

Only one thing to do...return to the scene and surrender! Just then, I saw a pair of headlights approaching. I started jumping up and down, frantically waving both arms and yelling, "Help!"

The driver, a youngish dude, stopped, looking confused. I didn't explain, only pointed at the wreckage and asked him to take me back down the road. He acquiesced, never said a word as we sped along. The trip back to the scene didn't take more than a few minutes. I scanned the darkened highway for the KARATE! TAE-KWONDO! sign, but its glow'd been swallowed up by a swarm of swirling cherry tops and glaring headlights. At some point after my departure, State Police, County Sheriffs, and Highway Patrol had responded en masse.

The driver's face turned ashen. Before we reached the strip mall parking area he slowed, pulled to the side of the road, coughed politely into his hand. "Uhm, hey, I gotta let you off here. I've been smoking weed, and...you know."

"Hey, sure, no problem. You better get going. I mean, I think you're okay, though. It's me they're looking for, I'm pretty sure. Right?" I jumped out. "Thank you!" He nodded, pulled back on the road and drove off, both hands anxiously gripping the wheel, and carefully observing the speed limit.

Oh well. Better get on with it. I bounded forward into the parking lot, calling out to the cadre of cops. "Don't shoot! I SURREND-EEEER!!" I held both hands over my head, the way I'd always seen desperate fugitives do it on TV cop dramas, hoped they'd hold their fire.

The law enforcement guys turned and stared, perplexed. One cop in a State Trooper hat aimed his flashlight in my direction. "So, it was you?"

I started shaking all over. "Yes, I had a wreck, lost control of the car. I didn't realize how bad it was till I started driving. I'm sorry I left the scene. What're they gonna do to me? WHAT ARE THEY GONNA DO TO ME?"

Another cop, a Sheriff, strode toward me. "Miss, where is your vehicle?"

"It's a little way down the road." I hung my head, shook it from side to side. I held out my hands. "I guess you better cuff me."

The Sheriff looked quizzical. "With all of this damage, we thought you'd be dead, but we couldn't figure out how you got your car out of the store. What were you driving, a front end loader? I mean, you crashed through a plate glass window, wiped out a big display of liter-size Coca Cola bottles—looks like they'd been stacked into a pyramid, maybe, and then smashed into a freezer case. One thing is, it looks like you tried to clean the place up a bit, like you started tryin' to re-stack 'em."

The State Trooper looked like he was trying to smother a chuckle. "You're gonna get in trouble with your insurance provider. A one-car collision, and all the damage, not only to the 7-Eleven store structure, but to the equipment. That freezer'll cost a bundle."

A third cop, also State Police, chimed in. "Yep, a bundle. And you're responsible for loss of inventory. See, after you left, the alarm went off at some point, but apparently not soon enough. Maybe the crash impaired the alarm's function in some way. Seems as though some folks came in, grabbed up a heck of a lot of the stock right off the shelves, and made off into the night. And when the alarm went off, we all responded. We were out here checking tire tracks, trying to figure out why somebody'd stage a smash and grab using a vehicle as a ram."

Sheepish, confused, I somehow managed to look each cop in the eye and mumbled, "I'm really sorry."

The Sheriff turned to the State Troopers. "Okay, you want to take her?"

The third one nodded his assent. "Sure." He turned to me, pointed at one of the State Police cars. "We're not going to arrest you. There'll be an investigation, and you'll be contacted by your insurance company, the law, or both. Right now, we're going to give you a ride home."

At the time I didn't think about it, but they seemed to understand I'd been in shock, and to my surprise, they arranged to take me home. The cops didn't arrest me. I never figured out why. But one thing I'm pretty sure of—they all had a good laugh over it.

The crash changed all my plans. My insurance company dropped me the next day. The representative informed me by phone. He also told me that I'd destroyed city, county and state property as my car ricocheted across the deserted freeway. According to the damage assessments, I'd spun through a drive-in movie theater and taken out a couple of those steel poles, and the speakers that people attached to their cars for sound. And then, the report said, I'd clipped a big light pole on the freeway, an interstate highway. I'd also damaged some curbing. That was the right side of the road. The left side...well, that was the strip mall. The total cost of damages would be covered by my liability policy. The insurance rep's voice rose a notch as he concluded our conversation. "You won't be able to buy any auto insurance for a very long time, Miss. Not unless you win big in Vegas."

I'd lost my Dodge Charger, since I didn't have full coverage. But I didn't lose my license. There'd been a light rain falling that night, and the road'd been slick. The cops never took a statement from me, and the store owner never pressed charges. The insurance rep said there was a little trailer court next to the strip mall, and that the residents were poor elderly couples, too old to retain their driver licenses, subsisting solely on social security checks, who'd been forced to rely on that 7-Eleven for all their groceries at radically inflated prices. When the alarm went off, they'd seized the moment, cleaning out the inventory of their oppressor in a burst of senior vengeance.

But, unlike the senior citizens in that trailer park, I missed my moment. The day after the accident, I couldn't show up for my new job. Because of the loss of the car, and the high price of insurance, I lacked the means to purchase—let alone insure, a replacement vehicle. Caroline, my babysitter, who'd become a very close friend, invited me and Anne Marie to move in with her, temporarily. I felt grateful for the opportunity to spend more time with my daughter. After all, I was unemployed. I figured since I had some savings, I'd take a week or two to be with my baby and find solutions to my problems. I know now that one of the main problems was my drinking, but back then I didn't know enough to factor substance use into the equation. If I hadn't gone out to party with friends after work, the accident wouldn't have happened. But I didn't think about it. My denial was growing stronger. And I could not bring myself to confront the early sexual abuse and other trauma that was fueling my desire to blot out my feelings.

That's when Derek stepped in. He showed up after the accident, when I was feeling very vulnerable, loving the time with my child but ashamed of having wrecked my car and, I figured, possibly my future. He used all his charm and convinced me that we needed to be a family again, that it would be so good for Anne Marie. He told me he planned to move to Florida and asked if I wanted to come along. "We'll rebuild our lives together," he told me, looking deep into my eyes, "We'll be a complete family again." Derek lacked cash, but possessed a running vehicle, insured and registered. I had saved about $1500, and when I told him how much I had in the bank, he suggested we take off immediately. "What the hell, Marti! We've got nothing to lose. We can drive down there, rent a place, and I'll start looking for a job first thing. I promise."

"Well, you're right about the nothing to lose part." *He's got a point. I've crashed my car and fucked up my insurance, and I wanna get outta this town. He's not perfect, but he's the father of my child. And he was my first love. Maybe we can make a new start...together... if not—well, I'll cross that road when and if..."* "Okay, I'll do it."

CHAPTER 5

SOUTHBOUND

THE DECISION TO MOVE TO THE SUNSHINE STATE WAS AN EVEN bigger fuckup than totaling the Dodge Charger. We drove down to West Palm Beach, spent my entire savings on the first month's rent and deposits on utilities, then Derek, true to his word, started looking for a job right away. The problem was, Derek's idea of a job was playing bass in a rock band, which meant contacting a dude named Jerrod, who'd been Derek's lead guitar player in the short-lived but audacious band they'd formed in high school. Jerrod, now in his early twenties, showed up on the threshold of our unfurnished apartment in an alcoholic haze, cradling a fifth of Jack Daniels, stumbled in, and sat down on the kitchen floor. We'd brought only sleeping bags and the baby's things, a few cooking utensils, and Derek's guitar and amplifier. Derek and Jerrod commenced tuning their guitars, chugging the entire bottle of Southern Comfort.

I found a job as a cocktail waitress in a fancy nightclub on Worth Avenue in Palm Beach, and located a child care center that held a number of certifications and endorsements from local sources. They kept toddlers like Anne Marie overnight, since the club and restaurant business was a big part of the economy in South Florida. The shift was a long one: 6:00 p.m. till sunrise. Each morning, I'd come home with our baby, exhausted, and find Derek and Jerrod passed out on the floor, empty bottles of booze scattered nearby, the amps still buzzing.

After about a week, while the guys were passed out, I called a crisis hotline, packed up our things into a trash bag, and checked into a safe house with Annie. Social Services furnished us with a bus ticket for my hometown. Boarding the Greyhound with Anne Marie, I fought back tears. The day after arriving in Florida, our little family had celebrated Annie's second birthday with a fancy little cupcake I'd bought at the Winn Dixie. Derek and I'd been trying to put our lives back together. I figured the love we'd had in the past was good and true; that only a good and true love could create such a sweet and lovely child as Annie. *And anything good is worth fighting for! I'm not giving up without a fight.* Tenderly, I picked up my baby, held her tight, grabbed our de facto luggage, got off the bus and called the apartment. Derek answered, sounding shaky but surprisingly liquor-free. "Where are you? Marti, I'm sorry."

"Now listen to me, Derek. I called a crisis center, because I could not stand to bring our baby home to that situation, and they gave me a bus ticket. I don't have enough money on my own, because all my tips have been going to pay the child care center. Anyway, I'm not leaving. Not without you. You're going to drink yourself to death, get evicted, or arrested, or some other thing, and I can't leave you here and let that happen. Now pull yourself together, get rid of Jerrod, and let's get out of Florida."

I called one of the people I knew at my former waitress job, and they wired me fifty dollars for gas via Western Union. Derek decided to join the Navy, found out he'd be doing basic training in Orlando, and asked his parents for help with a down payment on an apartment. We still had to sleep on the floor, and our car only started intermittently, but Derek would be getting pay during boot camp, and I got to stay home with the baby. Anne Marie and I spent a lot of time at the apartment complex pool, and we met other young moms and kids there.

Upon graduating from boot camp, Derek got assigned to Great Lakes Training Center, where he'd soon begin studying to be an electrician. We needed money for the move to Chicago. Derek asked me to go back to work, and told me he could stay home with the baby. I landed a job at an exclusive restaurant downtown, serving cocktails. My coworkers were primarily students with clear-cut goals and a bright future. Comparing myself to them, I felt frustrated, locked into a life with little purpose. I wondered if I'd ever obtain an education or do anything other than wait tables. After work, one drink barely took the edge off my desperation; I needed several, it seemed. Some nights I drove home drunk, and always felt guilty—or terrified—about it in the morning.

For years, my marriage hadn't been a happy one, but I'd accepted that fact as part of domestic life. Even though he'd asked me to go back to work, Derek often made reference to a common negative stereotype of the times: that women who work as cocktail waitresses are stupid and promiscuous. Some days, when I'd be getting ready for work, my husband would say, "Remember, you're married to me, and if you mess me around, I'll get custody of our daughter. I'm fighting for my country, you're serving drinks to a bunch of rich tourists. And you're mentally ill. My dad's been prescribing Lithium and Haldol for you all this time, and you've been taking it. Nobody's going to help you if we go to court. You'd better watch your step if you want to keep your baby."

Secretly, I started to hate Derek, and took revenge by spending some of my tip money on myself instead of bringing it all home for the three of us. But I felt like a traitor, because the way I saw it, lack of money was the main problem in our marriage. I found myself wishing I could get out of the relationship, yet on a very deep level, felt that if I did, I would kill something very important, something I couldn't even find words to describe. I'd been in an intimate relationship with Derek since fifteen years old; it seemed to be a fact of life for me, and together we'd brought an adorable little girl into the world. Our marriage and family seemed so worthy of saving, I dug in my heels and determined to stick it out.

Day after day seemed to drag by, until finally Derek received orders to relocate to Chicago for training. From what he told me, he'd first be in school, learning a skill, then they'd assign him to another base, or a ship. We moved to Illinois and found a furnished apartment in a boarding house. Derek started school. His classes began early and ended by 2:00 p.m., and since his pay wasn't going to kick in right away, he suggested I go back to work as a cocktail waitress. "I'll be here with Anne Marie."

I found a job in a Sheraton Hotel down the road, started work immediately after filling out the application. The place was run by a cadre of Greeks, who instantly impressed me as thugs, possibly even Greek Mafia. The murky cocktail lounge, obscured by cigarette smoke and adjacent to the restaurant which proudly served "Authentic Greek Cuisine," employed five bartenders and two waitresses per shift. Only one bartender seemed to speak English but he poured solely for the head waitress. The rest of those guys seemed to do little more than lurk in the shadows.

As "new employee" they posted me at the subordinate station—the one manned, for some strange reason, by not one but several swarthy, scowling, hulking brutes who grunted in annoyance when I submitted drink orders. At first, I thought the process of filling and delivering orders in this place seemed halfway normal—well, at least outside the realm of food service phantasmagoria—but I was dead wrong. I ordered up my first round of drinks from a towering hoodlum who appeared to be wearing an overcoat. "Three Cutty/water tall, two Jack/soda tall, one Seven and Seven tall, two Smirnoff/tonic tall." I smiled politely, then set my tray down with the neatly written drink order on top, according to house protocol.

Overcoat glared, thrust a hammy fist under the bar, snatched a few liquor bottles, and started pouring. I avoided his gaze, turned my attention to the tables in my station while he filled the order. *No way do I want to get off on the wrong foot with this guy...* Overcoat worked fast. It only took him a few seconds to get it done. *Wow! He's not chatty, but he's quick on the draw...*

I walked briskly in my high-heeled pumps, delivered the drinks, moved on to the next table, and began taking their orders. Within a surprisingly brief span of time, I heard shouting from the original table. "HEY WAITRESS! GET OVER HERE!"

"Just a moment," I smiled at the customers seated around the second table. "I've got your order, I'll be back soon."

The entire first table regarded me with scorn. "Listen, Hon'," a guy with an oily comb over and a bushy mustache jabbed a pudgy finger at his tall highball. "Either do your job right, or get your GED, or find some dude to marry you. You totally screwed this up." I stared at him, weighing the consequences of verbally shredding him. I decided I needed to keep my lousy job.

"How can I help you, sir?"

Comb Over, now red-faced, shouted, "THIS is NOT a CUTTY and WATER TALL!" His tablemates joined in, the other two Cutty drinkers nodding angry assent. A woman with platinum hair, wearing a leopard-print jacket and tight sweater, knit her brows accusingly, and leaned in with plenty of cleavage, thrusting her libation skyward.

"And THIS is NOT A VODKA-TONIC, Darlin'!" The rest of the party followed suit, indignation on their faces, voices shrill.

"YEAH, I mean, C'MON, HOW DIDJA FUCK UP A SEVEN 'N SEVEN?"

"JACK DANIELS an' soda! THAT'S what I TOLDJA, AN' THIS is NOT JACK, Babe!"

"Er, I'm really sorry," I began picking up all those tall glasses, setting them on my tray. "I'll take these back and bring another round, with the right stuff."

Confused, I scurried back to the bar to find Overcoat, glowering.

"Uhm, excuse me, but," I took a deep breath, pulled myself up to my full height, "Uhm, these drinks are, um, they're not what I ordered. The customers complained. I need another round, to replace them." I smiled deferentially, set down my tray, then gestured at the original ticket. "See? It's right here."

Overcoat shot me a blank look, threw up his hands, turned, and stomped away. Dumbfounded, I stood at the bar for a minute or two. *Oookaay.* "Excuse me! Hey, I have an order!" I raised my hand, but not one of the swarthy, hulking lurkers manning the bar paid me any mind. In fact, three made a show of turning their backs on me. *That does it.*

I picked up my tray of mis-poured cocktails, marched over to the head waitress' station and addressed her special guy, the English-speaking bartender. "Listen, I need help. This round of drinks, it's all wrong. I ordered according to house protocol. All I need is a replacement round. I asked the uh, the other bartender, the one with the overcoat, the guy that poured them all wrong in the first place, and he...he walked away. Here, I brought the ticket. See for yourself."

"Sure. I'm Jimmy. Marti, right? You're new." Jimmy emptied my tray of the erroneous round, grabbed the ticket, set up new tall glasses, and started pouring. "Okay, here's what: Stavros—he's just passin' through, he's fresh from Sparta, you prob'ly won't see him again, y'know? Drinks aren't really his thing. Don't ask any of the other guys for anything either. Not tonight. I'll fill all your orders. Just don't say anything—to anybody." He threw me a meaningful look. "Now get out there on the floor."

I finished my first shift, even made some tips. Jimmy was right. I never saw Stavros again. And the cast of characters behind that bar seemed to change nightly, except for Jimmy, who appeared to be a fixture. The pace in that place was frenetic, so I scarcely had time to think, but I couldn't shake the nagging feeling that Stavros and his crew'd been imported from Sparta to work behind the scenes, away from the public eye. Perhaps the owner owed the Greek Syndicate a massive gambling debt, and was coerced into providing a conduit for Gangland muscle. Maybe Stavros had been merely hanging out, waiting for a signal from the capo, and my drink order'd put him on the spot. Then he'd clomped off to the basement to clip the fingertips off a corpse, pull out the teeth, and after sawing it up and bagging it, headed off for Lake Michigan in the dead of night, to drop it off a boat. Or, he could've been the owner's brother-in-law.

Anyway, none of that mattered in the end, because I stayed with that job no longer than a couple of weeks. The situation quickly proved unbearable. Since Derek's school day started early, I got up with the baby after only four hours of sleep, and when he got home I had to make dinner and get ready to go to work again. Within a week of this routine I was physically exhausted, depressed, and emotionally drained. One morning, when I got up to make coffee and breakfast for Derek so he could go to his classes on the base, I told him how I felt: that I didn't like working at night, and that the people I waited on in Chicago seemed meaner, more sarcastic than the people back in Florida. He looked at me sharply. "Are you taking your Lithium? Maybe we oughta call my dad and see what he thinks."

"Maybe I should go to a psychiatrist on the Navy Base instead. Maybe your father is wrong and I'm not supposed to even take Lithium."

He shook his head, making a show of looking disappointed, as if I were a naughty middle-schooler who'd been caught cheating on an algebra test. "I don't think that's a good idea. It'll make me look bad on my Navy record if they know I have a wife with a flaw like yours...a mental illness. That'd definitely hurt my career. No, it's like dad says, we gotta keep this in the family."

Anger, shame, fear, and anguish rose up inside me, but I didn't process it, I pushed it down. That'd been my coping mechanism since my first traumatic experience. Now, caught in this unhappy reconciliation with Derek, I yearned to break free but was hobbled by abject terror and unfathomable self-doubt.

I looked at Derek, exhaled sharply, straightened my shoulders. "Yeah. Okay, we'll...we'll keep it in the family." I washed up the dishes. After that, I played with Anne Marie, opened up one of her favorite books, "The Hungry Hungry Caterpillar," and read it aloud to her, three times in a row. In a couple of months, she'd be three years old. I thought about how I wanted to keep her safe and happy, but how would I do that when I was tired all the time, and taking this awful medication with its horrific side effects, and living in an unhappy marriage?

When I went to work that night, I began to think about filing for divorce again. As I carried drinks, I grew more and more desperate to make an exit plan. I needed to get out—out of my dead end job waiting tables, out of Chicago, out of the Midwest entirely! For months, I'd been thinking about moving to Texas. And I wasn't the only person thinking this way. People from the Rust Belt were moving to Texas, Arizona, Florida and California in droves in search of work, a trend pundits dubbed "The Sun Belt migration." I'd never been to Texas, but I figured the weather would be warm, and they had lots of jobs. The Seventies had seen a deep recession, and the OPEC cartel, formed in the early Seventies, sparked a dramatic hike in fossil fuel prices. Industries that had formerly been situated in the Midwest and Northeast had picked up and switched to sunnier climes. Media talking heads used terms like, "The New South" to describe economic and social changes taking place.

I began to believe that in Texas, I could make a better future for myself and my daughter. I'd heard about all the construction jobs and labor jobs. *Why not get one of those?* I didn't own any suitable clothes for office work, but I had plenty of jeans and T-shirts, even some old cowboy boots to wear to work. I could get out of waiting tables, pull down a man-sized paycheck, maybe even go to college. I reckoned California was too far away; the airfare too costly. But I knew somebody in Houston. Kathy, a friend from high school. It was a stretch, but I still remembered her parents' home phone number.

The next day, I called Kathy's mom and got her number in Texas, then called Kathy that night, from a phone booth at work. She and her husband'd moved there after graduating college and were living the good life. They'd both found jobs, and the weather was perfect. She went on to tell me all the wonders of Houston, how even someone with only a high school diploma could get a high-paying job. "You just have to get here," she said. "Hey, are you still with Derek?"

"Yeah."

"I can't believe it! Really? Why?"

"We have a baby. A girl, named Anne Marie. She's beautiful."

"Oh." She sniffed. "I was going to offer to let you stay with us when you first get here, but with Derek, and a baby...sorry, no room. We're in an apartment."

"That's okay, I won't need help, I can do it anyway. Maybe I'll see you in Houston."

"Yeah, okay. Good luck!"

I hung up the phone. The conversation had galvanized me. *Texas!*

As soon as I got a chance to talk to Derek, I filled him in on my plan. "See if you can get a transfer to a Navy Base in Texas," I took his hand, squeezed it. "We could move there, I can get work. Kathy and her husband moved there, and they're doing really well. She says the job opportunities are endless."

"Kathy? I never did like her."

That's all he has to say? Desperation washed over me like a tidal wave, and with it, the full realization that I'd been existing in misery for many years. My young life had been dominated by Derek and his family. I'd suppressed all my own feelings and dreams and desires to be a good wife at eighteen, after being a good girlfriend from fifteen on…taking his father's birth control pills in high school, then blindly accepting his father's de facto psychiatric diagnosis, taking the Lithium and Haldol, stamping down my anger because my fear of going insane overshadowed my outrage. I'd reached an impasse. No turning back.

"Okay, but I'm going, and I'm taking Anne Marie, and you can visit her any time you want, but I am making this move. I've got enough money for a one-way ticket for me and the baby. I'll save a few more paychecks and have enough for a first month's rent and utilities. And I'll get a job right away even if I have to wait tables."

"This is crazy talk. I'm calling Dad. I won't let you go because I'll never be able to visit her! I'll never travel that far for visits, never! My family stays with me, no discussion." Derek clenched his fists, then stabbed a finger in my direction. "You. YOU can go. But I'm gonna take the baby. You will never see your daughter again!" He stalked out of the room.

True to his threats, Derek called his father, and together they began the process of cutting me out of Annie's life. For decades Derek's father had retained a personal attorney nicknamed Dirty Dan, a guy with a reputation for greasing palms and cutting deals under the table. Derek's dad and Dirty Dan were friends; they'd done each other favors over the years. Derek and his father informed me they'd built a case against me, and were prepared to have me committed if I didn't sign over custody.

In those days, if you had been treated for a mental illness, even as a juvenile, you were not allowed to see your psychiatric records.

People with mental illnesses had no rights, even suspected mental illness could get you committed to a state hospital indefinitely. Derek's father had the power to have me committed, based on his diagnosis and the fact I'd been taking those psych meds for years. And when I was still in high school, I'd had that seizure that'd landed me in the psych ward at the local hospital. Derek's dad could access those records, and I had no idea what those records said. Terrified, I visited an attorney in Chicago—took the baby with me to the appointment. The guy refused to represent me, I didn't have the money to fight it, he said. And he confirmed my worst fears, that my father-in-law and husband could have me committed and get away with it. "Young lady...have you ever seen a snowball?" He chuckled.

"Yes."

"Well, picture a snowball...in hell. Those are your chances." He chuckled again, waved me out of his office.

Making my way home on foot, carrying my toddler daughter, I wrestled with my emotions. Rush hour traffic zoomed by. At one point, I stopped at a busy street corner to watch for a chance to cross. I set the baby down for minute, clutched her hand, and we stood together; she'd gotten tired of being held. The light changed, traffic stopped, it was now safe to cross. I hoisted Anne Marie into my arms. A motorist rolled down the window and stuck his head out. "May I help you, Miss?" With all the traffic noise, I thought he'd said, "Bitch," instead of "Miss."

I glared at him. "Don't call me 'Bitch.'" He stared back, stupefied. I crossed the street, hugging my baby close.

We made it home, and I fixed Anne Marie something to eat. Then we read "The Hungry Hungry Caterpillar" over and over again until she fell asleep. My father-in-law's and husband's words and actions had eaten away at my self-confidence over the years, but I still possessed a kernel of hope for the future. I had recent proof of my own self-sufficiency and resilience. I knew I was a hard worker, outgoing, good with people. I could get a job and hold a job. They had destroyed me today, but I would triumph tomorrow. *All I need is a chance...*

I looked at my very young daughter. I wanted the best for her. It was now time for me to think objectively, to be a good mother and make the right decision. If I fought them, or took the baby and ran, I'd only make it worse for myself, and for her. Running would take connections and money—I had neither. I'd be charged with kidnapping, or it'd make me look insane and totally irrational. Getting committed to a mental hospital or going to jail would not help my child. Derek and his dad had backed me into a corner. *I will have to stand up and accept this defeat...for now. I will take it on the chin, give up custody. But then I will move to Texas, land a high-paying job, save my money for an attorney, and fight to get my baby back.*

———————

Derek drove the car from Chicago to his parents' place, so he and his father could get a head start on the custody and divorce process. Our earlier divorce had never been finalized, then we'd reconciled, so with this it'd be official. Derek was getting an additional perk from the divorce: a hardship discharge from the Navy, on the grounds of abandonment. His dad had worked all of that out for him. He'd be moving in with his folks—his mother would care for Anne Marie.

I stayed behind in Chicago with Anne Marie; was expected to arrive at the attorney's—Dirty Dan's—office the following day. Since I had no vehicle I called my brother, who lived in Southern Illinois, and he agreed to pick us up and give us a ride to our parents' house. I never told him the purpose of my visit. My heart was ripped into pieces, but I kept up a strong front. We chatted in the car on the way down. Anne Marie loved her uncle. We stopped for a little picnic in a park, and the baby played in the sunshine. I never took my eyes off her, knowing these were my last moments, treasured memories to carry when I fought my way back to her.

Prior to my brother's arrival, I'd talked softly to my daughter, telling her how much I loved her, how her dad loved her too, hoping that even though she was a month shy of three years old, that she'd retain some remnant of a memory of it. I told her I was going away to Texas—only because I had no choice, but I'd be coming back soon, no matter what. I didn't cry or give any signal of distress; I knew it wouldn't be right to do that. But I felt an urgency to tell her what was coming, even if she didn't understand. I was adrift, wounded, acting mainly on instinct.

Anne Marie and I spent the night at my folks' house. The divorce proceedings were set for noon the following day. My brother gave me a ride to Caroline's, Anne Marie's former babysitter. This was the woman who'd cared for her when she was a baby, when I'd worked to save a foreclosing mortgage. Anne Marie loved Caroline and she loved Anne Marie. I'd called her from Chicago a few days before and arranged for her to keep the baby for two hours, and if Derek hadn't contacted her by then, to call my mother's house. No way was I going to simply hand Annie over to Derek's father. Taking her to a friend, a childcare professional, was the most dignified thing I could do in the circumstances. I would say goodbye to my child—my reason for living—in the presence of an ally, someone who respected me.

And I did it. I did this awful thing, the unthinkable, a young mother's nightmare. I did it because Derek and his father coerced, threatened and manipulated me into it. But I mustered my courage, believing that I could rebuild. From Caroline's house, I called Derek, then started walking, carrying my suitcase. He picked me up along the road. He drove me in our car—not "our" car now, his—to Dirty Dan's office. I signed a custody contract that stated I had,

117

"...all reasonable rights of visitation," words that inspired a glimmer of hope in me. I gave Derek Caroline's phone number and told him to call her right away and pick up the baby. He asked if I'd paid her and I assured him I had. "Good. Oh, and Marti? Here are the utility bills from Chicago. You need to pay these right away." He handed me the envelopes, unopened.

I put them in my purse. "Derek, I'm only taking some clothes with me to Texas. I can pack everything up, pretty much, but I'm leaving it all with you, so Anne Marie can have some remembrances of me: my teacups from Holland, and my books and stuff. I hope you'll take care of them...for her." My ex-husband only stared at me. But at least he gave me a ride to the Amtrak Station, where I caught a train to Chicago.

A few hours later I stopped at my bank and withdrew all my savings, a few hundred dollars. Then I dropped off my suitcase at the lonely furnished apartment and walked to the Greek Mafia Sheraton to work my final shift. As soon as I put in my first drink order, the despair began to chew at me, devouring my focus. The beefy assassins behind the bar glared uncomprehendingly, the music sucked, and the customers seemed to reek of Marlboros, whiskey sours, and urban misery.

One table was different. Three guys and a chick, my age. They smiled and laughed a lot. Instead of barking orders, they asked me my name and how I was doing. "I'm cool," I lied. Slapped on a grin. "And my name is Marti. Where are you from?"

They introduced themselves in turn, Billy, Dave, Ron, and Terri. Terri bought the first round. I immediately liked her for that. She seemed to be the spokesperson. "We're from all over the place. I'm from Minneapolis, Billy's from Houston, Dave's from Newark and Ron's from Buffalo. We work together; we're here on business." They tipped me in cash each time I brought the drinks, instead of at the end of the night. The cash made me feel better. Tonight was my last night; tomorrow I'd be at the travel agency, purchasing an airline ticket, and I needed all the cash I could get for my new life in Texas.

Another cool thing about Terri from Minneapolis' table was that they all ordered St. Pauli Girl beer. The thugs behind the bar could swing that, no prob, so I didn't have to suffer the consequences of carrying mystery highballs to these nice people. *That's it, Agamemnon, the green glass bottle with the blonde on the label... Eeeaasy does it...*

Billy from Houston ordered the next round of beers. When he handed me my tip, I leaned in. "May I ask you something? Do you like Texas?"

He gave me a half smile, shrugged. "Sure. Houston."

"See, I plan on moving to Texas tomorrow, but I'm not sure whether to settle in Corpus Christi, or Houston. But it's either one."

"What's your plan?"

"No plan, really, except I gotta get outta here, and fast. I heard there're lots of jobs in Texas, and I don't wanna be a waitress anymore."

"Well, Houston's the place to go. Skip Corpus. Nothin' there."

I went back to my other tables, made it through the night without crying over my daughter. The pain of separation began setting in. Since the signing at noon, shock had insulated me somewhat, but now the pain insisted, it throbbed, screamed at me. *No crying. I'm in the fight of my life, and fighters don't cry. At least not in the ring...*

My table of newfound friends hung in till last call. Terri approached. "Hey Marti, we're staying in this hotel, on the company tab. Wanna come up to my room after you're done here? We're all gonna hang out, play some music. It's cool."

"Policy is, we don't go to the rooms. But this is my last night. I'm quitting right now, moving to Texas tomorrow. Sure, I'll come up, if it's your room. I'd like to hear how you got your job working with these guys, and what you do. Is it construction?"

"Sort of. Come up. My room is three-one-four." She passed me a cocktail napkin with the number written on it, and smiled. "Just in case you forget."

I took a deep breath, walked briskly to the head waitress' station, occupied by Jimmy, the only English-speaking bartender. "I'm quitting, Jimmy. As of this moment. Tell management they can keep my last paycheck, because I haven't got a forwarding address. In exchange, I'd like to cash my current paycheck, it's only twenty-three dollars and seventy-six cents."

"Uhh, well, um, management's here tonight, so you gotta talk to Mr. Papadopoulos." He jerked a thumb over his shoulder.

Bummer. Mr. Papadopoulos, a beefy, silver-haired guy with thick lips, a perpetual smirk, and eyes like black buttons, was the General Manager. I'd only interacted with him a couple of times, but I figured he resented the fact that I didn't act desperate for the job and kiss his ass all the time. I approached him and delivered the same pitch I'd given to Jimmy. "Mr. Papadopoulos, I'm quitting as of this moment. You can keep my last paycheck, when it comes, but in exchange I hope you will cash this current paycheck now, it's only twenty-three dollars and seventy-six cents." I pulled the check out of my purse and handed it to him. He sneered.

"You quit now, noh nohtiss and you ask to cash your paycheck now? NOW? Maybe you bllooow meee and I thiiink about it. Ha! I heet you Marrth-ti and how 'bout you blow me, how 'bout that? Hah!" He turned to his troops—the hoodlum henchmen newly arrived from Sparta—seeking affirmation. They guffawed in unison, enthusiastically bellowing support.

Coolly, I returned the check to my purse and exited the smoke-stained lounge. Good thing Terri'd jotted down her room number on that napkin. Ol' Papadopoulos'd made me so mad I'd forgotten it. I marched to the nearest elevator, in the hotel lobby, pushed the "UP" button. The doors opened immediately, and I stepped in and ascended to Terri's room. I knocked once and the door swung open. "Hi!" She motioned me in. "I am so glad you quit working there! What a feeble excuse for a bar. Hey, you smoke weed, right?"

"Um, yeah, but only a little, okay? Like I said, I'm getting up really early to go to the travel agency. I need to buy my airline ticket and take off."

Terri raised an eyebrow. "Yeah, Billy told me you're moving to Texas."

"I got divorced today, at noon. And I, uh...I want a new start, wanna put some miles between me and the guy I was married to. He really, well he really screwed me over. He, he got, got—" The pain and grief began to well up, but I pushed it deep down. *Do NOT act crazy. Do NOT cry. Do NOT tell her about Annie.* "Where's that weed, anyway?" Terri lit a joint and passed it to me. I thanked her, took a hit, exhaled, then waved a hand as if brushing away a minor inconvenience. "He got everything. But I'm gonna rebuild. I'll make a new life for myself."

"You can do it. You remind me of friends of mine, up in Alaska. Steely strength." She did a hit of weed, held it, exhaled. "I worked on the Alaskan Pipeline. I was in nursing school in Minnesota, and when I heard about the money to be made, up in the Arctic Circle, I jumped on it. Quit school, totally upset my father; he's a doctor, wanted a career for me in medicine."

"Terri, I want that. I want a man's job, like hard hat construction, or whatever. Something with good pay and benefits. I don't have any money, only a couple hundred bucks, and I'm spending that on a one-way airfare, but I can wait tables when I get to Houston and save money till I can join a union or something and get an apprenticeship."

"You figured out where you're going to stay when you get there?"

"No, but with the tips I made tonight, I should have enough money for a couple of days in a fleabag motel, and each day I wait tables I'll make more tips, and I'll slowly get it together..." It suddenly struck me how crazy this plan might seem to Terri, and wished I hadn't said it. *After all, I might be crazy. No. No, I am not...*

"Look, Marti. Those guys I work with are okay. They're in Bill's room, down the hall. I'm going there for one more drink, come with me."

In Billy's room, the group seemed to be celebrating something. The room, a suite, offered a sofa, armchairs, a coffee table, and a desk and office chair in addition to the bed, so we all had plenty of room to sit and hang out. A boom box played cassette tapes, first Jackson Browne, then Randy Newman. We smoked a few hits of weed. After that, Billy put on some George Carlin, and we all laughed really hard. I liked Billy's readiness to laugh. Terri had a great sense of humor, I loved the way she exuded confidence and strength. She was really pretty, too. They were all good looking, and young, and full of enthusiasm. I felt I'd known them for a very long time. For the first time in many years, I began to feel like myself. I started making funny remarks and getting laughs, too. I felt wealthy in knowing these new friends, lucky I'd met them in the midst of the loneliest day of my life.

"Hey Billy," Terri said, "Marti's moving to Texas tomorrow. One-way ticket to Houston."

Bill looked up from cleaning some weed. "Yeah, she told me somethin' like that." He cocked his head in my direction. "She told me she was thinkin' of either Corpus Christi or Houston, but I told her there's nothin' in Corpus." He chuckled, turned to me. "Glad you took my advice."

I laughed, and so did everyone else in the room who had not passed out yet, i.e. Terri and Billy. Dave and Ron were toast.

I asked Terri and Billy about their occupations. They told me they did welding inspection, using ultrasound, a new technology. Billy'd worked on the Alaskan Pipeline with Terri, that's where they'd met. Here in Chicago they'd been inspecting the welds at an industrial plant, but they'd finished that day, and that's why they were partying.

"Wow." I longed for something brilliant to follow, but no luck. "How do you get a job like that?"

Terri set a mirror on the coffee table and laid out a couple of lines of coke. "You just do it, Marti. When you get to Houston, you follow your plan and stay with it." She grabbed her purse, pulled out an address book, and started writing on one of the pages. "Here's my phone number, address, and also my parents' phone number. If you can't reach me at my place, my mom will take a message and get it to me. I like you and I think you've got what it takes. Call me if you need any help." She tore out the page and handed it to me.

Carefully, almost reverentially, I folded the piece of paper and put it in my wallet. "Thank you! But I won't call unless I really get into trouble. I want to do this all on my own."

Billy chimed in. "I've got another job after this one, and I'll be traveling for about three weeks. Tell you what, I know a place in Houston where you can stay for free, but only for that three weeks. It's not fancy. Actually, it's my place. I share an apartment with two other guys, I've known 'em both for years, so they won't mess with you. You can have my room till you get settled. And when you get your plane ticket, give them a call and somebody'll pick you up at the airport. I'll set it up for you."

Astonished, I accepted his offer. *All I need is a chance. And my chances just got better.* "Thank you, Billy. And Terri, thank you again. I gotta tell you something, it's only fair to be honest. You know I just got divorced. Well, it's a long story, but I married my high school boyfriend, who later became an adversary. His father is a psychiatrist, and they've got a lot of money, and that's how they...how they got everything. We had a baby, a girl, and I got really depressed after she was born, but I love her so much—it had to have been the hormones. But anyway, the father says I'm mentally ill and I don't know, he may be right, I mean, he's been giving me Lithium for years, I hate it but I take it because I'm scared I might actually BE crazy and if I quit the medication I'll go wacko for real and the loony squad'll come and lock me up. And the husband and his dad sued me for custody." I looked at the floor. "And I gave her up because I was so afraid they'd be able to lock me up forever, I know it's horrible...And now that I'm divorced, I can't get the Lithium from my father-in-law anymore and I'll have to go without it for awhile and in case I am what he says I am—"

Billy interrupted me. "And what exactly does your father-in-law say are the symptoms of this supposed mental illness? Like, what'd he say would happen, anyway? DID anything happen?"

"Yeah, well, short version, a few years ago when I was gonna leave the husband, he went off to his parents' house down the road, and then he came home with a bottle of Lithium and said his dad said to tell me I'm manic depressive and I gotta take the Lithium and not go to anyone else to get checked, we'll keep it in the family. And I was so intimidated I just went along with it. Er, I went along with it, uh, after I got really mad and threatened to kill myself, which did make me tend to doubt myself. I mean, if I'd been in my right mind I'd have threatened to kill my father-in-law."

Billy and Terri started to laugh, and I suddenly burst out laughing, too. I laughed until tears came into my eyes. Terri spoke up. "Look, it sounds like your father-in-law and your husband were using the psych meds in a last ditch attempt to rein you in, corral you. My father's a doctor, I know a little about the laws. They could have had you committed."

Billy cut in. "What do you think would happen if you quit taking the pills?"

"Hey, Billy...I won't go off at your place, just give me a chance...I reached for my purse, pulled out the meds I always carried with me. I shook the bottle. "See, it's more than half full. By the time this bottle is empty, I'll have my own place. You won't be in any danger."

He laughed again. "I'm not a bit worried about that. What I'm trying to say is, why not just quit the shit right now? I don't think you need it—you never did, most likely. I agree with Terri, it's a control thing."

"But my father-in-law told me my mind moves too fast, that it moves fifteen times faster than a normal mind!"

A grin, like a sunrise, spread across my new friend Billy's face. "Fifteen times faster, huh? Well, I would think that'd be an advantage! You were a threat. The father-in-law needed control, for his son, and to grab up the grandchild. Toss that shit and go to Houston. You've got friends now!" He laughed. "Once you're a Texas transplant, you can get goin' and set those assholes straight."

Hope bubbled up in me, bringing with it a sane, steady self-confidence. "Will do." I walked to the hotel room's waste basket, tossed the pills in. "You mind?"

"Not a bit. Housekeeping'll take out the trash."

I never took another dose of Lithium, ended the medication without consequence. Billy was right. I never needed it—it turned out my father-in-law was way out of hand, his diagnosis incorrect. And that made me all the more determined to fight for my child, my future, and myself.

CHAPTER 6

DYNAMITE, DISCO, AND DEER BLINDS

Landing the first job had taken some effort. I'd left Chicago for Houston with about thirty-seven dollars in cash, some clothes, and three weeks to stay at Billy's apartment while I got on my feet. His roommate Richard picked me up at the airport, just as Billy'd said he would. Purchasing my one-way plane fare'd exhausted all my savings. My plan was to get a job working in the oil field, or in hard hat construction. I was burnt out on waiting tables, but when I hit town, I'd first applied for a job at the premium Houston night club, Elan, on Westheimer near the Galleria, and they hired me—a good thing, since the tips provided me with cash for day to day living and helped me kick in on my newfound friends' rent.

I worked at Elan for a couple of weeks, serving cocktails to nouveau riche good ol' boys and Saudi sheiks, equally misogynistic subsets of the Texas urban male species in the late 1970s. The good ol' boys, oilmen, wore string ties and Stetsons, boots crafted from the skins of endangered species, and slaphappy grins powered by Jim Beam and Coke—'ca-Cola, that is, not 'caine. And the Saudi oil millionaires? The sheiks proudly sported their traditional Arabic desert garb and appeared to disdain all American females, their attitudes dismissive and their sneers contemptuous.

Even though the dresses we wore at work were modest, with hemlines just above the knee and necklines tasteful, the American and Arab oilmen alike tended to misbehave, both subtly and unsubtly, and made disrespectful comments. Back then, the term, "sexual harassment" was virtually unheard of, used only among female activists for the first time during the early to mid-1970s. We dreaded waiting certain tables. Management attempted to bolster the morale of female staff by spinning yarns about this or that cocktail server who'd been tipped twenty grand by this or that cowpoke or sheik, but we doubted the veracity of these accounts, with good reason.

I saved up some money, quit Elan, and took a job at the Stouffer Renaissance Hotel in Greenway Plaza, close to Rice University and damn near adjacent to the Summit, an indoor arena and home of the Houston Rockets since 1975. On my first day at work, I met Robert, an openly gay bartender who was looking for a roommate. We hit it off, and after the shift ended Robert showed me the apartment. The place was beautiful, spacious, gated, and located only a few blocks from work. Robert held the lease in his name, and Jeff, the other roommate, worked part time at the Houston Fire Department and was engaged in a lawsuit against a fire station in Georgia, where he'd worked till they fired him after he came out publicly.

Now that I'd found a place to live, I saved every bit of money I could toward my long-range goal. I missed Anne Marie, and the pain of separation, nearly visceral, tore at me, but I coped with it by spending a portion of each week's wages on gifts for her. I shipped clothes, toys, and books to my in-laws' address, with a letter or card attached to each package. I hoped that my ex-mother-in-law would give the presents to my daughter and maybe even read the letters aloud to her. But I never received a single reply or acknowledgment. Still, I kept sending things. Her birthday passed, then Christmas, with no contact. When I phoned my in-laws' place, Derek's father would answer, and each time, refused to let me talk with her.

I bottled up my pain and threw myself into learning more about Houston, and what was going on in the world. For the past three years, as a young working mom, I'd barely kept up with current events or issues. Now I lived in a gay neighborhood, with assertive gay roommates who lived large, loud, and sassy, during a stormy period of social change and cultural upheaval. The circumstances suited me, since my former existence had been blown to smithereens. New beginnings.

Moving into the Montrose district intrigued and thrilled me. The fact I lacked a vehicle did not prove a drawback in that area of the city; I could walk everywhere. And the Montrose was gay/bohemian/misfit headquarters! This part of town rocked with festivity, cultural diversity and artistic innovation. In the 1960s, the fledgling counterculture movement developed in the Montrose district, and it became the center of the gay and lesbian movement in the 1970s. Progressive radio stations like KPFT, KLOL and KILT, pioneers in the underground FM radio movement, established themselves in the area, and KPFT's radio transmitter was bombed—twice, by the Ku Klux Klan—earning them the distinction of being the only American radio station to be literally blown off the air by terrorists.

And the white-hooded wizards of KKK weren't the only hate group around the neighborhood. Forays by vigilante homophobes abounded in Houston, but gay activist groups like the Gay Liberation Front, based in Montrose, didn't stand for that. They organized and united the community. I heard about groups of gay men using CB radios for communication—that they'd notify one another when a hate crime was in progress. Word on the streets was that these big butch gay guardians would jump in their four-wheel drive Broncos, race to the scene and retaliate, driving the attackers away and assisting the victims of the violence.

Only a few weeks after I arrived in Houston, news of the horrendous Jonestown massacre hit, with accounts of infamous cult leader Jim Jones, who ordered his followers to commit mass suicide-by-cyanide-laced-Kool-Aid. The tragedy occurred on Nov. 18th, 1978, and more than nine hundred people died, three hundred of them children. That same month, followers of an obscure Muslim cleric named Ayatollah Khomeini attacked the British embassy/El Al office in Iran, and the U.S., France, Great Britain, and U.S.S.R. all performed nuclear tests. To pessimists and apocalypse fans, these events seemed to be ushering in an Armageddon.

In pop culture, Farrah Fawcett, Suzanne Somers, Lynda Carter, Iman, and Christie Brinkley were the hotties, Oakland Raiders' John Madden became the thirteenth coach to win one hundred NFL games, and "Question of Love," the first lesbian-themed TV movie, starring Gena Rowlands and Ned Beatty, aired nationally and was later nominated for a Golden Globe.

Things definitely seemed to be shaking up, and I counted myself lucky to be living in that climate of change—after all, I planned on making an impact myself, crashing through gender bias, exploding stereotypes, and ultimately shattering the glass ceiling. My plan was to get the butchest, most high-paying job I could. So every day, before donning my little black dress, black pantyhose and spike heels and reporting to work at Stouffers' cocktail hour, I'd slap on my jeans, Acme cowboy boots and a denim work shirt, hike to a major oil company or high-rise construction site, and attempt to land a hardhat job.

My first prospect was a huge skyscraper under construction near my apartment. The big boss on site was Ned Sullivan, aka Sully, a genial, white-haired Irish guy with a great sense of humor, who appreciated my enthusiasm and actually granted me an interview instead of dismissing me at the outset. Mr. Sullivan appeared to keep an open mind regarding hiring women. Another plus with Sully, I figured, was that he didn't appear to have a hidden sexual agenda. He talked about his grandkids and his wife—a real family guy.

Sully told me that corporate employers, such as the one overseeing his project, would be receiving tax cuts and other incentives to hire minorities, including women. This was all part of the new world of EOE—Equal Opportunity Employment. If they were to hire me, I'd have to start out doing grunt work—picking up fallen bricks and pieces of rebar around the lot, but if I stuck it out, I'd move up. "Are you okay with heights?" Sully'd asked me. "You gotta be sure-footed and not get spooked. When you're seventeen stories up, walking along a girder..."

"I'll have to think about it, Mr. Sullivan, but I'm pretty sure I can do anything. I don't scare easily." After leaving the interview I worked my shift waiting tables, took a taxi home, drank a couple of Heinekens and went to sleep. That night I dreamed I was sitting high up in the framework of Sully's building, my feet dangling off an iron girder, a black-painted metal lunchbox on my lap and a hardhat atop my head. A burly coworker sat on either side of me, clad in gear identical to mine. In the dream, I glanced down at my dangling feet, then beyond them to the street below, a distance of about a half-mile or more, it seemed. And I turned to one of my coworkers and said, "Last night I dreamed I fell from way up here. Isn't that weird?"

My coworkers in the dream replied in one voice, and the voice echoed eerily, tossed by the wind. "Don't look down! A guy fell from here yesterday..."

But in the dream, I didn't heed them. I looked down. The girder began to sway in the wind, and I'd jerked awake just in time to avoid hurtling to my dream death...and certain that I didn't want to continue the application process. In the morning I stopped by to talk to Sully, told him about the vivid, crazy dream. Sully shuddered. "Oh. I dread having dreams like that. And I have 'em...every once in a while. So you need both feet on solid ground? Nothin' to be ashamed of, and there are plenty of good jobs in Houston."

So I'd embarked on my tour of oil companies, determined to brazen my way into something good. Most of big oil—Amoco, Shell, Chevron, and others—had set up their corporate headquarters in the same general sector of the city where I resided, so I could hoof it, and since I was applying for labor jobs, it'd been both kosher and logical for me to wear jeans and boots. I took a cheerily assertive approach, breezing through the glitzy glass double doors of each corporate stronghold, slapping a smile on my face and hailing the receptionist or security guard with a hearty, "Hi! My name is Marti MacGibbon and I need to talk with the President, please."

To my surprise, this strategy produced some results. At each stop, staff appeared to be nonplussed by my audacity; they'd issue me a security badge and send me back to talk to some muckety-muck in the personnel department or some higher-up in exploration. And through this crazy, haphazard process, I began to collect industry jargon, and insider tips on which of the decent-paying jobs held the lowest requirements for experience and education. I began to refine my search and learned that working in seismic exploration might be a good place to start. The pay would probably be far lower than a roughneck's, but I wouldn't need the brute strength and ability to zone out and trip pipe all day or all night—or both—that roughnecking required. Also, I would never be called upon to stand hundreds of feet up the derrick on a tiny little square of steel. I was still reeling from that dream of falling.

One executive at a smaller oil company referred me to Lance Thatcher, head of operations at a big exploration company. When I called Thatcher, he informed me his company wouldn't be hiring for a few months, but he'd keep me in mind. When I told him I needed immediate work, he was kind enough to refer me to a short list of big seismic exploration companies, suggested I use his name when inquiring about work, and promised to back me up with a reference when they called him. "I like your attitude, Marti. Tell 'em you worked for me in the field at Triah-Dayelt a couple of years back." He chuckled. "Yeah, tell 'em that. And if you don't get somethin' real quick, remember later on we've got a big job comin' up in Wyoming. The site's pretty remote. They lower you in a harness out of a helicopter onto a butte. Never boring."

Triah-Dayelt? With his pronounced Texas accent, I wasn't sure what company Lance was referring to, but didn't want to hobble my good fortune by asking him to repeat it. "Wow. Thanks, Mr. Thatcher."

"S'Nothin'. Keep in touch. That Wyoming project might come through early. And let me know how it goes."

My search soon brought me to Seismodyne, an international seismic exploration company in Houston. I gave the receptionist my usual pitch and gained access to the Head of Field Operations, Hank Patterson. Mr. Patterson was tall, fit, silver-haired and charismatic. He wore a genuine smile; his green eyes crinkling up around the edges. "Sit down," he said, and took a seat opposite me. "What can I do for you?"

"I'm looking for work on a seismic crew, and I'm willing to travel anywhere. If you hire me, I can start immediately." I began telling Hank my story: how I'd come to Texas with a one-way ticket and something like thirty-seven dollars to my name. I started working up the courage to deliver my best rendition of Lance Thatcher's drawled "Triah-Dayelt" reference, but Hank cut in.

"You know, Marti, you remind me of me when I first arrived in Houston. Long time back. I rode out on the bus from Decatur, Illinois. Had about sixteen bucks in my pocket when I got here." He chuckled. "My life savings..." He shook his head slowly, chuckled again. "I took a job with a seismic crew, and I never looked back. Started out as a juggie." Another amused chortle. "Anyhow, I like your attitude, and I'm gonna hire you." He pulled an application out of his desk drawer and slid it across the desktop. "Go ahead and fill that out." I began scribbling in earnest. He continued. "So, here's what you do, Champ. You let me get your paperwork processed, and then wait for the call. The company's got a crew on the ground up in Conroe. Y'know where that is? It's up north of the city, around Sam Houston National Forest. They're running a shot line up there. Here's what seismic is like. The crew chief is like a king, what he says goes. There're about sixty men to a crew, and not all of 'em are gonna be what you'd call refined, but if you know how to handle yourself you'll do okay. And I've got a feeling you know how to command respect."

I looked up from my scrawling and nodded, glad of his confidence in me. "Thanks, Mr. Patterson."

He held up a hand, as if to stem the tide of any superfluous gratitude. "So, when you get the call, you'll travel up to Conroe and check in at the field office. Every seismic crew travels from place to place, following the work. It's sorta like the carnival in a way." He paused to chuckle once more. "You report to that crew boss. Your paperwork will have already arrived, and they'll issue you your per diem, that's your living expenses. Be careful with that money—it'll have to last you till your first paycheck, about two weeks. You'll need to find a temporary residence, and you'll stay there until the crew moves on. If you decide you like seismic work, you'll move on with 'em." He rose from his desk.

I glanced up from my application, sensing that Hank Patterson was now terminating the interview. Unsure of how to spell, "Triah-Dayelt," I hastily scratched in, "Tri-Delta," under past work experience and handed him the completed form. Later, I discovered to my dismay that Tri-Delta was another name for a sorority, but I guess it didn't matter. The job was already mine.

Hank handed me his business card and graced me with another smile. "Remember, Champ, I started out as a juggie. Keep your eyes on the prize. And stay in touch."

I strode out of Seismodyne on winged feet. My heart pounded with joyous anticipation as I contemplated my new career in the oil business! I scurried off to my paltry waitress job, thrilled to know that my days there were now few, very few in number.

When I got to work, I told Robert the news, expecting him to be impressed. He sniffed, "Oh, Mary, puh-leeaase. Working out there in the wilderness with those yay-hoos? Girl, you'll have skin like an alligator by the time you hit thirty. But I guess wading through the mud in those bayous'll tone up your thighs." He glared at me for emphasis. "You'll be cellulite-free from all the exercise, so you might still be able to get laid at thirty...as long as you slap on the sunscreen. Skip that sunscreen, and you'd better keep a bag over your head." He rolled his eyes, an exaggerated expression of boredom. "Gimme your drink order."

On January 5th, I departed Houston for Conroe, sitting proudly behind the wheel of a dilapidated, sludge-green Plymouth Fury III, loaned to me by my friend Billy Ray Castor, who'd assisted me in relocating to Houston from Chicago. Billy, an adept backyard mechanic, had planned to give the car to his mom for a second set of wheels once he'd fixed it up, but he'd agreed to loan it to me for a stint, prior to restoring it. "You're gonna have to take your chances. It's kind of a community-you-gas-it," Billy'd told me, his poker face working overtime, "You gotta pump the brakes real easy, though— it fishtails." The car's upholstery was pretty ripped up, and it lacked a radio, but the big, wide seats would afford me room to stretch out and sleep if I had to actually spend the night in it. The heater worked, another essential to survival. And even better, it boasted legit plates and registration, something every car needs, especially in Texas.

I rolled into Conroe in the afternoon, and located the field office, a shabby-looking storefront building on the main drag. The weather was really cold that day, and windy, so I buttoned up my coat to ward off the chill as I jumped out of the old Fury III and made for the door. I knocked once, then decided it'd be silly to stand outside on the doorstep like some Girl Scout selling cookies. I grabbed the doorknob, turned it, pushed, and stepped inside to see a burly man with a buzz-cut seated at a massive, battered oak desk. He wore a khaki shirt, a flight jacket and a disapproving scowl. His pale blue eyes appraised me, then cut sharply—in the direction of the huge Doberman Pinscher sprawled on the floor to his right. He hissed, "Don't move."

I froze, then took a second glance at the Dobey. Its stumpy little tail wagged, and my muscles relaxed. "What a beautiful dog!" I slapped on a grin in order to relay a definite lack of intimidation, and sauntered slowly toward the desk. The dog sat. "Hi," I offered. "I'm Marti, and Houston office gave me orders to report here."

The Sarge said nothing for a moment, then muttered, "She's an attack dog. Watch yourself." He jerked his head to the left, barked at a guy in a flannel shirt who sat at a smaller, metal desk. "Vince! The paperwork." Vince jumped up, marched to a pair of metal filing cabinets along one wall, and extracted a couple of sheets of paper. He walked to Sarge's desk, set the papers down, and stepped away. Obviously, this uptight, crew-cut-wearing dude was the big boss, lord of his domain, ruling his fiefdom with an iron hand. He turned to me. "Sit down." He swept a hand toward a wooden chair to the left of his desk. I sat, my back to Vince, folded my hands demurely in my lap, and waited while the Sarge looked over the paperwork. "Hmmm. Alright, Miss—oh, but I s'pose it's Ms., isn't it?" He chortled, and a menacing gleam crept into his eyes as he surveyed my responses. "MS.! Yep. Of course, because you're a PROGRESSIVE PERSON, right?"

I smiled again, unsure of what to say, exactly, but confident I could handle this asshole. I might not like him, but I could handle him. After all, I'd dealt with much bigger misogynists as a waitress.

"Yes, I am." I drew a breath, smiled, and waited. I'd been hired in Houston, and no matter how much he hated it, this guy couldn't fire me without an excuse. I would stand my ground.

"Heh. Yep, well, home office told me you were comin,' and here you are." He let out his breath, a huffing sound. "My name is Bo Gilsup. I'm the Field Supervisor, and U.S. Army Drill Sergeant, retired. I run things around here, and as far as I'm concerned, I'm still military." He grinned slyly. "Well, you're dismissed. Be here tomorrow at oh-seven-hundred. We'll try to find some way to put you to work. Oh, and MS.? You'll need to find somewhere to stay, and show up with your lunch. We're in the field all day."

"Sounds good. Houston told me I could pick up my per diem tonight, for relocation expenses."

"Heh!" His laugh sounded more like a cough. "Houston told you wrong. You'll get your per diem in two weeks, with your paycheck. No exceptions." Gilsup's glee was palpable as he delivered his final shot, "Oh, and don't even think they'll stop for a restroom. You'll have to go in the woods, like everybody else. Heh. Heh."

"See you tomorrow, Mr. Gilsup." I waved at Vince for good measure, and headed for the door. On the way down the front steps, I noticed a young cowboy type with curly brown hair, ice blue eyes, and muddy boots strolling up the walk. He stepped aside to let me pass, then continued on into the office.

I reached the dented old Plymouth, jumped in and started the engine, preoccupied with thoughts of survival. I'd only brought about fifty bucks with me on the trip, since I'd been expecting to pick up the per diem. The rest of my total cash assets, close to four hundred bucks, was stashed in my bank in Houston, and I didn't have enough time to drive back home and get it before the bank closed. Besides, I couldn't risk missing work in the morning. That would be exactly what Gilsup was hoping for, and I promised myself I wouldn't allow him the satisfaction. *I'll sleep in the car.*

I steered the Fury III out onto the street and started driving. A few blocks down, I saw a real estate office on the right, next to a Dairy Queen, and grabbed a parking space. I strode briskly to the door of the real estate office, stepped inside, walked down a dimly lit hallway to another door with a sign that read, "Bill McNamara, Real Estate." I tried the door, but found it locked. I rang the doorbell but no one answered. Just then I noticed a bulletin board on the opposite wall of the hallway. An index card tacked to the board advertised an apartment for rent, and a phone number. Ecstatic, I grabbed the card from the bulletin board, shoved it in my coat pocket, and shot back down the corridor looking for a payphone.

I exited the real estate building and made for the Dairy Queen. The drive-in was a little rundown, but the counters and tabletops appeared fresh-scrubbed, and the young woman behind the counter smiled engagingly. I threw my shoulders back and marched up to the counter, surveying the menu for the cheapest item I could find, which turned out to be a ten-cent small beverage. "Small Coke, please."

"Sure, just a minute." The smiling counter attendant turned to fill a small plastic cup at a soft drink dispenser, and I noticed she was more than a little bit pregnant. Very pregnant, in fact, and she looked very young, maybe eighteen. She handed me the soda, and I gave her a quarter.

"Keep the change," I said, then laughed, a little embarrassed, but the counter chick laughed with me. Encouraged, I pulled the index card out of my pocket and waved it nervously. "Hey, do you have a phone I can use? I'm new in town, and I'm looking for an apartment, and I saw this ad on the bulletin board at the real estate office, but there's nobody around."

She glanced at the card. "You don't want that apartment, believe me." She rolled her eyes, then leaned forward, dropping her voice. "The realtor owns this Dairy Queen, and it's his apartment, too. The place is crummy and it's way too expensive. Besides, he's... not a very nice guy, really."

"Oh, well, um, do you know of anything? I've got some cash for a down payment, and on the weekend, I can drive to Houston and get some money out of the bank..."

"How much are you thinking of paying for rent?"

"As little as possible. See, I've got this job with an oil exploration company, and tomorrow's my first day. We don't get paid for two weeks, but I've got about forty bucks on me now. If I have to, I'm gonna sleep in the car."

"I'll tell you what," she ventured, "My husband and I have a spare bedroom, and I need help with housework—just dishes and vacuuming. If you can do that, I'll rent it to you for ten dollars a month."

"Wow! Really? Of course I'll do it. Here." I pulled a ten-dollar bill out of my purse and handed it to her, but she pushed it away.

"I can't take your money yet." She looked at her watch. "My name's Maria. I'm off in a half hour. Hang around, and when my husband comes to pick me up after work, we'll show you the house and you make your decision then, okay?"

I nodded. "Nice to meet you, Maria. I'm Marti." We both laughed. I liked Maria, couldn't believe my good fortune. When her husband, Joaquin, showed up, he turned out to be a really sweet guy, and not much older than Maria. The couple told me they hailed from Eagle Pass, a border town, and that they'd come to Conroe in search of work and a better life for their baby. They'd been in town four months and things were going pretty well for them, all told. Joaquin had a job in construction, framing.

I followed them down a side street and across the railroad tracks to a tiny wooden house with a spindly pine tree in the yard. The exterior paint clung to the siding in patches, like fur on a mangy dog, and the roof sagged, but inside, the house was snug and warm, and Maria had obviously spent time and effort scrubbing the shabby furniture. My room was a tiny alcove off the living room. Its walls had been painted teal blue, and the twin bed looked lumpy, but I didn't care. Maria told me I could make a peanut butter and jelly sandwich to take in my lunch the next day. That night, when I turned out the light in my bedroom, the cockroaches swarmed all over those teal blue walls. I flipped the light switch back on and slept in my jeans, socks, and a T-shirt. I got up at 6:00 a.m., packed my lunch, tiptoed out of Maria and Joaquin's house, jumped in the Fury III and showed up for work early.

Gilsup blanched when he saw me walk into the office, my lunch in hand. He tried to regain his composure, smiling weakly and fumbling for words. "Sooo. You...uh. So, you found a place to stay?"

"Yes, I found one right away, thank you." Although I did make some effort, I couldn't contain my smugness, so I turned away from the boss and waited outside in front of the office for a minute or two, till I got my smile under control. *That's right, I'm still here, Mr. Gilsup...and I'm not scared of peeing in the woods, either. You gotta do a lot better than that if you wanna get rid of me. Guess I'm your feminist nightmare...*

When the other workers began arriving, I walked back into the office. Some of the guys stole sideways glances at me, then shifted nervously from foot to foot, no doubt wondering what the hell I was doing there. Others adapted a more aggressive posture, narrowing their eyes to slits and homing in on me from across the room. I couldn't decide whether they did this in an attempt to make me uneasy, or reassure themselves. Others chose to ignore me. *It's okay. I'll show 'em I can keep up.*

When all sixty-some crewmembers had gathered together in the office, Gilsup unleashed his Full Metal Jacket drill sergeant act, full force. "Hyaarrhhright, men! He snarled, "Formation!" My co-workers, many of whom appeared desperately hungover, having sloshed, stumbled or staggered into the office only moments earlier, now snapped to full attention, all but saluting our boss, who strutted back and forth like a small-town cracker sheriff and lynch mob instigator in a B movie, barking orders. "Now, men—" Gilsup began, then, with exaggerated emphasis, stopped stock still, stared at me pointedly, and corrected himself, adding, "Oh, and Marti..." He continued on with his orders, dividing everyone up into crews, then dispersing everyone with, "Dyiiis—MISSED!"

The boss'd assigned me to the explosives crew that first day. "Okay," he'd smirked, "Ever'body's got at least six men to a crew. Except for the shooter crew, an' they've got Marti, she's half-a-person, so it's five-and-a-half. Heh." On hearing that, I'd privately rejoiced, but tried to seem disappointed, and hoped my act was convincing enough. No doubt Gilsup, who, I'd noticed this morning, kept a framed black and white poster of General George S. Patton—in jodhpurs, no less—on the wall in the office, figured the shooter crew'd be waaay too butch for a "little ol' gal"—as if he could frighten me off with loud noises, thereby purging his man-army of the newly-arrived female scourge. *He'll need to ramp up his scare tactics...*

As it turned out, the shooters went out with the juggies that day, because they needed more hands to set things up on the shot line. Lucky for me, Hank Patterson had briefed me on the basics of seismic work, and I knew what a shot line was. A seismic crew's objective, Mr. Patterson had told me, was oil exploration, and in those days, this generally involved obtaining an accurate reading of the earth's crust via sound waves gathered from explosive blasts strategically set off from points on either a grid or a tangent. The word "seismic" means "of or relating to an earthquake." The blasting, or shaking by heavy machinery in some cases, would simulate a sort of mini-earthquake, and then the seismic crew's technological equipment would pick up the sonic waves as imagery, then send it back to the geophysicists for analysis.

The way I understood Hank's summarization, it all started with the client's team of geophysicists, back in the city, who'd target a general area they figured might have oil and gas. The area the oil company targeted, of course, would be land where they'd already leased the mineral rights from the actual landowners. Enter the seismic crew. First, the permit man gets in contact with the targeted landowner. He knocks on doors and hopefully finds an upbeat way to tell the ranchers that a bunch of workers, heavy equipment, and explosives are going to be coming through, and convinces them to sign a permit. The permit man's gotta be a charmer, or a persuasive guy who can get this done. Sometimes the landowner greets the permit man with a smile and a glass of sweet tea, sometimes the landowner brandishes a loaded shotgun.

Next, Hank Patterson'd told me, the survey crew goes in and sets up the shot line or the grid, and the points thereon, the "shot points," designating the stations with stakes and flagging. The drilling crew follows with heavy equipment—a drilling rig, such as they might use to drill for water wells, and a "water buggy," a massive truck containing enough water to make the drilling process possible. The drilling team pierces the earth's crust and drills down to a depth designated by the geophysicists in the city. It might be fifty feet, a hundred feet or so, and at a designated distance apart, a hundred, two hundred, or so.

After drilling, the seismic workers drop sticks of dynamite into those shot holes, and the crew's electrician wires the shot line and attaches the blasting caps. Then the juggies come along and string cable and set the geophones all along the shot line. Geophones are the key to the whole thing. The juggies push them into the ground, and, once the explosives on the shot line detonate, those little devices pick up the vibrations of the earth, which are in turn recorded by the computer in the Observer's truck.

The coolest part of the explosives crew, I thought, would be the chance to detonate the charges. I determined to pay close attention and work diligently, so that someday I'd rise up the ranks to a position of responsibility and get to trigger the blasts. Gilsup gave orders for the shooter crew, survey crew, and juggies to combine efforts along one stretch of the line, clearing brush and loading the holes with dynamite at the shot points. We all climbed in the back of an enormous vehicle with gigantic tires. My co-workers called it a "brush buggy."

We bounced along in the back of the buggy on the way to the job. I kept quiet, hoping my silence would project confidence and toughness. A couple of the guys, Boots and Jimmy Joe, asked me my name and introduced themselves. Another guy, Earl, asked me where I'd worked before signing up with Seismodyne. "Triah-Day-elt," I replied, taking a stab at what I hoped was a convincing drawl, and smiled. The guy nodded, apparently satisfied with my answer.

The country around Conroe, Texas was heavily wooded, thick with underbrush. The work day passed quickly, with the brush buggy pounding through brush and saplings to get us to each segment of shot line. We'd all jump out and begin walking the line to make sure the grass and turf was clear enough around each shot point, so as not to obscure the geophones' reading and transmission of data. The forest's beauty and the scent of the pine trees refreshed me and kept things fun. I'd always loved hiking, and this job offered plenty of that.

At one point in the day another huge piece of heavy equipment pulled up to our brush buggy, and a bunch of guys started unloading sticks of dynamite. Boots and Jimmy ran over and started helping them, so I followed. I'd never seen a stick of dynamite before that day. Up till then, my knowledge of explosives'd been confined to the cartoon world as I witnessed the tireless efforts of Wile E.

Coyote to apprehend the Roadrunner, using bundles of TNT mail-ordered from the Acme Company, his favorite source of supply.

But this dynamite wasn't even faintly cartoonish; it was the real thing, and everyone on the crew appeared to respect it, even though some joked around while working. I'd never worked with men before, and I noticed that they pulled together to get the job done, without asking me any questions about why I was there. I felt relieved that these guys didn't give me a hard time or try to harass me into quitting. I'd showed them a willingness to work as hard or harder than anybody else and demonstrated an ability to focus and learn the skills required. I kept my eyes and ears open and spoke very sparingly. I figured I must be earning their respect. The day ended and we rode the buggy back to the office, where the boss stood in the parking lot, talking to Bob Estrada, the driller.

As I dismounted from the brush buggy, Gilsup turned and half-smiled, half-sneered at me. "Hey there, Half-a-person...er, Marti. Get on over there and grab a hose. You ain't done workin' yet. Tires on the drilling buggy need rinsed off. Do it." He extended a calloused finger in my general direction, then back to the drilling buggy.

I slapped on a smile, sauntered toward the hose. "Yes, sir, Mr. Gilsup!" I shouted cheerily, then set to the task at hand. *If that dickhead thinks he can get me to quit by throwing extra work at me, he's in for a surprise.* When I finished, I headed into the office, still sporting that smile, and found the boss seated at his desk. The Doberman glanced in my direction and wagged her stumpy tail ever so slightly. "Anything else, Mr. Gilsup?"

Gilsup studied his paperwork. "Tires done y' can go on." He waved a hand dismissively, almost a shooing motion. I turned, bounced out of the office and down the steps. And as I made my way down the sidewalk, I again crossed paths with that young cowboy-type, the one with curly brown hair and ice blue eyes. He glanced my way, nodded, and flashed a quiet smile. I smiled back, tentatively, and marched toward the old Fury III.

Over the next two weeks, I settled into the job. Yes, I was roughing it, but I loved every minute of the challenge. For the first week I had to scrape by with only a few dollars for food, but Maria and Joaquin shared their evening meals with me and I reciprocated by doing the dishes, vacuuming, and sweeping the kitchen floor. And I'd had enough cash to purchase a jar of peanut butter and some bread from Conroe's grocery store, the Piggly Wiggly.

On Friday, the end of the first week, we got off work at 2:00 p.m., allowing me time to make a run to Houston. I purchased enough gasoline for the old Fury to wheeze into the city on fumes. I made it to my bank moments before it closed, withdrew half the cash from my savings account, and headed back to Conroe. First thing, I reimbursed Maria and Joaquin for groceries, then peeled off a couple of twenties for carrying money, and stashed the remainder in my right boot. *One more week till payday, Yee-haw!* The way I figured it, my paycheck, boot stash, and what was left in the bank would add up to enough to get a place of my own. Well, maybe.

Over that first weekend, I resisted the urge to spend. The entire sixty-hand crew worked Saturday and a half day Sunday, the shooter crew working along with the survey crew and juggies, finishing up that shot line. Boots, Jimmy, and Earl I'd already met. On Saturday, Scott, James, and Kevin introduced themselves. James was cool, the only black man on the sixty-unit crew, and he took no shit from anybody, seemed to be having fun doing the work. I modeled my attitude after his—it made perfect sense to me. Like James, I was the solitary representative of my demographic.

A lot of our work that day involved walking between the shot holes, or waiting for word to come down the line from Bob Estrada, the driller. At each shot hole, Kevin, the electrician, would connect the thin wires to the explosives, and the juggies would run cable and push the geophones, aka jugs, into the ground at each shot-point, enabling the equipment to pick up the vibration when they shot—blasted—the line.

Kevin's hair was longish, and strangely, pure white, even though he looked no more than twenty-six or twenty-seven years old. He seemed pretty cool to me because, except for executing his electrical wiring tasks with precision, he acted like he simply did not give a damn. He exuded a vibe of blissful relaxation. As the day drew on, I noticed a pattern with Kevin—every hour or so, he'd halt his steps, reach in the watch pocket of his Levis and pull out a battered Excedrin travel pack. Back then they were made of metal, sturdy, with a tight seal, an ideal and widely used stash container for uppers, downers, hits of acid, bindles of coke, or whatever. He'd pry open the aspirin tin, select a round white tablet from the pack, and pop it in his mouth. Sometimes he'd meander back to the truck for water to gulp down the pill with, but most times he'd dry-swallow it. *Hmmm. Maybe they actually are aspirin...*At one dose point, Kevin caught me watching him, looked me right in the eye. I stared back, raised my eyebrows, and smiled ever so slightly. "Ludes. They're Quaaludes. Want one?" He extended an astoundingly steady hand, open Excedrin box nestled in the palm of it.

I threw my head back and laughed. "Cool! No thanks. I was worried you had a migraine or something. Now I know you're okay. No sweat."

He chortled. "Damn right." He snapped the box shut, pocketed it. We marched on ahead, in silence, and I contemplated Kevin's seemingly infinite capacity for Quaaludes. *Why hasn't he passed out by now?*

Boots caught up, and Scott. James strode several yards ahead. We'd been traversing the pine forest all morning and along the way I'd noticed a wooden structure built into the trees, not too far up, with a ladder extending from the structure to the ground. I'd wondered what it could be. I reckoned it had to be a tree house for the landown-ers' kids to play in. Just then I looked up and saw another one, so I took a chance and commented, figured they could fill me in on the details. "Hey," I pointed upward. "I saw one of these earlier. I think it's kinda cool that the landowner builds these tree houses for his kids to play in, but how come they're so far out in the woods?"

Boots'd been chugging an Orange Crush, and he burst out laugh-ing, spraying a little of the soda into the air. He wiped his mouth. "TRAY-ee-haahwses!!" He slapped his knee and guffawed again. He poked a plug of Skoal into his lip. "They ain' trayee-haahwses," he began, accentuating his already heavily twanged Texas coun-try drawl for emphasis—or maybe the Skoal was impairing his lip mobility—"Thay-at's a DEER-bhlaan'—Woman, you AIN'T from aroun' here, are ya?"

His speech'd been muffled, but I thought I got it right; the thing was a deer barn, some sort of storage place for hay in case deer had a rough year. "Oh, man, that is so nice. A deer barn? Texas is so friendly the farmers even feed the deer." I wasn't being sarcastic. I had grown up in college towns, never'd been hunting, hadn't the slightest notion how Texans bag their deer.

Scott explained, speaking very slowly as if I might be intellec-tually deficient. "Marti, it's called a deer blind. Hunters hide inside there, sprinkle corn on the ground or put a salt lick out front, and when deer come for the bait, they stick the ol' rifle barrel through a spot in the blind, and blast Bambi to smithereens. End o' story."

"Oh. Uh, yeah. Got it."

The shot line had moved into a scenic pasture now. Gently rolling hills and warm afternoon sun. I'd been joking around with Scott, James, and Boots. I introduced myself to the two Mexican guys, Freddy and Blacky, noticed how the white guys didn't talk to the Mexicans much, and at first had thought maybe that was be-cause Freddy and Blacky only spoke Spanish. But their English was perfect. Before leaving the shelter of the forest, we'd all stopped for a smoke break. Boots'd fashioned a pipe out of his empty Orange Crush can, using his thumbs to make indentations in the middle of the can, a safety pin to poke tiny holes into the indented area to create a filter. Finally, he'd deftly poked a hole in the side of the can for air flow, removed the pop top, and we were in business. Freddy'd generously donated some killer weed, and we'd all taken a couple of hits.

The mood lightened, I threw away some of my caution and composure. I kept musing about how I'd thought the deer blinds were deer barns. I started laughing, trying to suppress it, because I lack the skill required to laugh silently, or even softly. Suddenly, music lunged into my head. Disco, too...really strange, since I prided myself on being a rocker, and really only listened to disco when dancing at gay clubs with Robert and Jeff, my former roommates back in Houston.

But the song, entitled, "Boogie Oogie Oogie," seemed irresistible to my brain waves in that moment. The song, a very popular crossover hit, had been a 1978 Billboard chart-topper by the disco/R&B group, Taste of Honey, who'd won a Grammy that year. Now, in January of 1979, DJs still played it frequently. In fact, I'd heard it twice on the radio in the ol' Fury III during my drive back from the bank run. And now the lyrics slipped in, hooked me.

Get down, boogie, oogie, oogie. Get down, boogie oogie oogie... Suddenly I felt like dancing—an urge so potentially humiliating, yet so powerful, that I murmured a furtive prayer to help me resist the temptation. My lapsed Catholic petition fell flat, but the song didn't miss a beat. The bass line of that disco tune throbbed relentlessly in my synapses. *Fuck it. I can at least hum the bass out loud, can't I?*

I cut a few strides away from the others. "Daaa-da-da-da-da-da. Da-da-da-da-dada-da-da," I hummed it under my breath. I momentarily increased my pace, in time with the base line, then dropped back, mentally scolding and shushing myself. *Shut up, shut up! Be cool, BE COOL.* With that inner remonstrance, the lyrics came back to me again, loud and clear, tantalizing. I laughed out loud, and, to my inner dismay, caved in to the urge and raised my voice in song, way off key, too. "Iiif you're thiinkin' yoouu're too cooool to boogie..."

To my left, and up the line, James' voice rang out clear, perfectly in tune, adding the next line. "Boy oh boy have I—got—news for yoooouuuuu."

I jogged a few steps, closed the distance between myself and my singing coworker. We did the next two lines in unison, my off-key voice and his perfect pitch. "Eeeverybooody heere to-niight must boogie...Let me tell you you are no excep—tion to the rule..."

In a flash, Freddy and Blackie blew my mind by chiming in! "Git on—uup—on the flooor, Cuz we're gonna boogie oogie oogie till you just can't boogie no mooore."

Kevin stopped twisting his electrical wires together, turned, and loudly joined his dry-swallowing-Quaalude-parched throat to the refrain. "BOOGIE NO MORE...YOU CAN'T boogie no moooore... BOOGIE...Boogie no moooore."

Scott and Boots stared. Earl slowly shook his head, eyes closed. Scott started laughing. "Man, y'all are STONED!"

Boots spat some Skoal on the ground. "Stoned or craaazy, ei-thah one.

I smiled, because I knew for sure I wasn't crazy, and it felt good. We all knew we were stoned. Acting silly, stupid even, but nobody cared. I remembered how I used to worry about being crazy all the time, and how I took those psych meds out of intimidation. I discontinued that avenue of thought, knowing it would take me to my pain center, to missing my baby. I resisted plunging down that tunnel. Out here, not one of my co-workers asked me if I had kids, and they would not, so I didn't have to worry about breaking down and crying uncontrollably. It struck me this new work environment was somehow emotionally safe. But physically safe? Yes, if I walked the chalk line. I did need to be on my guard at all times, do my work well, keep my distance, stay out of harm's way. But I'd come to recognize my capability and I relished it.

As the shift wound to a close, we connected with the chief surveyors, who'd been farther up the line planning the next morning's work. Scott stepped up and introduced me. "Y'all met Marti? She's learnin' on the shooter crew, but also works as a floater right now." They were Roger, a stout, red-faced guy with iron gray hair, and Jake, the guy I'd noticed before, the one with the ice blue eyes. Today, instead of a cowboy hat, Jake wore a ball cap. Roger nodded to Jake, then jumped into a company pickup truck. Jake told us to walk up to the brush buggy and catch a ride back to the office. Although he spoke very softly—I strained to hear him—Scott, James, Kevin and all the others immediately responded, marching on up the line. I followed, and never looked back, but as I moved ahead, I thought I could feel Jake's eyes on me. I tossed my head. *Who cares?*

Back at the office parking lot, I met a smiling, friendly chick about my age, named Faye. I hoped she was a new hire from Houston. "Hey, are you working here too?

"No, I'm picking up my husband, Joey. He drives the powder truck. It's a real important job." Faye smiled again. "So, you work here? That's great, we can hang out together. None of the other guys are married except Mr. Estrada, and his wife is up in Dallas. Besides, they're kinda old." She laughed. "Do you party? Joey and I go out on Saturday nights, I mean, there's not much to do here in Conroe, but there's a bar real close to the office. Everybody goes for a drink after work. You wanna come? You can ride with us."

"Okay, but I don't need a ride. My car's parked just down the street. I'll have one drink, that's all."

Faye touched me lightly on the shoulder. "Hey, will you come sit in my car for a minute? I want to ask you something."

"Sure."

She led me to her car, a blue 1976 Chevy Nova, and we both got in. "Nice car," I smiled. "So new."

"Thank you. It's Joey's pride and joy. An' I like it a lot, too." She caressed the steering wheel and giggled. "Okay, here goes. You're single, right?—I don't see a wedding ring..." She looked at me. I nodded.

"Yep. Single." My stomach started twisting, my chest felt constricted. *Oh no, she's gonna ask me if I have kids. I have got to get outta this car...*

"Good! I wanna fix you up with a friend of ours, his name is Larry Frazier, he's good lookin' and sweet, and he makes good money; I mean, he works here, do you know him? He drives heavy equipment. Marti, the two of you will hit it off, I know it! C'mon, tell me you'll go out with us, I'll bring him along, okay? Lately, Larry's been drinkin' a lot, prob'ly because he's kinda down right now, and he's Joey's best friend, so Joey's drinkin' more than usual. It won't hurt, we're only going for one drink, okay? I'll owe you one!"

There was something about Faye, her openness, her ready smile, that persuaded me. "Okay, but let me meet you guys over there in an hour, okay? I'll go home and change clothes, get cleaned up a bit." I didn't really care about impressing a guy right now, but I'd agreed to go out on a Saturday night, and I had my standards. Even in a podunk town.

"Marti, go ahead and do that. But, you look cute right now!"

I laughed out loud. "See you soon, Faye."

I went home and showered at Maria and Joaquin's, then traded in my work clothes for a pair of designer jeans, a cobalt blue blouse, and some chunky platform shoes. Leaving the light on in my room to scare away the roaches, I grabbed my good coat from the tiny closet and headed out the door.

The bar was on the main drag, a stone's throw from the field office. I stepped inside and saw Faye waving enthusiastically, sitting at a stainless steel, Formica-topped table with two ruggedly handsome young men. The jukebox blasted strains of George Jones' "He Stopped Loving Her Today." I took a deep breath and walked over to the three of them. "Hi." I smiled. One of the guys stood up and pulled out a chair for me. He was my height, with shoulder-length light brown hair and dark brown eyes. I sat down, but kept my coat on. "Er, you must be Larry. Faye's told me some good things about you." Larry smiled shyly, glanced down at the table. I noticed how long and dark his eyelashes were. I didn't feel attracted to him, instead, I felt...tender toward him and I wondered why.

"Marti, this is Joey." She looked lovingly at her husband, a lean, cheerful type with collar-length platinum blond hair and lots of scars on his hands. I smiled, nodded.

Joey stood up, looked my way. "What're you drinkin'?"

"Beer's fine. Budweiser or Miller, either one'll do."

Faye was bubbly, a fun hostess. She talked loudly enough to be heard over the montage of jukebox plays. One good thing about that honky-tonk was, the jukebox contained a surprisingly eclectic collection of tunes. George Jones' lonesome crooning gave way to Blue Oyster Cult's "Baby, Don't Fear the Reaper," followed by Led Zeppelin's "Stairway to Heaven," then we heard Tammy Wynette belting out, "Stand by Your Man." The four of us joked and made small talk, and the others went for a second round, but I held back, nursing that one beer. I needed to keep my wits about me, I figured. If I got loaded, I might start crying over my daughter, and that would ruin my new career in the Oil Patch. I worked with Joey and Larry and absolutely could not afford to appear emotional, or worse, emotionally unstable!

Somebody played the Commodores' "Brick House," and Faye and Joey got up and started dancing by the jukebox. Then they stood in front of it, pushing in quarters and selecting songs. *I hope they don't play the Bee Gees...no, they don't seem like the type. Good people.*

I turned my attention to Larry, tried to draw him into conversation. I asked him a few questions, about how long he'd worked at Seismodyne, things like that. Nothing personal. He'd been drinking Jack Daniels on the rocks, looked as though he'd gotten a pretty heavy buzz on by now. He knocked back his current drink, rested both arms on the table, and began opening up about his life. He told me he was divorced, that his ex-wife lived up in Dallas, and I could feel the pain radiating from him as he confided he had a son from the marriage, a toddler not quite two years old, and that his ex wouldn't let him see the boy, talk with him on the phone, or anything. "It damn near kills me to think about him." Larry ran a hand through his hair, shook his head as if trying to rid himself of a heavy weight. "Sorry, Marti, I, uh, I didn't mean to be such a bummer. I'll get us another drink." He rose to head for the bar.

I touched his wrist. "No, stay. Let's talk."

Larry nodded, sat back down, slid his chair nearer to mine, and leaned in close. He turned to me, his gaze intense. "Larry, I got divorced a couple months ago. And I've got a little girl. She's three years old, and my husband and his father sued me for custody; his family's got money and influence, and I couldn't fight it. They won. They won't even let me talk to her on the phone. But you know what? I'm gonna work hard, and save my money, and make a way for myself. And I'm gonna get a lawyer and fight and try to get her back, or at least get visitation rights. That's why I'm working on this seismic crew, way out here. There's money in oil, right?"

"Yeah." He was paying attention now, pushing his drink away.

"Larry, you can do the same thing! You've got a good job here. Save up your pay and invest it or something like that. Build up a fortune, that's what I'm gonna do, and THAT way, if the worst happens and my lawyer doesn't win me custody or visitation, I can still leave my daughter a substantial sum of money when I die, or when she grows up and they can't dictate whether I can contact her, or, or whichever comes first. Life is all about fighting, right?"

"That's right." A light came into those sad brown eyes. He looked like he just might smile...maybe.

"Well, Larry, there's more than one way to fight. You fight by living, and working, and showing your kid how much you care, in any way possible. And you wait, and watch, and when your time comes, you're ready. You can do this. I don't know the details of how, even for myself, right now. But I'm goin' one step at a time, and I know how this is gonna end up. I will prove my love for my child." I drew in a sharp breath, abruptly halted my speech. I'd said too much, dug too deep, shown my hand. I had to be wary, or the pain within my soul would leap up and devour me, crush me, and bury me so deep I might never climb back out.

I pushed back from the table, tried to make it casual, to close the door on it. "That's all I'm saying."

Larry grabbed my wrist, squeezed it gently. "Thank you."

Faye and Joey came back to the table, carrying a round of drinks. "Hey, you two! You've got a lot to talk about, huh?" She grinned and elbowed Joey.

Larry put his arm around my shoulder, drew me to him, and hugged me lightly. "Yep, we've got a lot in common, right, Marti?"

I looked in his eyes, and thought I saw hope. "You bet!"

I said goodnight to my new friends, and Larry walked me to my car. As I drove off toward my little room at Maria and Joaquin's, I glanced in the rearview mirror. Larry stood in the road, waving. I stuck my arm out the window and waved back. *He IS really good looking...and sweet.*

The next morning, Sunday, we worked the same route on the shot line. Gilsup put me on the brush crew, along with James, Boots, and Earl. And there was a new guy, Darren, from New Jersey. He carried a backpack, and wore his down parka unzipped, as if to show off his Bruce Springsteen T-shirt. The job involved moving along the tangent Jake and Roger had flagged, and clearing whatever the brush buggy had knocked down. We pulled brush and heaved trees. The weather was really cold for Texas—Boots said it was twenty degrees, but I thought he might be exaggerating. We clomped around and tried to keep our hands in our pockets, or at least rub them together to keep them warm.

Boots and Earl started talking about the risks of seismic work and the dangers lurking in the wilds of Texas. "Y'all do right now, Darren, Marti. There's a lot o' things can go wrong out here," Earl growled. "Y' gotta watchyer step! Them dahhynamite charges, if they're shallow, they can go off an' blow you inta itty bitty little pieces, all over creation. An' if that don't getcha, the wild pigs WILL."

I figured they were trying to freak Darren out, since he was new and a "Yankee." My friend Billy, a native Houstonian, had laughingly told me Texans count anything north of Dallas to be Yankee country, but there'd been a ring of truth to it. Of course, I was a Yankee, too, having come from Chicago, but prior to that I'd been in Florida, so I'd told my coworkers I was from there. I also figured they were trying to freak me out, since I was the girl, and I'd recently demonstrated my ignorance about deer blinds.

"Right, wild PIGS!" I laughed so hard I almost choked. "Look out for P-P-P-Porky and his f-f-f-friends, they'll rip you a new one!"

Earl stopped working and glared at me. "Hey now, this is serious. Wild pigs are a threat. Tell 'em, Boots."

Boots launched into a tirade about wild pigs, his eyes big as billiard balls, his face flushed, hands gesticulating. "Wild pigs'll come up on ya in the woods, outta NOWHERE!! There's javelina, they're native to Texas, and then there's wild pigs, pigs that ran off from the farm, and've bred wild for generations. Both kinds got tusks, sharp ones, and they'll come barrelin' through the pines like a damn torpedo. They move so fast, you gotta run like hell if you hear 'em comin' through the brush, and if you run LAHK HEY-LL, maybe you might make it up a tree before they KILL YA! That's how serious it is!"

"Wow. Oh, hey, I'm sorry. I didn't realize. It's just, it sounded kinda silly to me." I started worrying a little bit. I could run, but I doubted whether I could get up a tree! I shot a glance around the clearing at the tall pines. No low branches to grab onto. *I'll be DEAD if a wild pig shows up.*

Darren chimed in. "Well, I grew up in Newark, and I survived that. I'm not gonna be trippin' about any pig, no matter how wild it is."

Boots shook his head. "Alright, but I warned ya. Keep an eye out for wild pigs. An' wild cows, there's wild cows, too. They run off from the farms'n ranches and live wild, in the woods. You come up on one o' them, an'—well, it's serious."

"Okay, I get it. Hey Darren, you get that Springsteen shirt at a concert?"

"Sure did. The show was killer."

The conversation dialed down to small talk. Everybody started discussing where they lived, or were staying, during the project here in Conroe. Earl and Boots revealed they were locals, married guys with houses and wives to go home to every night. Neither of them was certain whether he'd continue on with Seismodyne when the crew left for the next job.

Darren said he'd just arrived and was staying at a motel, but that he'd be moving into "The Bachelor Pad" as soon as he got his paycheck.

"What's The Bachelor Pad?"

Darren explained it was an apartment rented by about a dozen guys on the crew, a couple of blocks from the office. The place had no heat, but there was electricity and cold running water. "But it's real cheap. Guys're campin' out in there, sleepin' bags, hammocks strung all across this one room. You get to keep a lot more of your paycheck. How about you, Marti? Where you stayin'?"

"I've got a real good setup. I rent a room from a Mexican couple, Maria and Joaquin, and the rent is cheap. They're really nice."

Darren stared at me, his mouth agape. "You're in Mexican town, over there? I heard there's all kinds of shootings and robberies and stuff on that side of the tracks. You oughta watch out..."

"Right, the pine trees're fulla wild pigs, javelina, wild cows, whatever—and in my neck of the woods, lookout for the Frito Bandito. C'mon, you guys, gimme a break."

Darren pulled off his backpack, unzipped it. "Hey, uh, Marti, I got somethin' here, I can let it go for ten bucks, an' there's thirty rounds of ammo...woman like you needs protection." He slid his hand inside the pack, drew out a gun. "Besides, I feel kinda skittish carryin' it around. Yesterday, I left a couple in the chamber. Damn thing went off and blew a hole in my backpack. Had to mend it with duct tape. See?"

Man. He coulda shot himself in the back...or the leg, or... So far, I'd only seen one other firearm in my life, and that was during my high school years. I'd been out with Derek, on New Year's Eve. I was fifteen then. Our "date" consisted of Derek stopping us by his friend Gary's place. Gary, a twenty-one-year-old guy, was employed as an auto mechanic. Derek, Gary, and Gary's girlfriend Denise dropped acid, but I didn't; I had to be home by 10:00 p.m. or my folks would've grounded me. Denise put on a Steppenwolf album, and right in the middle of "Goddam the Pusher," Gary reached between the couch cushions, pulled out a pistol and waved it around, laughing, shouting, "Don't flip out, man, it ain't even loaded."

A few minutes later, while Derek was driving me home to my folks, he commented that the gun was "A bummer and no way to trip properly."

Darren's pistol looked similar to the one Gary'd yanked from the couch cushions and brandished so gleefully. It was dark rather than chrome-colored, and sported a cylinder, not a clip. "I got it
156

from a guy on a street corner in Houston." Darren refrained from picking it up, only pointed to it. "I'm not a gun guy, so you'd be doin' me AND you a favor. No bullets in it right now, but if you want, I'll show you how to load it up and fire it. Way out here, no one'll mind, right?" He looked to Boots and Earl.

Earl spoke first. "Hmmm. Y' can't beat that deal, Marti. It's a short barrel Smith n' Wesson .38 Special. Light recoil, an' you can't do better'n what the cops carry. Heh, heh. Can't hurt to have a piece on ya. Like me an' Boots were sayin'—it's dangerous everywhere, y'know? An' you bein' the only woman and all..."

I stared at each of my coworkers in turn—gave them what I hoped was an icy, forbidding stare. "I can take care of myself...But I'm interested." I turned to Darren. "Okay, so it's not loaded?" He shook his head. "May I?"

I dropped to a crouch and picked up the revolver. It felt heavy, but not too heavy. I turned it over and noticed a deep groove had been gouged into the side, but for ten dollars it seemed like a deal, and besides, although I'd never admit it to my coworkers, I felt a bit jittery about possible javelina attack. I knew for sure I was no tree climber. "I'll take it." I reached in my boot for my cash, pulled out a ten-dollar bill, stood up, and handed it to Darren. He passed it back to me.

"Hey, keep it till quittin' time. You don't have a backpack, so I'll carry it outta here."

"Okay." We walked out the rest of the line, working hard. As usual, I put all my effort into the job, feeling compelled to excel, to never slack off. I was beating down the door for other women who might come after, proving that females are strong, tough, and capable. And considering Gilsup's apparent misogyny, I couldn't risk even a chance of being viewed as weak by anyone. With a newfound consciousness of wild pigs, javelina, and other fierce four-footers, my eyes constantly swept the perimeter for any threat that might emerge from the surrounding forest. *Just in case...*

CHAPTER 7

HUNTSVILLE, A COLD CREEK CROSSING, DEERFLIES, AND DREAMS

I BIT DOWN INTO THE LEATHER OF MY WALLET TO STOP MY teeth from chattering, tightened my fingers around the folded clothing and boots stacked onto my head and continued, submerging my body neck deep in the icy cold, muddy water. *Think a woman can't do this? Think again, dudes.* Hustling along, half-swimming at the deepest point, I crossed in a flash, reached the grassy bank, climbed up it, then hunkered down, shivering, allowing the Texas wind to dry my skin a bit before pulling on my jeans, T-shirt, long-sleeved denim shirt, and jacket. I sat down, yanked my socks and boots on, then jumped up and ran in place to raise my body temperature.

I reckoned I'd better head back up the line, not even look toward the point on the creek bank where I'd split from the rest of the crew. I'd hiked a long way to get out of ogling range. Roger, our crew leader that day, had spent little time weighing the options when we'd reached the swollen, turbulent stream. Few trees lined its banks, and we'd been traversing open pasture land, so a sweeping glance in each direction told him we couldn't hike around it. The creek seemed to stretch to the horizon, both ways. "Alright, y'all, we gotta do this the hard way. We're on a deadline, and Gilsup said we gotta get to Huntsville ASAP. We're gonna cross this, but it looks deep. Anybody here don't know how to swim?"

He'd looked at each of us in turn. No one'd spoken up. Roger'd fixed his gaze on me. "Okay, Marti. This is it. You gotta cross, too." His face flushed red. "Uuhmm, not with us, of course. I'll make sure nobody follows you. Meet us up the line, there." He'd pointed to a fence line in the distance, with thick brush and trees immediately beyond that.

"Not a problem. I'll walk that way, over the rise, till I find a good spot." I'd turned and stalked off downstream, eventually arriving at my crossing point.

Now, having made it out of the stream alive, I looked around to get my bearing, marched straight ahead awhile, then began angling back toward the line. I felt a thrill of satisfaction when I reached the fence at the same time Roger and Scott did. The other guys—Jimmie Joe, Boots, and James, arrived soon after, and all my coworkers seemed to regard me with a smidgeon of awe, a sort of unspoken respect they hadn't shown me previously. *Amazing what a cold creek crossing'll do for your street cred.*

Roger checked the map, pointed to the fence corner several paces to our right, and stepped off the distance to it. "We gotta work this side of the fence, set a few stakes, and flag the line ever' once in awhile. We gotta cut any brush that'll obscure the flaggin' too, so let's get on with it." On the way along the fence line, we cut back the brush with machetes. Progress was slow, and when we stopped to eat our lunches, Roger let Jimmie Joe fire up a fat joint and smoke the whole thing. He'd offered each one of us a hit, but no one had taken him up on it, not even Boots, a stalwart stoner.

The thing was, we'd abstained because the brush along the fence line proved so daunting. We all needed to keep our wits and our energy sharp and at a high level. After lunch we hacked, hewed, and chopped away at mesquite, yaupon, and other scrubby stuff that was wiry, tough and aggressive, slapping at our faces and hands in retaliation for each attempt to cut it back. The woods immediately beyond the fence corner soon thinned out into thorny saplings, and we had to thread through them single file, to cut the brush alongside the designated line of demarcation. Later on, the brush buggies would drive in and knock them down so the driller and juggies could do their thing. We'd come a few hundred yards when Scott noticed the lack of brush on the other side of the fence. "Hey, uh, Roger. Check out the property on that other side! It's fuckin' manicured."

Roger stopped hacking, averted his gaze to the lush green meadow, devoid of bull nettles, mesquite or other botanical foe. "Heh. Manicured. Yeah, it is." He pulled the map from the back pocket of his Ben Davis workpants and stabbed a finger at a couple of squiggles etched in red Marks-A-Lot. "It's nice over there, but it's the wrong side o' the fence. The line's on this side, map shows it specifically. Keep on."

We'd resumed our tedious chore and gained another couple hundred feet, when Roger got a mesquite thorn stuck deep in the palm of his left hand. He dropped his machete, grabbed his wounded left hand in his right fist, seething. "Goddam it!!"

Boots sidled over, whispered in his heavy Texas twang, "Mesquite thorns got poison in 'em, an' ma-aa-aan, do they hurt lahk all hey-ll."

Roger shot Boots a withering stare, then powered on a while longer and we followed, but finally, he stopped stock still, looked over at the proverbial grass-is-always-greener side of that barb wire fence, and called it. "This is crazy. That's it, we're crossin' over the line. We'll walk it out nice an' easy, flag the fence from yonder clear pasture. C'mon, y'all."

We climbed over, and practically tap danced the next thousand yards. My coworkers' mood lifted, some jauntily twirling their machetes over their heads, others cracking jokes and slapping their knees on the punchlines.

"Hey Boots," I waved a hand in a 180-degree arc to denote our unencumbered view on this benevolent side of the barrier. "Check this side, man. Not a wild pig or a javelina for miles! Easy Street, right?"

"Well, yeah. But ya can't never be too sure." He shook his head slowly. "You packin' Sister? I hope so, cuz we—Hey-ll!!! Run lahk hey-ll, y'all, it's a damn Do-bruh-mun!" He jumped up and down and waved his arms. I was preparing to ignore him, when I saw the Doberman Pinscher, black and tan, sleek and muscled, heading our way, its ears pricked up. *Could this be Gilsup's dog? Way out here?*

"Hey Scott, Roger, is that Gilsup's Doberman? Do you think he's come way out here to check on us?"

The dog ran past, seemingly oblivious, and headed up over a slope that lay further ahead.

Boots exhaled slowly. "That was close. Don't like Do-bruh-muns. Sneaky dogs. I'm glad he's gone, but I gotta feelin' he might be waitin' for us up yonder."

Jimmy Joe chimed in. "Right on, Boots. Dobermans're high strung, jumpy. I got bit on the hand by one once, I was takin' a girl, Sherry, to the junior prom, her daddy never did like me, an' I know he prob'ly let that dog out in the front yard on PURPOSE, just in time to slither up on my blind side. I jumped and dropped her corsage on the ground. It shook me up. Her mama was nice, though. Poured some peroxide over the teeth marks'n wrapped it in a bandage. Me an' Sherry made it to the prom, an' later I made it to home base." Jimmy Joe chuckled.

Scott scoffed. "Don't act so proud. She musta felt sorry for ya, Dude. Gave it up outta guilt."

Jimmy Joe feigned outrage, then laughed harder. "Maybe so, maybe so."

Now that the conversation had turned to "making it to home base" and females "giving it up," it struck me I'd benefit from vacating the scene for a while. I didn't want any of my coworkers to begin fixating on me as a prospective home run.

I picked up my pace, striding boldly in the direction the Doberman had gone. *Better to face one lone dog than a pack of men.* A deerfly hummed over my head. I carefully resisted the urge to duck, it would make me look like a sissy. *I swam across a freezing cold creek this morning, with my wallet in my teeth, carrying my boots and clothes. I'm a badass. Yeah. I AM a badass, and nobody can—*Another deerfly buzzed past my right ear, annoying, pestering. I made a conscious effort to ignore it and soldiered on up the rise. Another one buzzed my left side, a little closer this time, and I swatted at it, but yet another whizzed in behind it, so fast I felt a breeze along my left jawline. I swatted again and set my sights on the top of the crest. *Weather's cold, even for January, better keep moving.* Besides, I liked staying ahead of the guys. No way did I want to risk them thinking a chick couldn't handle this work. Another deerfly, this time on my right; I felt the wind from it, again heard that odd whining buzz. *These are the biggest deerflies I ever...Wait a minute—it's January... and deerflies don't...*

Jimmy Joe's voice cut in, sharp and urgent, "Marti! MARTI! Git DOWN!"

I hit the dirt, facedown in the grassy turf. *Wow! Bullets. Now I know what it feels like to be shot at.* I turned my head to the left, a few yards downhill, saw all five of my coworkers prone, heads down, and as I heard more bullets zinging, lifted my head just enough to catch a glance at two redneck farmers in the distance, silhouetted by the late afternoon sun, shouldering their rifles and taking aim.

"Marti, GIT YER HEAD DOWN n' KEEP IT DOWN!" Scott hollered. "These RANCHERS think we're ESCAPED CONVICTS!"

Wow. We ARE pretty close to Huntsville. Scott'd told me all about the Penitentiary that morning. His brother was doing five-to-ten for possession.

Roger, the crew's leader who ran the transit, weighed in, his hoarse bark emphatic, "JIMMY JOE, grab your GODDAM WALKIN' STICK, an' TIE some flaggin' on it AN' WAVE THE SUMBITCH AROUND as high as you can without gettin' y' HAND blown off, so they can see we're with the COMP'NY! We're on the WRONG SIDE o' the fence, remember?"

Jimmy Joe moved lightning-quick, like a cobra, amazing considering how stoned he was. Earlier that afternoon, in the woods, he'd fashioned the walking stick from a tree branch in order to keep from staggering. In milliseconds, the fluorescent orange flagging was waving in the air, like a neon Cheetos-brand flag of truce, and the rustic snipers momentarily ceased fire. Suddenly Jimmy Joe's bloodshot eyes widened in inspiration as he shouted, "MARTI! TAKE OFF YER BALL CAP! C'MON!"

I knew exactly what he meant, and without thinking, tore off my baseball cap, shook out my long blond hair and jumped up, waving the cap frantically at the paused shooters. I tore off my jacket for good measure, hoping that, even though I was dressed in a work shirt, just like the guys, the hayseed killers might recognize my female form and hesitate before gunning me down. Scott and Jimmy Joe, in a somewhat delayed act of chivalry, jumped up with me a moment after I took my stand.

The ranchers lowered their rifles and broke into a run, rapidly closing the distance between us, one of them shrieking at the top of his lungs, "IS THAT A GUUUURRRRLLLL?" When the yokel militia jogged within earshot, Roger stepped up and introduced himself as our crew chief.

The leathery gun-toters snorted derisively. Both wore Bull Durham ball caps, Wrangler jeans, western shirts and denim jackets.

The one with the beer belly spat tobacco juice on the ground and barked, "Don' y'all know yer s'pose to stay on the other side o' the fence? Y'all damn near gotcherselves killed, y'know that? We get a bounty fer every escaped convict, dead or alive, it don' matter! Heh. Heh..."

"Yep. That's raht. Good thing we seen you had a gal along. We shoot first an' ask questions later," growled the other rancher, the leaner and more menacing of the two. He turned, jabbed a gnarled finger in my direction and rasped, "Hey there MISSY, what're YOU doin' way out here?"

I met his jaundiced gaze with what I hoped was a steady, stone-cold stare, but inwardly I wavered. *Yeah...Come to think of it, what AM I doin' out here?* But I gained my composure, pulled myself up to my full height, and answered. "I work for Seismodyne, sir, and the company is running a shot line through these parts, for seismic exploration. We are the preliminary crew to traverse this area, and soon we will be followed by heavy equipment." I waved a hand toward Roger. "He's the boss here, he's running the crew."

Roger cleared his throat. "She's correct, we represent Seismodyne, and our company has obtained permits to make our way through this area. Er, the mistake we made was to cross over to the wrong side of the fence. See, the brush is real heavy on our side, and we're on a deadline, so I, uh, I made the mistake of thinking we could walk on this open side for awhile. We never meant to trespass. We'll get back over yonder where we came from, and that'll be it." He stared at the ranchers and they stared back. Then they nodded their assent, and Roger gave the sign to retreat. We all stepped slowly away, mindful of the shotguns, anxious to avoid being target practice for redneck, beer-bellied, Bull Durham-chawing bounty hunters.

The next morning, I brought my .38 Special, wrapped in a T-shirt and shoved under the seat of the ol' Fury III. I intended to stop at the Piggly Wiggly after work, to see if they sold back packs. With stray Dobermans, wild boar, javelina, wild cows, and psycho vigilante redneck riflemen—with plenty of firepower—on the loose, a person can't be too careful, right? And ruling out the possibility of earning a black belt overnight, why not resort to one of the Lone Star State's most abundant natural resources, firearms, for protection?

Gilsup lined us up for our marching orders. "All right, men." He glanced in my direction, grimaced, and continued. "We're headin' for Huntsville. Gonna run a shot line right through the joint, and I've assured the warden there'll be no trouble. I'll be there to supervise, so heads up." He scowled and stomped off.

Scott, James, Jimmy Joe, and I traveled to the jobsite in one of the company pickup trucks, with Scott at the wheel. "M' brother's in there, y'all know that. It's only fair to tell y'all, after we get done today...I'm gonna circle around to the fence at a certain spot, and chuck some hash n' white crosses over the fence. Got the whole package sealed and hid in this tennis ball!" He slammed the heel of his right hand on the steering wheel, threw back his head and guffawed. "Any of y'all wanna come along?" He shifted his eyes from the road to scan our faces.

James folded his arms over his chest, looked straight ahead, resolute. "Nah, I'll stay in the truck, Scott."

Jimmy Joe sat up ramrod straight, eyes bulging. "Damn, Scott! You tryin' to kill us all? Them high riders got shotguns, and how about them guard towers?"

Scott smiled. "It's all arranged. I know exactly where to throw it, and I'll park the truck far enough from the scene of the crime for y'all to claim ignorance."

I spoke up. "I'll go with ya, Scott. I mean, I'll let you throw it..."

Scott looked startled, then grinned. "Man, thanks Marti! How fast can you run?"

"Pretty fast, and I'll probably break my record if we get shot at again like yesterday." I laughed.

At the penitentiary, they opened the gates for trucks and equipment to drive in, then closed them behind us. The prison, nicknamed "The Walls," was the oldest prison in Texas. It seemed to stretch on forever, all thick brick walls and forbidding guard towers. The inmates had been cleared from the huge area where the line was going to go through. I could see a big crowd of them in the distance, standing at the high, razor-wire-topped chain link fence at one side of the perimeter. I thought about the execution chamber at the heart of the complex, and felt a chill down my spine.

"Hey! Marti. Git over here, on the double!" Gilsup's face looked red and contorted, he was obviously trying to provoke me. *Good!* I suppressed the urge to smile, jogged over to where he stood talking with some grizzled old boys, one of whom wore a sort of cowboy-ish hat, most likely some kind of high official from the lockup. Gilsup seemed to enjoy being here at the oldest prison in Texas.

"Yes, sir, Mr. Gilsup." I felt crazy laughter skittering around inside me, somewhere near my solar plexus, inching its way up, and willed it down deep. Gilsup threw me a rancorous stare and placed his hands on his hips.

"Can you drive a truck?"

"Sure."

He snorted, pointed to a massive truck parked nearby, then jerked a thumb toward the farthest corner of the clearing. "Go fire that one up, and drive it over there. Then come on back. Keys're in it. Move."

I nodded, turned, and started running toward that big ol' truck. I'd known we'd be going to the prison, so I'd worn an extra baggy shirt that day, and had my hair shoved up into my ball cap. Camouflaging my gender, for safety. And I'd figured my asshat boss would call me out, give me a hard time. *Suck it, Mr. Gilsup...I got to the* vehicle in seconds, reached way high to grab the door handle, pulled it open, and leapt into the driver's seat. One look at the floor shift and my heart sank. Rows and rows of gleaming metal levers. *Fuck it. Too late to turn back now.* I fumbled for the key, turned it in the ignition, and applied a little pressure to the gas pedal. The truck roared to life, and to my amazement, began rolling over the grassy, uneven turf. After a minute, I sensed the engine needed me to shift gears, and decided to pick one at random. Suddenly I heard two sharp banging sounds on the passenger door.

I leaned to the right and shoved the door open a crack, then snapped my gaze back to the windshield. *Hitting some dude is not an option.* "Marti!" Scott climbed into the moving truck, flattened onto the seat, and pointed to one of the metal levers. "Pull that one, right there. That's it, now, that one..." I followed his instructions, and he got me across the field. I parked it sidelong and killed the engine. "Marti, jump out and run on back. I'll hide here on the floorboards for a minute, then make my way over. He'll never know I helped you out. It'll blow his mind, you driving a truck like that. Funny as hell!"

"Yeah, it is. Thanks, Scott. I'm coming with you to the fence, to toss that hash inside."

I hopped down from the driver's side and hit the ground running, but not too fast. I didn't want to look scared or too eager. As I bounded up to where Gilsup stood, he barked, "Where're the keys?"

"I left 'em where I found 'em, Boss. You need me to get the keys for you?" Gilsup's face fell.

"Naw, that's good." He looked crestfallen. All I could make of it was that he'd hoped I'd brought them. Clearly I'd done what was the right thing, and he'd missed an opportunity to deplore the fact that the home office'd sent him a "half a person" instead of a male. All of a sudden he brightened up. "You left a lot o' tire ruts in that field, it's a big mess." I looked, but couldn't see any ruts. "Yep, Marti. You tore it all up. It'll prob'ly cost the comp'ny a whole lot in damages." He sauntered away, shaking his head.

The workday zipped by. Gilsup surely wanted to avoid even the slightest whisper of a problem, so he pushed every single employee to the limit. I kept my eyes on my work, made every effort to blend into the background as we crossed that big clearing, juggies unwinding cables. Kevin hooked up the wiring, and we dropped the sticks of dynamite down the holes. I noticed that our electrician had been shrewd enough to leave his Quaalude-laden aspirin tin at home. Today, he appeared wide-eyed, stone cold sober, even a tad on edge.

Back when I'd first worked with him, on that day we'd sung "Boogie Oogie Oogie" together at work, Kevin'd shared some of his past with me, so I understood his penchant for Ludes and other substances. Kevin Goforth Thibodeaux had been born the eldest son of a filthy-rich Louisiana sugar plantation magnate, a staunch ultra-conservative. Enter the Sixties. Kevin tuned in, turned on, and dropped out, along with zillions of other guys his age. On his first truly epic LSD trip, Kevin attained a stratospheric level of psychedelitude, got so inspired he dropped three more hits, and kinda lost it. Flipped out, but in a fun kind of way.

"I remember having a surreal vacation in Maui. I flew in on my daddy's American Express Gold Card, an' checked into a luxury beach resort. Drunk up the whole mini bar an'ordered up three fifths of Southern Comfort, then locked housekeeping out for a string o' days. I maxed out the card, and when the concierge called, they got hip to the fact I was Kevin JUNIOR, and it's ol' Kev SENIOR that's got the dough. The details're a little sketchy, prob'ly because of the shock treatments, but all hell broke loose, and m' dad had me committed."

"Oh, man. What a bummer. I'm sorry, Kevin." I'd been filled with shock and sympathy for my coworker.

Kevin'd nodded. "Damn straight, it was a bummer, Marti. Freaky old-style insane asylum, and they did hydrotherapy, shock, padded cells, isolation cells, all the stuff that's banned now, bona fide Cuckoo's Nest/Nurse Ratched kinda stuff, worse even! My hair turned white, but I never gave in and apologized to the old man. They let me out, and here I am." He'd chuckled. "Still enjoy a good acid buzz, y'know? My fave is Orange Sunshine but it's hard to get these days; Ludes'll do. They doubled down, gave it hell, but the bastards couldn't break this old dog. Hah."

Today, Kevin would walk the straight and narrow, along with every other hand on the crew. Laboring under the shadow of a guard tower puts a damper on things. We could sense the inmates staring at us, the guard tower's gun barrels trained on us. Hardly a festive atmosphere. I turned to Kevin, smiled incrementally. "You doing okay?"

"Yep."

The layout continued, with only one blip on the radar. At one point, I heard a shout from the mass of inmates on the fence. "Is that a GIRL?" I ignored it, and the commotion that followed. Then everything died down.

Back at the entrance gate, the Observer sat in the recorder truck, ready to shoot the line once all was in order. The shot, which would feel like a little earthquake, was set up to happen later on, after almost all personnel had exited the hot zone. Only Rob and Johnny, two shooters from Florida—both of them former professional wrestlers and current bodybuilders—would remain to coordinate with the Observer. They were muscly and stout, easy going, and could handle all the heavy lifting in the world.

Now that we'd accomplished the layout, all but those few and Mr. Gilsup moved on to the trucks, with orders to wait for Gilsup's call to pick up and finally clear the prison once the Observer got the recording. We'd be logging tons of overtime on this shift, and everybody was stoked about the big paychecks we'd get.

The day ended well after dark, a convenience for Scott and me as we trotted up a rise to that place along the Huntsville perimeter. James and Jimmy Joe waited in the truck along the highway, and James'd promised to whistle if they saw any sign of trouble. I felt a little bit psycho for accompanying Scott on his mission, but he'd come to my aid with that truck, so I backed him up. I saw Scott's arm wind up, pitch and snap back, then watched the ball hurtling high over the razor wire and dropping on the other side. We turned and ran like hell for the truck, never once looked back.

Scott jumped in, put it in neutral, and rolled forward, lights off, for a bit before turning the key in the ignition and revving the gas ever so slightly to get clear of The Walls. We drove in silence back to Conroe and the field office. Another day, another dollar, another step toward my dream, and my baby Anne Marie.

———————

THE EAGLE FLIES ON FRIDAY—THAT'S WHAT THE OLD BLUES SONG calls it—and that particular Friday, my wages landed. There's nothing like an ample paycheck to fix things that need fixing. I received my two weeks' pay, with plenty of overtime, and the long-awaited per diem. Heavy rain pounded Conroe for the last few days of the pay period, but we'd been able to work in spite of the weather, because the deluges came intermittently with spurts of sunlight in between. Nightly rainfall throughout that second week had finally created a flood situation, and the buggies and big trucks started getting stuck.

Friday afternoon, Gilsup called us in, lined us up, gave us our pay, and declared a rain out. Everybody's mood soared; I could feel the vibe in the room, but no one said a word. The crew members filed out into the parking lot, and I followed. Scott filled me in. "Rain-outs are good, Marti. What it is, we get fifty hours guaranteed pay, rain or shine. Now it's a rain-out, so we get the weekend off, and

Monday we report in the morning, but we don't work. He'll tell us to come back on Friday. If the ground's still too wet, we get another week of guaranteed pay. And we get our per diem."

"Wow. That's good news." Thoughts of what I could do with all the spare time pinged around my brain. "Have a great weekend, Scott." I took off straight for the Fury III, eager to cash my paycheck. But first I stopped at Faye's place. I liked her, and her husband, too. Even though it was a temporary residence, Faye'd decorated their apartment, creating a real home. She and Joey were obviously in love; it cheered me up to be around them. And with Faye, I could talk about clothes and lightweight topics—I could let my hair down, so to speak.

"Marti, c'mon in." Faye waved me inside. "Didja get paid?" I reached in my wallet, produced the check with a flourish, and waved it around over my head. We both laughed.

"Gonna cash it ASAP. Hey, I just learned what a rain-out is! Gonna get some time to look for a better place to live around here, and I get to go back to Houston for a visit. What're you and Joey gonna do?"

"Joey's cashing his check right now, and when he gets back, I'm gonna help him pack a suitcase, so he can go to Louisiana with the guys. Just for the weekend." She smiled, showing her dimples. "Larry, Kevin, Joey, and Darnell are going. Kevin's got a cabin in Opelousas, Louisiana, it's a couple of hours from New Orleans, and they're gonna stop there tonight. Darnell's got a big Oldsmobile, and they're gonna drive straight through—about four hours. They plan to go into New Orleans to party on Saturday. Joey says they'll be back Sunday night. I told him he better be careful and stay away from those topless dancer places." She laughed. "But I do want him to have fun. He needs a break from the job."

I nodded, aware that Joey's position as powder man required a special license to deliver explosives, and to be responsible for the whole cache of dynamite, including the blasting caps. Faye told me that when the crew mobilized from location to location, Joey's job was to drive the powder truck—a dangerous mission if the route went through a city like Houston. Even a fender bender in heavy traffic could pose a serious risk. She added that they stored the caps in a special compartment, separate from the explosives, so an impact or spark couldn't cause the caps to trigger a disaster.

"Wow!"

"He won't be driving when they party, I know that for sure. His driving record's really important for his job."

Joey came in, smiling, and Faye gave him a hug. I headed for the door. "Have fun on your trip, Joey. Hey Faye, wanna get coffee Sunday morning, or lunch?"

"Sure. Call me, or better than that, skip the call. I know you don't have a phone. Just come on by around nine, or earlier if you want. I'm going to the Laundromat by ten, gotta get all our clothes washed."

I left Faye's place, stopped at a local grocery that accepted oil patch workers' checks, then called Billy in Houston, and asked him if I could keep the ol' Fury III till I saved up enough for a junker of my own. Bill, one of the best friends I ever had, extended the loan. I filled the gas tank, washed my laundry, stopped at the grocery and bought food. I ducked into a discount store, where I bought a few towels, a cheap clock radio, and an insulated vest to wear at work—the weather'd been so cold—then stowed everything at Maria and Joaquin's.

As a payday celebration, I took myself out to dinner. On the main drag, I'd noticed a newly-opened seafood restaurant with a sign promising "Fresh Gulf Shrimp and Oysters." The food was insanely delicious: chilled shrimp as big as your thumb, enormous fresh oysters. The owner, a buff young guy, sported a frizzy chestnut mane neatly tucked into a hairnet. When I asked for hot sauce, he cheerfully slid a bottle of Tabasco down the bar. "My name's Adam," he grinned.

"Marti." I drank some beers, we joked around, and I told him about my job on the seismic crew. He told me about his plans for his restaurant, how he was living in a tiny Airstream trailer, but expected great things to happen once the place got going.

"Hey Marti, wanna drive over to Galveston with me tomorrow? There's an old piece of a fishing boat out there, and I'm gonna salvage it. It's solid oak or somethin' like that, the prow and a big hunk of the bow. I'm gonna put it in front of the restaurant, like it's beached, y'know? And then I'll toss the dried oyster shells all around it. Cool idea, huh?"

"Hmmm. Sounds interesting. I've been in Texas a few months now, and haven't seen the coast yet. I'll go for a couple of hours, but I need to get back by five...I've got a date." I added the part about a date for insurance, testing his reaction. Didn't want him to think our trip to Galveston would be romantic or anything. *I don't know this guy...should I bring my gun?*

He shrugged. "That's cool. Stop by here tomorrow morning around 10:30. We'll have to take my truck, to haul the boat hull. It's a '66 Chevy, runs great. I'm restoring it gradually.

"Okay."

The trip to Galveston with Adam proved very interesting. He acted as tour guide, pointing out historic old Victorian mansions, homes of 19th century sea captains, and the wharf district, where we saw ships from all over the world. We drove his vintage truck onto a ferry and made the crossing from Galveston Island to the Bolivar Peninsula, a thirty-mile sandy strip of land separating the Gulf of Mexico from Galveston Bay. Dolphins bobbed alongside the ferry, and gulls wheeled overhead.

Adam, a Houston native, grew up in foster homes and, as he put it, "Came of age in the Houston City Jail." He told me he'd pulled himself up, saved money while working as a heavy equipment operator, and now'd invested his life savings in that seafood bar. I kept my guard up, but revealed that I was rebuilding my life, too. The ferry docked, and Adam navigated along the shoreline till he found the boat remnant. He pulled the truck alongside it, and somehow managed to lift it enough to rest part of it on the tailgate. It was huge, must've weighed a ton. He pushed the wreck, and I stood in the truck bed and guided it in. I couldn't believe how strong he was.

When we got the truck back on the ferry headed for home, I threw back my head and laughed. "That was crazy! You owe me."

Adam smiled. "Guess I do. Come by anytime, free seafood." We arrived in Conroe during the late afternoon. Pretending I had a date, I said good-bye, jumped in the Fury III and split. I drove around on some of the back roads for a bit, feasting my eyes on the pine forest, and feeling hopeful about the future. I got a burger at a Mom n' Pop joint, and bought a six pack of Miller High Life at a country store. Then I returned to my roach-infested rented room at Maria and Joaquin's. I fell asleep early, around 9:00 p.m., with the lights and my clothes on...as usual. Cucarachas be damned.

I woke up suddenly, my heart thudding in my chest, eyes wide open, consumed with an ominous sense of mortality—my own, anybody else's, and everybody else's. *What the f*—I sat upright, grabbed my new clock radio. *2:47 a.m.!* What I felt wasn't dread—more like awe—but with it, an inkling of alarm, high alert, as if something very important needed to be said...I felt a sensation, an urgent need to bid farewell.

During the first few moments after I awoke, I thought it was me who was going to die, and I panicked, thinking of my daughter. *Annie!* I closed my eyes, envisioned my child's sweet face, focused all my love and hope and mother-strength, reaching out to her across time and space. *I love you with all my heart, and I am so sorry for what happened to us...*

In that moment, I felt a wave of peace and safety and knowing. She would be safe, she would make her way. I felt a deep sadness followed by a sense of peace. *I'm not dying, I will live to fight for my daughter, I will see her again.* But if I weren't dying, then who was? Someone close. I squeezed my eyes shut, willed myself to breathe slowly, began striking out across the ether, visualizing the faces of loved ones, waiting for a sign. My father? Mother...grandparents? No. Finally, I resolved to accept the presence, and the feeling, and honor the one who'd awakened me so urgently. *I hear you, I respect you.* After about ten minutes, the pressing sensation faded away. After another twenty-five minutes, sleep returned.

Sunday morning, I awoke wondering what had happened the night before, then recalled how Faye'd said to come over early. It was only 8:00 a.m., but I felt fidgety, and hell, I slept with clothes on for fear of the roaches, so all I had to do was wash my face and brush my hair. I figured Faye'd go for coffee with me.

At Faye's place, I knocked on the door, but no one answered. I double-checked on the Nova, and it was parked right in front, so she had to be home. "Faye! Hey, you home? It's Marti." I peeked in the kitchen window and saw her. She was sitting at the tiny kitchen table, her head resting on her arms. I could see her shoulders shaking. *Dammit! What's going on?* I pounded on the door with a fist, and it opened.

"Marti, they had a wreck!" Faye pushed a strand of hair out of her eyes, sobbing. "I got the call just a couple of hours ago. All of the guys were in that big Olds, they musta been goin' real fast—Marti, they hit a big light pole on some...bridge in New Orleans. Joey broke his leg, he's in critical condition, and the other guys're in the hospital, too. And—LARRY'S DEAD!" Paroxysms of grief enveloped her.

I held Faye's hand while she wept. Faye lifted her head, pulled herself together. "Poor Larry! And poor Joey. I know his heart must be broken. Larry was his best friend. I've got to drive to that hospital an' be there with him."

I nodded. "Yes, you've gotta go there. Faye, I'm so sorry. Do you know when it happened?"

"Yeah. It was around 2:30 a.m., but I didn't get the call till hours later. The police had to use the Jaws of Life to get them out of the car. Larry died on the scene."

Faye told me she had to get ready to drive to Louisiana. I offered to help her pack, but she told me she'd rather be alone. I went out to my car, sat behind the wheel. It was 2:47 when I woke to that sense of high alert, and that gentle, awe-inspiring presence. *It's so strange, and so sad...what was the connection?*

Monday morning, the whole crew reported to the office. I got there early and so did a lot of my co-workers. Guys milled around the parking lot in front of the office, waiting for Mr. Gilsup to show up, call us in. Everybody was talking about the accident. The word'd spread quickly. I figured Faye'd called Mr. Gilsup; she probably had a way to get hold of him, since her husband held a key position on the crew. Or maybe she went over to the Bachelor Pad and told whoever was closest friends with the other guys. Maybe somebody called the hospital and talked to Kevin, or Darnell, or Joey. I never asked anybody how they'd found out, and didn't tell anyone that I'd known about it, never even made a comment. Instead, I listened to my coworkers' discussions.

Scott said they'd probably gotten really wasted at the hunting cabin in Opelousas. "I've been to that cabin with Kev before, it's more of a shack. Rundown, no electricity or water. That's why Kevin can go there, his dad doesn't care. Anyway, the time we went we did a whole lot of acid, man. It was weird after nightfall, trippin' in the dark. All we had to eat was stale tater chips n' warm beer." He chuckled softly. "Later in the trip, after we peaked n' felt like drivin' we took off for New Orleans n' got motel rooms, y'know, showered an' all, and then partied like hell on Bourbon Street. I guess Kevin an' Joey an' them were either comin' or goin' from Bourbon Street when they hit that light pole." He shrugged. "It's a god-awful thing what happened to Larry." He shoved his hands into the pockets of his jacket, gazed at his boots. Raindrops began falling. Scott glanced up. "Betcha we get another week's worth o' rain-out." He hitched up his jacket collar.

Rob and Johnny, the burly ex-wrestler, bodybuilder shooters, weighed in. Rob spoke first. "Gilsup'll call some rain-out days, you can bet on that."

Johnny nodded. "Hell yeah. They can't run a full crew without our powder man and our electrician." They seemed like nice guys, always relaxed and joking around. Johnny wore his black hair in a ponytail. Rob had more of a military haircut and had a tattoo that looked as if it might've been military. They hailed from Florida, and I figured they must be pretty badass, since they did all the important blasting.

The rain fell harder. "Hey," Rob smiled, "Marti, c'mon over to my truck, sit inside while we wait. No use gettin' soaked out here." He turned to Scott. "You too. C'mon, man." Johnny and Rob ran for a metallic blue, Dodge double cab. Rob sat behind the wheel, Johnny shotgun. I slid into the backseat, grateful for cover from what now appeared to be a burgeoning downpour. Scott climbed in the other side, pulled a pack of Marlboros out of his shirt pocket, selected one.

Rob smiled, shook his head emphatically. "No smokin' in here, man. Unless it's weed. My truck, my rules."

Scott stowed the cigarettes, sat back. "Oh. Yeah. Y'all're body builders n' athletes and all."

Both Johnny and Rob howled with laughter. Then the vibe grew more serious, and the conversation returned to our coworkers, their misfortune, and the outcome.

Rob rested his muscled left arm on the steering wheel. "I feel real sorry for Joey. He broke his leg, and his best friend is dead. Seemed like Joe and Faye were just about all the family Larry had."

*SEEMED that way, but...he had a family...*I kept silent, didn't tell them what I'd learned on my blind date with Larry, that he was a father. A father who yearned for his son. My heart felt like it would explode...the terrible pain of separation from my child. Panic rose up in me as I struggled to staunch the uncontrollable tears, to push them down, bury them. For now. *Do. Not. Cry. Do not cry. Do not cry.*

Johnny leaned back in his seat. "Yeah, that's what everybody thinks. Gilsup's gotta be pissed. Just last week, Larry took out a big life insurance policy, somethin' like three hundred grand, the max—he worked here a long time and was eligible. We were in the office, doin' our timesheets when it happened. Gilsup was helpin' him with the forms, an' the ol' snake was actually tryin' to talk Larry into makin' HIM the beneficiary! Gilsup tried to play it like he was goofin' around, but he meant it. Didn't work, though. Larry's got a little boy up in Dallas, an' he left it all to him."

"Yeah!" Rob grinned. "That's the one bright spot. The paperwork just finalized on Friday at five, so they'll have to pay out. Gilsup's GOTTA be PISSED!"

I smiled, and my thoughts drifted back to Sunday morning, 2:47 a.m., when I woke up with that sense of urgency, that gentle nudge from some other realm beyond what we see and hear and touch with our physical senses. It'd been Larry, waking me to say good-bye. When that big Oldsmobile crashed and splintered and wrapped around that pole, and he felt his life receding, in that moment Larry'd known his son would receive his parting gift. And he'd thought of me, and taken a moment to reach out and thank me on his way out.

I looked out the window of Rob's truck at the rain, the wood-sided storefront that served as field office, and wondered at the mysteries of life and death and whatever lies between and beyond. Suddenly, the office door banged open and there stood Gilsup, wearing a yellow rain slicker and rubber boots, fists clenched at his sides, scowling. "Oops. Gilsup, y'all. Time to go in." Scott shifted, opened his door, and paused just before bailing out. "Johnny, Rob, you called it! Gilsup's totally pissed." We exited the vehicle and stepped out into the rain.

Sixty-odd employees crowded into the office, many of us rain-sodden, dozens jostling for positions closest to the exit. With an obvious rain-out, most of us had already made some sort of plans for the week, and itched to get out of town. A murmur of anticipation buzzed around the room. Gilsup stood at his desk and snarled, "Hyaarright, men! Line up for inspection." Workers began to shift position and regroup, forming rows as well as possible, considering the limited space. The boss seemed to be somewhat appeased by our efforts. "At ease." *At ease? Is he high?* Explosive giggles threatened to burst from between my clenched teeth. Gilsup's tantrums triggered hysterical merriment in me, a good thing, since the alternative would be rage, and I felt certain that was the reaction he relished.

"Men—and Marti." He paused for emphasis, staring angrily in my direction. "The ground is still wet n' muddy, can't risk getting equipment stuck. And, as some of you may know, as of this weekend I am short a powder man, a buggy driver, an electrician, and a juggie. I'm declaring a rain-out for this week. Report in on Friday morning. Diiis-missed." Everybody started filing out, faces blank. I figured I wasn't the only one trying hard not to laugh at the quasi-military lingo. I felt a light tap on my shoulder and turned to see Jake, one of the head surveyors, smiling at me. Wearing that cowboy hat again.

"Hey, um, may I speak with you for a moment?" His voice was so soft and low. I'd noticed it before, and it intrigued me, since I'd always been loud and boisterous, and grew up in a family of loud talkers and even louder laughers.

"Sure. I'm going out to my car. You can walk with me for a minute."

Outside the office, on the steps, Jake spoke again. "I was wondering if you'd like to get coffee with me. There's a little diner here in town, it's real quiet. Will you meet me there?"

For reasons I couldn't have explained at the time, I accepted his invitation. He gave me the name—The Horseshoe Diner, and simple directions involving driving three blocks west of the office, then five blocks south. I watched him stride toward a little Mazda pickup truck and drive off. Not wanting to arrive first, I took my time driving that handful of blocks, and parking. I stepped inside the door, scanned the room, and saw him sitting in the farthest table from the door, his back to the wall. He'd set the cowboy hat on the chair next to him.

When I walked toward the table, he stood up and pulled out a chair for me, the one directly across from him. "Thank you." I smiled at Jake. A young woman in a waitress uniform approached the table. I smiled at her, too. "Coffee, please."

"Make that two, please." Jake smiled.

"So, you wanted to speak with me? Let's start with introductions. I'm Marti. And you are?"

He exhaled slowly. "Jake. It's Jake." He laughed softly. "I wanted to talk to you, away from work. Wanted to get to know you. I'm from Texas, a little ol' country town, but I've traveled all around. Been in the Navy. I came on this job as a clerk for Mr. Gilsup. Then I moved into surveying, but I still do some of the office work, too. Accounting, stuff like that." He chuckled. "Man, Gilsup was riled up when he saw what they're payin' you. And he's never had a worker he didn't personally hire. When they sent you from the home office...well, it was a sight to see. His reaction, I mean, when he got the news. Not that you were a sight to see..." He looked uncomfortable for only a millisecond, then regained his calm, self-assured air. He shrugged.

"So, you want to know what I'm doin' out here? Some rancher asked me that question last week, after shooting at me and the other guys." I laughed. "I'm working out here for the money. It pays a whole lot better than waiting tables, which is what I was doing before. And I can keep up, no doubt about that. Ask anybody."

He rested his forearms on the table, sleeves rolled up. His hands were thick and callused, and he wore a gold band on his left hand, a thick gold band with a small diamond in it. When I noticed the ring, I felt a twinge of disappointment. *Married. The best ones are taken, it makes sense. Anyway, who cares? I'm NOT in the market for...*

"I don't need to ask anybody about you. I can see you're sharp and tough and you can handle Gilsup and any other guy like that. Would you have dinner with me some night this week? I know a good steakhouse, real Texas beef. It's a nice place, almost nice enough for somebody like you." His ice blue eyes sparkled. He smiled.

"What about that ring on your finger? How about you take your wife out for some steak?"

He looked at his hands, as if seeing them for the first time. "Aaaww, I'm not married. I bought this in Singapore, when I was in the Navy. I just wanted to have a diamond ring. I broke the second and third fingers on my right hand once, in a fight, an' a ring doesn't feel good on that hand. So I wear it like this. That's the truth."

I leaned back in my chair. "Wow. That's a good story, and I almost believe it. But I just came out of a marriage, and I don't need to take chances. I'll pass on the dinner, Jake." I put a few dollars on the table, started putting on my jacket.

"Marti, I'm not married. Look, we've got the week off, how about you come have a steak dinner with me in the town where I grew up? I'll take you to meet my sister, and my parents. Ever'body there'll tell you I am not married, never been."

"Where's your hometown?"

"Not far. Grew up in Gonzales, it's a two-and-a-half-hour drive from Conroe. We can go tomorrow morning, be there by noon. My little sister lives on a cattle ranch, we'll visit her. She'll vouch for me. If you don't believe her, my folks'll tell you I'm not married. And if that doesn't convince you, my grandma will set you straight."

"Hmmm. Okay, but this is not a date. It's a road trip."

———

Jake wasn't married. I enjoyed the trip to Gonzales and meeting his relatives. We got a beer at a local bar, and he introduced me to some of his friends—Viet Nam vets, hard drinkers—and their girlfriends. One of his friends had worked for Halliburton, another for Schlumberger. From listening to some of their stories and jokes, and talking with him later on the drive back to Conroe, I learned a bit about Jake's life. He'd grown up fighting, drinking, working hard, riding bulls...and often these activities overlapped. In high school, Jake told me, he'd been pistol-whipped by a local cop. I didn't ask any details on that one. He seemed to know all the jails in the sleepy little Texas towns around San Antonio and the hill country.

On the way out of town, Jake and I stopped in for an early dinner at a steakhouse, but I insisted on separate checks. "Jake, I had fun today, but let's go Dutch, okay? We're coworkers, and I'm new to the company. I want to set myself apart. Not many women working in the oil field yet, I'm walking a thin line."

"No sweat. I respect that. It's not a date." Jake's blue eyes smiled at me. "We can go to San Antonio next time, if you want. Remember the Alamo, an' all."

"Maybe." My main concern was that I not get involved with anyone. I needed to maintain a laser-like focus and forge ahead.

The rest of the week flew by. I went to Houston and spent a few days with my former roommate, Robert. We went to a couple of gay bars in Montrose, and took a long walk through the ritzy River Oaks neighborhood. Robert made sarcastic remarks about my rough work, but I knew he loved me like a brother. "You don't look as butch as I thought you would. Not yet. Be careful. Wear sunscreen and walk in the shade when you can, Honey. Leather's not for faces, it's for chaps and studded cock rings. Keep that in mind."

I went to the Galleria and used some of my pay to buy new clothes for Annie, had them gift-wrapped, and mailed them to my ex-in-laws' address. I included a card with a note, and as always, hoped against all odds that they would read it to her and let her know the gifts were from me. After that, I used Robert's phone to call my ex-in-laws' place, hoping they'd let me talk to my child for a minute or two, but my father-in-law answered and refused my request. I resolved to return to work, and not to give in to despair.

On Friday, Gilsup announced another week of rain-out. After checking in on Monday, I called my parents' place. I talked with both my mother and my father, and told them about my new job. I also asked if I might be allowed to visit later on, in the spring, once I'd saved enough money for airfare. "I'm hoping I can go to Derek's parents' place, that they'll let me see Annie."

Silence on the other end of the line, then my dad spoke up.

"I hope so, Sweetie. It'd be good to see you."

My mom responded as she often did. "We'll see."

I knew the whole situation must've been heartbreaking for both of them, and I was sure they were worried sick. I felt a lump in my throat and savagely suppressed my tears. *I will not cry...*I said goodbye and went out looking for apartments in Conroe.

The week flew by, and on Friday, Gilsup called an end to the rain-out. Monday, we were back on the seismic line. Gilsup assigned me to the shooter crew, and this time, I collaborated with

Rob and Johnny, blasting. My work involved carrying a fifty-pound pack on my back which contained part of the equipment required for detonation. We carried a radio so we could communicate with the Observer's truck, and set off the charges at intervals, whenever the Observer ordered it. The work involved a lot of waiting, but the blasting proved very entertaining. Little geysers of mud and water blew out of the shot holes all down the line, and I could feel the earth shake. I loved working on that crew.

Over the next few months I got a taste of rural Texas culture— most of it fun. Texas people are friendly, hardworking, and tough. The mom n' pop grocery stores, and the little towns with their honky-tonks and dance halls, fascinated me. I loved the way people would take their kids with them to the dance halls on Friday and Saturday nights. Couples would two-step their way through a song or two, and you'd see moms and dads dancing with their children. When the band took a break, the kids would kick off their shoes and get out on the polished wooden dance floor to slide and skate back and forth in their socks. It was hard not to imagine Annie there, having fun. All of it triggered the pangs of separation, but I became adept at suppressing the deep emotions. And if my skills at burying feelings failed, I used alcohol.

Back then, racism didn't lurk in the shadows, it raged openly, rearing its ugly head in a variety of situations. Martin Luther King had carried our country closer to the dream, but we still had a long way to go. During my time on the job, I heard some people using the N-word often and without compunction. I'd never heard that word used in my family, or my extended family. My parents taught us to respect all cultures, and to treat individuals with the same regard we hoped to receive.

When our crew stopped at a store in Cut and Shoot, Texas, a tiny hamlet near Conroe, a drunk-as-a-skunk local approached the truck and asked Rob the age-old small town question, "Y'all ain't from around here, are ya?" Clutching a brown-bag-wrapped pint to his chest, he bragged that his town still maintained a "functioning sweatbox," then added a comment describing its use in the town square, which included the N-word. And strangely, he turned and glared/leered at me, as if for emphasis. *Is he trying to scare me, or impress me?* The racist boozehound swayed ever so slightly, knitting his dandruff-flecked eyebrows in concentration. "Heh. Hey, Missy, what's YER job on the crew? Hyuk, hyuk..." Rob rolled up the window, put the truck in gear and backed away from the guy.

I never verified the crazy redneck's claim about the sweatbox in Cut and Shoot. I did learn from Scott and Boots that Cut and Shoot acquired fame when local boxer Roy Harris fought Floyd Patterson for the heavyweight title in 1958. Harris got a lot of press—appeared on the cover of Sports Illustrated and was featured in Life Magazine. A landslide of fan mail addressed to, "Roy Harris, Cut and Shoot, Texas" prompted the U.S. Postal Service to assign the burg a local post office.

In February, I found a furnished apartment for rent, cozy and affordable, situated directly above the local Laundromat. I continued to mail cards and gifts to Anne Marie, and occasionally called Derek's parents from a telephone booth, doggedly sliding the coins into the slot at the prompts as I entreated Derek's dad or mom to let me talk to my daughter. I also called my folks at intervals, trying to keep in touch, unsure of whether they still loved me after what'd happened. I could never even begin to explain, to describe all the trauma I'd endured in the years leading up to Derek's dad threatening me, and the fear that drove me to signing over custody. But I clung to the hope of seeing my child again. The contract I'd signed had stated I'd have "...all reasonable rights of visitation," and I naively thought that granted me access. At that point, I didn't know that it was legalese for "Nada."

I welcomed the backbreaking, muddy, dangerous aspects of that job as a way to prove my capability to myself, to focus my hurt and my anger on meeting challenges. Gilsup let me stay on the shooter crew, and I gained a general knowledge of explosives work. I also worked the brush crew with Boots, Scott, Earl and James. One day, Gilsup sneeringly assigned me, James, Freddy, and Blacky to a crew, and gave us a nearly impossible deadline for clearing miles of heavy brush, pine saplings, and kudzu vines. It seemed pretty obvious why we got the shit detail. Freddy and Blacky were Mexicans, James was the solitary black man on the sixty-man crew, and I was the lone woman.

Busting my ass, I channeled my anger at Gilsup into labor, and experienced the sweet-revenge-feeling that comes from having fun at work in spite of your dickweed boss. James was a role model for me; I learned by his example how to project a steady badassitude under pressure. Freddy and Blacky cracked a lot of jokes. At one point, Blacky asked me, "What're you doing way out here, Marti? You're pretty AND tough. You coulda been an airline stewardess." I laughed so hard I almost dropped my machete.

That Sunday, I called Derek's parents' house and his mom answered. I persuaded her to let me come to visit Annie some time that spring. "But only here, on the property, Marti. And you can't be alone with her," Derek's mom warned. I thanked her, and even though my access would be heavily restricted, I felt a thrill of gratitude. When I hung up the phone I jumped up and down, ecstatic. Now all I needed was another rain-out, and the heavy black clouds had been dumping torrents of rain all week. *Fingers crossed...*

Joey, Kevin, and Darnell got released from the hospital in Louisiana, and came back to work. Faye told me that because Joey's broken right leg would be out of commission for quite a while, he'd been assigned to help out in the office. Both Faye and Joey looked a touch sadder, their faces looked a bit pinched. I stopped by their place from time to time, never mentioned Larry, and neither did they. I knew I'd never forget him and was certain he held an important place in their hearts, too.

On Friday morning, during a ludicrous, pseudo-soldierly "drill" before work, Mr. Gilsup announced a new hire. "Hyaaright! Attention, men." He refrained from adding, "And Marti." I figured his message excited him so much he'd momentarily abandoned sarcasm. "I've hired a good man, real hard worker, he's gonna start Monday. He's an ol' Army buddy of mine, we go way back." He cleared his throat, glared accusingly at all of us and in some cases, took time to stop and administer the evil eye individually. "He just got outta Huntsville—deserves a fair shake." Gilsup straightened his spine to ramrod setting, raised a finger and pointed at us workers, stabbing the finger for emphasis, leveling an implicit threat. "I do—not—want...to see any token of disrespect toward this new man. From anybody. Hear me?" Bemused, we nodded in unison. This behavior marked a whole new level of wacko, even for Bo Gilsup. We shuffled out into drizzling rain and headed for the line.

After a stormy weekend, I wasn't the only one hoping for a rain-out. I showed up extra early Monday morning, and hung out in the parking lot, hoping to hear some of the buzz about a possible rain-out. Jake strolled over, shoved his hands into the pockets of his Carhartt jacket and leaned my way. "We're gonna get a rain-out this week. Suarez, what d'you think?"

Raul Saurez, a water buggy driver with waist-length back hair and a wild reputation, was a man of few words, but popular on the crew. Of late, Suarez'd gained celebrity. Our permit man, Don Olivetti, constantly flaunted his higher salary and elevated status, so most everybody thought he was an asshole. Whenever possible, Olivetti went out of his way to drive his vintage Porsche 911 to work, then park it conspicuously and yell at anyone in the vicinity, "Keep your hands off my ride!" On Friday, after the boss announced his new hire, the Army buddy, Suarez was firing up his buggy when Olivetti stalked by. The stuck-up permit man accidentally dropped his Porsche key ring on the rain-soaked ground, and Suarez "accidentally" ran over the keys. The massive buggy's tires squished those vintage keys deep into the mud, and Olivetti, red-faced and seething, needed a shovel to dig them out. In fact, I heard he'd collared a couple of juggies and made them do the dirty work.

"We might..." Suarez tossed his long hair, laughed softly. "Hope so, man!"

A Greyhound bus pulled up and a man in a cheap-looking blue-grayish suit jumped out. He made his way up the walk toward the office. Just then, Gilsup opened the front door, signaling the start of another shift. Inside, as we waited for work assignments, the guy in the suit slid toward me, a predatory grin plastered across his face. "Whoooaa! Hey, Blondie, you look good to me," he muttered, adjusting his lapels. I stepped away from him, and he trailed behind me, rasping, "Hey Missy, want to know where I been? Prison! Heh. Heh. Yup. Wanna know what I was in for?" I ignored him. "Rape! That's right. Heh, heh, heh. Oh yeah! Heh."

So this is Gilsup's ol' Army buddy. Perfect."

I drew myself up to my full stature and stared straight ahead, staunchly refusing to acknowledge him. Eventually he gave up and shoved his way to stand in the front row as Gilsup barked out orders. "Men...and Marti," the boss smirked, "We'll work today and take stock of the situation. I'm not callin' a rain-out yet. As long as our vehicles can penetrate to the line, we will have boots on the ground."

As it happened, the trucks got bogged down that morning, and the drill buggy and water buggy started getting stuck, too. At noon, Gilsup drove up in his pickup truck, his Doberman perched on the seat beside him, and witnessed the sloshy devastation first-hand. That evening, he declared a rain-out and told us to report in Friday morning.

Driving rain pelted me as I hightailed it to the Fury III. I jumped in and drove to a phone booth, called my parents to ask if I could visit them for a day or two. Dad answered and mom picked up the extension. I thought I heard my father's voice crack as he told me, "Come home. We miss you." After that, I called my ex-in-laws, and my luck held. Derek's mother answered and assured me I could see my child on this visit, if only briefly.

I called Delta Airlines and made a reservation for the next day. When my plane landed, my father picked me up at the airport and drove me home, to the house where I grew up. My mother and father treated me kindly, although my mom seemed very tense and anxious. Hell, I felt tense and anxious, ready to jump out of my skin, in fact.

Derek's parents lived on an expansive piece of property—wooded acres with a barn that stabled several Arabian horses—about twenty minutes from Mom and Dad's. I phoned Derek's mother and arranged to see Anne Marie. My father got on the phone and told her he'd be giving me a ride over there. Mom said she'd rather stay home. "I'll get started on dinner," she said. I figured she might be suppressing her feelings—much the same way I'd been doing in order to survive the last few months. But I couldn't be sure. As we drove to my ex-in-laws' residence, I wrestled with intense emotions: shame, agony, fury, and grief, pushed them down deep. Dad parked in front of the house. I hopped out, jogged to the front door, and knocked.

The door opened, and there stood Derek, his mother, and one of his sisters. No one invited me in. Not a sound from any of them. "Where's Annie?" I peered inside, straight over Derek's shoulder, searching, scanning for a glimpse of my baby.

Derek's mom spoke now. "I'll go get her. She's down at the office with her grandfather."

My heart sank, my knees buckled, but I stood strong, forced a smile. "Okay. I'll wait right here." I turned and walked back toward my father's car, and for the first time, noticed he'd been standing beside me all along. I felt wobbly, unsteady, chilled...as if a very strong wind had buffeted me, nearly knocked me down. I decided to look at the ground, at the gravel in the driveway, till I could gain some kind of footing, a way to keep my cool. I counted from one to one hundred, then began counting backward from ninety-nine....*Ninety-eight, ninety-seven, ninety-six...*

"Mommy!" I heard joy in her voice, looked up, and then—I saw her, and all the love inside me came rushing up to greet her. She was smiling, laughing, so glad to see me, and I didn't feel that chill wind any longer, only the sunshine of her smile. My beautiful little girl ran toward me across the lawn, tiny arms outstretched. I ran to meet her, fell to my knees, arms open wide, and after long months of heartache I held her in my embrace. I forgot everything except maternal love and happiness. Later, on the way home with my father, I would try to recall the words my daughter and I had exchanged but couldn't. We'd played in the yard for a while, maybe fifteen minutes. I held her and swung her around—one of our favorite games—and we ran races.

Derek and all his family stood around and watched us, but I didn't care. I didn't even notice them until Derek's father tapped me on the shoulder. "Okay, it's time for you to go now."

I nodded, dropped to my knees again, gave Annie another long hug, and said good-bye, looking into her sweet face, memorizing every detail...for later. Derek walked over, took the baby by the hand, and led her away. I turned, determined not to weep, not to show weakness. My father walked with me to his car, opened the passenger side door for me, and when I was seated, closed the door and walked around to the driver's side. He slid behind the wheel, started the engine, and drove off. We rode in silence, and when we got back home, my mother had dinner waiting. That night, I dreamed of my daughter. The next day, Derek's parents refused to let me see her a second time. I returned to Texas on the next available flight.

———

Back in Conroe, Mr. Gilsup declared a rain-out till the following Friday. Jake asked me out to dinner again, and I accepted his invitation. This time I let him pick up the tab. I had to admit I liked Jake. He was macho-handsome, soft spoken, and smart. We drove to Houston, ate gulf shrimp at a seafood bar, and talked. He told me about his life growing up in a small Texas town, and his time in the Navy—or, as he put it, "The Tonkin Gulf Yacht Club." After Viet Nam, he'd studied at the University of Texas. As we talked, I realized that this was the type of guy I might want in my life, but I waved the thought away. I wanted to tell him about my deep trouble, my struggle...and my dream of winning my daughter back, but I resisted the desire to unburden myself. *Someday, maybe...but not now.*

I spent the next several days reading paperback books. Rain fell intermittently, and when it did, it came down in torrents. Finally, Friday rolled around, and the entire crew assembled in the field office, eager to collect our paychecks. Gilsup stood in front of his desk, scowling. "Line up, men. Marti, you too. We've got a disciplinary matter on our hands. This is a SERIOUS SITUATION!" He clenched both hands into fists and began pacing back and forth. "Last week was inventory, an' we recorded a full cache of explosives in the powder truck. I sent that REPORT to HOUSTON." He quit pacing, turned, and for no apparent reason, glared at Suarez, then switched his accusatory gaze to Kevin, who pulled out his Excedrin tin full of Quaaludes, then apparently realized it wouldn't be cool to swallow one at that moment, and stuck it back in his pocket.

Gilsup was pacing again, looking at the floor. "And THIS WEEK, on Wednesday, I arrived here at OH-SEVEN-HUNDRED, only to find...OUR—POWDER TRUCK—MISSING!" Red-faced, the boss stopped, turned, and frowned at all of us. "This incident has precipitated an internal inquest, and I have ordered a complete inventory of all vehicles, equipment, and supplies ASAP!" (Gilsup didn't spell out the letters in "ASAP," instead he spat it out as one word, "A-SAP!") Pacing again, he continued. "I've requested a change of all locks—ALL LOCKS, trucks, buggies, toolboxes, office doors, desks, EVERYTHING, as a precautionary measure. And I will not rest until the CULPRIT is found. All o' this has been especially rough on Bob Elgin, the new hire, he's an Army veteran, high standard o' discipline, he was in training to fill in as powder man while Joey's leg's outta commission. I regret to inform you that when he learned of the powder truck's disappearance, he left town. The whole thing musta put too much pressure on Bob, him bein' on parole. It's a tragedy." He sighed loudly. "Rain-out's still on. DIIIS-missed." He turned his back on us, waved a hand in Joey's direction. Joey pushed himself up from his desk and onto his crutches. He hobbled forward and began dispensing the paychecks.

Out in the parking lot, I expected a brouhaha over the powder truck heist. But no one said much, at least not openly. No doubt everybody picked up on the fact that Bo Gilsup's crony from his days in uniform had mysteriously disappeared during the same week that the loaded powder truck had gone missing. Rob, Scott, and Johnny offered their opinions, quietly and discreetly, of course. Scott adjusted his CAT Diesel ball cap and shook his head. "That's some craazy-ass shit."

Rob snorted. "That powder truck's in Mexico by now, and Bob Elgin the Army bro is sittin' in a bar in Mazatlan, sippin' Tequila Sunrises."

Johnny guffawed. "Yeah, an' he traded in the prison suit for shorts n' T-shirt n' a pair o' flip flops."

"That was a prison suit?"

Rob stared at me, incredulous. "Hell, yeah, Marti! Guys get outta the joint, they get a prison-issue suit n' shoes, an' some gate money. That ol' buzzard prob'ly had just enough for the Greyhound to Conroe, an' now...well, bet he could get a quarter mil for the explosives in any border town, not to mention what he can get sellin' the truck. It was brand new."

Scott looked annoyed. "It's shit like this that gives us oil industry workers a bad reputation. Just one more reason fer people to call us "Oil field trash."

"Oil field trash? Is that a thing?" I stifled my laughter.

Scott nodded. "Yep. Been doin' it a long time. The locals know we move from place to place—they call us oil field trash, an' blame us for damn near everything bad that happens. And some guys in this line of work deserve that rep. For most o' these sumbitches, oil field theft is one of the perks of the job. But lots of us take it as a compliment. You ever hear somebody say, 'Oil field trash and proud of it'?"

"No."

"Well," Scott smiled, back to his laid-back self, "You've heard it now. Be proud, Marti—you're O.F.T." He chortled. "Not everybody can claim that title, we're an elite group."

No one ever mentioned the powder truck heist again, and I never asked. I learned a lot that day, about prison suits, gate money, oil field theft, and the crazy-ass life in the oil patch. Seismodyne had plenty more work to do in the Conroe area. I invited Jake to move into my apartment with me. On our first night together, I told him about my daughter, and my dream of winning her back. To my relief, he reacted in a positive way. "I had a feelin' you were fightin' for something...or somebody. There's a deep strength in you, and it radiates out. Strength can be scary, that's why none o' these guys are messin' with you."

I smiled at Jake. "You think I've got a shot at this? I'm going up against a psychiatrist with a lotta money."

"Marti, if you've got a plan, you've got a shot. Right now, your plan is to save money for an attorney. It's a solid strategy. You've inspired me to think more about my long range goals. Since I got outta the Navy, I've kinda been drifting. Now I'm gonna start making a list. I'm gonna put my dreams on paper."

I grinned. "Wow, you're so organized. Now you're inspiring me. I'm gonna make a list, too."

"There ya go. We're a mutual inspiration society." He chuckled, put his arm around me, and held me. I rested my head on his shoulder.

CHAPTER 8

SUMMER OF DREAMS AND ALL THINGS TEXAN

Jake and I formed an alliance, supporting each other as friends, partners...and lovers. At Seismodyne, our sharing an apartment didn't seem to make any waves with our coworkers or with Gilsup. Since we split utilities and rent, each of us benefited. Jake escaped sleeping in his hammock in the Bachelor Pad, and I had more of my wages to put into savings. We told each other it was temporary.

I continued to use a payphone to call my parents, and my ex-in-laws' house, in hopes of keeping in touch with my daughter. A couple of times, Derek's mother let me talk with Annie for a minute or two. I even made it back there for another one of those weird, supervised visits with my baby—furtive moments of joy and love, hemmed in by my ex-husband, his parents, and one or more of his siblings. Looking back now, I understand how traumatic the whole thing was for me and for my child. I lived for those fleeting glimpses of her, and in between, I donned my woman warrior badass persona and threw myself into my job. Oil field trash and proud of it.

Gilsup assigned Jake and me to work together on a survey project, running elevations on a huge piece of acreage owned by a rich Texas wildcatter named Mitchell. Jake told me the land, which was chock full of piney woods, rolling hills, and beautiful scenery, served as a private wildlife preserve for the famed oilman. We saw flocks of exotic deer, curly horned sheep, and other rare animals while collecting data for the geophysicists and geologists back in Houston. We climbed over towering fences that separated some sections of the land from others. I enjoyed the work and admired those animals, but couldn't drive away the uneasy feeling that the ranch might be more hunting preserve than wildlife preserve.

One morning, Jake came out of the bathroom in our little apartment. "Gotta lay off the Jack Daniels for a stretch. Blood in my urine again."

"Huh? Whaddya mean by 'again'?"

"Awww, don't worry, Marti. I've been pissin' blood on an' off since Viet Nam. On leave, the military'd fly you around on big ol' transport planes for free, if you didn't mind bein' a strap-hanger. Back then I was drinkin' really hard, and the transport flights are hell on your kidneys. That was the first time I noticed the blood. It's nothin' to worry about, happened to a lotta guys back then. Like I said, when I see blood, I lighten up on the bottle, and it fixes me up tough."

"But Jake, it's been a long time since Viet Nam, and you're still having these symptoms? Blood in the urine is a serious danger sign. Have you seen a doctor?"

He laughed, stared at me. "Naw, it's nothin', I told you. It's on and off, not all the time. Course I never saw a doctor."

"Hey, please make an appointment. It can't hurt to get checked out."

"Okay, but I'm only doin' this to make you feel better."

A week later, Jake took a day off to see a doctor in Houston. He returned stoic and laconic as ever. "The Doc told me to thank you," he half-smiled, "Says you mighta saved my life. I already liked you, Marti. Now I owe you, too."

"What is it?"

Jake shrugged. "They gotta do more tests. And I gotta see a kidney specialist."

After seeing the specialist, Jake filled me in, sparing his words, as usual. "Surgery, no way around it. One of my kidneys is blocked—they may be able to fix it, may have to remove it." He took a deep breath. "I gotta make plans for some time in the hospital, and maybe a month to recover. Might have to quit Seismodyne. Hope not."

"Jake, put in a request for sick leave. Don't sweat it, I get the same pay you do. And I'm not goin' anywhere."

That night we talked about how to handle the situation. I told Jake I'd support him financially and otherwise. He didn't like the idea. One of his mantras in our relationship'd been, "No free ride." I had no qualms about helping him out—we now co-owned a vehicle, a four-wheel drive Toyota Land Cruiser, and had planned to lease it to the company, our first entrepreneurial effort. Long-range, we figured we'd start an oil-field-related business together. We'd both tap danced around the concept of romance though, both of us too tough for that...at least in our own minds.

Instead of driving me away, the impending major surgery turbocharged my involvement with Jake. I liked him, respected him, and couldn't ignore the electric spark of physical attraction. And I knew he felt the same about me. I weighed the pros and cons of sticking with Jake, and in the end I sided with the pros.

Jake filled out the paper work requesting sick leave, the specialist urging him to push through the company red tape to begin his kidney overhaul, pronto. At the same time, events in my life took an abrupt turn.

Through keeping in touch with my parents on a regular basis, I learned my brother's wedding was coming up in a few months, and that I'd be invited if I could make it. *Hell, yeah. I will find a way to make it. And maybe I can get a chance to see the baby...*

I called Derek's parents' line, and Derek answered. Somehow, I resisted the nearly overwhelming urge to slam down the payphone. "Hello, um, Derek. I'd like to talk with Anne Marie, please."

"She's with my sister right now..."

I took a deep breath. "Well, uh, I want to talk to you, too, Derek. My brother's getting married in June, and I'm going to the wedding. I'd like to take Annie with me to the ceremony and the reception. My parents will be with us, and I'll bring her right back to you." I held my breath, hoping...

"Sounds good, uhhm. How about if I come to the wedding, and I'll bring the baby with me?"

"Well, no, I don't think that'd work." I felt stifled, smothered, as if an invisible hand was pressed over my nose and mouth. My heart started pounding.

My ex continued. "Okay, well. If you want her with you at the wedding, that's the only way. Hey, I've started dating someone. I've been thinking it'd be convenient for me if I could spend some quality time getting to know her, without the baby. Maybe you could take Anne Marie for a couple of months. Remember we talked about joint custody?"

No, I don't remember having that conversation with you, your father, or his corporation lawyer...the day you railroaded me. Dickwad. I stemmed my anger, exhaled, and forged ahead with the conversation, adopting a breezy, matter of fact tone. "Uh, yeah, uh, okay. Sure, I'd love to spend more time with Annie, Derek. But I'd need to bring her to my house here in Texas. I can fly in for my brother's wedding and fly back with Anne Marie for the summer. And then, when you're ready, I'll fly her home to you. How does that sound?" *I gotta think fast. I'll need a house for the summer, a different job with shorter hours, safe, responsible child care...*

Silence on Derek's end of the telephone line. Then, "I'll consider it. Call back here in a couple of days."

After white-knuckling through the next few days, I won verbal permission from Derek for a summer visitation. Ecstatic, I told Jake the news, and he smiled. "Hell, I'm up for it...As soon as I get my stitches out. And guess what? I got three weeks' paid sick leave." We cracked a couple of longnecks, celebrated our good luck, and determined to make a nice home for the baby's visit.

———————

JAKE'S DISTRUST OF HOSPITALS RAN DEEP, AND HIS INITIAL experience at the hands of the urologist and his staff hadn't helped matters. Describing his ordeal, Jake went all cowboy on me. "Y'know what they did right outta the chute? Stuck a damn rod up my dick! Hurt like fuckin' hell, and it AIN'T gonna happen again! That shit just ain't my kinda rodeo." As the date of his surgery approached, he grew antsy, agitated. I'd never seen a ripple in his cool before.

The night prior to the scheduled procedure, as instructed by the surgeon, we arrived at the hospital for "admission and prep." Jake pulled us into a space in the parking lot, killed the engine, jumped out, walked to the back of the Land Cruiser, reached in and pulled out two leather bags. Then he handed me one. I thought it felt heavy for an overnighter. *And why two?* He turned and loped toward the hospital's side entrance. I followed, lugging that hefty valise.

Jake slipped inside the hospital and waved me to a staircase. "Sshh. Marti, I packed my Colt .45 in this one." He patted his suitcase, then jerked his head in the direction of the bag I clutched at my side. "Your .38's in there." He took a deep breath, set his jaw. "Both of 'em're loaded. Okay. We check in, and the doctor's meetin' us up in the room. If they whip out any sharp instruments, or ask me to take my cock out, I'm gonna draw on 'em! You pull your Smith n' Wesson, cover me, and we're gonna shoot our way out! Got it?"

At first, I thought he was joking, and started to laugh. Then I looked in his eyes. *He's not kidding!* I tried to talk Jake into walking back out to the car and stashing the handguns, but my boyfriend remained adamant. He'd been pre-admitted, so we took the stairs to the appropriate floor, and on our way to the nurse's station to find out Jake's room number, we saw the specialist, Dr. Steinberg, standing near the elevators.

In the room, the doctor talked with Jake and told him what to expect. I broke the ice by asking about whether there'd be any more tests. "No, we've got all the information we need. Well, you get settled in now, and I'll see you in the morning, Jake." The surgeon hustled off, most likely in a hurry to check on the next patient.

"Feelin' better now, pardner?" I laughed. "You need me to cover you?"

"Damn it, Marti, I had to make sure."

"I, uh, see that...Now, quick: gimme your Colt, Jake. I'd better get all this firepower outta the building before we both get busted."

———

JAKE'S SURGERY YIELDED SUPERB RESULTS. THE SURGEON reconstructed his kidney and built a new, functional valve. No dialysis, no kidney failure, none of the scary possibilities we'd been required to consider. I visited the hospital every night after work, and on weekends. Eventually, Jake returned to work part time, in spite of abdominal pain and back pain. Concerned with Jake's health and my summer visitation with Annie, Jake and I wanted to take a few months' leave of absence. But Seismodyne didn't grant breaks like that. If you wanted time off, you had to flat out quit and take your chances at hiring back on at a later date.

So that's what we did. I turned in my notice first, Jake a few days after. We found a house for rent in Seguin, a little town near San Antonio. I took an entry level job with a property surveyor at a fraction of the pay I'd been pulling down at Seismodyne. But I knew I could return to the oil industry. The cantankerous Bo Gilsup astonished me by turning in a glowing evaluation on my job performance. I never would have guessed that, but my ally Hank Patterson, who'd originally hired me at home office, clued me in when I called to thank him for giving me a chance in the first place. "Sorry to hear you're quitting seismic, Marti. Ever want to come on back, door's open. By the way, your field supervisor, Mr. Gilsup, rated you at the highest possible level. In fact, he added some comments I can't pass on, for fear you'll get the big head. Guess you gave him the what fer. I had a feeling you'd keep up."

I hung up the phone, marveling at the superlative rating, and couldn't help but laugh. *There's gotta be a hitch.*

Jake hired on at the same company I worked for, but we didn't mention our connection to each other. The head of the company, Ernie Benkowski, a licensed surveyor who'd graduated from Texas A & M, owned a cattle ranch on the outskirts of town. Ernie was a good-natured guy, easy going. I learned some basic surveying skills that are old school today: how to identify a property corner, how to chain distances, and how to use a plumb bob for accurate vertical alignment. Today data collection is done with GPS. Back then, a three or four-person crew gathered everything station by station, on the ground, using a transit or theodolite, tempered steel chain, and plumb bob. Bigger companies than Benkowski's used a distance meter, but even the big surveyors knew and valued the basics.

Our party chief, Jasper Dobbs, chewed Bull Durham, and tended to spit the juice all over the base of the transit's tripod. Jasper, a good ol' boy, expounded on his fear of rattlesnakes—well, all snakes—daily. "Y'all best get higher boots, or better, snake guards. Molting season is on, and they're especially dangerous." Dobbs' eyes widened. He glared at me, then at Harley, the other guy on the crew. "When they molt, they're blind, and their skin's real sensitive, so they're jumpy an' apt to strike at the slightest provocation. They hide in the grass, along the fence lines...places WE WORK."

I thought I saw him shiver. "Watch out." He picked up the tobacco-splattered tripod and marched ahead, swinging a stick through the grass as he went.

Texas is a cornucopia of snakes, and according to some sources there are seventy-six different varieties of snakes statewide. Rattlesnakes, water moccasins, copperheads, and coral snakes are the venomous species native to the Lone Star State. Jasper lectured on the defining characteristics and behavior of each and every one of the poisonous ones. Some of his stories seemed over the top, but I couldn't discount anything he said. Being from the North, my snake sightings were limited to one live garter snake on a camping trip in second grade, and beyond that, I'd only seen pictures in Encyclopedia Britannica.

The daily grind was pretty much soporific, and the bucolic little South Texas towns seemed narcotic after life in fast-paced Houston, the adrenaline-accelerating process of setting off dynamite charges, working in and around Huntsville Penitentiary, and getting shot at. But this summer I'd be with Annie, and a safe, quiet little town'd be the ideal backdrop for our summer visitation. Jake had come of age in nearby Gonzales, and on the weekends he taught me some things about South Texas: barbecue and rockabilly, armadillos and buzzards and different breeds of cattle, and how to identify the psilocybin mushrooms that grow in the cow patties. We agreed to refrain from tripping on shrooms till summer's end, a savvy move, and highly disciplined, considering they grew abundantly in many of the fields where we surveyed.

I indulged in all things Texan—gobbled down fajitas, devoured raw jalapeno peppers, and knocked back shots of tequila or mezcal. I went slightly redneck on the job: bought a tooled leather work belt with my name on the back, a buck knife, and a pair of Wranglers. On Saturday nights, Jake and I went to dance halls around San Antonio. I knew the long list of Texas rock and blues artists: Buddy Holly,

Lightnin' Hopkins, Roy Orbison, ZZ Top, Janis Joplin, Johnny Winter, Edgar Winter, Doug Sahm, Augie Meyers, Townes Van Zandt, Delbert McClinton, and more. I reveled in the scenery, too. Texas wild flowers are beyond compare. The bluebonnet-covered pastures took my breath away, and the huge live oak trees gracing the rolling hills never failed to thrill me.

Texas people impressed me as down to earth, no bullshit types, straight talking, cards-on-the-table. I felt safe where I'd landed and began setting down some semblance of roots. For me, at the time, those roots consisted of identifying with a culture; I'd arrived in Texas with only a traumatic past, nothing to lose, and a future bright with dreams.

Downtown Seguin's gift shop offered a range of choices for wedding presents. I wanted to buy something nice for my brother and his fiancé. Silver was too expensive, but I did find a pewter serving platter, and asked the shop owner to gift wrap it. With my savings in the bank, I had enough to cover rent, utilities, and groceries till September. I'd set aside specific funds for airfare for me and Annie, and some cash to buy her toys, books, or new clothing during our summer visitation. I requested a few days off to attend my bro's wedding, and Mr. Benkowski allowed it.

Derek hadn't reneged on his offer to let me bring Annie to Texas—he still wanted time alone with his new love interest, Linda. But any interaction with him or his family felt like tiptoeing on eggshells. In parsing out our utilities budget, Jake and I had decided against putting in a phone. Instead we used the payphone down the street. I pumped some quarters in and called my parents first, then Derek, to confirm travel plans and dates, and arrangements to pick up Annie for the wedding. Payphone calling being hit-or-miss, I made several trips up and down the street that afternoon and evening before scoring a hit. Mom answered, and after a moment, Dad got on the extension. "I got Friday and Monday off for travel. My plane lands Friday, early afternoon. Can you pick me up at the airport, Dad?"

"Yes, I'll be there, Sweetheart. We're very happy that you're coming to the wedding."

My mother's voice chimed in. "Yes, we are! And we can all drive together. Three and a half hours is a long drive for Annie at her age. But we can stop along the way."

Next, I rang Derek's parents' number. Since he still lived on their property with Anne Marie, I had to go through them. When Derek's father picked up, I shuddered, then strapped on my bravado. "This is Marti. Is Derek available?"

"Yes, I'll go get him." Coming from my former father-in-law, even those five words sounded patronizing. Stoically, I reminded myself to stay focused.

Derek picked up. "Hello." Silence followed. I caught my breath. For a second, a memory flitted across my brain—of how it felt handling the explosives, standing by while Qualuude-fueled Kevin wired up the charges. *Eeeaasy does it...*

"Hi! I've made all the arrangements, and I'll be flying in on Friday, in the early afternoon. My dad's picking me up. We'll be heading for the wedding on Saturday morning. How about you bring Anne Marie to my folks' house Friday night? Or Dad and I can stop by on the way back from the airport and pick her up."

"No, Marti. I'll bring her over there." Another sullen silence.

"Okay, Derek. Sounds like we're set. See you then. Bye!" I hung up and walked slowly back to my house.

My plane landed on time, Dad picked me up, and when we got to my parents' place, Mom embraced me. "This is a big weekend, Marti! Are you ready?"

"Yes, Mom. And I'm ready for a summer with Anne Marie. I hope Derek doesn't change his mind."

My mother squeezed my hand. "No, how could he change his mind now? He's still planning on driving over to the wedding with you and Annie tomorrow. He'll be bringing her suitcase with him."

"What? Derek's not invited to the wedding!"

My mother looked surprised. "Well, he called me a few days ago, asking for your brother's phone number. He said you told him to call because you have to use a payphone and you forgot the number. Honey, he asked your brother if he could drive you and Annie over there, and your brother added him to the guest list at the last minute."

That asshole!!! He knew my brother'd be too nice a guy to say no.

"Mom, why in the world would you think I'd want my ex-husband with me at the wedding?"

"The way Derek explained it, it made a lot of sense. Your daughter has been in Derek's care for quite some time now, and she may need the extra time to adjust to you again."

My blood boiled, but I maintained silence, swallowing my rage.

The next morning, Derek called and said they were running late. My parents couldn't risk missing the rehearsal dinner, so they headed out, left me the keys to the house, and told me to lock up. An hour or so later, Derek knocked on the front door. I ran to open it, thrilled to see Annie again. But my ex-husband stood alone on the doorstep. I looked over his shoulder at his car. "Where's Anne Marie?"

"She's with my mom. We've got plenty of time."

"Plenty of time? For WHAT?"

Derek pushed past me into the living room. "You're gonna do something for me. If I'm gonna let you have Annie all summer, you have to show me I can trust you. Do you want to do it on one of the beds upstairs? I guess the carpet might do just as well." He locked his gaze on me, his face expressionless. Waiting for my response.

I slipped into survival mode, detaching myself. My eyes darted around the room, and I realized I was seeking out a household object I could use as a weapon. In that moment I awoke to the truth: that the anger within me now approached homicidal levels.

I took a deep breath, met his gaze. "No."

"Okay." Derek turned and sauntered toward the door. "I didn't think you loved Annie enough. And I was right. A REAL mother would do ANYTHING for her child." He snickered. "Good luck trying to get visitation again."

Something inside of me twisted, then broke in two. "Wait."

My ex turned and walked back toward me, a mix of triumph and self-pity in his eyes. "Like I said, the carpet's as good a place as any."

I'd brought an old sweatshirt with me, so I ran upstairs, got it out of my suitcase, and laid it down on the carpet beforehand. I refused to feel the shame that welled up in me. Instead, I embraced my white-hot rage. Afterward, I buried the old sweatshirt in one of the garbage cans in my parents' garage. And I slowly smothered my anger—as much as is humanly possible. I'd coexisted with rage long enough to know that it makes you stupid. And stupid was a luxury my long-range plan could not afford. Today, I know that this sort of abuse is not uncommon, that ex-husbands often do this to their ex-wives in custodial situations. But then, I felt as though I was the only one who'd been put through it.

Derek waited while I showered and changed clothes. I grabbed my luggage, locked up my parents' house. We got into his car and drove to his parents' estate. Annie stood at the front door, holding my ex-mother-in-law's hand. As I observed Derek interacting with our daughter, it struck me how gentle and loving a father he appeared to be—or actually was. I struggled to reconcile this aspect of the man with the coercive oppressor who'd stood there in my folks' living room and demanded that I "pay" for visitation with my body. He'd done it out of spite and aggression, not loneliness or physical need—after all, he'd found a new woman to replace me.

But all troubling thoughts took wing when Annie ran to me, smiling. I swept her up in my arms and held her tight. During the long drive to my brother's wedding, I spent all of my emotional and mental attentions on my child. Derek acted as though nothing had happened. I determined not to show any signs of distress in front of my parents, grandparents, and other family members who attended the ceremony. My brother's bride's family graciously provided a hotel room for Derek on Saturday night, and Annie and I slept in my hotel room. During the wedding ceremony and the reception, Derek blended in with all the other guests, and some probably assumed we were a family. I kept conversation superficial and bland as a protective measure. Everybody adored Annie. She seemed to have fun at the wedding reception, running around and playing with the other kids. My mother and father seemed happy to witness what looked like an amicable relationship between me and my ex. I never let them know the truth.

Annie and I returned from the wedding in my parents' car. Derek maneuvered the situation so that he could accompany Annie and me to the airport on Monday morning. I felt I couldn't refuse to go along with it. But when Annie and I boarded the Delta Airlines jet and took off together, I was free from Derek's grasp. Flying fascinated Annie. She looked out the window excitedly, and the flight attendant gave her a wings pin to wear.

When we landed at Austin airport, Jake greeted us at the gate. I introduced him to Anne Marie and they solemnly shook hands, smiling shyly. I knew it would take some time for my daughter to adjust to Texas, but she loved animals, so I asked Jake to stop by a couple of horse ranches. We got out of the car and walked to the fence to watch a mare and her foal graze in the meadow. We also stopped to look at cattle. My love for Anne Marie was so fierce, and my desire to spend every moment with her so strong, that I immediately turned in my notice at work, even though I'd previously lined up a babysitter. My savings provided for all of our needs. I didn't have enough for luxuries, but little children don't need luxuries. They need love and quality time. And so do moms.

Summer in Texas means sweltering heat and unflagging humidity. Annie spent a lot of time playing in the backyard, and I watched as she splashed in an inflatable wading pool I'd set up under the shade of a poplar tree. The days flew by. We visited the San Antonio Zoo on weekends, and ate watermelon and popsicles. Nights were long and steamy hot, and my rented house didn't have air conditioning, only window fans. But Anne Marie slept all through the nights, which made me happy since I figured she must feel safe.

Halfway through the summer, on one of those nights when it's 88 degrees at midnight with 90 percent humidity, the dream crept up on me. It started—suddenly—with me looking out the corner of a screened-in porch. I crouched, naked, peeking outside and down a long dirt road that led away from the house. Immensely tall evergreen trees lined each side of the road as far as I could see, and the woods on each side of the road were dense. I could smell the forest.

At the moment I smelled the forest, a realization swept over me in the dream, and I knew I was naked, hiding from a mass murderer who held me and my friends prisoner in that house. I knew, in the dream, that he'd already killed all of my friends and cut them up into pieces with a power saw. I could hear the saw's motor running behind the house, so I knew the killer was busy, and if I started running immediately, there'd be a chance I could make it to the main road and escape. I looked out that window, gauging the time and distance...then the dream ended as abruptly as it began and I woke up, sweating. That was the first time.

I took comfort in knowing that my daughter was not with me in the dream. She was somewhere else, safe and secure and happy.

I wondered if the dream could possibly be the result of someone reaching out to me, relaying a message through the ether. Larry'd reached out to me as he left this realm. I puzzled over it, but ultimately let it slide away, determined to focus on spending the bright Texas days with my sweet little girl.

That first dream returned every night that summer, reenacting itself until I grew accustomed to its terror and stopped wondering what it meant. The purpose of the dream, I figured, was to warn me of some upcoming danger in my life, some situation I must avoid in order to be spared the mass-murderer-and-saw horror. *I'll stay away from houses with big pine trees and screened in porches...that oughta help, right?*

Soon a second dream sidled in, flickering across my brain waves in the wake of the first one, and it rendered me petrified—because my daughter was in it with me. In this second, fever-dream scenario, events whipped by at panic-stricken pace. The dream started with my daughter and me adrift in the middle of a vast ocean, standing on a candy-apple-red swimming pool air mattress. Suddenly a huge dorsal fin sliced through the water toward us. I grabbed my daughter, held her in my arms, looked toward the horizon, and saw a massive steel bridge spanning the expanse of sea.

Crowds of people stood on the bridge, all of them friends. They waved at me and shouted advice, but I couldn't distinguish any of the words. Still cradling my child, I sat down, began paddling the red air mattress toward the bridge, looked back, saw the dorsal fin had vanished, and exulted in the hope that I'd outrun it. I heard one of my friends on the bridge holler, "WELCOME TO CALIFORNIA!!" And all of a sudden a massive shark surfaced and attacked us, its scimitar-sharp fin slashing the floating mattress in two and separating me from Anne Marie. I saw myself reaching out for her. In the final scrambled, blurry instant of the nightmare, I saw myself and my daughter lifted out of the waves, away from the shark, toward the bridge and our waiting allies. The dream ended; I woke up sweat-soaked, chest heaving.

This scrambled, almost-silly-yet-oh-so-disturbing phantasm haunted me every night that summer, hot on the heels of the serial killer nightmare. As with the first dream, I viewed this recurring dream as a portent of things to come—events that could be averted. And as it replayed itself night after night, my body became inured to its horror. I accepted it as a warning, and resolved to never, ever set foot in California. *Why would I wanna go there anyway? I've lived in Florida, seen the beach and the orange trees. Same thing! No reason to go. Right. Case closed.*

The summer zoomed past like a starved coyote chasing a black-tailed jackrabbit. In mid-August, Jake and I and Annie relocated to Austin. We found an apartment on the south side that bordered walking trails leading to Zilker Park. The park offered lots of activities for children, including the Zilker Zephyr Miniature Train. Annie and I could ride all around the park, a forty-minute tour, or we could disembark at any of the stops on the route. My daughter liked the playground best of all, so we spent hours on the swings, slides, and merry-go-round. Our apartment complex had a swimming pool, too.

And with this new apartment, we splurged and installed a home phone. Throughout the summer in Seguin, I'd walked to the phone booth with Anne Marie at regular intervals, and would hold her in my arms while she put quarters into the slot. It seemed right that she stay connected with both parents.

The first several times we called, Derek answered the phone, and carried on a brief conversation with our child. But one night, when I dialed my ex-in-laws' number and we asked for Derek, he never came to the phone. His parents chatted with their grandchild for a minute or two, but I couldn't hear what they were saying. As we walked home, Annie turned to me. "My Daddy's on 'cation!"

"Oh." I dropped to a crouch, gave her a quick hug. "Well, I hope it's a fun vacation for him. How about a piggyback ride?" She giggled and climbed onto my back. We trotted back to my place.

Throughout the next several weeks, Derek continued to evade all attempts at communication, including both calls from the phone booth and a letter or two. Now, calling from my home phone in the new apartment, I reached Derek's mother, and gave her my new number. "Oh, er...thank you. I'll be sure and let my son know you have a phone now."

"Is he still on vacation?"

"I'm sorry, dear, but I can't share that information with you. Bye now." Abruptly, she hung up.

At first I felt extremely anxious over the whole situation, but then I began to look at the details in a more positive light. Nobody had set a date for Anne Marie's return to her father. *There's no visitation contract stating a return date. Maybe she can stay with me a little longer—or maybe I can find an attorney...*

I began to entertain a wild hope of winning back custody of my child. I wondered if Derek's lack of engagement this summer signaled a cessation of enmity, or at least indicated he'd lost interest in depriving me of contact with Annie. *He mentioned joint custody. It's possible!* Elated, I fell asleep the minute my head hit the pillow, and the recurring nightmares didn't seem as vivid as usual. That morning, I called some Austin law firms, requesting a free consultation with an attorney. The lawyer I talked with informed me that I was in a very vulnerable position, since I'd signed over custody, and that whenever my ex requested it, I would be compelled to return my child to him immediately or face consequences. I told him my ex had mentioned joint custody. "That sounds positive," the attorney said. "But a verbal agreement is nil. You'll need an attorney in the state where you were divorced, to draw up a joint custody agreement. It's all gotta be legitimate. No gray areas."

Three days later, a phone call from Derek burst my joint custody bubble. "I'm ready for Annie to come home now, Marti. I need her with me. Buy a ticket and put her on a plane."

"Derek, you mentioned joint custody a few months ago. I'm very interested in working with you on that. I can fly back with Annie and we can draw up a joint custody agreement."

"Right now, all I'm interested in is getting my little girl back home. Call me as soon as you get her travel set up. Let's see if you can work with me on that. I want her back here by the end of the week."

My chest tightened, and my lungs seemed to freeze up. A part of me wanted to beg him for a little more, a day, a week maybe. But I was fierce, and I held onto my wits. *Never let him hear you beg. This is a war of attrition.* I mourned the fact that my ex-husband used our child as a weapon in that battle, a way to maim, cripple, and punish. Still, I strapped on my armor, steeled myself, and faced the truth: I was legally compelled to return Annie to the custodial parent immediately—or face consequences.

And that's how my bright summer ended. Once again, I surrendered my daughter. Carefully, deliberately, I dealt with the aftermath. First, I went into her room, and lovingly packed up her things—every artifact, every item connected with memories of our time together. I held back one photograph, stowed it in the top drawer of my bedroom dresser, a memento to cherish until I saw her again. I allowed myself one day to cry. And the day after that, I powered through the agony and started looking for work.

Jake had hired on with an engineering firm, working as an instrument man doing property surveys in North Austin. I pored over the Classified Ads section of the Austin American Statesman till one listing jumped off the page. "Workers needed immediately for pipeline survey. Excellent pay and benefits. Samuel L. Benson & Associates, Surveyors and Engineers, San Antonio." The ad included a phone number. My pulse pounded in my ears. *Pipeline Survey! Hell YEAH!!! I can do THAT!* I picked up the phone and dialed. My mouth felt suddenly dry. After only two rings, a man picked up. "Benson and Associates, Dan Priestley here."

I'd gotten hired at Seismodyne in person, never had tried cold calling. With this job, I knew I needed to win them over in the first few syllables. And that meant creating the auditory illusion of possible masculinity—lowering my naturally husky female voice just a skosh, enough that Mr. Priestley might assume I was a guy named Marty looking for a job, instead of me, Marti the badass chick, seeking employment. I dropped my voice to its lowest register, slathered on tons of Texas drawl, and mumbled for good measure. "Uuuh— Yeah, this is Marteeeh, Ah'm callin' 'bout the PAAHP-laahn work. Aah've worked fer Seismodaahyne, n' Triah-Dayelt, n' done some propuhty surveyin' too. Ah'm livin' in Austin here lately, but Ah'm willin' to relocate or travel."

"Marty, you're hired. We can use experienced hands like you. Can you be down there at the job on Monday?" The enthusiasm in Priestley's voice triggered a giddy, balls-out confidence within me.

"Yessur."

"Good. Now, the field office is right down on Main Street, in Giddings. Report to Phillip Carvey. Seven sharp. Be ready to put in a full day's work."

"Can do." I paused a moment, decided to push the envelope. "If yer lookin' fer experienced hands, I know an instrument man that's lookin' fer oil field work."

"Son, we'll hire him, too. Consider it a done deal. You can fill out the paperwork in Giddings. All I need now is a phone number, an' your name, and that instrument man's name. Now, if you're comin' from Austin, there's a party chief name o' Dave Ryder that lives in Austin, and he's lookin' for folks to carpool with him. Want Ryder's number?"

"Yessur. I'll give the ol' boy a call. Either way, Ah guarantee Ah'll be there." I hung up the phone and sat still for a minute, relishing my good luck. Back to full-time pay! And on top of that, I'd scored a gig for Jake, too.

Jake dragged in late that afternoon, looking weary. Property surveyors in the city only pay a fraction of what oil field work pays. When I broke the news about Benson and Associates, Jake's eyes widened. I clapped him on the shoulder. "I know it's hard to believe! They're hiring right offa the phone, man! The pay's gonna rock! They've got hourly wages and per diem. Better call your boss and quit first thing tomorrow."

"Marti, I can't do that. Gotta give a few days' notice."

"Okay then. I'm going in there on Monday, though. There's a surveyor I can carpool with, lives here in Austin. You take the Land Cruiser to work till you finish out, then we'll ride together."

I called Dave Ryder later that night and talked with him, careful to converse only in my faux-testosterone-toned voice. We arranged to carpool on Monday. On the phone, Dave sounded like a soft-spoken stoner. "Cool, man. I'll pick you up at your place around quarter to six. Sound good?"

"Yep."

The next day, Thursday, Jake turned in his resignation, promising to work Friday, Saturday, and Monday. He would begin work on Tuesday. The temperature spiked over the weekend. Weather forecasters predicted Monday'd be blistering hot and drenchingly humid.

Monday morning at quarter to six, Ryder showed up at my front door, smelling faintly of cannabis smoke and only registering mild surprise that I wasn't a dude. He wore his hair long and topped it off with a cowboy hat. The mellow vibe in his Chevy pickup truck during the commute set me at ease. The town of Giddings turned out to be a little spot in the road about an hour's drive from Austin. Dave Ryder pulled into a newly-asphalted parking lot off the Giddings main drag. A dozen or more vehicles, mostly Chevy Suburbans, but also a few Ford Broncos and Dodge Rams, stood parked and empty, or sat idling with passengers visible through the tinted windows.

Ryder and I got out of his truck. Dave led the way through the side door of a two-story office complex, then up a carpeted staircase to an open workspace. File cabinets and shelves full of maps lined the walls. Beside a Formica-topped, built-in cabinet stood a dark-haired man wearing black jeans, a black tooled-leather cowboy belt with a silver buckle, and a white cowboy shirt with black piping and shiny jet-black snap fastenings. Dave turned to me and pointed at the man, then meandered off through a doorway at the other end of the room.

I turned, crossed the room to face the dark-haired man, flashed what I hoped was my winning-est smile ever. "You must be Phillip Carvey. Good to meet you, Sir. Mr. Priestley told me to report to you at seven sharp." I extended my right hand and he shook it, dumbfounded.

"YOU'RE MARTY?!"

I dropped my voice an octave and hit him with my best impression of an industrial-strength redneck, badass motherfucker. "That's RAAHT!!"

Carvey laughed, long and hard, and I joined in—couldn't help myself. "Mr. Carvey, I spell it, M-a-r-t-i, by the way."

"Well Marti, you're experienced...and qualified...And we're short-handed." His weathered, craggy face cracked a smile, then morphed into a mask of angst. "I don't know how to say this, but... well, you're gonna be workin' waaaay out in the woods, with guys that are WILD an' even kinda CRAZY, they might act like—er, I mean, you bein' a woman, they might—"

I interrupted him. "Mr. Carvey, I've got experience in the field. I can handle myself out there. We've got chainsaws, right? Machetes?"

Carvey's jaw dropped, he looked flummoxed. "Oh HEY NOW, don' SLICE any of 'em up! My insurance'll go through the ROOF!"

Now it was my turn to trigger a burst of laughter. "Naaw, I won't CUT anybody, Boss. I'll just BRANDISH a weapon, er—a piece of EQUIPMENT, that is—an' BACK 'EM OFF. Works every time."

Phil Carvey's grin lit up his leathery visage like Christmas lights in downtown Dallas. "Okay, siddown over there an' fill out the paperwork." He waved a calloused hand toward a worktable with two plastic chairs beside it. A couple of blank forms lay on the table. I pulled out one of the chairs, sat down, and began scrawling away.

"Oh Marti? Priestley told me you connected us with an instrument man, Jake?"

"Yep. He's good. I worked on a coupla jobs with him at Seismodyne. He told me he can start tomorrow. I gave him the number to call Mr. Priestley."

"Well, thank you for spreadin' the word. If you know anybody else with experience that might be interested, point 'em this way. We do seismic, pipeline, and perimeter surveys. Our clients're all the big oil companies, an' we're lookin' at YEARS of work here. Everything's BOOMIN'."

I finished the forms, handed them to my new boss. He looked them over, turned, and walked toward the door Dave Ryder'd exited a bit earlier. Carvey motioned me to follow. He led me into a hallway, then into a supply room. "I saw on your application you've got experience as a chainman." I nodded an affirmative. "And you worked seismic." I nodded again. "I'm puttin' you on Billy Joe McKenzie's crew. You're gonna work head chain." He handed me a small, spiral-bound field notebook, turned and walked back out into the hallway, again motioning me to follow. "The chain, pencils—hell, chainsaws n' machetes too, ever'thing you need'll be in the crew truck. For a prelim, we do a minimum mile a day if it's woods, and more if it's open pasture. An' I need detailed notes." He continued down the hallway, through the big office where I'd filled out my forms, and down the carpeted stairway I'd ascended a while before. I hustled along behind him.

"Yessir."

At the base of the staircase, Mr. Carvey stepped out into the parking lot and headed for a two-tone beige and tan Chevy Suburban. A beefy, farmer-tanned, crudely tattooed arm dangled out the driver's side window. Phil Carvey approached the truck. "Billy Joe, Marti here's your new head chainman. She's got all kinds of experience in seismic, property survey, everything."

Billy Joe McKenzie, my newly designated party chief, stepped out of the Suburban, extended a hefty arm, shook my hand, smiled at me, and nodded. He wore a MACK truck ball cap, shaggy, shoulder-length brown hair, and a faded Lynyrd Skynyrd "Gimme Back My Bullets 1975 Tour" T-shirt with the sleeves torn off it. "Okay, let's git goin'. You rahde shotgun." He jumped in the Suburban and fired it up as I climbed aboard. Carvey'd already disappeared into the office building.

Billy Joe backed up the vehicle, one hand resting lazily on the steering wheel, rolled us out of the parking lot and down the Giddings main drag, amping up the stereo, turning up the AC to the max, and once we left the town limits, punching the accelerator. The in-dash eight-track cassette player blasted Black Sabbath at ninety decibels as the Suburban lurched, then leapt forward, careening down Highway 77. In minutes, we reached an intersection where Billy Joe executed a tire-squealing turn onto a narrow two-lane road, hardly slacking up on speed at all. He swiveled his neck in order to address me in the front seat and the rest of the crew in the back, guffawed, and hooted, "TELL ME IF YOU'RE SCAAYERED!!!"

No one uttered a word. I fixed my eyes on the road ahead and willed myself to relax against the vinyl upholstery. *Damn if I'm gonna act skittish.* A gravel road dog-legged off the paved one we were currently hammering down—I found myself hoping we wouldn't be taking that route, but made peace with the possibility and focused on Ozzy Osborne's vocals. Billy Joe glanced down at the aerial map spread out on the seat between us, traced a finger along a section of it, looked back up at the road and grinned. "HYERE WE GO!" He nosed the crew truck onto the gravel road and we bounced along at high speed for a few miles, up and down slopes and around curves, churning up cumulous-sized clouds of chalky dust on either side of the Suburban, and a typhoon of dirt and gravel in its wake.

Billy Joe turned off the gravel road and onto a narrow dirt road that led up a rise. At the highest point, he stopped in front of a cattle guard and gate. As head chain, the task of hopping out and opening the gate fell to me. He drove the Suburban through and I shut and latched it, then jumped back in. Billy Joe parked the truck on the dry, hard-packed ground to the right of the gate. He poked a button on the dash, abruptly quenching the blistering inferno of a heavy metal lead guitar bridge, the ensuing silence marred only by the faint mooing of distant cows. He looked in the rear view, pointed his index finger in my direction, and in his Dixie accent, addressed the men in the backseat. "Boehys, this here's Mahrteh." Then he turned to look at me, jerking his thumb in the direction of my coworkers. "Mahrteh, meet the crew." He rattled off their names: Floyd, Casey, Rebel, Elrod, and Dog.

I turned to face my fellow laborers, leaning a forearm on the top edge of the backseat. "Hey." I gave them each a nod. They responded in a variety of styles. I'd seen it before at Seismodyne. Elrod and Casey looked askance, Rebel and Floyd met my gaze and mirrored my nod of acknowledgement. With three rows of seats in this truck, we totaled a seven-member team. Dog, the guy in the third row, raked his gaze over me and smiled, revealing blackish, mossy-looking teeth. I felt a slithery vibe emanating from him, but repelled it, shooting him an icy stare that stomped out the spark of gang-rape-y lust in his eye.

Our party chief, Billy Joe, got out of the truck, walked around to the back, opened the doors and started unloading tripod, transit, and a couple of chainsaws. The others got out too, began unloading lathes, sharpening machetes, and other equipment. I reached into the glove box, found a mechanical pencil and a stub of a wooden one. I stuffed them into the front pocket of my work shirt, shoved the field notebook into the left back pocket of my Levis and a plumb bob in the right back pocket, and joined in the work prep. I grabbed a machete and a file, honing the long blade edge into a wickedly sharp weapon, pausing at intervals to deliver a casually murderous glance at Dog, then set to work covering the top three inches of wooden lathes with fluorescent orange spray paint.

Our work that day consisted of clearing and setting up a tangential line through diverse landscape, including deep woods hung with kudzu, mosquito-dense creeks, and open grazing land. We hammered wooden lathes into the ground at intervals to mark stations. I knew that a seismic contractor would follow, and the results of the blasting would tell geologists where to drill, but a few of my coworkers seemed completely unable to grasp, or were oblivious of, the big picture. Elrod, Casey, and Rebel were local good ol' boys who'd hired on solely for the substantial paycheck. Floyd, like me, knew what the fuck was going on. Dog, I figured, might be a convicted sex predator, escaped from a lockup and on the lam, drifting through the Southwest in search of prey, bad dope, or both. Apparently Samuel L. Benson and Associates was eager to toss any and all available grist into their personnel grinder.

I cut dense brush with a machete, took a turn with a chainsaw, then doubled back up the line to find Floyd, my tail chainman. We chained the distances from station to station, and I drew sketches to record all measurements and distinguishing landmarks, such as cattle guards, fence corners, fence lines, and isolated stands of live oaks. Each page of the field notes needed an arrow sketched in, to show true north. This being a preliminary survey, the information could be useful in a number of ways.

I paid close attention to maintaining a pace and intensity that topped any of the men that labored at my side—a necessity—I knew that first day was my litmus test. Throughout the morning, the heat and humidity soared. Around 11:00 a.m., when we'd hacked our way through the woods to some open pasture with only a few scattered trees, Billy Joe stomped his way up the line, motioning me to follow him. "C'mon. Gotta move the truck an' I don' lahk openin' mah own gates." I left Floyd on line to wind up the chain, which was actually more like a steel tape, about a hundred feet long and tempered to withstand extreme heat and cold without expanding or contracting. When it's pulled tight, applying sufficient pressure, and both ends are leveled with a plumb bob and centered over a nail set into the ground, a chain can get an accurate reading. Any error on a loop is cumulative, so at each point, accuracy is key.

Billy Joe walked as fast as I did, a surprise to me since he looked so stout. Along one stretch of cleared brush, he stopped and stared at me with an exaggeratedly serious expression, hands on hips. "Ah heard 'bout you, Misseh—'bout how YOU had SEX with Phillip Carvey, an' that's the ONLEH reason you got hahred."

I stared back, kept my expression blank. "Oh yeah, I did! That's how I got the job. In fact, I had sex with EVERYBODY. Except for you, Billy Joe, because they told me YOU were GAY." For a nanosecond, Billy Joe's face registered shock. Then he exploded into gut-busting laughter, actually doubled over for a moment, wiped a few tears from his eyes. I kept my deadpan on, then cracked a smile. As we began walking again, he slapped me on the back.

"Heh. Youah all raht, Mahrteh!"

We covered the rest of the distance to the Suburban in no time. He turned the key in the ignition. As the V-8 engine sprang to life, he cranked up the air conditioning, and plucked a field notebook off the dash. "Pass me one o' them pencils outta the glove box, will ya?"

"Yeah, sure." I appreciated the fact he'd refrained from reaching across me to grab a pencil—he was respecting my space. I rummaged around, pawing through time sheets, a snake bite kit, and a couple of bags of Planter's dry roasted peanuts until I finally laid hands on a mechanical pencil. I handed it to Billy Joe.

"Took ya long enough! If it was a snake, idda bit ya!" He grinned at me. I chuckled. Billy Joe riffled through the pages of his notebook and carefully began jotting things down. He held the book close to his chest as if he might be self-conscious.

I pulled my notebook out of my back pocket and my pencil out of the front pocket of my shirt, and began adding to what I'd already compiled. "I'll catch up on my notes, too."

Billy Joe turned to me. "How do ya spell, 'gate'?"

"It's g-a-t-e."

"Thanks."

"Any time."

We scrawled for a minute or two in comfortable silence. Then he turned to me again. "You lahk Lynryd Skynyrd?"

"Sure."

He slid a Lynryd Skynyrd tape into the deck, set the volume low and pushed a button to select a track. Guitar riffs from "Sweet Home Alabama" drifted from the speakers. Billy Joe leaned back in his seat, smiled. "Ah'm from Dothan, Alabama. Robbed a country store outside o' town when I was fourteen. Walked up to the counter an' pulled out a .45—stuck it in the ol' lady's face, an' asked her for a piece of bubble gum." He chortled, shook his head slowly back and forth, reminiscing. "Ya shoulda seen 'er face!" He laughed.

"They put me UNDEH the jail." I listened, nodded, smiled, tried to think of something to say but decided against it. *Is he trying to impress me? With a bubble gum story? What the fuck?*

Billy Joe closed his field notebook, carefully placed both it and his pencil back on the dash, revved the engine slightly, drove forward a bit, then began maneuvering the Suburban into position in front of the gate. I put away my field book and pencil, exited the truck and opened the gate, then closed it and jumped back in. Billy Joe turned onto the dirt road, headed for the gravel road, and picked up talking where he'd left off. "Ah grew up in the jailhouse. Learned a whole lotta things, but spellin' wasn't one of 'em." He smiled, nodded to himself. "'Nother time, Ah stole a chainsaw—it was a Stihl, that's a real good saw—an' ah did anotheh stretch for that, with six months in solitareh. But they didn' break meh." He tapped a finger on one of his temples. "Ah kept it togethah."

I looked him dead in the eye and nodded, recalling my time locked up in the psych ward. "That's tough. And you came through it."

"You ever done Thorazine?"

I stared at him. *This is WEIRD, but HELL, no use lyin'.* I inhaled, readied myself. "Yeah." I exhaled. "Why?"

"It's a GOOD drug."

I did a double take, figured he must be joking around. But the look on his face told me he meant it. *What the FUCK is he TALKIN' about? Thorazine freezes your brain waves.*

"Yup. Ah'd love to get me some moah o' that...know wheah Ah can get some? You live in Austin, raht, Mahrteh?"

"Er, uhm. Yeah, I do live in Austin, but I don't know where to get any Thorazine, Billy Joe." *Whooo! I was right. This IS weird...*

"Well, if y' find any, lemme know." He turned up the volume, and Southern rock music flooded the Suburban as Billy Joe turned onto the gravel road, drove at a clip till we reached another gate.

Again, I opened, closed and latched it, and he drove through another pasture until we reached the place where we'd left our co-workers. They'd assembled and gathered all the equipment, and loaded it up. Billy Joe took us back to Giddings for lunch at the City Meat Market, a brick building on Highway 290. The barbecue was outstanding—brisket, steaks, chops, chicken, sausage, you name it. They served the stuff on white butcher's paper instead of plates. I forgot all about the bubble-gum-larceny-solitary-Thorazine conversation with my crew chief.

Heading back to the job after lunch break, Elrod fretted about the hot weather. "Forgot my damn baseball hat, an' m' forehead's gettin' sunburnt. Can you stop at the store, Boss?" Elrod was a little baby-faced redneck with a naturally whiny voice, like a mosquito buzzing in your ear. Casey leaned on the backseat and seconded the motion.

Billy Joe pressed his lips together, drummed his fingers on the steering wheel, and said nothing. As we approached a country store on the right-hand side of the road, he gunned the motor and speeded up as if to pass it, then immediately slammed on the brakes, swerved off the highway, and screeched to a halt in the gravel parking lot. "Ever'body out! Go git yer hat, Elrod." Elrod, Casey, Rebel, Floyd, and Dog exited the vehicle and headed for the mom n' pop shop, their boots crunching in the scorching-hot gravel. Billy Joe looked my way, waved a hand in the direction of the store. "We gotta fill up the tank anyway. Ah gotta go on in theah an' take caeh of it. The comp'ny's got a chahge account heah." He tossed me the keys. "Back it up to the numbah three pump."

I backed the Suburban in and lined it up, and when I saw the pump switch on, I twisted off the gas cap, reached for the pump nozzle, stuck it in and started filling it up with regular. Billy Joe sauntered back to the vehicle and stood next to me while the gallons rushed into the Surburban's big fuel tank. "Ah love the smell o' gasoline—used to snort it till Ah got dizzeh."

"Yeah? I always liked the smell of it when I was a little kid."

"Me too—lahk Ah said...hey, that Elrod's a weenie. He's got his pantehs all in a wad ovah a sunbuhn! Heh. Heh!" He looked at the gravel under his boots. I heard the glugging sound of a near-full tank followed by the thunk of the pump disengaging, stepped to pull the nozzle out, and replaced it in his moorings.

We walked to our respective front seat side doors and got back into the truck. Billy Joe started the engine, set the AC to the absolute maximum capacity. I saw my crewmates straggling back across the parking lot. Elrod reached the Suburban first, hopped inside, and piped, "Thanks, Boss!" He sported a brand spankin' new, bright yellow, CAT Diesel Power baseball cap.

Billy Joe stiffened, leaned forward, and took a long, slow, disapproving look at Elrod through the rearview mirror. He fished around in his collection of tapes and found a David Allen Coe album. The rest of the guys had arrived by now and were taking their places in the vehicle. "Ah don' lahk yellah CAT hats." He gave me a lopsided grin. "Ah stabbed a boehy oveh one jus' lahk Elrod's. Ah was on Quaaludes, an' we was wranglin' over it—Ah wanted it, an' he wouldn't give it up. Ah damn neah killed 'im, they was gonna chahge me with muhdeh but he pulled through—stabbed 'im in the haht. But the blade missed the aohta bah a fraction of an inch, so they reduced it to assault in the fihst degree. I cut 'im with a Puma. That's a GOOD knahfe, a Puma. You ever wanna buy a buck knahfe, getchou a Puma. You boehys ready t' go?" A chorus of yeahs and yeps issued from the second and third rows. Our crew chief punched it and we peeled out onto Highway 290.

When Billy Joe parked in the pasture, we bailed out of the air-conditioned Suburban and gasped as the full weight of late August heat slammed us. We unloaded equipment again, set out the Igloo water cooler and cups in the back of the truck. This crew traveled with an additional ice chest filled with aluminum cans of soda and even some beers. Billy Joe reached into the ice chest, pulled out a Pepsi, popped the top, and guzzled it. "Damn! It's hotter'n HEY-ull out heah!" He slapped Elrod on the back. "Ain't you glad you wuz BALLSEH enough to ask me 'bout stoppin' at the stoah? Now yer FOAHHEAD won't get all blistahed in the sun!"

Elrod looked peeved, but didn't answer. Dog laughed. Floyd and I unrolled the chain and resumed the work of recording stations. The long afternoon dragged on, with only one interruption. Rebel, Casey, Dog and Billy Joe began harassing Elrod. At one point, Rebel threw a rock at Elrod, knocking his new CAT Diesel hat into the dust. Visibly flustered, Elrod picked it up, gingerly brushed it off, and glowered at the others. "Dang it, I'm gonna report this when we git back to the office!"

Billy Joe snorted. "Repoaht it? Boeyh, you CRAZEH?" He chortled and looked around. "REPOAHT it. Don' be a PUSSEH."

Dog picked up a rock and zinged it at Elrod. The missile hit him in the left knee. "Ow! Y' hit m' knee!" He turned to face Billy Joe, pointing at Dog. "He hit m' KNEE! That's a fire-able offense!" Billy Joe laughed. Elrod stamped his foot, pointed at each one of us in turn, his face a show of haughty disdain. "Whadday'all think will happen when I report this incident? Think y'all can get away with this??"

A volley of small stones pelted Elrod in reply. He ran, and as he ran, additional projectiles peppered the middle of his back. He climbed a tree and perched on a branch, his coworkers heckling, catcalling, and tossing sticks and pebbles up at him until Billy Joe called a halt. At that, all hands returned to work. At first, Elrod refused to come down from the tree. From where I stood, I couldn't make out what our party chief said, but a few muttered words from Billy Joe precipitated Elrod's hasty descent.

We knocked off work around sundown, about 7:00 p.m., and piled into the Suburban. Billy Joe headed toward the office, but stopped at a beer joint on Highway 290, a newly-built, corrugated

225

steel building featuring loud music, ceiling fans, and pool tables. Thirsty and tired from working long hours in hundred-degree heat, we pounded down beers. I only drank Miller Lite, because it contains less alcohol. Billy Joe and Floyd started shooting pool. Casey and Rebel set up a game at an adjoining table. I sat on a bar stool along the wall, sipping slowly and taking in the surroundings. The place was packed with oil field workers, and except for me, the only females appeared to be bartenders and waitresses, which came as no surprise.

Billy Joe chalked his cue and leaned over the pool table to assess possible shot options. A petite, pretty woman with long, jet-black hair and brown eyes strode into the bar, approached Billy Joe, began talking to him. I thought she might be his wife, or a girlfriend. Interested in introducing myself to the only other chick in the bar that wasn't staff, I stood up and made my way over. As I drew nearer, one glance told me this woman was royally pissed off at Billy Joe. He looked down at her, grinned, and shook his head. She immediately assumed a fighting stance, squared her shoulders, hauled back, and punched him in the face. The big redneck staggered back a few paces, a look of astonishment spreading across his features. "I beat you fair and square, McKenzie! You owe me FIFTY BUCKS!!" He reached in his pocket, pulled out a sweaty wad of crumpled bills, and handed it over. She grabbed the cash, whirled, and marched out of the room.

Billy Joe saw me standing there. "Her name's Brandeh. She was raht about me owin'. She kicked mah ass in heah, shootin' pool. Ah know Ah'm not the shahpest tool in the shed, but Ah know bettah than to fuck with Brandeh Broussard. Her brothah Blaise works for Benson an' Associates, you'll meet him. Brandeh makes her money in pool halls, hustlin' hicks lahk me. Three nahts ago, when Ah met her, Ah didn't know who she was, thought she was flihrtin' with me. Asked me to teach her how to play, all sweet an' nahce. Purty soon, she was battin' her eyes, askin' if we could try playin' fer a little money." He raised his voice register to a falsetto. "'Oooh, Billeh Joe, let's trah bettin'! It'll make it moah excitin'!'" He dropped back to his normal voice. "She shoulda KISSED me that naht, cuz she shoah did FUCK ME SAHDEWAYS."

"All I can say is, I'm impressed! I've heard it's really hard to punch upwards like that and still connect."

"She's from Louisiana. Same town Phil Carvey's from. And she's Cajun. All them Cajun women can pack a punch."

"Wow. She's a badass! I don't even know how to shoot pool."

Billy Joe guffawed. "Naw, I ain't gonna buy that one, Slick. Ah betchouah a stone cold pool shahk."

I found an empty pinball machine and played a few games to help pass the time. After another hour or so, Billy Joe rounded up the crew and finally delivered us to the office. Our crew being one of the last ones to report in, I wasn't surprised to see Dave Ryder hanging around talking with Phil Carvey. I turned in my field notes and asked Dave if he'd been waiting long. He said everything was cool. Dave's eyes looked bloodshot, but I figured mine did too, and his pickup rolled steadily along in the correct lane. When we got to my apartment, he asked if he could come up and take a leak before driving on to North Austin. "Sure, c'mon up. You can meet Jake. He just hired on with Benson and Associates."

"Cool, I'd like to meet him." Ryder and I started climbing up the concrete-and-steel steps to the second floor apartment I shared with Jake. We both had to steady ourselves by gripping the wrought-iron banister—exhaustion, inebriation, or both. When I reached the apartment door, the place looked dark and empty, the door unlocked. I opened it, stepped inside, and as the porchlight gleam spilled into the darkened living room, I caught a glimpse of Jake, slumped in an armchair in the corner, swigging the last dregs from a Bottle of Jim Beam, face slack and eyes downcast. I flipped the wall switch, and light filled the room. He lifted his gaze, barely blinking, and waved an arm in a vague gesture.

"Hey Jake, I'm home. This is Dave, the guy I carpooled with today. Dave, meet Jake.

Jake didn't get up from his chair. "Good to meetcha Dave."

"Good to meetcha, Jake. Marti told me you're startin' at Benson tomorrow. Hey, can I, uh, use the facilities?"

Jake waved his hand in the general direction of the hallway. "First door onna right."

Ryder disappeared, returned moments later, and headed out the door. "Thanks. G'night."

"Jake, did you eat yet?" He stared off in space, seeming preoccupied. I realized I hadn't eaten since lunch, but was too exhausted to care, figured the beers had enough calories in them to get me through the night. I headed for the bedroom. "Jake, you comin'? We gotta get an early start in the morning."

Jake stood up, took a step, wobbled, and sat back down. He muttered something like, "Whachamuzzoozzllefwerktwoozlle." *Man, he's totally WASTED!!*

"Okay then, but I gotta crash out now. I've been workin' my ASS off in hundred-degree heat." I stumbled off to the bedroom, stripped off my clothes, collapsed onto the bed, and congratulating myself on a rough day's work well done, slipped into sweet oblivion.

CHAPTER 9

CHAINSAWS, MACHETES, AND STEEL-TOED BOOTS

Ice cold water—a lot of it—splashed on my face, jarring me out of sleep, soaking into my hair and the pillow beneath my head. I sat bolt upright, spluttering. "WHAT the FUCK!" Jake stood over the bed, the empty Jim Beam bottle clutched in one hand, an empty quart Mason Jar in the other. I noticed a few ice cubes strewn across my pillow. *He actually added ICE CUBES to the water before he threw it at me!! MotherFUCKER!!*

"I was tryin' to TALK to you, an' you WOULDN'T WAKE UP! So I WOKE YA!!"

"Jake! ICE? Really??" Beginning to shiver, I jumped up, grabbed the bedspread, and wrapped it around my naked body. "I got you a JOB! It STARTS TOMORROW! WHAT are you DOING??"

"I NEEDED to TALK to you! He tossed the Mason jar onto the bed. It bounced off, landed on the shag carpet with a muffled thump. He raised the empty fifth of Jim Beam to his lips, then with a look of disappointment, realized it was empty. He cradled it under his right arm and began gesticulating with his left. "I was gonna ASK you to BE MY WIFE!"

Flabbergasted, still half-asleep, with half a dozen beers in my system, and physically exhausted, I shifted into sarcasm. "Ooooh, you're gonna PROPOSE to me? Well then, by all means, sling another quart of ice water my way! I wanna be super-alert, don't wanna miss one syllable of your romancin', Cassanova!!—oh, and you'd better pinch me too, so I can be sure I'm not DREAMIN'! Don't forget to drop to one knee before you ask the Big Question! Oh yeah, and—word to the wise: in most cases, the ice you throw around in a nuptial situation is the DIAMONDS kinda ice. Like, on a RING! Definitely NOT cubes-of-frozen-water kinda ice. Get it straight, Einstein." I drew the bedspread tighter around me, pulled myself up to my full height, and with what I hoped was the epitome of grace and decorum, made my exit. At first, encased in the heavy quilted bedspread like a caterpillar in a cocoon, my movement was limited to keep my feet from entangling themselves in all that fabric. But after covering a couple of yards of carpet at that pace, my wits kicked in, and gathering up the front of the comforter in my arms, I freed my long legs and strode into the kitchen, congratulating myself on my sizzlingly snarky rejoinder. *Hmmph. I fixed HIS little red wagon.*

I leaned against the kitchen counter in front of the sink, suddenly aware of how thirsty I was. I turned on the cold water tap, and water gushed from the faucet. Holding the bedspread around me with one hand, I reached into the cabinet with the other, selected a tall glass, filled it to brimming, held it to my lips, and began gulping it down. Man, did it ever taste good!

He came up on my blind side. I never saw his hand, only felt his knuckles as he back-handed me once—the thick glass shattered in my mouth—twice, as the broken chunks of glass slashed my lips—three times, the splinters cut into my chin—four, my ears rang and I saw stars. The shots seemed calculated, as if he knew exactly how hard to hit me without knocking me out cold. Stunned, I turned around to face him—I'd never seen this man before, never this side of him, anyway. His blue eyes widened in surprise, then horror, as he saw the damage he'd done. The flash of recognition struck us both at the exactly same moment.

"You killed me! YOU KILLED ME!! YOU—KILLED—MEEEEEE!!! I dropped the bedspread, stumbled out of the kitchen. Jake followed close on my heels, his voice remorseful, ashamed, begging my forgiveness.

"Oh my God Marti! I didn't mean to do that! I've never hit a woman before, don' know what CAME OVER me. I am so sorry, I'm so sorry, I'm so SORRY!!!"

"GET AWAY FROM ME! YOU KILLED ME!" My shock and rage billowed like sails in a trade wind, propelling me forward and away from him. All my exhaustion evaporated, replaced by boundless energy. I ran into the bathroom, slammed the door, locked it, and leaned my back against the wood, feeling his fists pounding, sensing rather than hearing his pleas for forgiveness, his entreaties to come out and talk it over. I approached the mirror over the bathroom sink. One glance revealed my face: swollen already and continuing to swell. The glass cuts made my upper and lower lips appear to be blooming, the shape of the lacerated tissue surrounding my mouth resembling a lily in the way the ends seemed to curve outward. Ghastly. I reached inside my mouth, gingerly running my index finger over and around the lining of each cheek, the insides of my lips, my tongue...looking for any stray bits of glass. I bent over the sink, cupped my hands in the water, rinsed my mouth, spit. *Only blood. No glass. Good.*

I'd only been in the bathroom a minute. The pounding stopped. I heard his boots clomping on the floor as he paced back and forth in the living room, and thought I heard him sobbing. I grabbed my bathrobe off the hook on the wall, donned it, tied the belt, then opened the door and shot out into the hallway. I saw Jake sitting on the edge of the couch, his head in his hands. Barefoot, I scampered into the kitchen, unfazed by the overwhelming possibility that I might step on shards of broken glass. I knew I needed to create a distraction. I didn't know what to do, so I set the house on fire.

I grabbed up all my tea towels, hand towels, and dish cloths, heaped them into a mound on the gas range top, and switched on all the burners. Flames leapt high, instantaneously igniting the cotton fibers, and smoke billowed toward the ceiling. I snatched up one of the big black Hefty garbage bags from its package under the sink and sprinted from the kitchen. I ran around the bedroom and bathroom, grabbing all of my belongings and some of Annie's, and stuffed them into the trash bag. Jake shouted from the kitchen. "HEY! WHO STARTED A FIRE IN HERE?!" I heard slapping, thumping, and water running, and knew the distraction'd worked. Jake was now fully occupied with trying to extinguish the flames.

I ran to the phone, picked it up, dialed a friend. "Lulu, it's Marti. Jake HIT ME!"

"I'm on my way."

I slammed down the phone, twisted up the neck of the bulging Hefty bag, and threw it over my shoulder, Santa Claus-style. I raced out the front door, leaving it wide open, and hauled ass off into the night, never once looking back. At the moment I reached the edge of the parking lot, Lulu's canary yellow 1968 Cadillac convertible swooped in and picked me up. I'd met Lulu and Mason from Jake; they were classmates of his at the University of Texas. When Lulu pulled the big Caddy into their driveway, I saw Mason standing on the front porch, and worried that he'd already told Jake where I was. But they didn't betray my trust. Once inside the house, Lulu wrapped some ice in a washcloth and handed it to me. "Hold that on your mouth, Honey. It'll take the swelling down."

Her kindness moved me so that I broke down sobbing. I couldn't talk very well, because my mouth was so messed up, so I didn't bother to recount the incident. Lulu combed the tangles out of my wet hair and made up a bed for me on their living room couch, but I didn't sleep much. I was too worried about my new job. I sat at the table in the kitchen, applying ice to my lips and chin. The swelling'd gone down only a fraction. Around 5:00 a.m., Lulu and Mason's one-year-old son, Justin, woke up crying. Lulu tiptoed into the kitchen, carrying the toddler. "I'm sorry Lulu. Did I wake the baby?"

"No, it's not you. His molars are coming in and it drives him crazy." She opened the freezer, pulled out an ice-cold gel teething ring, rinsed it under the kitchen faucet, and held it to Justin's mouth. He stopped crying and began chomping on it. "This'll fix him up. Did we wake you?"

"Are you kidding? I can't sleep. Every time I close my eyes, I think about how I'm gonna have to miss work today. And Jake'll be going! If I call in sick, I don't know if they'll let me stay on with the company. Yesterday was my first day."

"Girlfriend, you can't drop outta that oil field gig! The money must be phenomenal."

"Yeah, the pay rocks. But I work with crazy redneck felons, and I'm the ONLY female out there. Look at my face! If I show up like this, those guys'll take one look and start thinkin' that if one dude can hit me, it's open season."

"Marti, you gotta follow through on this opportunity, no matter what. Why not just go on in there?"

"You're right! I'm not gonna let Jake or any other man run me off! I'm gonna show up over there and...oh, but I need a ride to Giddings, where the office is, gotta be there by seven sharp. Jake and I were supposed to drive in there together. But I am NOT gonna call HIM and ask for a ride!" I stood up, reached into the freezer to replenish my ice pack.

"Honey." Lulu cocked her head to the side, made eye contact, smiled slowly. "Mason'll drive you to work. He's an early riser, and he's got today and tomorrow off. He's up already and shaving."

"Oh wow, that's perfect! Thank you. Can I uh, take a shower in your spare bathroom? I'm gonna start getting ready for work now. It'll take a while to find my stuff in that trash bag."

"Sure. I'll fix breakfast."

I dragged the distended Hefty bag, my de facto luggage, into the guest bathroom, showered, fumbled through my wadded up clothes and selected a pair of jeans and a T-shirt. I pulled out a pair of thick, cotton crew socks, and gripping them in my fist, dragged the black trash bag back into the living room. I folded up the sheets and blanket neatly, stacked them on the floor on top of the pillow Lulu'd supplied, and sat down on the couch to put on my socks. I pawed to the bottom of the Hefty bag for my work boots.

Lulu stuck her head out the kitchen door. "Marti! Mason! Breakfast is ready—I made bacon and eggs."

Mason strode through the living room, kissed Lulu on the cheek. "My favorite!"

"Be there in a minute!" A feverish search for my rugged foot-wear failed to yield results. I turned the Hefty bag upside down, spilling its contents onto the floor, to no avail. In my exodus from the apartment, I'd cadged a couple of pairs of high heels, some strappy sandals, and a pair of foamy rubber flip-flops, but by some crazy twist of fate, had failed to toss in my Timberland work boots.

Despondent, I shuffled barefoot to the kitchen, took a seat at the table with Lulu and Mason. Lulu passed a plate of toast my way. "Looks like you're ready to show those ol' goat-ropers a thing or two."

I didn't feel like eating, but politely took a piece of toast and nib-bled on it. "Uh, yeah. Except for one small detail. I forgot to pack my work boots. I've got a pair of flip-flops, though, and I'm gonna show up wearing those things! I've made up my mind. They'll have to fire me before I'll back down."

Mason's eyes lit up. He set his fork down. "Hey, wait a minute! I've got a pair of steel-toed work boots. I'll loan 'em to ya. They'll be way too big, but if you wear thick socks and lace 'em up tight, they'll do."

We finished breakfast. Mason headed off to get the boots while I helped Lulu clear away the dishes. Mason called out from the living room. "Marti, c'mere and try these on."

I hustled into the living room. Mason stood holding a battered pair of enormous boots. "These boots will bring you luck, Marti. I wore 'em in Huntsville, and I keep 'em as a reminder of what I've overcome." I knew Mason'd done time in the late Sixties and into the first years of the Seventies, for manufacture of LSD.

In 1967, when Mason majored in chemistry at U.T., he and another student had learned the recipe for Orange Sunshine, from a renegade Californian who'd worked with the famed Owsley of San Francisco. They soon began making their own Sunshine, in quantity. One night, the cops raided their lab and arrested Mason and his partner—caught them red-handed with seven pounds of LSD, in crystalized form. Somebody'd snitched them off. Back then, Texas law enforcement had no idea what acid was, so there were no laws dictating prosecution of crimes relating to it. The State of Texas pushed for harsh retribution, and the judge handed down life sentences for the two young chemists. Mason and his lab partner did hard labor in Huntsville's infamous Ellis Unit until finally, as the law began to evolve, their appeals won them reduced sentences and early release for time served. Lulu had waited for Mason all those years, and they married when he got out of Huntsville.

He passed me the boots. "Wow. Thank you, Mason!" I sat down on the couch, pulled them on. "Oh man, my feet are SWIMMING in these!"

"Well, yeah. They're size thirteens. But like I said, slap on enough pairs of socks, and lace 'em tight. I've got some super-thick socks I can loan ya. Buck up, Badass Chick! It's almost time to go."

"Er, uhmm, okay." I piled on layer after layer of socks, yanked the boots on, strapped up the laces, stood up, and tried stumping back and forth a few times. "Ready."

Lulu and Mason let me leave my trash bag full of belongings in their house, and Mason told me he could pick me up that night after work. I thanked them for all their help. "By tomorrow, I'll have a carpool arrangement set up, I think."

Mason pulled his El Camino into Benson and Associates' parking lot at 6:55 a.m. I glanced out the passenger-side window, recognized the tan and beige Suburban I'd worked out of the day before with Billy Joe's crew. And to my chagrin, I caught a glimpse of Jake stepping up to the Suburban and taking a seat in the back. *Fuck! They assigned us to the same damn crew!* "Thanks for the ride, Mason." I opened the passenger door of the El Camino, set my feet on the pavement, and lurched to a stance, swaying slightly in those massive steel-toed clompers. Seeing my wobbliness, Mason helped me out by reaching across the seat and shutting the passenger-side door behind me. He drove off.

Setting my sights on Billy Joe's Suburban, I kicked my right foot forward, then my left. Encased in the Ringling-Brothers-Barnum-and-Bailey-sized clodhoppers, and highly self-conscious about the appearance of my bashed-and-slashed face, I appropriated the most hard-ass, belligerent attitude I could muster. I threw my shoulders back, held my head high, narrowed my eyes to slits, glaring around the parking lot as if eager to eviscerate any unwitting fool careless enough to sneak a glance in my direction. Satisfied that everyone either didn't notice or didn't care, I relaxed a little. Then I tromped over to my crew's truck, opened the front seat passenger side door, and sat down on the front seat. The trouble with making this entrance was that the weight of those prison-issue hoofs required me to sit sideways at first, and then—those boots were so big I had to haul back and swiiiing 'em into the truck. The thick leather soles hit the rubber floor mat with a ka-thud.

Dead silence reigned in the Suburban. Intensely aware of Jake's presence in the backseat, and uber-vigilant of my other co-workers' reactions to my beat-up face, I stared straight ahead, arms crossed over my torso. A split second later, Billy Joe broke the palpable tension. "Damn, Woman! WHAT SAHZE SHOE DO YOU WEAH??!!" The entire crew, including me—and minus Jake—burst out laughing. *Good ol' Billy Joe.* After pausing for a beat, I resumed my staunch posture and don't-fuck-with-me attitude, staring stoically out the windshield.

Billy Joe fired up the Suburban, backed the truck out, and exited the parking lot. He hung a right, zipped down Giddings' main drag, and floored it. On the way back to the previous shift's point of departure, our party chief maintained his signature driving style: stomping on the accelerator, executing sharp turns onto each and every gravel road or dirt road, and slamming on the brakes, often with both feet on the pedal. Billy Joe's road techniques coerced the bulky vehicle into jaw-dropping displays of vehicular misconduct—lunging from zero to seventy on take-off, fishtailing on turns, careening all over the narrow, unpaved roads, and stirring up cyclones of dust and debris capable of sandblasting the hide off a rhino. With Billy Joe, arrival at any destination involved screeching tires, the stench of burned rubber, and the rattle and crash of loose items and equipment.

This second day's weather promised to be hotter and muggier than the first. Billy Joe barked out orders in his good-ol'-boy, Ah'm-jes'-half-ass-jokin' tone of voice. In spite of his breezy style, every one of his regular crew snapped into action. Billy Joe's team was a tightly knit one. Jake and I were the neophytes, I figured. Then I reminded myself that Jake was more newbie than me, at least by one day. I threw myself into the work, completely ignoring Jake and refusing to make eye contact with anyone else, either.

Billy Joe called for a mid-morning break. "Hey y'all, it's too damn HOT! Ever'body grab somethin' to drink, an' we'll sit in the truck for awahle. We got Pepsi, Sprahte, Doctah Peppah, Bud, Schlitz, an' Millah Laht. Take y' pick." All hands scrambled for the ice chest, pulled out a beverage, and boarded the Suburban. Our crew chief parked the truck under the shade of a massive live oak tree. He let the engine idle with the AC going, and for a moment, the only sound other than the hum of the V-8 and the whoosh of the fan was the sound of aluminum can pop tops opening, or the occasional slurp.

Fixing my gaze on the scenery ahead and deliberately paying no attention to the others, I merely pretended to sip my Pepsi. With my swollen face, the process of drawing liquid into my mouth through the tiny opening in the aluminum can wasn't easy. But the cold can soothed the still painful wounds. Billy Joe turned to me, a lopsided smile on his face. "Who slapped the shit outta ya?" Stony silence pervaded the atmosphere in the Suburban. Refusing to dignify his question with even a smidgeon of a reaction, I continued to stare straight ahead, unmoving and unmoved. Billy Joe took another run at it. "Somebody knocked the shit outta ya, didn' they?" I turned my head only a fraction of a degree and saw the lopsided smile had morphed into a slaphappy grin. I stood my ground in belligerent silence, returned my gaze to the forefront. Inwardly, I embraced and rehearsed assorted acts of mayhem, and assumed an attitude that I hoped radiated menace. Undaunted, Billy Joe continued. "Onleh reason Ah'm askin' is, Mahrteh—is cuz we LAHK YOU! It's cuz YOUAH ALRAAHT!" He straightened, looked into the rearview mirror to address his team in the second and third seats. "AIN' THAT RAHT, BOEHYS?"

A chorus of, "HELL YEAH," and "DAMN STRAIGHT," rang out from the back of the Suburban.

"That's raht, we lahk you Mahrteh, you got HAHT, an' WHO-EVAH it is that HIT YA—WE'LL FUCK HIM UP!!!" He again addressed his posse in the rearview mirror. "WON'T WE, BOEHYS?"

The thundering refrain from the "boehys"—a collective round of, "HELL YEAH," followed by hoots, rebel yells, and random hollers of, "LET'S CUT 'IM!!!" increased in volume, finally reaching a crescendo that seemed to rock the vehicle.

Billy Joe chuckled softly. "So who done it, Mahrteh? DOES HE WOAK HEAH?"

A hush fell over the Suburban. I knew which spot Jake occupied in the backseat, and in that moment I felt certain I could sense the distressed vibes coming from him. I kept on looking straight ahead, but relaxed a little. "Well, he MIGHT work here." I leaned forward, set my Pepsi on the dash, took off my baseball cap, smoothed my hair, put the cap back on again, luxuriating in the tension from Jake. "And—he MIGHT NOT." I didn't intend to give him up, but couldn't resist the urge to snatch a tiny, sweet morsel of revenge. I turned to face Billy Joe. "Y'know, HE JUST MIGHT WORK HERE." I paused for another moment. "But he MIGHT NOT." I turned away, reached for my Pepsi again. "I appreciate your offer, Boss. And I'll THINK IT OVER." I managed to take a sip of the Pepsi without it dribbling down my bashed up face. "Right now I can't say."

Billy Joe nodded, lifted his can of Budweiser, chugged some, and reached for his tapes. "We need some MUSIC up in this sumbitch!" He popped in AC/DC's newly released Highway to Hell album, selected the kinetic tune, "If You Want Blood (You've Got It)" and whipped off his MACK Truck baseball cap so he could throw his hair back and forth while headbanging to the hard rock sound. I didn't look back, but figured that if their crew chief was headbanging, so were Casey, Floyd, Dog, Elrod and Rebel. As for Jake, I didn't even give him a thought.

The song ended with AC/DC lead singer Bon Scott screaming the last line, "IF YOU WANT BLOOD, YOU GOT IIIIIIIIT!" followed by the ferocious riffs of AC/DC lead guitarist Angus Young. Billy Joe silenced the stereo with a jab at the power button, killed the engine, bailed out of the Suburban, and waved a hefty arm, motioning us to follow.

"Break time's ovah, boehys!" We set all the chainsaws and machetes in motion, clearing right of way through the iron resistance presented by thick mesquite, huisache, buckthorn, and trees overgrown with spiny greenbrier vines. Shortly before sunset, Billy Joe called a halt, and this time, he didn't stop at a beer joint. He took us straight to the office. I turned in my field notes, caught Dave Ryder in the hallway and asked if he'd like to carpool. He told me he would, so I gave him Lulu and Mason's address for the next morning. Feeling strangely carefree, I thudded down the stairway in my loaner, ex-con boots to find Mason's El Camino pulling into the parking lot.

As I scooted into the front seat and swung my legs inside, hearing the now-familiar and even comforting ka-thud of the size-thirteens onto the floor mat, Mason asked, "How'd it go?"

"Okay. It went okay."

"Lulu's fixin' chicken fried steak." He pulled the El Camino out of the parking lot and headed toward Austin.

I pointed to the battered steel-toeds. "I'd like to say I've walked a mile in your shoes, but I know better."

He chortled. "You can borrow them till you get a day off."

"You and Lulu get a cut of my first paycheck."

"Sounds fair enough. But be sure and hold back enough cash to get you on your feet. No pun intended." He switched on the radio and turned the dial button, searching for a station with a strong signal. He settled on a rock oldies station.

A few songs down the highway, the DJ played a 1966 classic by Nancy Sinatra, "These Boots Are Made For Walkin.'" I laughed till my eyes filled up with tears, wiped them away. In spite of everything, I felt lucky. Later that night, after Lulu's kickass chicken fried steak dinner, Mason drove over to the apartment I'd been sharing with Jake and picked up my Timberland work boots. "He asked me to tell you he's sorry."

"Okay. Thanks for going over there, Mason. It can't be easy for you, Jake's an old friend. I don't want you and Lulu to get stuck in the middle of this."

Lulu spoke up. "It's not a problem. Jake fucked up and you're welcome to stay."

Mason folded his hands and cracked his knuckles. "That's right. Jake knows he did wrong. He said he won't give you any trouble at work, either."

"He's telling the truth. He definitely will not do that." I picked up the bedding I'd folded and stacked early that morning, started making up a bed for myself on the sofa. And this time, I had no trouble sleeping. The next morning, Wednesday, I wore my own boots and carpooled with Dave Ryder. Nobody at Benson and Associates asked me what happened to my face that day, or any other day after that. When I reported to work on Billy Joe's crew, Jake wasn't there.

Billy Joe told Floyd and me to stock up the truck with lathes, flagging, and other supplies while he talked with Phillip Carvey up in the office. Floyd arranged the sledgehammers and machetes on one side of the Surburban's rear bed. "The new guy went out with Harley Heenehan's crew, they needed an instrument man." I nodded in reply. With my face still healing, I kept my conversation to a minimum. Floyd continued. "We're doin' a rush job in Fayette County today. Phillip only wants Billy Joe doin' this one, nobody else."

Billy Joe McKenzie and Phil Carvey approached the truck as Floyd and I finished stocking the back. Rebel, Casey, Elrod, and Dog piled in, and Floyd and I took our seats. Billy Joe got in and slid behind the wheel. Phil walked to the driver's side of the car parked beside the Suburban, a midnight-blue Cadillac Seville. He opened the driver's side door, ducked his head in, extracted a brown paper grocery bag, walked back around the Seville, and leaned in the driver's side window of the Suburban. Phil inclined his head in my direction. "Can you shoot a gun?"

"Yeah, sure I can."

Phil passed the grocery bag to Billy Joe. "Take this, and give her that hogleg." Billy Joe reached under the seat, pulled out a sawed-off shotgun, handed it off to me. "Stash that under the seat, Marti. It's for security. Lotta crazy shit goin' on." I nodded assent, concealed the weapon as directed. *Now I'm ridin' shotgun. Literally.* Billy Joe opened the grocery bag, whipped out the other piece, a .357 Magnum with a six-inch barrel, and shoved it under the seat on his side. He crumpled the paper bag and tossed it on the floorboards. Phil pounded a calloused hand on the roof of the Suburban, gave us a thumbs up, turned and headed back into the office. Billy Joe put the Suburban in gear and in minutes we'd blown out of Giddings, sailing along the roads of Lee County on our way to Fayette County.

At one point, Billy Joe pulled off onto a rutted, one-lane dirt road, and we bumped and rattled along for a stretch. Dense woods and thick brush lined the road on either side, and we narrowly missed clipping a flock of buzzards as they panicked at our approach, rising hastily into the air from their fetid feast of roadkill. Billy Joe wore the slaphappy grin that I now began to realize was his default facial expression. "Buzzahds make good tahget practice, but sometimes when y' shoot one, it'll bahf all ovah the place, an' that ain' pretteh." He gunned the V-8, barreling down the road about a mile before stomping the brake pedal. The Suburban swayed, heaved, and ultimately emerged unscathed from a partial spin-out. As the truck decelerated, Billy Joe swerved it onto the shoulder and parked. We disembarked amidst a mini-tornado of dust and gnats stirred up by our abrupt arrival, the bucolic early morning atmosphere shattered.

When the dust settled, I noticed Billy Joe held the .357 in one hand. "Mahrteh, git that hogleg out from undeh the seat." I retrieved the gun from its storage place. The other guys opened the back doors, rummaged under the seats, produced several empty cans, and tossed them on the ground. They stood, arms crossed over their chests, regarding me with an air of careful scrutiny and mild skepticism. Billy Joe nodded in the direction of an aged barbed wire fence line that ran alongside the road. "Rebel, set up some o' them cans."

Rebel grabbed a Bud can and an RC Cola can and placed them atop the thickest of the fence posts. Billy Joe turned to me. "Head chainman gotta know how to shoot. Theah's a LOTTA CRAHM out heah, an' theah's crews hahjackin' crews, stealin' trucks an' sellin' 'em in Mexico. Shit lahk that. Youah rahdin' shotgun, you gotta show us you can hold up in a fahrfaht. If it comes to that." He guffawed. "It's the damn truth." He glanced around at Dog, Rebel, Casey, Floyd, and Elwood, and all hands nodded in affirmation.

Floyd muttered, "Mmhm."

Billy Joe's shit-kicker grin expanded as he pointed at the weapon I held in my hands. "It's a sawed-off. All you gotta do is hit from close range. Ah wanna be suah you can keep a steadeh hand."

This all seemed like an exaggerated game to me. *Ohfuckthisis... so...crazy. Concealed weapons, highway robbery. It's like the Wild West.* I stifled the urge to laugh. *But when in Rome...*I gripped the stock in my right hand, steadied the truncated barrel with my left, and took aim at the RC Cola can. I exhaled gently, squeezed the trigger, and felt the kick in my shoulder as the blast from both barrels decimated the aluminum cylinder. I heard stifled laughter from my coworkers. Billy Joe grinned. "You did alraht. Hit the tahget. But y' staggahed back a foot or so. Y' gotta anchah youah LEGS, so y' can handle the recoahl bettah. Fahr a few moah rounds, and this tahm—stand y' ground!"

For a short spell, Billy Joe coached me through the nuances of sawed-off shotgunnery. I obliterated various brands of empty pop top cans until he and my other coworkers were satisfied with my skillset. Our crew chief, Floyd, and Casey set up some cans on more distant fence posts, and each fired one round from the .357. All bullets hit their targets. This demonstration struck me as an encouraging display of our crew's security potential. Shooting over, we jumped back in the Suburban and rolled on down the dirt road until we reached a gated turn-off. The taller-than-customary gate was latched and encircled by a heavy-gauge steel chain and oversized padlock. Billy Joe parked in front of the gate and consulted the aerial map spread out on the front seat. He pointed a finger at the thin thread of road captured in the photo. "This is it."

A maroon Ford Bronco approached from the opposite direction, moving at a good clip. Billy Joe held up a hand. "Ever'body stay insahd till they pass." The tension in the Suburban was tangible. The Bronco sped by us, braked, and slowly reversed until the driver side window was parallel with Billy Joe's, its occupants invisible behind darkly tinted windshield and windows. The Ford's driver rolled down his window. Billy Joe's hand drifted toward the .357, pulled it into his lap. I leaned slightly forward, placed a hand on the hogleg, set it on my knee.

The driver of the Bronco, a brawny dude with long, wildly wiry blond hair, leaned out, smiled lazily, and addressed Billy Joe. "Hey, you got a spoon?" He glanced behind him momentarily, appeared to be caucusing with his passengers. "We'll give you a taste. It's uh, an emergency." He threw back his head and laughed. Hoots of laughter exploded from the Bronco's backseat.

Billy Joe relaxed, tilted his head in the other crew leader's direction. "Naaww, we ain' got nothin' lahk that. You can cut off the bottom of a beah can, caintcha? I got plenty o' cans in heah. An' if you got any crank, Ah'll take a taste."

The burly blond driver slapped a hand on his forehead. "Oh fuck, I forgot about usin' a can!" He laughed, again turned to the backseat of the Bronco. "We got one in here, so we're good." He scratched his chin. "No crank today. We're goin' downtown."

Billy Joe waved a hand. "Ah'll pass."

"I'm Trigger Jim, I'm the driller on that rig back there over the hill. We switch out, crystal and junk, dependin' on workin' conditons. If you ever wanna score, stop by the rig on second shift an' lemme know."

Billy Joe chortled. "Thanks, man. Ah'm Billy Joe. We woak f' Benson an' Associates. Stakin' wells, pahplahnes, shit like that. See y'all around." He returned his focus to the aerial map.

"Later." Trigger Jim and his crew drove on down the road. Billy Joe watched in the rearview as the Bronco disappeared in a cloud of dust. Billy Joe stashed the .357 and I ditched the hogleg under my seat.

"Ever'body out! Floyd, grab me a ten-pound sledge. An' a fouah-poundeh." He turned to me. "Mahrteh, we gonna show you how a good ol' boeyh picks a lock." Floyd and Rebel held the heavy chain taut, so that the lock pressed tight against the gate post, and Billy Joe braced the padlock between the four-pound and ten-pound sledgehammers. Then in one fluid motion, he pulled the hammers back and simultaneously smashed them against the lock, breaking it. Now that we could open it, I held the gate while the Suburban drove through, then closed it, draped the chain back in place and hung the remains of the lock from one of its links. I jogged to the Suburban and hopped in.

"We ain't comin' back this way, boehys. This ain't nothin' more'n a shoahtcut." Billy Joe drove slowly and smoothly, the Suburban trundling along through bull nettles and clumps of grass. "We'ah onleh skihtin' this ranch to get to anothah piece o' propehty. The ownah don't WANT us heah, but the pahp-lahne is comin' through anyway. They call it the Law of Imminent Domain." He turned to me. "We'ah packin' today on account o' the OWNAH told the landman HE'LL be ready—with a twelve-gauge." He drove a bit further, turned to me. "And yondah sawed-off is a ten-gauge, so don't get triggah-happeh."

Our main goal on that stretch of line was to mark a rough tangent across the recalcitrant and hostile landowner's pasture. We didn't have to cut brush, it was mostly low-lying scrub and prickly pear cactus. We passed a house on our right, perched atop a hill, and I half-expected to see a shotgun barrel poking out from between the front window curtains, like in some of the hokey old Westerns I watched on television as a little kid, or to hear the crack of warning shots fired. But the whole thing went down without a hitch.

The next piece of property was home to a herd of dairy cattle, and the land in one pasture had obviously been tended with the utmost care. Billy Joe handled the Suburban as gently as he might cradle his newborn son—or a bindle of his favorite dope. "Home office in San Antonio sent us oahdehs NOT to SPOOK the cattle. So heads up, y'all." We took a side trip off line, drove through a couple of cattle guards, then climbed a rise and parked. A pad for a drilling rig had been staked out, and the heavy equipment had begun the process of clearing the ground. Our crew had been charged with the task of taking elevations and setting marked stakes for the heavy equipment operators to follow when leveling it out. Next, gravel trucks would deliver enough aggregate to create a solid drilling pad. We used a transit and Philadelphia rod to set the grade.

Elevations completed, we packed up, returned to the pipeline survey. Later that afternoon, and farther down the line, on another parcel of property, we saw a massive piece of Caterpillar machinery parked on a hill. I'd seen things like this on the highway, hauling rigs or pumping stations around Conroe area, back when I worked for Seismodyne. The machine looked brand new, its bright yellow paint gleaming in the hot sun. Billy Joe slapped on that gleeful-southern-psycho smile. "Damn! You know how EASEH it is to HOT-WIAH one o' them sumbitches?"

Floyd spoke up. "Hey-ull, yeah! Y'know, if somebody steals one off the location, they'll pay a thousand-dollar reward or more for information of its whereabouts. There's a coupla guys around town that hot-start Caterpillars like that, move 'em around, wait a few days, and then collect. They get old guys or Mexicans to call in the tips, an' give 'em a coupla hundred a piece. You can't make steady money that way. It's a side business."

Billy Joe crowed with glee. "Whooo-weee! Ah'd lahk to get m' hands on summa that sahd moneh! Ah'd get me some crank an' some acid, an' take a trip to New Oahleans! Las' time Ah picked up some extra was down around San Antonio. Y'know them big ol' reels o' tape from the Obsehveh truck? On a sahsmic crew, I mean. Mahrteh, you woaked sahsmic, you know what I mean, doncha?"

"Yeah, I do."

Billy Joe nodded, continued. "Well, me an' this ol' boehy Ah knew, we hiahed on with a sahsmic crew, just fer a week or so, an' we waited till the Obsehveh stepped out to take a leak. An' Ah snatched up one o' the finished reels they was gonna ship to Houston. We drug up off the job that naht, it was payday. Nobody knew the shit was gone till we was down the road! Heh, heh."

Rebel laughed. "So how'd you make out?"

"We did alraht. Sold it to some boehys at the bah fer a couple grand. The boehys that bought it, they woaked fer a competitah, I reckon. Coahporate espionage. Haw, haw!!"

None of this sounded likely to me, but then I reminded myself that I had absolutely no criminal experience—a good thing. And I wasn't looking to get any experience like that, either. So I sat back and listened to Floyd and Billy Joe swap a few yarns. After they finished jawing, Billy Joe slid a David Allan Coe tape in the dash, and selected "My Long Hair Don't Cover Up My Redneck." This being a rush job, on the drive in Billy Joe'd taken a vote on working through lunch and eating at the end of the day. The only crewmember that voted against that idea was Elrod, and when beaten by an overwhelming majority, he'd gotten a burr under his saddle.

"My momma forgot to wake me up on time this mornin' so I had to skip breakfast, or be late to work. An' I ain't never late to work. If we don't stop fer lunch I'm gonna be starved!!" He rolled his eyes for dramatic emphasis.

Billy Joe snorted with laughter. "Youah MOMMA DIDN' WAKE YOU UP ON TIME?! Whas' the mattah with you, Boehy? Cain't you git an ALAHM CLOCK? Haw!" He shook his head slowly, back and forth, and adjusted his grip on the wheel. "Yo' MOMMA didn' wake you up...Whaayh, you little STUMP JUMPAH! Don' that jes' beat ALL." Still, Billy Joe'd stopped at a country store, and waited while Elrod bought himself something to eat.

Late in the afternoon, Billy Joe and I sat down in the Suburban and put the finishing touches on our field notes. The rest of the crew goofed around and cracked open a cold beer or two. "Mahrteh, Ah'm takin' y'all out to dinnah at the Cottonwood, it's a steakhouse in LaGrange. Ah keep mah crew happeh."

"That's nice. You're all right, Billy Joe." I felt self-conscious about going out to dinner with my face still swollen. But I figured the place'd be jammed with grizzled old cattle farmers, truck drivers with white line fever, and local yokels out for a night on the town. All the denizens of the place'd be drunk as skunks. I figured nobody'd give me a second glance, and felt better. La Grange is a little town on Highway 71 between Houston and Austin. It's the Fayette County seat, famous for being the home of Sheriff Jim Fluornoy, a pot-bellied, gun-totin' redneck lawman. Despite being a raving racist, and implicated in criminal activity, Ol' Sheriff Jim stayed in office for thirty-four years. Sheriff Jim was retired, elderly, and frail now, but still had a reputation as The Meanest Sheriff in Texas.

Billy Joe jerked a thumb toward the back of the Suburban. "Mahrteh, check in the back an' make shuah all the sledgehammahs are in theah."

I stepped out, walked around to the back, took a quick inventory, and returned. "All there."

Billy Joe closed his field notebook, set it on the dash. "C'mon, boehys!" The guys began ambling toward the truck. Billy Joe turned to face me. "Ah keep a close watch on them hammahs." He took his Mack Truck hat off with one hand and pulled his hair up off his forehead with the other, exposing a wicked-looking scar at the hairline. There appeared to be four small, deep dents in his skull, at the hairline, although the skin had closed over them. "See that? Them mahks're from a claw hammah! Theah's moah of 'em fahtheh up, undehneath m' haieh."

"Wow! A claw hammer. Man, what happened?"

"Ah was runnin' a construction crew in Panama Citeh, Flohrida. Ah was drahvin' the crew back t' the office, an' one of 'em rared up from the backseat an' stahted beatin' on me with that goddam hammah!"

"Wow! He attacked while you were driving? Did somebody grab the wheel when you passed out?"

Billy Joe howled with laughter. "Grab the WHEEL? PASSED OUT? Hell no, Mahrteh! I pulled the truck up on the shouldeh, put it in pahk, an' jumped out an' pulled that summabitch outta the backseat, an' BEAT THE FUCK outta him."

"And THEN you passed out."

Billy Joe guffawed again. Then he changed the subject. "Hey Mahrteh, Ah lahk talkin' to you. Y'know, Ah keep a scrapbook of all my arrests an' shit. Ah got a lotta newspapah ahticles they wrote about me during my legal proceduhs. Ah'm gonna bring that damn scrapbook to woak tomorrah, an' Ah'll show you what Ah mean."

"Sure." On the way to the Cottonwood for dinner, as I reviewed the events of my third day at work, I mulled over the logistics of attack by claw hammer. Or any kind of hammer, for that matter. I figured Billy Joe's skull must be about three inches thick in order to withstand an onslaught like that. I'd learned some cool stuff, though—even though I didn't plan to put most of it into practice. How to fire a sawn-off, double-barreled shotgun and handle the recoil. How to break a heavy steel padlock using two sledgehammers. Ways to make "sahd moneh." And I learned that sometimes, felons proudly keep a record—of their criminal record—in a scrapbook.

The next morning, Thursday, Billy Joe didn't show me his felony scrapbook, because Phillip Carvey assigned me to a different crew. I figured he might be testing my mettle, skill, and ability to work with others. Phil told me Bart Bodean, the party chief, worked only pipeline surveys.

"Bart's one o' the long-runnin' employees of Benson. Spends a lotta his time doing pipeline in Louisiana, and Oklahoma here lately. You can learn a lot from 'im."

"Okay, Mr. Carvey."

"Do me a favor an' lose the 'Mister.' You can call me Phillip. Phil's okay, too."

"Okay, Phillip."

When it came to driving, Bart Bodean's skills rivaled any stock car racer or moonshine runner. Fast and fearless, he coaxed our crew truck, a two-tone metallic-blue and white Suburban, to near red-line velocity on Highway 290. Bart hailed from Mississippi and, like Billy Joe, seemed barbaric but easygoing. He negotiated a hairpin turn onto a gravel road, spewing geysers of rock and dust into the woods on both sides. Lighting a Kool non-filter, he gave us the plan for the day. "We're only doin' a prelim, but we gotta get some miles in befoah Millah Tahm. We gonna WORK ouah ASSES OFF."

The route to the jobsite required a long jaunt on the gravel road, with plenty of potholes. I bounced around in the backseat along with three others—Aaron, Roy Lee, and Bryar. We were packed in shoulder to shoulder, which partially cushioned the impact when hitting potholes at sixty miles per. Devo, the head chainman and instrument man, rode up front with Bart. Devo had worked for a pest control company in Amarillo prior to hiring on at Benson, and today he sported a khaki shirt emblazoned with the extermination company's name. He'd sheared the sleeves off it, and wore it unbuttoned, with a wife beater T-shirt underneath. Devo wore horn rimmed glasses, and hair slicked back in a pompadour reminiscent of Elvis.

Roy Lee, a heavily muscled dude with shaggy, shoulder-length black hair, was one of several workers who'd relocated from Louisiana when Phil Carvey'd come to set up the office in Giddings. Roy Lee smiled frequently and radiated an air of savagery. Bryar was a Tennessee native with arms and neck as thick as an NFL offensive tackle. Victor, a lean-and-mean, chain-smoking Mexican guy from Chiapas who looked to be around forty years old, sat in the third row back.

Like me, Aaron was new to the crew. In fact, it was his very first day, and strangely, he'd reported to work in a polo shirt, having mistakenly assumed he'd be employed in the office. Aaron was a local Giddings guy with neatly-styled blond hair, who repeatedly reminded his coworkers of his importance, and bragged about his rich daddy. I couldn't figure out whether his garrulousness stemmed from arrogance, ignorance, fear, or all three. "My dad's President over at Southwestern Bell, an' he wants me to work in the field for a while before I go to college, to learn about the oil business from the ground up."

Although his comment was met with stony silence from all his coworkers, Aaron prattled on. "I don't need the money, really. But it'll come in handy when I start at U.T. in the spring." I considered taking him aside and cluing him in to the fact that most of the crew likely harbored a keen disapproval of "college boehys" and "rich boehys." But I rejected the idea, thinking Aaron'd pick up the vibe on his own. Many laborers I'd worked with at Seismodyne had demonstrated virulent resentment of anyone who'd obtained any kind of education outside the walls of State or Federal lockups, and I felt certain this crew harbored a similar acrimony.

Bart Bodean brought the Suburban to a shuddering stop alongside a barbed wire fence tied with fluorescent yellow flagging. Beyond the flagged fence line, a wall of trees, brush, thorny greenbrier, and thick kudzu vines opposed us. Bart stepped out of the truck and hollered, "FIFTEH-FOOT RIGHT OF WAY, Y'ALL!" His regular guys—Bryar, Vic, Devo, and Roy Lee, hopped over the barb wire, fired up their chainsaws, and hurled themselves into the work at a frenetic pace. I had no trouble keeping up. The morning coolness had flitted away at sunrise, and now the heat and humidity pressed down on us with a remarkable ferocity.

Aaron proved himself a sturdy and steady worker. I figured he picked up on the mood of the crew. No longer a wordster or braggart, he hove to and pulled brush for three chainsaws at once, dragging away the thorny vines and branches, and stacking them up on either side of the cleared right of way. After a few hours, when his sweat-soaked polo shirt hung in tatters, he didn't utter a peep in complaint.

Up ahead, Bryar shouted, "HORNETS!!!" He dropped his still-running chainsaw and sprinted down the line, a buzzing swarm of fury in pursuit. Vic, Roy Lee, and Bart leaped out of the way. I did the same. Only Aaron didn't seem to know the protocol for hornet attack. He stood stock still in the middle of the clearing. When Bryar ran past him, he tore off the blue T-shirt he was wearing, and the hornets clustered around and over it, stinging the fabric with a vengeance. I'd learned this technique at Seismodyne, and for that reason, always wore a work shirt unbuttoned over a T-shirt. If bees or hornets attack, you can run, throw off the shirt, and keep on running while the cloud of stinging assailants sets to on your discarded garment. For some reason, Aaron had been advised of a different strategy, one I've never tried. I have heard it said that if you freeze up and don't move a muscle, bees won't sting. Maybe it only works for bees. All I know is, quite a few of the hornets got bored with stinging the shirt, noticed Aaron standing there, and zapped him viciously.

Bart yelled at the top of his lungs, urging Aaron to run. "BOEHY! AARON! GIT THE FUCK OUTTA THEAH!!" Others shook their heads in disgust, muttering that the new guy had no sense, no sense at all. Eventually, all the hornets flew away, ostensibly in search of a suitable place to begin construction on a new nest. A shirtless Bryar moseyed back up the line toward us, his torso covered with jailhouse tattoos. The ones inked onto his chest and shoulders included racial epithets, and featured imagery characteristic of white supremacist prison gangs. He plucked his T-shirt off the ground, bent to pick it up, pulled it on over his head.

Red welts peppered Aaron's arms, neck and face. Devo showed off some of the extensive knowledge he'd acquired in pest control school. "Dolichovespula maculate, the bald-faced hornet, has left its mark on you!" He walked down the line toward the Suburban. "We got a first aid kit in the glove box. But I recommend whiskey. And Coke. If you can afford it—the Columbian shit is up to $110 dollahs a gram these days!" He guffawed, and the rest of the crew roared with laughter. I joined in.

Aaron chuckled half-heartedly, straightened his back. "Aaww, I'm alright. Not allergic." We continued hacking and sawing away through the woods. At one point, we entered a clearing, and Bart called a break. We marched back down the line to the crew truck, and drank Dixie cups full of water. Bodean's crew carried bottled Coke, Pepsi, and Bud longnecks in an ice chest in the back. Everyone except me chose beer, I stuck with Coca-Cola. Devo rolled a joint, passed it around. Young Aaron took a hit, too, and immediately started talking about how he might get his dad to donate the cash for Benson and Associates to equip their crews with special insect sting first aid kits. "Just in case somebody IS allergic."

Roy Lee turned and meandered up the line. Bryar, Vic, and I followed. Bart and Devo hung back a bit, lit a second joint, then raced each other to the clearing, hooting and cackling with wild laughter. Aaron chugged his beer and hustled after them. Once we reached the clearing, the work grew less intensive for a bit. Devo paused by a clump of brush, stooped down, then stood holding up his right hand at eye level with a pale green katydid balanced on his index finger. "Ah, Tettigonia Veridissima! Of the class Tettigonioidea. Outstanding!"

I'd been avoiding calling attention to myself, since my face was still cut up and a little bit swollen, but I couldn't resist approaching Devo to satisfy my curiosity. "Do you know all the scientific names for insects? That's pretty cool."

He shrugged. "We learned it in pest control academy. If anybody on this crew gets bit or stung, I can identify the perp, tell if it's poisonous. I've studied the swarm behaviors, life cycle, you name it—of any varmint in the Lone Star State." He barked out a goofy stoner laugh-giggle, waved his finger and released the katydid.

Under Bart's directive, our crew breached the clearing and launched an offensive on a new barrier of thick green that included scrub oak, huisache, mesquite, yaupon and other badass brush. The ever-present kudzu vine vexed us, and the stickery greenbrier vines oppressed us. Roy Lee waded into the wall of thorny, slapping branches, swinging a Stihl chainsaw like it weighed no more than a toothpick. He led the pack. Then suddenly we heard a deep-throated scream. "MOTHERFUCKER!! There's ASPS in this damn tree!" He cut off his saw, set it on the ground, and hands shaking slightly, doffed his shirt, turned and pointed a finger over his shoulder. "Devo!! Check out my back, man. Is it a ASP?"

Roy Lee's back was broad, hard as oak, with the words "WHITE POWER" tattooed in three-inch-high jailhouse ink, in an arc-shaped curve across his bulging rear delts, lats, and upper traps. Below the lettering, a tattooed image of a penitentiary covered all the rest of the available tattoo real estate, with the words "ANGOLA PRISON" inked in under the building's image. With all that ink screaming off his back, it was tough to figure out what he was pointing at, but I looked again and saw a couple of fuzzy things fall off him. In fact, one of them seemed to bounce off the Angola Prison guard tower on the way down. *These can't be the asps he's talkin' about. They look like cotton balls! An asp is a snake, from Shakespeare. Cleopatra held the asp to her breast...*I lurched out of my reverie, forbidding myself to speak a word. *It's not like I'm workin' with poet laureates or champions of chivalry.* I knew if I mentioned "Shakespeare," or "breast," in present company, I likely ran the risk of enduring suspicion, angry bafflement, gang rape, or all three.

Devo strode to the spot where the fuzzy blobs had dropped off Roy Lee's back. He crouched, examined something on the ground, nodded solemnly. "It's an asp that got ya, Roy Lee. Ya mighta got bit by more than one o' those fuckers. Technically, it's a caterpillar—the larval form of the Megalopyge opercularis species of moth."

"It hurts like a son-of-a-bitch. Feels like more'n one asp stung me! I was cuttin' back branches with my chainsaw, an' saw 'em fallin' outta the trees. Then I felt the stings."

Bryar chimed in. "I've heard of a asp, but never seen one. One ol' boy on Lonnie Thibodeaux's crew, he got stung on the neck, and later, at the bar, he got a fever, an' his head started spinnin' an' he almost passed out. We thought he couldn't hold his liquor! Ended up with the dude going to the hospital, and they said it was the asp venom."

Devo turned to Bart. "Boss, we got any duct tape in the truck?"

"Yup. In the back, with the spray paint."

"Good. Marti, go to the truck, an' bring back that roll o' duct tape. S'posed to use scotch tape, but we'll try duct tape."

Roy Lee laughed out loud. "Whatchou think you're gonna do, Devo? Tie me up?" He chuckled. "I'll kick your ass."

I walked back to the Suburban, thinking how many uses rednecks seem to find for duct tape. When I got back to the crew, Roy Lee's condition looked a bit worse. Three red spots, resembling small burns, had appeared on his back. Asp stings can cause intense, throbbing pain, nausea, vomiting, headache, abdominal pain, and shock or trouble breathing. Roy Lee appeared to be experiencing the first on the list, and enduring it stoically. I handed the duct tape to Devo. He turned to his asp-stung coworker. "Okay, get ready, Roy Lee. We're gonna stick the tape onto your back, then strip it off real quick. If you're lucky, the tape'll pull some of the spines out. The venom's in the spines."

Roy Lee dropped to a crouch, braced one arm against a tree trunk. "Git 'er done." Devo stuck lengths of the duct tape on Roy Lee's back, waited a moment, then abruptly tore them off. Roy Lee winced. "Anything else you recommend, you goofy summabitch?"

"Yes. Heroin." Roy Lee, Bryar, and Bart howled with laughter. Devo grinned. "But for now, you'll have to make do with beer." That got a big laugh from everybody.

We finished the job, in spite of two casualties due to insect attack. Roy Lee and Aaron carried their weight through the afternoon, even though they probably felt like hell. At the end of the shift, Bart Bodean treated us to another display of NASCAR-grade driving, followed by dinner and drinks at the Cottonwood, the same restaurant and bar where Billy Joe'd stopped the night before. Aaron'd chugged down several Bud longnecks before boarding the truck. The alcohol, combined with probable fatigue, produced a dramatic impact on him, and when the Suburban rounded the many curves in the Fayette County backroads, he began to sway slightly in his seat. We were packed in shoulder to shoulder, the same way as en route to the jobsite that morning. I sat on the far-right-hand side, by the window. Burly Bryar sat next to me, then Aaron, then hefty Roy Lee next to the window on the far-left-hand side. Each time Aaron oscillated in his seat, both Bryar and Roy Lee jabbed Aaron with their elbows, but Aaron seemed oblivious to the rising tension.

When we arrived at the Cottonwood and bailed out of the vehicle, I breathed a bit more easily. We tromped in, and the hostess seated us in a large, round booth lined with red vinyl, overstuffed upholstery. Bart Bodean and his crew regulars insisted on buying round after round. Roy Lee, Bart, and Bryar switched to Jack Daniels. Devo and Vic stuck with beer. Bodean raised an eyebrow and glanced around the table, pausing to glower at me, then Aaron. "Y'all bettah keep up!" Aaron ordered Budweiser longnecks and guzzled them down. I ordered Miller Lite, because of the lower alcohol content and the fact that this establishment served them in cans. I could sip a little bit of each beer, leaving most of it in the can without anyone knowing I didn't finish it. The waitress, a grim-faced, wiry redhead, brought the drinks right on top of each other. The hard-ass regulars on this crew consumed mass quantities of booze, and astonishingly, not one of them displayed any of the common signs of impairment.

Unlike his fellows, Aaron's alcohol consumption transformed him into a mumbling, drooling zombie. At a critical moment, he wobbled to the left, and his head lolled forward, then jerked back. Eyelids drooping, he grabbed the table edge with one hand, righting himself momentarily, then listed toward Roy Lee, who sat beside him on the right. Again Aaron's head lolled, but this time in Roy Lee's direction, then sagged onto the hefty ex-con's shoulder. Roy Lee stiffened, looking peeved, then shoved the polo-shirted new guy with an elbow. Aaron's eyes opened wide. His shook his head as if to clear it. "Mmmph. Gottatakealeakmizzlemorphen. Twzzfizle. S'cuze." He stood up and exited the booth, stumbling twice and pitching headfirst toward both Vic and Bryar in turn.

During Aaron's absence, Roy Lee, Bryar, Vic, and Bart exchanged a volley of comments, expressing their outraged macho sensibilities. Bart slammed a fist on the table. "Did y'all see THAT? The new guy's a PUSSY! Can't even handle a few beers without floppin' all around the joint."

I wanted to interject a comment in Aaron's defense, but couldn't risk aligning myself with him, since I was also a "new guy" and actually possessed genuine lady parts. No need to draw attention.

Roy Lee's eyes nearly bulged out of his head. The muscles in his neck stiffened, and his face turned red. "Motherfucker's not only a PUSSY. He's QUEER."

Vic swigged his brew, then set the bottle down hard. "He doesn't belong here. PINCHE PENDEJO!"

Bryar straightened his back and squared his shoulders. He inhaled abruptly through his nose, bloodshot eyes wide. "Roy Lee, you're right—He's a PUSSY an' a fuckin' QUEER."

Devo dropped his goofy stoner demeanor to weigh in. He slapped the flat of his hand on the tabletop. "That MothahFUCKAH."

The waitress approached our booth. Bart turned to her. "Honeh, bring me the check."

She hurried back with the tab, no doubt relieved to be rid of our party. Bart peeled off a pile of twenties. "Keep it."

She beamed at him. "Thank you!"

Bart growled, "Let's get the fuck outta heah. Now." All hands rose, exited the booth, and trooped toward the door. I thought they were going to ditch Aaron, but he returned from the men's room in the nick of time, and departed along with the rest of us. We marched through the dark parking lot to the truck. To my surprise, Roy Lee and Bryar took the same places in the Suburban for the drive back to the office, positioning themselves on either side of Aaron.

Bart Bodean put the key in the ignition and the V-8 engine sprang to life. He peeled out of the parking lot and sped down the winding country roads. Way out in the middle of nowhere, on one particularly sharp curve, Aaron lurched hard toward Bryar—I couldn't see it in the pitch dark, but I felt the extra weight in my shoulder. I felt Bryar's steely right arm draw back, then heard a thud followed by a grunt of pain. Bryar turned his body in Aaron's direction and barked, "PUSSY!!" A series of thumps and punches followed. I heard a click. The sound of rushing air and rolling tires filled the Suburban's interior as the door on Roy Lee's side flew open. Bryar, Vic, and Roy Lee pushed Aaron out onto the road. The V-8 roared as Bart gunned it, and the truck surged ahead into the night.

We rode in silence for a minute or two, then Roy Lee snickered. Bryar chortled. Vic snorted, "Chingado!" All three exploded into guffaws.

Roy Lee scratched his chin. "Man, Vic! You're quick with that blade. Nicked him in the ass on the way out, I think."

"Bullshit. I cut him higher. But not too deep."

Bryar smoothed his hair with his hands. "You fuckin' Mexicans! Always gotta cut somebody."

When Bodean pulled the crew truck into the parking lot at Benson and Associates, Dave Ryder called out to me from his Chevy pickup. "Hey Marti! Ready to roll?"

I hesitated. Bart looked up from the time sheets he was filling out, glanced at me in the rearview. "Go ahead. Y' gettin' fifteen houahs today."

I joined Dave in his truck, and we began our commute back to Austin. "Thanks for waiting for me. I think our crew got in late."

"No later'n any other crew, all told." He adjusted his grip on the steering wheel, fixed his gaze on the road ahead. "Be good to get back to Austin, won't it?"

"You bet." I looked out the passenger window, into the night. I figured Benson and Associates would surely be handing out some heavy retribution to Bart Bodean, for losing a new guy on his very first day.

Dave and I arrived early the next day, Friday. Payday. Unsure which crew I'd be assigned to, I began climbing the stairs to ask Phillip Carvey, but Billy Joe stopped me on his way down. "Ready to woak, Mahrti? Phillip's puttin' you back on mah crew. We got about six weeks o' woak in the Brazos Riveh Basin, ovah in Buhleson Counteh!" At Samuel L. Benson and Associates in those days, we often worked seven days a week. Sam L. paid us per diem, too. At the bottom of the staircase, Billy Joe stopped and pointed. "Damn! Somebodeh hit that boeyh with an ugleh stick." I looked. A male figure in fresh, clean clothes walked slowly and painfully across the parking lot toward us. The man's head, so swollen it appeared oversized, was covered with bruises, scrapes, and small cuts. His eyes looked like slits in his face. I wondered how he could see. As he drew closer, I recognized him.

I strode over to him. "Aaron!"

He laughed a little, then winced. "Yeah, it's me. Man, I was so drunk last night, I uh...I blacked out. I do remember getting tossed out of the truck, though. Lucky for me, there was a farmhouse in the distance, so I walked toward the lights. They let me use the phone. My dad told me to show up this mornin' and go back to work. He's says when a bronco throws ya, ya gotta get back on or ya never learn to ride."

Wow. That's tough love if I ever saw it. I had no words to say. He walked past me and headed up the stairs to the office. I admired his strength of character for not only surviving it, but for showing up at work the next day.

I never saw Aaron again. But according to talk among Sam L. employees, Phillip had fired him that morning, given him a paycheck, and sent him away. Word was that Bart Bodean'd already sent a negative report about Aaron to the home office in San Antonio the night before.

If this first four days was any indication, Giddings, Texas rivaled the legendary cowtown, Dodge City. When it came to unchecked savagery, abject ignorance, unabashed racism, unmitigated misogyny, rampant alcoholism, and down-and-dirty-redneck insanity, Giddings might even win hands-down.

But the pay was good, so I figured I'd stick around and take my chances.

CHAPTER 10

BOOMTOWN AND PAYBACK

I stood outside the door marked LADIES, crossed my arms over my chest, and casually glanced left, then right. Jackson'd been in there for several minutes, but I refrained from knocking. I'd stood guard for him the previous day, and knew he needed time to find a vein. Jackson Langford, like many of the guys at Benson, hailed from the bayou country of Louisiana. Langford was a Viet Nam vet whose outstanding marksmanship skills had landed him in cadet academy, where he'd trained as a medic, then headed for the front lines. Jackson had witnessed the horrors of modern jungle warfare and sometimes felt the need to self-medicate. He'd been completely honest with me when he'd asked me to stand guard while he shot heroin each morning in the women's restroom at the Circle K. "Ah'm gonna kick this stuff, but Ah gotta take it easeh. If Ah go cold tuhrkeh, Ah won't be fit to woak." So here I loitered, faintly amused at the situation, but growing restless. Jackson emerged. "Thank you, Mahrteh. Ah won't ask again. Ah think this's the last time Ah'll be chippin' before woak. Bahy tomorrow Ah'll be in the cleah."

We strode quickly toward the waiting Suburban, me in my work boots, Jackson wearing the same pair of flip flops he'd shown up in a few days before. Each night after work, Jackson slept in the back of one of the Suburbans, and each morning he reported to work a little less strung out. Carvey assigned Jackson to work the brush crew along with me, Billy Joe McKenzie, and a motley assortment of burly, rowdy, and often downright ignorant coworkers. One hulking new hire sported a tattoo on his arm of a naked woman with a hatchet buried in her skull, a couple of arrows in her thigh, a dagger protruding from her chest, and a sword through her abdomen. On his wrist, I could see an inscription, but never got close enough to make out the words. I figured they said something like, "Let's Party."

Jackson was alright by me. He handled a chainsaw like a pro, even in those flip flops, and somehow managed not to lose his footing in the deep woods. Today would be payday, and tonight Jackson could buy a pair of boots and find a room to rent. Jackson was one of hundreds of other hopefuls streaming into Giddings in those days. Employers welcomed the tide of applicants—companies scrambled to fill their employee rosters. Lack of cash, lack of lodging, or in Jackson Langford's case, a heroin habit and lack of shoes? No problem. You're here, you're hired. And if you make it to your first paycheck, you're golden.

In August of 1979, when I began working in Giddings, the bucolic little town was fast becoming the epicenter of a historic oil boom known as the Austin Chalk. The Austin Chalk Trend is a stratum of limestone running from Texas to Mexico and into parts of Florida, and this geological formation got its name because of its outcrops around the city of Austin. Exposures of Austin Chalk are mainly visible in rock quarries, roadcuts, and streambeds where the water has eroded the soil. The outcrops can be seen around Dallas, and south along I-35 around Austin and San Antonio. Oilmen had been drilling the Chalk since the 1930s, but the fragility of the chalk and marl, and the porosity of the limestone layers rendered the process frustrating and cuss-worthy. The focus of attention was a strip about fifteen to twenty miles wide, anywhere from two hundred to eight hundred feet thick, and located at depths of eight thousand to twelve thousand feet. Over the years, vertical drilling occasionally resulted in huge gushers that poured out payloads like gangbusters, then quickly diminished.

In 1973, a wildcatter named Chuck Alcorn successfully drilled the deep chalk in the Giddings area. Alcorn poured acid down a near-dead well named No. 1 City of Giddings and brought out 300 barrels a day. He noticed that the oil coming from that well was golden, almost honey-colored. For generations, oilmen and geologists had known there was a treasure trove buried in the earth's crust in that region, but the delicate chalk formations created complications and risks that proved nearly insurmountable.

But in 1975, a geologist named Ray Holifield arrived in Giddings. Usually it takes a geophysicist to decipher the images culled from seismic readings. But Holifield was one of those rare geologists who can read and interpret seismic data, and he proved to be a master at it. Holifield knew how to pinpoint the fracture systems, or "sweet spots" in the chalk. He also discovered a way to use horizontal drilling to access the deep reservoirs of oil, and found ways to use massive amounts of sand and water to bring the oil up from the fracture systems.

Drilling in the Chalk was expensive, with the average well costing about a half million dollars. Still, with Ray Holifield's technique, when oil companies drilled, the strikes yielded huge, steady payloads of honey-colored bounty that kept on producing. Three neophyte oil investors from Dallas kicked off the surge: Max Williams, a former pro basketball coach, Pat Holloway, a lawyer, and Irv Deal, a real estate developer. All three men worked with Ray Holifield, the magician of the Austin chalk. These guys mined their investment capital from wild card sources, including Mary Kay Cosmetics and New York real estate. A boomtown was born. With Holifield's guidance, Holloway's Humble Exploration, Deal's Windsor, and Williams' U.S. Resources hit gusher after gusher.

By spring of 1981, the Giddings boom would reach gold rush proportions. Dirt farmers morphed into millionaires in a few days' time. Millionaires got a leg up on becoming billionaires. Midland oilman Clayton Williams was a major player, along with locals such as Garland Gerdis, a cattleman and landowner. The Giddings oil patch attracted Kuwaitis, Canadians, high rollers flush from Alaska's North Slope, and anyone with the cojones and the cash to get in on the action. And all the major players hired Sam L. Benson and Associates, Surveyors and Engineers, to stake wells, and run pipeline, seismic, and perimeter surveys.

Over a period of about a year and a half, as OPEC ushered in a second round of major cost increases, world oil prices jumped from twelve to forty-one dollars a barrel, an astronomical price in those days. Thousands of people and over a hundred companies stampeded to work in the Giddings area. New arrivals slept in their cars or in tents short term, then scrabbled for longer-term housing while chasing their dreams of big bucks in the black gold business. One enterprising outfit converted overturned oil tanks into living spaces and rented them out to workers.

My work for Sam L. provided me a ringside seat to witness Texas oilfield history in the making. As one of the first women to work as a laborer in the Austin Chalk, I honed my technical skills amidst a climate of machismo. I cultivated the knack for keeping my cool in dangerous working conditions, and with rough-edged coworkers whose raging testosterone levels occasionally pushed them to violence. I developed the art of interacting with big city oil investors, notorious oilmen, and redneck rubes with finesse, and when the situation called for it, with my own brand of feminine ferocity.

When I first hired on, I worked twelve hours a day, seven days a week, for five straight weeks, got one weekend off, then resumed a seven-day schedule. At a certain point, I decided to reconcile with Jake. Since I still possessed the keys to the apartment we'd shared in Austin, I arranged to meet him there one night after work. Careful to arrive early, I brought along my wildly illegal Smith and Wesson .38 revolver, the one I'd bought for ten bucks back in Conroe.

I sat opposite Jake, loaded pistol in hand and aimed at his chest, while we talked. Finally, I forgave him and moved back in. We created some ground rules and some boundaries, and Jake never once stepped over the line.

The serial killer dream returned, and so did the one with the shark. Both had ceased when I'd hired on with Sam L., replaced by dreams of endless falling, or work-related nightmares featuring me stumbling and pitching face forward onto my still-running chainsaw blade. After the summer visit, when Derek had demanded I return Annie to him, I was bereft. Once a week I tried calling Derek's folks, asking to speak with my daughter, but Derek's mother continually refused, telling me that neither my ex-husband nor my daughter were available. Undaunted, I mailed letters to Annie in care of both grandparents, hoping some word might reach her. My heart ached for her. My first thought upon waking each morning was of Annie, and each night before I fell asleep, the yearning for my child filled my consciousness, often flooding my eyes with tears.

I pushed myself to continue rising at dawn, driving to Giddings, and powering through each workday. I'd gotten in on the ground floor of the Giddings oil boom. In the early days my employer, Samuel L. Benson and Associates, shared its building with Ray Holifield, and the new oil millionaires bustled in and out of the same doors we Benson employees used to access our office. The Austin Chalk boom taught me that multi-millionaires and billionaires, at least in the oil biz, tended to be unassuming—regular guys. For a time, we gassed up our crew trucks at Clayton Williams' oil company's pumps, down the road from the office. Filling the tanks took some time, so most of us would get out of the trucks and stand around in the parking lot. Sometimes we'd talk to the Clayton Williams employees, catching up on the latest news.

On those mornings, an older man with a touch of silver in his hair would amble out among us and engage in conversation. He was lean, and always wore a khaki shirt and pants, a well-worn pair of brown leather lace-up work boots, and a genial smile. Since he was so much older than most of us workers, I went out of my way to listen politely to everything he said. I never asked his name and he never asked mine, but over a string of mornings, the guy taught me a lot of really interesting things about how oil is extracted, how the topography of an area can be an indicator of where the pockets of oil and gas lie beneath the surface, and other cool stuff. The guy in khakis impressed me, because he spoke both English and Spanish fluently, and seemed to take particular care to talk with everybody on the lot each day. I felt he deserved respect for that, and figured he might be some old retired guy, or soon-to-be-retired guy. One morning, while walking back to the truck after chatting with the khaki-wearing guy, a young dude approached. "Looks like you're some kinda bigshot."

I stopped walking. "Whaddaya mean by that?"

He jerked his head in the direction of the old guy. "Well, I figure you got some kinda connections—every day I see ya, you're talkin' with Clayton Williams."

"What? You mean that old guy is Clayton Williams?" He smiled and nodded. My head almost exploded. I'd always thought of rich oilmen as city guys in pin-striped suits, sipping martinis and whiskey sours in Dallas and Houston. My encounters with Williams, one of the richest Texas oilmen of that era, taught me that he knew his business inside and out.

The Cottonwood Restaurant and Lounge in Fayette County was a popular spot for oil workers, and a favorite of Billy Joe's. Billy Joe, Jackson, Rebel, the dude with the psycho tat on his arm, Floyd, and I stopped by the Cottonwood for lunch and a couple of rounds of beers. Billy Joe asked for the check, and we all threw down cash to cover it. The guys jumped up and began traipsing out to the truck. I stayed behind to make sure the tip was adequate. Our server, a slim, pretty brunette around my age, began clearing the table. I added some bills to the pile, pushed them in her direction. Her wise brown eyes met mine, and she raised an eyebrow. "How'd you get that job?"

"They're hiring. You interested?"

"Might be."

"Talk to Phillip Carvey. Samuel L. Benson and Associates, in Giddings." I smiled. "It'd be cool to see another female working there." I smiled, stood up, headed for the door.

A few weeks later, as October gave way to November, Sam L. threw its first company party, a shrimp and crawfish boil in the Cajun tradition, with an open bar. All employees, supervisors, and clients had been invited to the wingding. Phillip told all of us to knock off work an hour or so early. Workers who lived in Giddings would go home, wash up, and change clothes before heading to the soiree. Since I lived in Austin, I'd brought along a pair of designer jeans, a silk blouse, and sandals to change into, and Jake planned to don his best cowboy shirt in the restroom at the office. Billy Joe's wife, Ruthie, invited me to use their house to get ready.

We located some property corners on a ranch near Winchester that morning, flagged some fence lines, and met with a representative from a major oil corporation, a tall, skinny engineer from Houston. As we prepared to measure a distance for the rep, he ran ahead of us uphill. I noticed his close-cropped black hair was damp with sweat, and he ran with arms raised and palms open, zigzagging slightly. Billy Joe nudged me with his husky arm, leaned in, and muttered, "Ah don' believe he'd suck one, but Ah'll bet he'd hoooold one in his mouth foah awhahle." He gave me another jab and giggled. "Wouldn' he, Mahrteh? Wouldn' he?" I cleared my throat and stepped away.

"Billy Joe, the man's an engineer. Give him a break."

Billy Joe snorted. "Engineeah? That boehy wouldn't make a good pimple on a REAL engineeah's ASS! Whahy, Ah bet when he was growin' up, his mama had to hang a hunk o' salt poak aroun' his neck so the dog'd play with him." I'd heard lots of Billy Joe's ludicrously folksy insults. But I'd also seen his scrapbook of violent felonies, and heard him revel in his ignorant motives and swell with pride at the prison time he'd served.

The engineer collected his data and exited the pasture. We toiled on, skipping lunch. Around mid-afternoon, Billy Joe fired up the Suburban and peeled out of the main gate onto the gravel road. He slapped a tape into the stereo, maxed it to ninety decibels: Hank Williams Junior's "Whiskey Bent and Hell Bound."

Billy Joe's hands caressed the steering wheel. He smiled, adjusted the rearview so he could address the troops. "Boehys, we gonna scoah some weed, and some Preludins foah the comp'ny pahteh. Ah put in the oahdeh with my dealah two weeks ago. Can y'all say, 'Yee-haaw'?"

From the backseat, the crew howled in unison, "Yeeee-Haaaw!!!"

Billy Joe stomped the accelerator. The truck fishtailed, righted itself, shuddered, then sped onward, heavy-duty rear tires flinging what seemed like tons of dust, aggregate, and debris into the air. We stopped under a bridge, where the Colorado River flowed toward Smithville, Austin, and beyond. Trigger Jim, the driller who'd introduced himself to Billy Joe a few months before along a backroad, after he and his posse'd asked us for a spoon, stood waiting. His fellow roughnecks lurked nearby, looking grim and badass. Maybe he'd brought his crew along for backup, maybe they were on their way to work—I couldn't tell. Trigger Jim and Billy Joe strode to the water's edge, engaged in discussion. Billy Joe stuck something into the breast pocket of his frayed work shirt and walked back toward the Suburban, looking satisfied. "C'mon, y'all." He slid into the driver's seat, grabbed the wheel, and grinned. "We got the goddam Preludins! Now we goin' up t' Triggah Jim's house an' git the WEED."

We followed Trigger Jim's Bronco to his place, a cabin atop a hill near Winchester. Trigger Jim invited all of us inside, and I recognized the brunette with the thoughtful eyes, the waitress from the Cottonwood. "Hey, I'm Marti."

She smiled. "Suzie." We stepped away from the guys for a few minutes so we could talk in private.

"Hey, remember me? I work on this crew. We stopped into the Cottonwood a couple of weeks ago, and sat in your section. You asked me about the job. I was looking out for you to stop by the office and put in an application. Hey, why not come to the company party tonight? I'll give you directions, and when you get there, I'll introduce you to the supervisor. They're hiring."

She shook her head once. "Now that you mention it, I do remember you. I'm interested in the job. But I'd rather show up on Monday morning to apply."

"You're right, it makes more sense. When you apply, tell 'em you know me—tell Phillip Carvey you worked with me at Seismodyne. I'll back you up. Nice meetin' you, Suzie."

"You too, Marti."

As it turned out, Billy Joe invited Trigger Jim to the company party after scoring the weed. "Come on bahy, Triggah Jim! You can sling some dope in theah, afteh folks git all liquoahed up. Heh. Heh."

"Uh, yeah. Maybe." Trigger Jim didn't seem too keen on the idea. "I stepped on a copperhead last week, an' it bit m' foot. Ah'll hafta see how I feel tonight. Can't promise anything."

The company party took place in the backyard of a beer joint called Hawkeye's, and rapidly accelerated into a raucous redneck bacchanal. A huge cauldron of gumbo, and another reserved for boiling shrimp and crawfish, sat side by side in the center of the yard. They'd set up a canopy, with plenty of tables and folding chairs. Kegs of draft beer abounded, and bartenders stood by ready to pour a panoply of mixed drinks, including shots of mezcal. Strings of lights illuminated the scene. Samuel L. Benson was there, and so was his son, James Benson. Trigger Jim and Suzie showed up around ten o'clock. I felt grateful that she didn't want to be introduced to the boss.

I thought I was keeping a low profile despite having swallowed half a Preludin tablet, washing it down with RC Cola just before making the scene. I'd split my hit with Jake, and now felt ready to jump out of my skin. Preludin was the brand name for phenmetrazine, an appetite suppressant prescribed for morbid obesity. Today it's banned from the market. My coworkers had gobbled down whole tabs of it, and a few guys ingested two. Determined to take the edge off the popeyed agitation welling up in me, I guzzled one beer after another.

Phil Carvey's slimy brother, Lou, crept up on my blindside. "Havin' fun?"

I shot him a warning glare. Lou's dirty blonde hair hung down his back in a limp ponytail. Unfortunately, he never let his beer gut dissuade him from wearing shiny disco-style shirts, with the top three buttons undone to reveal plenty of porcine flesh. Unlike his brother Phil, Lou was not cool. At the office, he went out of his way to make lewd and highly unwelcome comments, which I steadfastly ignored. Tonight, in no mood for longsuffering, I eyed him, mentally gauging the weight of my draft beer mug and how much force it'd take for me to break his nose. No doubt the liquor'd rendered him incapable of picking up my signals, because he spoke again. "Wow, Sugar! You clean up good! I hardly reco'nized ya in them girly duds. Hee, hee." His bloodshot blue eyes wriggled over me, all the way down, then back up, coming to a stop at my rack. "Course I'd spot them headlights o' yours anytime. An' you're a—"

"Shut it, Lou." I made a chopping motion with my right hand. He flinched, then regained his cocky swagger. He swiveled his eyes over my torso again. "Okay, DICKweed. Enough! I will NOT tolerate this from you. Not tonight, not EVER again. From now on you will keep your eyes up here—" I held my hand at eye level, fingers together, as one might when preparing to administer a bitch slap. "Understand?"

Lou Carvey's lopsided grin dissolved, and I saw terror in his eyes. *Hey, I'm pretty good at this. Shoulda set this fucker straight a loooong time ago...* I held my hand level with my collarbone. "That's right. And you better make sure you NEVER let your eyes stray lower than THIS, or there'll be hell to pay. Y'hear me?"

Lou gulped. His chins quivered as he nodded a fervent affirmative.

"I wanna hear ya say it out loud. Do you understand?"

"Yup, uh, YES!"

"Good. We're done here." I turned, anticipating my grand exit, and saw why Lou's gleeful attempts at sexual harassment had disintegrated into paralyzing fright. Two of the biggest badasses in the company, Johnny Deveau and Matt Kendrick, had been standing behind me, fierce expressions on their faces, backing me up as I delivered my speech to Lou Carvey. I gave each of them a nod of acknowledgement, marched off to refill my beer mug, primarily so I'd have an excuse to carry it around. I figured I might need to brandish it as a weapon against the freak chance of Lou regaining his false bravado. I felt disappointed at discovering it wasn't me that struck fear in Lou's heart, but my coworkers. Still, I liked the idea of them backing me up—it was a sign of respect.

I hadn't worked alongside Deveau or Kendrick. But their reputations preceded them. I'd heard the stories swapped among Benson and Associates employees—men of a lower level of badassery. Goggle-eyed, furtively glancing to the left, then the right, these lesser dudes would warn newcomers not to mess with Deveau or Kendrick, and why. Lester Coggins, a scrawny Arkansas redneck with a scraggly beard, loved to expound on the peril of crossing

Mr. Deveau, who commuted to and from work on his chopped Harley Davidson. "Johnny Deveau, he's a EXPERT with a buck knahfe! He can toss a apple up in the air, whip that blade outta the sheath lahk lahtnin' an' cut that apple into itty bitty pieces before it hits the ground! Ah swear it! Seen it mahself." Johnny was a man of very few words, and seemed very laid back. But I knew Lou Carvey dreaded even the whisper of a chance of crossing him.

I'd heard stories about Kendrick, not only from Lester, but from other guys. Reportedly, Matt had been on a fast track to a pro baseball career when a sports injury'd snuffed out those gleaming aspirations. A heavy hitter in baseball, he'd retained nearly all the strength in his forearms, shoulders and biceps. Kendrick's rep among Sam L. employees was that nobody could throw a harder punch. Matt wore glasses, a fact that led many a drunken brawler in the Giddings bars to cross him. I'd seen it myself once, in a bar called the Derrick. A big bruiser had goaded Matt Kendrick, challenging him to a fight so repeatedly that Matt finally agreed. "Okay, but I gotta take my glasses off first."

The bully'd sneered at Matt. "Sure, Princess." Kendrick removed his wire rims and carefully set them down on the bar. Then he calmly headed for the exit. The tough-talking idiot followed. Outside, as soon as the door snicked shut, Matt clocked him. Knocked him out cold, flat on his back, then walked slowly back to the bar, put his glasses on, paid his tab, left a healthy tip, and departed. Another story about Kendrick involved him kicking the windows out of the backseat of a police car while handcuffed.

Jake and I left the party sober enough to traverse the distance to Austin without incident, catch some shuteye, and head back to work at dawn. As we approached Giddings, we caught a glimpse of Johnny Deveau silhouetted in the headlights, straddling his Harley in the emergency stopping lane. I slowed to see if he needed help. When our vehicle drew alongside the wild-haired Mr. D., I realized he'd actually parked the bike and appeared to be passed out over the ape-hanger handlebars. When Jake rolled down the window, Deveau roused himself from sleep, kickstarted his ride, and roared off toward the office.

The seven-day workweek began to take its toll, especially when the half-tab of Preludin wore off. I swore I'd never use stimulants at work again, and managed to keep my promise. I finished Sunday's shift by sheer force of will. That night, my sleeping brain entertained a phantasm no doubt born of frustration from overwork. In the dream, I grabbed a Stihl chainsaw from the back of one of the Suburbans in the Benson parking lot, walked into the office, and launched an assault on Lou Carvey, cutting him into neat horizontal slices. I woke up feeling strangely satisfied with my gory achievement, but relieved that the scene ended before my dream self could butcher any more of the creeps employed at the company.

I missed my baby. The carefully suppressed yearning, like shrapnel, refused to stay buried within, and the intense pain of separation worked its way to the surface at regular intervals. Monday was one of those days when the agony, sharp as a surgeon's scalpel, lanced through me so that I could barely hold myself together. I charged up the stairs to the office, where Phil greeted me enthusiastically. "Hey Marti, Suzie Judson just left." I slowed my pace.

"Yeah?"

Phil's smile widened. "We hired her. You know Suzie? She worked with you at Seismodyne, right?"

"Oh, yeah! Suzie, right, we've worked together. She's steady."

Phil reached for a topographical map from one of the shelves. "I've always liked the idea of hiring female surveyors. You're the first, an' you worked out just fine. You can match any man, toe to toe. Now we got Suzie." He stared at the topo map, but I could easily see his mind was somewhere else. "Back in the day, I tried to get my wife, Donetta, to work on a crew with me. She didn't want to."

He shrugged. "Turns out she's made a career of helping kids, and I'm proud to be her partner. So far, we've adopted seven. Foster kids—the ones the system labels as incorrigibles. Donetta's got a gift. No child belongs in the system."

"Wow, that's—that's beautiful, Boss."

Phil held up a hand, as if to wave away my admiration. "Aaww, it's nothin'. Anyhow, I appreciate ya, Marti. And Suzie, too. In my way o' thinkin', women tend to be organized and efficient. I look forward to hiring more."

That night, as the serial killer nightmare began snaking its way through my neural pathways to create another fright parade, the phone rang, rattling me out of fitful slumber. Jake turned, but didn't awaken. The clock on the bedroom dresser read 3:00 a.m. I walked into the living room, flipped on the lights, picked up the receiver. "Hello?"

"Marti, this is Derek."

"Uh-huh." *What now?*

"I need you to take Annie for a while."

My heart swelled, and I felt my breathing speed up. As the non-custodial parent, with no rights at all, I couldn't afford to ask questions, feared being cut off from the tenuous chance of seeing my child again. "Oh, okay. Sure." I held my breath.

"Good, she needs you now. And—I need some time to myself. To process. See, when I gave you a chance at visitation last summer, I, uh...I got married. Her name's Wendy. I took her on a cruise for our honeymoon. While Annie was with you."

I exhaled. "Oh. Yeah? That's nice."

"At first everything went great. Wendy was perfect, such a loving mother."

I felt the scalpel of pain. "Oh. Uh-huh?"

"But, see—Wendy was married before. To a big cocaine dealer. And she had a, a habit. I couldn't keep her supplied like he did.

Anyway, she drank. A LOT. And she'd BLACK OUT, see, and—well, you've heard of battered wives? Well, there are battered husbands, too, and I'M one of them. She'd get drunk and black out and ATTACK me. It was horrible."

The pain scalpel twisted inside me as I thought of my little girl being subjected to domestic violence and chaos. "Derek, did she... hurt Annie?" I held my breath again.

"No. No, that never happened. But Wendy scared her." He paused a moment. "Anyway, Annie's fine now. Wendy's gone, and Mom n' Dad're helping me take care of her. What I need is to get some time to recover from what I've gone through. I need some alone time. Like I said, to process."

Anger bubbled up, threatened to shape itself into words I'd regret later. I pushed it down. "That must've been so hard for you."

"It was. I'm still shattered."

Now I felt elated. A chance to see Anne Marie again. "Derek, I'd be happy to help. I'll drive. I'll apply for a leave of absence from work, and I'm pretty sure I can get there in a few days." My mind reeled at the possibility that Annie'd been hurt and Derek hadn't told me. I began to wonder if this situation might give me a chance to sue for custody, or at least visitation.

"Okay. Just hurry, will ya?"

"I'll come as fast as I can. Goodnight, Derek."

I set the receiver in its cradle, flipped off the light, and sat down on the couch till my body stopped shaking and I'd quelled the urge to break down sobbing. Then I went back to bed and an hour or so of dreamless sleep before the alarm went off. On the way to work, I told Jake about Derek's phone call. "I'm going to ask Phil for a leave of absence. If he won't give it to me, I'll have to quit. Maybe I can hire back on later."

"Aw, Marti. Whatever it takes. I know I ain't no PRIZE, but I'm fully employed and I care about Annie. I'll help you in any way I can."

"Thanks, Jake."

When I arrived at the office, I asked Phil for a moment in private. Very succinctly I told him about my situation, my daughter, and the struggles I faced. His reaction surprised me. "Well, you better get on the road tomorrow. Work a full day today. Take Jake with ya, too. He can help you drive. I'll give y'all a week off, with per diem. When you get back, see how your baby's doing. She may need you full-time for a stretch, and if so, I can give you a two-month leave of absence with per diem. After that, the per diem'll dry up. But I can promise you a job when you come back."

I thought of it as luck, my getting this break from my supervisor. Back then, I didn't realize that Samuel L. Benson and Associates was a de facto family, a dysfunctional one, but one that took care of its own. Besides, aren't all families dysfunctional? I stepped out of my meeting with Phillip Carvey filled with joy and hope, yet struggling to manage nearly overwhelming feelings of grief and loss. On the way down the stairs to the parking lot, I passed Johnny Deveau coming up. He gave me a collegial nod. I was working on Billy Joe's crew again, this time in Caldwell County. When I reached the Suburban, all my coworkers sat waiting. Billy Joe turned the key in the ignition, revved the V-8, and began transporting us to the worksite. I fixed my eyes on the centerline of the road ahead, trying to keep my face blank.

When we reached the site of our perimeter survey, Billy Joe parked the truck, then turned to me, a slaphappy redneck grin plastered all over his face. "YOU LOOK LAHK HEY-ULL! What was you an' Phillip talkin' about, anehway? You gonna quit this sumbitch and be a SECretareh? Woman, you'd make a piss-poor office gal." He shook his head in mock dismay.

My face felt hot, and my breath seemed to freeze in my lungs. I couldn't hold it anymore, so I told Billy Joe what was going on. The short version, but I told him about the psychiatrist father-in-law, and the corporate lawyer, and how I was saving all my money to get an attorney and fight for custody. The whole crew heard me, but I'd passed the point of caring. I crossed my arms over my chest and stared straight ahead, out the windshield at the big blue Texas sky.

"Ah'll kill 'im foah ya." Billy Joe's aw-shucks-ma'am-Ah'm-jes'-funnin' tone and lopsided grin didn't hide his earnestness, his gleeful willingness to commit murder. To commit murder for a FRIEND. And for a fleeting moment, the offer seemed attractive. I looked at him, but didn't say a word.

Billy Joe met my gaze and held it. "Ah said Ah'll kill the Yankeh summabitch. Ah'll drahve up theah an' do it f' fifteh dollahs an' a case o' beah." He stared at me for a beat, then haw-hawed his good ol' boy guffaw. All right, Y'ALL, let's git to WOAK, now. C'mon!!"

Jake and I took turns driving from Austin in the Sun Belt to the college town where I grew up. The city was only a few hours' drive from one of the Great Lakes, in the Rust Belt. Auto manufacturing plants and steel mills had all but shut down in many areas, decimated by the recession. Thanks to the university where my dad was a tenured English professor and head of the Humanities Program, my hometown maintained its economy. We drove the Toyota Land Cruiser that we now leased to Benson and Associates. While Jake and I'd been split up, I'd purchased an old 1972 Plymouth Fury III, one in much better shape than the battered old heap Billy Castor loaned me to drive to Conroe when I hired on with Seismodyne. Still, I didn't want to risk a roundtrip in the older ride.

We spent the night at a motel in the city, then stopped by my parents' place that morning, so I could introduce them to Jake. Derek had told me to come to his folks' estate in the afternoon. I hadn't told my parents much about Jake, only that I had a male friend and business partner. I'd told Jake plenty of things about my parents. He knew my father was a WWII veteran and a professor of English, specializing in British literature. I'd told him that my mother was active in the National Organization of Women and the League of Women Voters. As we pulled into the driveway of the house where I'd grown up, Jake sat up very straight. "When I get nervous, my grammar sometimes slips." He clenched his teeth, then exhaled sharply. "Hope I don't say, 'ain't' in front of your dad."

"Don't worry. My parents aren't intellectual snobs. They're nice people."

As I watched my folks draw Jake into conversation, setting him at ease and sincerely appreciative as he told them how he'd served in the Navy in Viet Nam, then majored in biology at the University of Texas, I felt proud of my heritage. And grateful for my parents' continued love and support through heartbreak. At first, I'd been too ashamed to tell them what Derek and his Dad had done to bully me into signing over custody. If they'd known, maybe they could have helped me. Most likely not, I reckoned. Derek's dad had a big corporation lawyer and the laws concerning mental illness had been stacked against me.

But working in the oil field had given me confidence, and through a series of telephone conversations, I'd eventually told Mom and Dad everything. "We're with you," my mother'd said over the phone, her voice wavering slightly. "I'm so sorry, I didn't understand." My father's voice had sounded deep and strong and clear. "We want you to speak from strength. We'll do all we can to support you in your efforts. You are not alone."

I drove the Land Cruiser to Derek's folks' place, feeling good about rolling in behind the wheel of a recently purchased, still shiny vehicle. I reminded myself that I now would be speaking from strength, loved by my parents equally as much as Derek was loved by his. Annie stood at the door of Derek's folks' house, smiling and waving excitedly. My spirits soared as I rushed to her, dropped to a crouch, embraced her, and felt her little arms around my neck.

The journey began. During the next few months I spent with Annie in Austin, I cherished the rare and precious moments, and the opportunities, to simply be a mom. I now earned enough money to cook a lavish Thanksgiving dinner for her in my home. I enjoyed the privilege of baking her a fancy birthday party cake, decorating it, and watching her blow out the candles. My prosperity enabled me to buy her any Christmas gift she wanted. But this year, I knew the joy of being present, watching her tear the ribbon and wrapping off each package under the tree, eager to discover what lay within. And we'd decorated that tree together, in my home.

New Year's Eve isn't a children's holiday. But when the clock struck midnight on January 1st, 1980, I celebrated quietly in our little apartment. My daughter slept soundly in her bedroom, safe and warm, surrounded by all her favorite dolls and stuffed animals. Jake and I sat on the couch, speaking in murmurs so as not to wake Anne Marie. We discussed our bright future. The Austin Chalk continued to boom. By 1980, local bank deposits in Giddings totaled a hundred million dollars, a staggering figure by pre-inflation standards. Filled with optimism, I dared to entertain a flicker of hope: that Derek might willingly concede custody to me, or at least grant me joint custody, without litigation.

When we'd first arrived in Austin, Annie'd found her room ready and waiting. She'd settled in nicely, but one night as we read storybooks and prepared for sleep, she asked me to sleep with her. I promised to lie down with her until she fell asleep. We resumed reading, but after a few pages, she extended an arm and pushed the book away. Her brow furrowed, she'd said something like, "Mommy was bad." At first, an electric jolt of shame and fear shot through me, because I thought she was talking about me. I didn't say a word, but gently listened. She continued. "Mommy hits Daddy. She's mean every time she drinks." I realized Annie was talking about Wendy, Derek's second wife.

"Honey, did she hit you?" My mind recoiled in horror at the thought of what my baby daughter might have lived through.

"No. I ran away and hid. When you're little, you can do that." I held back tears. *Be strong. Be fierce.* "Mommy—Wendy..." I noticed she was working her way through this, carefully correcting herself. "Wendy's gone now, but Daddy says he misses her and wants to take her back." Her eyes expressed a deep knowing, a burden of understanding far too heavy for her. Annie was worried, maybe even terrified that Wendy would return, and that she would eventually have to return to sharing a life and a home with her father and his raging, abusive new wife. My thoughts flitted back to how Annie'd referred to Wendy as, "Mommy," and how she seemed determined to correct that. It struck me that Derek, and likely his entire family, had programmed Anne Marie to address the new woman in his life with that title. Derek's clan had no doubt worked together as a unit, not only to replace me, but to erase me. *But I am here. I am alive. They can never erase me.*

"I'm here, Annie, Mama's here. I love you with all my heart."

"I love you Mama." I held her. We sat in silence a moment. "Mama, why did you go to Texas?" *How can I tell her?* I felt a stab of grief. *I can't. Maybe someday, when she's grown. But not now.*

"I had to go. I came to Texas so I could build a home and a future. For you. Do you feel at home now, with me?" Words failed me, and the flood of tears surged within, battering away at the dam of willpower that held them back. I looked down at my little girl. She struggled, managed a brave smile. Tears came to her eyes as she said the words.

"Oh, but Mama I need you! All the time!" And the dam broke. I cried, and she cried, and we held each other, sobbing. She gently pulled away, wiped her eyes with her hands, and the brave smile returned. "I couldn't hold it anymore Mama, and neither could you. But it's alright now. We're together." I smiled at her. *Together, we are the Brave Smile Family. I will fight for her as long as I have breath in my body. And beyond.*

Galvanized by that moment, I made my 1980 New Year resolution: to fight, but in a way that would not traumatize my child. I needed to be smart. And I'd sought legal counsel. The trouble was, Texas didn't share reciprocity with the state where my divorce from Derek had occurred. I would need to find an attorney in that state. Knowing that custody battles can be vicious, I hoped to spare my daughter from the anguish involved by seeking an amicable agreement with Derek. I began to consult with attorneys in Texas about my chances. I'd already been examined by a psychiatrist who concluded I was most likely not bipolar or suffering from any other mental illness. The attorneys advised me that since I'd signed over custody and then left the state, it'd be an uphill battle for me. Back in those days, stigma surrounded any divorced woman, and an especially heavy stigma surrounded a woman who did not have custody of her child.

In early January, Derek called and abruptly informed me he'd be arriving in Austin in three days. "I'm driving down, and I'll call you as I approach your apartment building. Be ready with all Annie's things packed. Don't try to stall around, it'll only make things harder." I made the most of my remaining time with my daughter, focused on savoring the moments leading up to letting go. Careful to stay light and upbeat while preparing both Anne Marie and myself for the upcoming separation, I refused to adopt anything but an optimistic outlook on the future. I told myself I'd see her soon, maybe next time we'd be together year-round. But underneath it all, a sense of apprehension grew. On the third day, around noon, when Annie and I'd gotten back from the playground and were making peanut butter and jelly sandwiches, the phone rang and I answered. Derek told me he was minutes away, calling from a phone booth at a filling station on South Lamar. Dread like a lump of ice leapt into the pit of my stomach, and I recognized the familiar impulse to grab my child and run—to Houston, to Mexico, to Australia maybe. But I knew better: better for her, better for the big picture.

I did the right thing. I mustered all the bouncy enthusiasm I could, slapped on a big smile. "Hey, Honey! Your Dad is on his way!"

She smiled and clapped her hands. "Daddy!" *Yes, we are the Brave Smile Family. I am the Brave Smile Mother, and my baby needs me, both now and all the time. I will not fail her...*I continued to exhort myself as I pulled open the kitchen drawer where I kept the Glad Sandwich Bags, pulled one out, slipped Annie's freshly made PB & J sandwich inside, sealed it, and packed a couple of homemade chocolate chip cookies into a second bag. *Brave Smile.* I took Anne Marie's hand in mine, walked into her bedroom, picked up her neatly-packed suitcase and a cloth bag filled with her favorite toys, and led her out into the foyer. I kissed her lightly on the cheek and we shared a goodbye hug.

Brave. I slung the toy bag over my right shoulder and clasped the suitcase in my right hand. I opened the door with my left, and stepped out of the second-floor apartment with Anne Marie by my side. A two-door sedan pulled into the parking lot below and sat idling. I could see Derek sitting at the wheel. He motioned to me to hurry. *Smile.* I took a deep breath, held Annie's right hand in my left, and slowly walked down the stairs, across the parking lot toward Derek's car. Somehow, I hadn't noticed the woman sitting in the front seat on the passenger side until she stepped out of the car, motioning Annie to climb inside the backseat. Derek opened his door, stood. "Annie, get in quick. Let's go!" He smiled encouragingly at our daughter.

The woman smiled at Anne Marie. "Hi Honey! Remember me?" The frozen ball of dread lurched in my stomach, and grew bigger. *So it's her. They've reconciled.*

Annie nodded. "Hi Wendy." Her voice sounded small and thin. She let go of my hand, boarded the vehicle. Leaving the engine idling, Derek walked around the front of the sedan and motioned me to hand him the bags. I complied. He turned and loaded them into the trunk, then jumped back in the driver's seat. As the car pulled away, I smiled and waved at Annie, framed in the backseat window. She waved back at me, smiling, until the car turned the corner and she disappeared from view. For a moment or two, I kept on waving. *We are the Brave Smile Family, Annie. You and me...*I squared my shoulders and ascended the staircase toward the apartment.

After allowing myself one full day to cry, I employed my only positive coping mechanism. I returned to work at Samuel L. Benson and Associates, Surveyors and Engineers. All my attempts to reach out to Annie via phone failed. The only number I'd ever had was Derek's parents, and they steadfastly refused to tell me where their son and my daughter resided. I had to assume they'd be living on his folks' acreage in one of the detached guest houses, but I knew I could be wrong. They could have helped him to settle elsewhere with his second wife and Anne Marie. When the pain pushed its way in, I reached for a negative coping mechanism, alcohol. I began to think of it as medicine, for emergencies, but deep down, I knew that drinking didn't help.

At work, my status improved. Phil Carvey transferred me off Billy Joe's crew and gave me a chance to move up from brush cutter and head chainman on seismic or pipeline, to rodman on Harley Heenehan's crew and others that specialized in perimeter surveys. Today, thanks to GPS, two workers can go into an area and gather all the data. Back then, a crew needed several workers. A party chief supervised the team. The chief of party, as he or she is still sometimes called, interpreted and recorded all data, and in our work, confirmed the location of property corners, landmarks, and bodies of water that tied into the survey. We needed to gather plenty of info for the Railroad Commission, the authority on who gets to drill where and when.

An instrument man was responsible for collecting data with the use of a telescope—theodolite, transit or distance meter, depending on what kind of job the crew was doing. The instrument man would set up a tripod over each exact point or station in the loop. The points were designated by a nail or piece of iron rebar driven into the ground, for instance. Once the survey instrument was mounted and leveled on the tripod and over the point, the instrument man would shoot the angles and distances.

A rodman's duty was to set up the special, high-tech reflecting mirrors on a leveled tripod at the different stations so that the distance meter's laser could bounce off the mirrors' surfaces and get a distance reading. The mirrors also served as a target for turning the angles. The rodman's work involved moving the mirrors from point to point, setting them up, until the crew could complete the loop. Most of our surveys tended to be simple enough. Sometimes, if we needed to record the curvature of a road, the survey'd get more complicated. Surveyors still use the reflecting mirrors and tripods today. Surveying involves basic trigonometry, and although math hadn't been my best subject in school, my laser-sharp eyesight and willingness to take initiative helped me to compete and advance.

Harley Heenehan, a sturdy redneck with a ruddy complexion and a volatile temper, proved a decent guy to work with. But the instrument man, Junior Freeman, a ferret-faced, wannabe good ol' boy who spouted racist, misogynist, and homophobic slurs, comments, and jokes all day long, tried my patience. It struck me that Harley, my new crew chief, wasn't fond of Junior either, especially because the instrument man often appeared to be extremely allergic to work. If the weather turned even the tiniest bit unpleasant, Mr. Freeman would stage a one-man strike. Occasionally, a light mist prevented Junior from functioning. "It's rainin'," he'd whine, "Ah'm not gettin' outta the truck!" On days when the temperature didn't suit him, Junior'd shut down. "It's too damn COLD! I'm not gonna work till it warms up." Harley Heenehan's face inevitably turned beet red when Junior boycotted, and sometimes I could see his lips moving as he counted to ten. Thanks to Junior, our crew always rolled in late to the office.

And when Junior actually did venture from the shelter of our crew's Suburban, he worked at a glacial pace. Although exasperating, his behavior offered me an opportunity. A quick learner, I mastered the art of selecting the best vantage points for the shots, and the skill of setting up the mirrors at each station. While Junior dawdled, I'd scout out the terrain, set up the mirrors, cut away any branches that might obscure the mirrors from the telescope's crosshairs, then double back in time to observe Junior as he turned the angles. Over the month of January, while waiting for the instrument man's sluggish completion of his tasks, I arrived at a point where I felt confident I could do his job from start to finish.

Each day as we headed to the work site, Junior Freeman would run through his annoying collection of over-the-top racist asshole comments. And every morning and evening, without fail, he would slip in some bullshit about beating his wife. "Ah'm gonna beat my ol' lady's ass when I get home! Kick 'er ass, she'll stay in line, that's mah motto. Yessiree." Then he'd erupt into squeaks and wheezes of laughter, as if he juuust couldn't belieeeve how funny that was. Then he'd launch into a string of racist one-liners involving watermelon, Moon Pies, etcetera. Junior loved homophobic jokes referencing the AIDS crisis. Mr. Freeman hooted with delight when telling his woman jokes, too. Hooted, and then swiveled his bony neck to turn and ogle me. He rode in the front seat, across from Harley Heenehan, slapping his thigh as if to amplify the punchlines. Each day, from my spot in the backseat, I endured the cavalcade of idiocy from this cretin, eschewing commission of first-degree murder by focusing on keeping my machete blade razor sharp. *I'm gonna keep on sharpening it, keep it handy. Just in case I snap...*

286

That winter, Sam L. Benson and Associates had suffered a shortage of competent instrument men, which was, I figured, the only reason Harley Heenehan hadn't fired Junior—or joined me and his other hands in disemboweling him.

My moment arrived on a cold, gray, Tuesday morning, in the middle of a rush job. Heenehan drove the metallic green Suburban up to the top of a hill. We needed to get long shots on this loop, because the job involved completing a perimeter survey of a pool of different ranches. I'd already set up the mirrors and had returned to the truck. The wind picked up, and the sky seemed to be spitting sleet. Heenehan glared at Junior. "It ain't rainin', Freeman. Git on out there and turn the angles." Harley grabbed his field notebook and mechanical pencil, to jot down the data. He jumped out of the truck, leaned in, and through the open driver side door motioned to Junior, his voice a low growl. "Do it."

Junior, glib and breezy, stuck his nose in the air, crossed his arms over his chest, and dug in. "It's too cold, and too damn windy. Ah'm not workin' in this shit!" I could see Harley's neck turn red, then his face, from chin to hairline, the scarlet hue inching upward by degrees like mercury in a thermometer. Our crew chief's lips began moving, I could see him counting: five, six, seven...

I jumped out of the backseat, shut the door, walked around the front of the Suburban and stood beside the party chief. I cleared my throat, spoke loudly enough to be heard over the rising wind. "Boss, I'll turn those angles for ya."

Heenehan turned, looked at me. His lips stopped moving, then widened into a smile. He nodded, jerked a thumb toward the back of the truck. "Go ahead. If you can set up right, I'll let ya give it a whirl."

I opened the Suburban's back doors, pulled out the tripod and the theodolite case, carried the equipment to the station, and set up. My work setting up the mirrors had taught me how to use a bubble level, dig the tripod's "claws" into the ground to anchor and balance the setup, and more. Once I'd put the tripod in place, I unlatched the theodolite case and withdrew the scope. Then I set the theodolite on the tripod, balanced and centered it over the point. Heenehan checked out the setup, then took a step back, satisfied. I moved in and began turning the angles, first shooting the backsight, then the foresight. The wind screamed and blew harder, its icy edge seeming to slice into my eyes as I focused the scope's crosshairs. In spite of the wind's distortion of visibility, I did pretty well. In fact, Harley Heenehan's voice trembled ever so slightly when I'd completed the shots and he calculated my accuracy. "You turned 'em flat." He stared, slack jawed. "Flat." I smiled. In surveying lingo, flat meant zero error.

Heenehan grabbed the front seat passenger-side door handle, jerked it open. He pointed at Junior Freeman. "Git out. Git in the backseat. I'm promoting Marti here to instrument man for the day. You're rodman."

I finished the day quickly and efficiently, and for the first time, our crew reached the office with time to spare. Heenehan charged up the stairs to show Phil Carvey the day's field notes. I'd completed the day's work with nearly non-existent error, at least according to field calculations. Later, when the supervisors fed the data into the computers, the results showed I'd closed the loop with an astonishingly low margin of error. Carvey promoted me to instrument man, complete with a nice pay raise. He transferred Junior to another crew, and put Floyd on Heenehan's crew as rodman. Over the next few days, work became fast-paced and interesting. A couple of times, I thought I saw Junior skulking around the parking lot, looking at me sideways, jabbing some other goat-roper with his elbow, pointing at me and talking behind his hand. Overjoyed at no longer being exposed to all his bullshit, I never gave it a thought.

Payday rolled around, and I gathered with the other employees in the parking lot of the Sam L. office in Giddings, eager to collect my bigger, better paycheck. The company's ranks had swelled to nearly thirty crews, and the scuttlebutt among workers was that Samuel L. Benson, Senior, now busied himself with constructing a new office building on the outskirts of Giddings. The boomtown attitude filled the air and field personnel hustled back and forth. Guys gathered in groups, hanging out. My friend Jackson Langford approached me. "Hey, you're on the theodolite now, that's cool. Harley Heenehan's calling you "The Hawk.""

"Huh. That's cool. Tell you the truth, Jackson, I'm feeling good about it."

"Yeah, you should. Hey, I want you to know, I was on a crew with Freeman yesterday. All he talks about is how you sneaked in and stole his job. He keeps on sayin' you ain't nothin' but a dumb broad, a sleazeh blonde piece o' ass, shit like that."

"Oh yeah?" I looked across the parking lot, saw Junior pointing at me and talking to Elrod. My long strides closed the distance between me and the weasel-faced, bigoted instrument man. Elrod cringed and scurried away. I stood, hands on hips, and glowered at Junior. He flinched, rubbed his scraggly beard stubble, narrowed his eyes, and croaked, "Ah NEVER said NOTHIN' lahk you think! Ah wouldn't even call my WAHF a dumbass broad. HONEST!!" Weeks of stupid, racist, woman-hating, anti-gay blather from Junior'd kept my rage simmering gently on the back burner. But the comment about his wife triggered my fury, and I backhanded him. He fell down flat on his ass, bug-eyed, mouth opening and closing in silent disbelief. I lunged, stood over him, and began smacking him with the back of my left, then my right—bitch-slapping him. Sweet justice for every time he'd used the B-word to describe his wife, or women in general. Payback for every time that dickhead used the C-word, or the N-word, or laughed at punchlines about AIDS. Each time my hand made contact with his scrubby little beard, I felt a jolt of elation. *Payback. Yeah, Motherfucker, how d'ya like THAT?!*

All of a sudden I felt hands grabbing my shoulders, pulling me off Junior. I heard a low voice near the right side of my face. "Marti! Ol' Man Benson's here. In the parking lot." Johnny Deveau had intervened, his timing perfect. He likely spared me from being fired, I realized. *Wow. I really lost it there for a minute...*I sauntered back to the other end of the parking lot, Deveau and Kendrick flanking me. When we'd reached a safe corner away from the crowd, they teased me relentlessly. Johnny rolled his eyes. "Muhammad Marti!"

Kendrick chuckled. "You're packin' some power. But you can't go around SLAPPIN' all the time. Cowboy up an' learn how to make a fist. You learn how to box, I'll bet money on you any day."

Deveau laughed softly. He made a fist, extended his forearm. "See that? You make a box with your fist, and then—" Johnny followed through, punching the air. "We can coach ya."

"I'm okay. As long as I can pick up a rock, or a piece of pipe, I think I've got it covered. For now, anyway."

Kendrick and Deveau shook their heads slowly, in mock outrage. Kendrick shoved his hands in his pockets. "Hmmph. Suit yourself." Deveau gave me a half-smile, and nodded acknowledgement. We headed in to the office to pick up our paychecks. Man-sized paychecks.

CHAPTER 11

BIRDS OF A FEATHER

"HOTTER'N' A FRESH-FUCKED MINK!" BIRD HOLLERED. "WHEN can we crack a brewski?" Bird, our rodman, newly-arrived from Willacooche, Georgia, constantly bitched about the heat, staggered in hungover, and whenever possible imbibed on the job. Who could blame him for kvetching? Bird'd only been with us a few days, so he hadn't yet become inured to the infernal heat that dogged us that summer.

During those days, the Lone Star State seethed and simmered under historic drought conditions and record high temperatures during what would become known as, "The 1980 U.S. Heat Wave." From June 23rd through August 3rd, in Dallas the mercury climbed daily to well over a hundred degrees, culminating in an all-time high of 113 degrees on June 26th and 27th of that year.

For all of us laboring twelve-hour shifts in the Giddings oil patch, alcohol and drug use became our common route to respite from weather conditions that felt positively molten. Well, maybe it was only an excuse to get loaded. After all, we were mere surveyors. We weren't roughnecks in searing steel hard hats, stuck on one of those broiling hot drilling pads, tripping pipe. The hard-packed caliche drilling pads maintained temperatures as high as 120 degrees during the heat wave. Most of the roughnecks I knew needed additional assistance—meth or heroin—to keep going.

Still, the blazing sun pounded steadily down on our backs as we set up tripods, and dust blew up off the gravel roads, clogging throats and obscuring vision so that it sometimes took twice as long to get the shot. And strangely, the drought did nothing to diminish the tick, gnat, and mosquito populations. They multiplied, exponentially, in the shallow stock tanks and listless sandy creeks.

I slathered on sunscreen obsessively, yet each night I returned home with a blister under my right eye from the heat radiated by my theodolite's telescopic site. Finally, I took to smearing zinc oxide under that eye, which solved the problem, but invited snarky comments from coworkers about my "eye shadow."

One of the toughest jobs that summer had been a pooled lease on which one side of the perimeter was railroad track. The heat waves distorted the backsight and foresight—the fluorescent-orange-painted lathes we used seemed to explode into squiggly fragments, like flames fanned by a psychedelic breeze.

To make matters worse, a half-mile stretch of track'd been littered with the putrefying corporeal remains—limbs, hooves, and hunks of hide—of some unfortunate bovine mowed down by a freight train several days earlier. Somehow, in spite of the obvious olfactory and visual distractions, I managed to close the loop with a very small margin of cumulative error.

Hard-won results such as those, earned during such mirage-laden, heatstroke-wielding workdays, lent longevity to my nickname: "The Hawk." Even my most badass, misogynistic co-workers gave me grudging respect. Still, in the arena of bridging the gender gap, I noticed room for improvement. To many of my peers and some of my supervisors, I was still just a "little ol' gal." I didn't care. My paychecks equaled those of my peers.

"Remember, y'all, no beers till afternoon. We've got company on this job." Jake, soft-spoken, authoritative, reminded us that our present standard of moderation with regards to alcohol—no beer till 10:30 a.m.—had been elevated to the pre-drought, pre-heat wave level. Weather conditions inflicted enough suffering that we felt entitled to swill beer, smoke joints, and in some of the more extreme cases, eat peyote or psilocybin mushrooms during the course of completing a perimeter survey. However, today would be different. Oh, yeah.

Today, for some god-awful reason, we'd been mandated to collaborate with two supervisors, Jim Presley and Augie Sellers. Presley, a civil engineer, was a good ol' boy from Tennessee who steadily cracked the whip over field personnel, cadging himself a reputation as a hardass. Augie was different. He'd been one of us until a promotion lifted him out of the searing sun and into the air-conditioned glory of the home office. Augie hailed from South Carolina. He dipped snuff constantly, and his consumption skyrocketed when he felt nervous. Now that Augie'd risen to management status, he appeared to exist in a state of perpetual angst over his responsibilities; some mornings, as he rushed around the office preparing work orders and printing out documents, his lower lip bulged with Copenhagen. On top of that, he'd swill coffee and eat peanuts simultaneously. Still, we liked Augie—he was okay.

The job, another lease perimeter, lay near Bryan-College Station, off a bumpy gravel road. Around 8:00 a.m., Jake, Bird, and I pulled our Chevy Suburban up to the gate indicated on our aerial map, then sat with the motor idling so we could keep the air on. The "bosses" arrived around ten minutes later in a Ford Bronco. Since I rode shotgun, I jumped out and opened the gate so we could enter the pasture. "Hold it, gal!"

This from Presley. "We're not drivin' in here. Landowners' request. We're gonna walk the fence line on this one."

I shrugged, walked to the back of the Suburban, grabbed my theodolite case, shouldered the tripod, and headed for the nearest flagged fence corner. I jumped over the fence and strode to the designated point of departure, a flagged nail driven into the ground and a "hub," a wooden stake pounded into the hard-baked earth beside it. I anchored the tripod by tamping down my booted foot on each of the steel "claw feet" at the bottom of the three wooden legs. I leveled it, using the built-in bubble level, then leaned over, unlatched the theodolite case, pulled out the instrument and mounted it on the tripod.

Head bent, I began leveling the theodolite. At first, I chose to ignore a strange swishing sound in the pasture's desiccated grass. When the noise persisted, I idly passed it off as the sound of Presley's long stride and figured he'd soon arrive to dog me. Annoyed, I inwardly rankled at his officious and sexist demeanor. *'Hold it, gal,' my ass! A hayseed with a civil engineering degree...is still a hayseed. Fuck him!* My hackles rose as I felt Presley looking over my shoulder. *What a dick! Is there no limit to his harassment?*

Suddenly, hearing a bizarre and primeval thumping sound, I froze. The velvety staccato reminded me of the rapid beats of mysterious jungle drums, or a runaway heartbeat. Hangover-induced irritability morphed into terror. Although my feet seemed rooted in place, I instinctively leaned forward, wrapping my arms around the expensive theodolite in order to protect the high-powered Nikon scope I'd come to love so dearly.

The pulsating rhythm increased in volume and tempo. I jerked my head around to see what the fuck was going on and found myself locking pupils with a gargantuan bird whose forest green plumage shimmered iridescent in the blazing sunlight. The huge bird's head drew back suddenly, then lunged forward, pecking at the theodolite and grazing my left hand in the process. I jumped straight up in the air but somehow managed not to scream. Gathering my composure, I detached the theodolite, snapped it back in its case, snatched it up, and hustled toward the fence corner with it. Once I'd set the instrument case on the safe side of the barbwire, I whirled and returned for the tripod, which I threw over my shoulder. I then retreated toward the fence, waving my arms wildly at the huge bird in a witless attempt to drive it away.

Now, standing with ample barbwire between me and what my instinct told me was a hulking raptor, my adrenaline level dropped enough that I could hear the raucous guffaws. I whipped around to catch a glimpse of Augie Sellers, doubled over with hilarity, his plump sides heaving, spewing chunks of Copenhagen from his lower lip. "Damn, Marti, but you c'n jump high! Wassamatter? Ostrich scare ya?" Behind him, Jake and Bird stood red-faced, arms crossed over their chests, trying hard not to snicker but failing miserably in that department. Presley stood a few paces to the left of the others, hands on hips, staring at some distant horizon and slowly shaking his head in disapproval until finally he sighed and shot a glance in my direction. He chuckled sarcastically.

"Well, this is what we get when we cave in to affirmative action, men. We get women who want to lead on the dance floor. We get lesbian bra-burnin' treehuggers takin' over the world and calling themselves, 'Ms.'s,' and 'feminists.' And right here on this very job, we get an instrument-PERSON who creates a work stoppage due to skittishness about POULTRY!"

I ignored the cold rage building in my sternum, steeling myself not to rise to the gender bait, and cleared my throat. "Er, but it's pretty big poultry, Mr. Presley." I straightened myself to my full height and thrust out my chin defiantly. "Look, I didn't want it to damage the theodolite. I can turn angles with the transit, okay? Transits cost way less, so if the bird pecks it, it won't cost the company so much money." I brushed past the supervisors, nodded to my coworkers, and strode to the Suburban. I grabbed the transit case, shouldered its wooden tripod, and marched back to the fence corner, noticing on the way that the enormous "poultry" was no longer visible. The pasture had shed its menace.

Presley advanced a step toward me when I arrived with the equipment. "All right now, Missy, let a man take over," he smirked, "I'll show y'all how it's done." Gleefully he stooped, created an opening in the barbwire by stepping on it with one foot, and ducked through. Once inside the pasture, Presley motioned for me to pass him the tripod and transit. He set up the equipment, centering it over the point with a plumb bob. A plumb bob is a weight made of lead, with a shiny brass exterior and a sharp point at the end. It's attached to a string, or plumb line. The polished brass caught the sunlight and flashed brilliantly as Presley completed the setup with a flourish. He returned his plumb bob to its leather holster, which clung smartly to the backside of his work belt.

Presley stepped up to the scope, rubbing his hands together. "Piece o' cake." He turned back toward us and grinned. "See? Nothin' to be afraid of! Now, rodman, get down there and set me a backsight." Our supervisor swung one hand behind him in a vague gesture. Bird ambled off to grab a hammer and a fluorescent-painted lathe. "Hurry it up now! Look sharp!" Presley barked at no one in particular, obviously relishing his power. He crouched and looked into the transit scope. I wondered if he had any idea how much he pissed off his underlings, and I marveled that he didn't seem to care.

But since Presley had in fact pissed off all of his underlings, including Augie Sellers, in the course of his illustrious career, none of us present that day had any desire to warn him about the three over-sized, iridescent-green-throated, ostrich-similar-yet-not-ostriches now galloping across the pasture. Several yards behind the first three, zipping along, came another trio of feathered aggressors. The birds moved like lightning, surrounding Presley in the blink of an eye. The flock now ominously regarded the civil engineer, cocking their heads, scraping their huge feet in the dry grass, apparently fascinated by his shiny brass plumb bob, his mirrored, steel-rimmed sunglasses, and his western shirt with its shiny chromed snaps.

Presley, having noticed the "poultry," stiffened his back, assumed his best stance, and attempted to stare each bird down, one at a time. This maneuver worked for about ten seconds; then one green-feathered head bobbed twice and shot forward, pecking at Presley's plumb bob case. Another strike went for his buttons. Now several beaks pecked simultaneously at his gleaming, mirrored, state trooper-esque shades.

Presley stifled a scream, desperately fending off the beaked assaults by ducking, bobbing, weaving. He spun, scooped up the oak tripod, transit still mounted on it, slung it over his shoulder, dropped to a crouch, and took one long stride backward, away from the point of departure and down the fence line. Maybe he was still trying to stare them down, or simply was loathe to retreat and surrender his backside to their relentless beaks. Whatever his intention, the birds reacted by unanimously taking one long stride forward, closing the distance between themselves and their hapless target.

Presley countered with three bold steps backward. The flock swiftly matched that with three equally bold steps toward Presley. Presley adjusted his grip on the tripod, whirled around, and began high-stepping down the fence line, his long-necked pursuers close on his heels. His gait quickened until he broke into a run, emitting a high-pitched wail as he looked back to see the eager beaks of the raptors closing in. The rest of us stood, transfixed, nearly stupefied by the unlikely scene unfolding right before our eyes.

Jake broke the spell. "C'mon, we gotta help him. Everybody get in the truck." We ran for the Suburban, jumped in, and slammed the doors shut. Jake started the engine and took off, steering the truck alongside the fence line, pounding on the horn—no, leaning on the horn, until the feathered peril, possibly confused by the noise but maybe simply bored, fell back from Presley long enough for him to hurl himself—still clinging to tripod and transit, over the barbwire to safety.

Once in the truck, Presley resumed his supervisory role without so much as a "thank you," for the rescue. Did he register any discomfort for having screamed in the pasture like a pre-pubescent girl? Not a chance. Instead, never missing a beat, he adjusted his glasses, smoothed his hair, and snapped, "All right, we gotta talk to the landowner. ASAP! Snap to it, Jake! Drive!" Jake obliged by turning the truck around and driving through the pasture to the landowner's residence: a two-story wooden farmhouse sitting at the end of a long, narrow, rutted gravel lane, its white paint cracked and peeling.

We pulled in, parked, and climbed out of the Suburban, flummoxed by the sight of dozens and dozens of imposing steel birdcages, each of which contained a different type of large exotic bird. I recognized macaws, toucans, mynas, peacocks, and parrots. Guinea hens, bantam roosters, geese, ducks, a few obese pigeons, and one enormous raven scratched and pecked around the yard. Presley grunted in disgust and lunged angrily toward the dilapidated farmhouse, instantly triggering a cacophonous barrage of cawing, screeching, trilling, squawking, and hooting. This was avian fury at its apex.

The flimsy screen door flew open, smacking the wood siding and scattering chips of paint. A lean, leather-skinned cowboy in a faded denim work shirt stepped out onto the front porch. The avian indignation came down a notch, enabling us to hear his voice over the noise. "Well, hey now! How y'all doin'? You with th' oil company?" Like most Texans, Delbert pronounced the word, "oil," as "aaawle." He favored us with a lopsided grin, trotted down the four creaky front steps, strode toward Presley, right hand extended for a shake. "Name's Delbert. Whatchy'all need?" Delbert's eyes were a faded blue, wreathed in smile lines and amiable squint creases. Strangely, his weathered face and leathery neck were studded with old scars—and newer, red puncture wounds. *Were they...bite marks?*

Was this guy repeatedly stabbed with a pencil in elementary school? If so, what present day bully has freshly assaulted him? Puzzling...

Presley scowled a moment, then regained his professional composure. He slapped on a smile and shook Delbert's hand, pumping it several times before dropping it. "Sir, what we need is access to your pasture, and, uh, you got some big birds out there that are spookin' my crew. They actually chased a few of us." *Oh. Yeah. A few of us...*

"Aaawww, dadburn it, that'd be m' emus. Y'know," he drawled, "Ah looove mah birds. They peck me, and they bite me, but ah looove mah birrrrrds." He fixed a faded blue eye on Presley. "That pasture ain't safe, with m' emus in there. They run a horse down in that pasture—kilt 'im—a week ago Sunday."

Presley's face paled. "E-emus? That's what those birds are? The ones that look like ostriches?"

"Yep. They're native to New Zealand. Same family o' birds as ostriches, though. 'Nother member o' that family, the cassowary, hails from Australia. Cassowary'll hunt a man down n' kill 'im with one strike. Emus, though, they just chase things till they drop. That's what happened to my horse. I'll round em' up and move 'em to a different pasture so y'all can finish up." Delbert turned and began loping toward a fenced-in area behind the house. "C'mere. Ah'll show y'all some o' m' emus up close n' personal. Don't worry—they're only dangerous in packs." He chuckled, smiling brightly and motioning us to follow. Hesitantly, we moved forward as a group, glancing nervously at one another.

"This is m' emu compound, y' might say." Another throaty chuckle from Delbert. We approached the fence, where several emus of varying sizes strolled easily. The landowner opened a small gate, approached one of the largest birds, swung his arm around its neck, and guided it toward us. The bird stood, staring emptily into space. "Emus are a livin' fossil. They've been around for millions o' years. See, their knees bend the opposite way that cows or horses do." Somehow, Delbert had trained the emu to tolerate him grabbing its leg and lifting its hulky, three-clawed foot to indicate how the birds' "knees" buckled in backwards. He described how an emu's formidable, taloned foot is its primary weapon. "One swift kick, an' it's over. M' poor horse." A flash of regret flickered across Delbert's scarred face, then vanished. "An' see? Here's where the ears are." He pointed a gnarled index finger at a forest green circular patch on the side of the emu's head.

"Um, Delbert, I heard a sound coming from one of them, when he first ran up on me in the pasture. It sounded kinda like drums, or—or a big heartbeat. What was that?"

"Heh. Heh. Yep, I've heard it, too. Well, that noise they make, it comes from an organ in their chest; it's sort of a form of communication. Purty sure they use it to call for their buddies when they spot prey or an intruder."

Bird chuckled. "Like in the movies, when the cops radio in for reinforcements?" Presley stiffened, and scowled at our rodman, as if to remind him he was a new hire, and to mind his Ps and Qs. No doubt our supervisor had taken umbrage at Delbert's use of the word, "prey," since he'd clearly been prey only minutes ago, in the pasture. Or maybe it was Bird's police reference that rankled—after all, Presley'd been a fugitive; "Pasture's Most Wanted" to the emus, you might say.

The leather-necked landowner continued. "Now, it ain't easy to tell male from female, but I finally figured it out, an' I know these in here are female. That's why I got 'em corralled in here, separate from the males. An' see over yonder? The littler ones, they're, well... teenagers, you might say. And young'uns." Delbert threw back his head and laughed. We joined in.

"Wow." That was all I could say.

Augie smiled and registered a comment. "Heck, yeah. This is all real...uh, interesting."

"Yeah," Bird offered.

"Yep." Jake's standard take on nearly everything.

Presley looked much more relaxed now. He barked out a laugh. "How'd you come by these animals? Did you have to go to New Zealand, or what?"

"Nope. Got 'em at a big sale in Bryan-College Station—the zoology department at Texas A & M had to liquidate some of their collection. All kinds o' animals there, and they auctioned 'em off. Like ah said, ah loove birds, so I couldn't resist biddin' on a whole lot of 'em. Y'all seen the ones out front. They're handy. Feathered doorbells—can't beat 'em! Better'n Brinks for security, I say!" The wiry Texan's good-natured chortle morphed into a guffaw.

Delbert's expression sobered. "Only one problem. Yep, one catch. One catch." He lowered his gaze, shook his head back and forth. "With these here emus, it's hard to tell their sexes, and what I thought was two females was a male and female! Before I knew it, I had a damn herd of emus instead of a pair! They breed like rabbits. Tell y' what, I'm fixin' to be overrun with emus!" The rancher's lopsided grin wrestled for dominion over his consternation, and triumphed. He turned on the charm, abruptly launching into a podunk sales pitch. "Say, y'all work for the aawle company; your money's good. Now, these emus make great pets. Just take one o' these, fence it in, a li'l water, a li'l feed, no problem. Kids love 'em! Or how 'bout a baby emu? They're cute as hell!"

"A baby emu? Where?" I couldn't help but ask.

"Why, right over here, Missy!" Delbert spun around, ambled toward the back of the corral, and gestured toward an exuberant flock of two-foot-tall, forest green-feathered creatures skittering and boomeranging around the barbed wire enclosure. He made eye contact with me, smiled and earnestly threw me a toe-in-the-dirt sales pitch: "You want a baby emu?"

"I'd like to think it over." *No use telling him I share a studio apartment with my boyfriend and don't have room for pets—the poor guy would be so disappointed. Besides, we're saving for a house! We could buy one then…Hell, why not?* "Hey Mister, can I have your business card, or a number where I can get hold of you?"

"Why, sure!" Delbert reached in his back pocket and pulled out an old, tooled rawhide wallet. He opened it, extracted some business cards, handed one to me, and presented cards to Presley, Sellers, Jake, and Bird. "Call me anytime, folks!"

Presley threw back his shoulders and stepped forward. "Thank you, Sir. I've got to get going and put my hands back to work on this perimeter survey. We'll drive back 'round to the gate while you redirect your, uh, livestock to another pasture."

"Fine, fine." Delbert grinned, then abruptly launched another pitch. "Say, y'all want a emu egg? How 'bout it, now?" He lunged toward some things on the ground that looked like a smaller, narrower version of a watermelon. The grizzled good-ol-boy stooped down, hefted one, and held it up with both hands. "Here, I got plenty! Make you a big ol' omelet!! See?" *Is that desperation in his eyes? Or monomaniacal persistence?* The colossal egg wore the color and patterning of a zucchini squash, looking a touch alien. For a nano-second, I glimpsed visions of little green men from Mars hatching out of its ovoid shell and wreaking planet-wide mayhem, extinguishing civilization in one fiendish stroke of extraterrestrial aggression.

Augie smiled, shrugged his shoulders, reached for his Copenhagen, and tucked a dose of it under his lower lip. "We'll be in touch." He waved to the rancher and motioned the rest of us to head for the trucks. We followed and set to work. By sundown, we'd finished our preliminary survey, so we headed back to the office to turn in our field notes.

Later that evening, Jake and I arrived at our tiny apartment, which was located in a repurposed Victorian-era bank building in Bastrop. We puzzled over the strange thumps and crashing noises we heard, coming from the apartment adjacent to ours. We tried to be laissez-faire about the whole thing, though. The unwritten code of the oil patch is that you pretty much mind your own business. And, typical of many garden variety heavy drinkers, we poured ourselves a couple of mason jars of Jim Beam, sat back on the bed and turned on the To-night Show. Suddenly, a thunderous crash obliterated Johnny Carson's monologue, followed closely by a brutal body slam. For a second, I felt certain I saw plaster dust billowing out from the point of impact.

I touched Jake's arm. "Hey, uh, think we'd better check in on Lucky? I mean, we're his neighbors! We can't sit around while he's getting his ass kicked, can we?"

Jake threw me a deadpan stare. "What if Lucky's the ass-kick-er, instead of the ass-kick-ee? What then?"

"Hmmm. Yeah, you've got a point. Well, I hope nobody gets killed, especially Lucky. It sounds really vicious."

"Aw, alright. We wait another half hour, and if it keeps up we're goin' over there, and we'll knock on the door. Okay?"

I nodded in agreement. We sat in silence, sipping our drinks, watching Johnny interview one of his guests, the winner of the National Cowchip Throwing Championship; something like that. My mind began to wander, thinking about Lucky, our crazy, hard-drinking, grizzled next-door neighbor—a welder who looked to be on the backside of sixty years old. Lucky, a rugged old redneck, perpetually Stetson-hatted and Justin-booted, worked as an independent contractor, welding the miles and miles of pipeline which criss-crossed the area between Austin and Houston that we'd come to know as The Austin Chalk.

Our first impression of Lucky had not been favorable. Lucky frequently came home drunk and passed out in his apartment with the radio on and tuned to a country station, inadvertently scourging our ears with the sounds of Lee Greenwood, Barbara Mandrell, and Tammy Wynette, at 90 decibels until 4:00 a.m., when he would awaken, shut off the hoedown and clomp down the stairs to work. Needless to say, we'd speedily made a "housewarming call," giving the old welder an earful of our special brand of profanity, registering our disapproval of his choice of music, and admonishing him on his lack of restraint in the noise pollution department. We'd also warned him that we could blow his country radio off the map with our new stereo speakers, adding that we loved the Ramones, the Sex Pistols, and other punk rock artists, which he might find aurally repugnant. Lucky'd been such a good sport! He'd slapped Jake on the back, his sides heaving with laughter, invited us in, and offered us each a bottle of his favorite beer, the Lonestar longneck.

My recollection of our meeting was interrupted moments later. A series of dozens of loud thuds in the wake of an earsplitting crash, intermixed with the tinkling of broken glass hitting the floor, prompted both of us to spring to our feet in alarm. We pulled on our boots and rushed next door. Jake rapped sharply on the old wooden door of Lucky's pad. No reply, but the tumult suddenly diminished, leaving us perplexed and feeling not the least bit more secure about our neighbor's welfare. Jake shrugged slowly, looked at me. "Maybe he—or...they—finally passed out." Then, lowering his voice to a whisper, he added, "Maybe Lucky's into rough sex. S&M, or...or something. Marti, we'd better let this go for now." Jake turned and sauntered back to our apartment.

"Okay. Yeah, okay." *Country Music and S&M? Weird. Unfathomably weird! But not beyond the range of possibility.* Momentarily, I envisioned leathery old cowpokes in ass-less chaps, wearing ball gags, astride a mechanical bull. Then, mercifully, I managed to stem the flow of painful imagery. I shook my head as if to clear it, then skedaddled back to our place.

The next morning, our alarm went off at 5:30 a.m., as usual. Jake and I showered, dressed and headed out for work. I tiptoed past Lucky's door, unsure whether to try to knock. I listened for sounds of life stirring within the lovable old sot's bachelor pad, but my ears met with stony silence. The two of us had agreed to check on Lucky after we returned from work, so I kept moving and caught up with Jake at the top of the stairs. Halfway down, I heard low groans and pitiful moans, coming from an area underneath the staircase. This alcove served as a de facto broom closet, tool shed, and storage area for all tenants. The groaning increased in volume. Jake shot me a look, said, "What the fuck?" and raced down.

Jake reached the bottom of the staircase first, I trailed him by mere seconds. I peered over Jake's shoulder into the alcove. My jaw dropped when I saw Lucky clambering over a box, struggling to his feet, his Stetson in one hand and an empty longneck beer bottle in the other. "Whooooa! I've had one hell of a night, and truth be told, I'm feelin' like fifty miles o' gravel road! I passed out here in the broom closet, on a couple o' boxes—Heh—hoooboy!" The welder managed a tremulous smile.

"Lucky! I'm so glad you're alive, glad you're okay, I mean. Jake and I heard all that racket from your place last night and...well, I was worried." I stopped short of asking the old renegade what had happened—didn't want to pry, or worse, make too big a fuss over him. In this situation, I felt it important to consider Lucky's macho redneck pride.

"Sounded like somebody opened up a big ol' can o' whupass." Jake commented.

"Can y'all help me?" Lucky's voice sounded plaintive. He leaned forward, motioned us closer. "You ain't gonna believe me, but, aaaww, hell—you gotta help me, this is too crazy for one ol' boy to take on single-handed!!!"

Jake spoke up first. "'Course we'll help you, Lucky. What's going on?"

The rowdy old welder began recounting his experiences of the previous twenty-four hours, occasionally casting frenzied glances up the stairs, as though half-expecting some hideous phantasm to descend at any moment. "We was drinkin' hard purty near all day, me and Ennis." Lucky paused, looked at Jake, attempted a rakish grin and failed in the effort. He looked down at his hands, which trembled slightly, rubbed them on his Wranglers, then clenched them into fists and dropped them at his sides. "Ennis, he's my helper, been workin' for me 'bout a year. He's a good ol' boy an' a hard worker."

Lucky stole an anxious look at the staircase, continued. "Y'all know how goddam hot it was yesterday. Well, we was puttin' away them longnecks, and after we knocked off work 'bout four-thirty or so, well, we hit the Jack Daniels. I was drivin' fast as my ol' double cab Chevy pickup'll go, an' that's fast as hell, even though the road we was on was rutted dirt n' gravel, an' there was plenty o' sharp turns. We was both about three sheets into the wind when we hit the summabitch. Sorry bastard ran out in the damn road, an' I swerved, and slammed on m' brakes, but it didn' do no good." Our besotted neighbor shook his head sorrowfully.

Jake shuffled his feet, looked down at the floor. "So—you ran over a guy? What was he doin' way out there on that dirt road on foot? Was he drunk? Or crazy?"

Lucky looked up. His bloodshot green eyes appeared fevered; a strange glint hovered behind their dilated pupils. "No! No, I didn' run over no...guy! It was a—a damn varmint! Craziest thing I ever seen. At first I thought I was hallucinatin', so I kept m' cool and steadied m' hands on the wheel. Wasn't plannin' on lettin' my helper know how bad the liquor—or the heat—was gettin' to me. But then all of a sudden Ennis, he screamed like a little ol' gal. An' then he hollered out, 'What the fuck is that thing? Hey! Lookout!' An' that's when I swerved an' slammed on the brakes, like I said."

After pausing a breath to collect himself, Lucky resumed his tale. "I heard a loud thump and gravel shot up onto the hood. Then it got real quiet. I waited till the dust settled, then bailed out o' m' truck. Ennis stayed in the cab. I think he might o' been scared or somethin.' Anyway, I hauled ass around m' truck to check out the damage and damn near fell over when I seen it layin' there in the road. Didn't know what the hell it was, just knew I'd kilt it. An' y'all know that spells trouble. Here in Texas, these ranchers n' farmers, they don't cotton to Oil Field Trash, 'specially if we run down livestock with our work vehicles. I knew an ol' boy, welder down in Beeville, hit a cow in his Dodge Ram and kilt it. Farmer got 'im for a big ol' fine n' he went backrupt. Lost his welding truck, his equipment, ever'thing."

Our neighbor paused a moment, and I spoke up. "Uhmmm, Lucky. You hit livestock, you say? What, a horse? A goat? What was it?"

"Well, damn if I know! I was drunk, and I didn't care. I only knew I wasn't gonna face charges for mowin' down livestock. Damn thing looked like an ostrich, only its head and neck was green, an' it had big long legs and big ol' clawed feet. Goofy lookin', once it was layin' there, but purty damn scary when it ran out on the road. I yelled for Ennis an' he hightailed it out o' the truck an' together we picked up the bird, an' we loaded it in the backseat of m' truck, an' then we jumped in an' I put the pedal to the metal. We put some miles between us and the scene o' the accident, an' when we reached Highway 71, I thought we was out o' the woods. By then, me an' Ennis was lookin' at each other, and laughin' about it—a little. I cranked up the stereo and popped in a David Allen Coe tape. An' then that damn monster bird woke the fuck up! I seen his face in th' rearview mirror an' almost pissed m'self! An' then all hell broke loose! That green-headed ostrich-fucker-bird-devil come up over the seat an' knocked fire from our asses, right there in the truck!!! He was kickin' an' peckin'—I know y' think I'm crazy—an' then Ennis, he grabbed up a wrench an' hit it over the head an' knocked it out. We drove quiet all the way to my place—no David Allen Coe, just in case that was what woke the bird. Then Ennis helped me wrap it in a tarp, an' we carried it up the stairs to my apartment. I don't remember much after that—I blacked out. Guess Ennis musta walked home."

"Uhuh. So...then what happened?" I asked the question, even though both Jake and I knew what must have befallen the hapless welder later that night.

The welder's lower lip trembled. Drops of sweat rolled down his forehead. "Next thing I knew I came to, sprawled flat out on the linoleum in m' kitchen. An' I seen that damn bird's beak comin' at me! I threw m' hand up in front o' my eyes!! Bastard pecked at my wristwatch a couple o' times, an' I jumped up. When I did that, the bird cut loose kickin' an' tore up m' kitchen! I ran outta there an' slammed the door an' turned the key in the lock. I ran downstairs an' passed out on them boxes. An' that's all she wrote—so far." The welder stopped speaking and glared defiantly at us, probably anticipating taunts and jeers in response to his story.

"Congratulations, man, you talked to the right people! We know what that bird is, and who it belongs to." Jake beamed at the shaken old welder, grabbed his hand, and shook it.

I chimed in. "Yeah, we do. It's an emu, and we surveyed the ranch where it came from, and we know the phone number of the landowner. I'll go up to our place and call him now. He'll know what to do. You can tell him you found it stunned in the road and brought it home to nurse it back to health or something. That way, he won't be mad." Lucky began to voice feeble objections, fearing possible legal ramifications, but I ignored him and ran up the stairs two at a time. I unlocked our apartment and stepped toward the phone. Suddenly I heard stirrings: thumps, and thuds from the grizzled old welder's domicile. *Uh-oh. No time to lose. The raptor awakes...*

Hastily, I dialed the phone. The rancher picked up on the second ring. "H'lo. This's Delbert." His voice sounded friendly and cheerful, breezy. Very encouraging.

"Uh, yes, sir. I met you yesterday at your um, your ranch. I... well, I was with the survey crew. My name is Marti, and you gave me your, um, business card. Uuhmm...I... wanted to talk to you..." I fumbled, trying to think of how to present things.

Delbert cut in. His voice sounded keen, eager. "Yeah, I 'member you, Missy. You want a baby emu, right? Or was it a emu egg?"

Still pitching! Er...no. Not, uh, not today, anyway. What I'm calling about is my neighbor over here in Bastrop, he...well, found an emu out your way. It was unconscious by the side of the road, and he's a bit of a Good Samaritan type, so he picked it up and...and brought it back to his apartment, and it, um, it woke up and made a terrible wreck of his kitchen, and now it's locked in his apartment. We were kinda hoping you could help us. Uh, sir, have you noticed any of your birds are missing?"

On the other end of the phone line, I heard a prolonged sigh. "Yup. One run off yesterday afternoon." He sighed again. "For some reason I...I thought this one wasn't comin' back." Delbert's tone was far from exuberant. I reckoned that whenever one of the giant birds broke loose, the rancher had high hopes it wouldn't return. And who could blame him? He seemed desperate to thin the herd, yet too tenderhearted to resort to slaughter.

"Delbert, will you help us out? I'd hate to call the animal control people." I waited, crossed my fingers, a silly superstitious ritual I still clung to sometimes.

"Well, hell, yes! I'm on m' way. I know how to handle m' birds. Ah loove mah birds! Gimme the address over there in Bastrop."

Delbert seemed to have rallied his spirits, and as soon as I gave him the street address, he swung into action. "Y'all stay put. I'll be there quick as I can." Before I could thank him, he hung up.

Jake called us in late to work and, since we were seldom late or absent, got no flack and no questions from our supervisor. We hung out with Lucky down at the bottom of the stairs. None of us felt comfortable about going upstairs and riling up the emu.

Delbert arrived in a white van with no windows. He'd come prepared, carrying a large, long-handled net and some sort of sedative in a syringe. We clambered upstairs with the emu rancher, but he cautioned us to stand back. Lucky unlocked the door to his apartment, then fell back as Delbert stepped inside and shut the door behind him. We heard muffled thumps and one crash, then all was silent. The three of us huddled together anxiously until the landowner emerged triumphant. He impressed us with news of his having subdued the emu, using the net and "just a touch o' tranquilizer."

Jake and Delbert carried the emu down the stairs and gently laid it in the back of the van. Delbert tarried a moment, taking care to smooth the unconscious bird's ruffled feathers. I peeked in at the sleeping form and thought how peaceful and serene it looked, lying there motionless. *Cute, sort of...Oh, what the fuck am I thinking?* Delbert shut the van doors and secured the lock. I glanced at my watch: 9:00 a.m. Even this early, the sun sizzled in the Texas sky, and heat waves shimmered off the van's chassis. We all stood for a moment in silence by the side of the vehicle, feeling the hot sun on our faces. Then Delbert spun to face me, a squirrely, desperate gleam in his eye. His voice, however, was smooth, silky, nonchalant, a perfect sales pitching style. "You want a baby emu?"

A few months later, Lucky lived up to his name. He began romancing a middle-aged widow who'd inherited a fleet of welding trucks from her late husband, a prosperous welding contractor. The last time I saw Lucky, it was on the staircase. He was wrestling a big cardboard box down toward a waiting U-Haul truck. He and the widow'd gotten hitched, he informed me, and he'd be helping her run the business. "An' I know this sounds crazy, but I ain't just married, now—I'M IN LOVE!!!" Lucky crowed. "Fer the first time in m' life! Never thought it'd happen to me—I'm the luckiest ol' boy in this ol' Lone Star State! HOT damn!"

As oil prices continued to spike, bank deposits in Giddings soared, reaching roughly $140 million in 1981. The spike in local revenue sparked a spike in local crime, and workers at Benson and Associates played a role in both. Personnel at Benson and Associates now included thirty survey crews active in the field. At our brand spanking new digs on the outskirts of Giddings, Sam L. crews could fill up the gas tanks of our thirty Chevy Suburbans at our own company pumps. The boss installed the pumps on the property when he'd constructed the new office building, on a pristine site dotted with shade trees. He'd also hired two new supervisors, enthusiastic young civil engineers with loads of expertise.

In order to enable crews to make the utmost of the daylight hours, top brass rolled out a new policy authorizing all party chiefs to drive the company vehicles home after work. This mandate proved a boon to many, and especially those crew chiefs whose thirst for rampant larceny, lunacy, and mayhem drove them to commit crimes before, during, and after working hours. The irony of the word "party" in our crew leaders' official titles wasn't lost on any of us. Party chiefs often morphed into chief partying motherfuckers on balls-out rampages.

More than a few of our thirty party chiefs were crazy redneck felons who robbed banks or liquor stores on their lunch hour, in the company truck, with the crew carried along during the ensuing high-speed chase from police cruisers and helicopters. Not only our survey crews, but oil field workers of every stripe made the nightly television news as they perpetrated largely dumbass, but startlingly bold, holdups. Samuel L. Benson, concerned for the hundreds of thousands of dollars of equipment in the trucks, took action. He hired a body shop to stencil huge numbers on the roof of each company Suburban, in bold, black paint. This way, when cops gave chase, the numbers could be spotted from the police helicopters. Mr. Benson arranged for law enforcement to notify him if the vehicle they were chasing turned out to be one of his company trucks.

Austin tended to be the city of choice for these heists, but oil field worker-generated crime in those days ranged as far as San Antonio, Houston and Dallas. Barroom brawls and fistfights abounded. Oil field theft, including tools, heavy equipment, even theft of the oil itself, became widespread, and billboards offering cash rewards for crime-stopper tips peppered the local landscape. Not all the crime could be classified as violent—the war on drugs, initiated by Nixon in the 1970s, and turbo-charged by Reagan in the 1980s, dubbed anyone who smoked a joint an offender.

At Samuel L. Benson, most employees did a lot more than smoke a joint in their spare time. Every so often, somebody snorted a line or two of cocaine. One crew hocked the theodolite and distance meter, equipment worth more than fifty grand, at a pawn shop for a hundred bucks, so they could buy a gram of coke. After firing that party chief, Mr. Benson etched identifying information into the metal surfaces on each and every scope and distance meter. He labeled the chain saws, too.

––––––––––

DURING THE LONG, RED-HOT SUMMER OF 1980, DEREK ONLY permitted me to see Anne Marie once. I flew to visit my parents at their house for a week, and he gave the okay for Annie to spend two days of that week with me. When I arrived on his parents' property to pick up my daughter, Derek informed me that he now studied full-time—a pre-law major at the university where my father taught. Recently divorced from Wendy, he'd been attending classes full-time for a year or so. "I wasn't going to let you in on it." He narrowed his eyes. "But I want this to eat away at you—in a few short years, I'll be an attorney. And I'll make SURE you never see Annie again."

That night, after tucking Annie into bed and reading stories with her till she fell sound asleep, I thumbed through my folks' phone book to the attorney listings. I closed my eyes, dropped my right index finger on the page, randomly selecting an attorney's name. I opened my eyes, grabbed a pencil, and jotted down the information. The next morning, I left a message at the attorney's office. On the last day of my visit, I met in person with Joe Clark, attorney at law. He agreed to take my case. "Lots of lawyers in the tri-county area know the reputation of your former father-in-law's corporation lawyer. He's known as a slippery sort. The first thing I'll do is file for a change of venue. This is going to take some time. Justice most always does."

I straightened my back. "Whatever it takes." I returned to Texas feeling lucky. And I was very lucky. My random pick in the phone book won me a first-class, ethical, bright young attorney with loads of empathy and good will. A professional referral couldn't have yielded better results.

Back in Giddings, I worked with Harley Heenehan's crew most of the time, and Jake's occasionally. While staking oil wells, I relished the opportunity to witness the landowners' transformation from middle class, working poor, or downright desolate, to filthy rich, crazy rich, or slap-me-silly, lap of luxury, tie-me-to-a-pig-and-roll-me-in-the-mud wealthy. As surveyors, we contacted the landowners during the preliminary survey, returned to stake the well location, and through our clients, the oil companies, we had the inside track on strikes and gushers. Even with the best of technology and expertise, oil, like the lottery and lightning, can be wildly unpredictable.

That spring, Heenehan, Floyd, and I completed a perimeter survey on a 250-acre dairy farm near Lake Somerville. The beauty of that land took our breath away. As we traversed the stations, we marveled at how neatly manicured all the pasture land appeared. Not one thistle or bull nettle marred the lush, green carpet of grass. Fat, sassy dairy cows sashayed around the meadow, munching contentedly, or lying down under the cool shade of the many huge live oak trees to chew their cud. Beholding this pastoral splendor, Harley's face reddened with astonishment. "This whole dang spread is like a great, big ol' postcard!" Floyd and I nodded, struck dumb with admiration for the farmer's land management skills and artistry.

Later, we returned to the property and staked the well. Harley pulled the Suburban into the driveway of the dairy farmer's house. We'd been instructed to check in with the landowner on the way out, and notify him we'd closed all gates and been careful not to spook the cattle. That's when we met Art and Velma, the elderly couple who owned the land. Hennehan shook Art's gnarled, arthritis-ravaged hand. "I hope your well's a blockbuster, Sir!"

Art exhaled sharply. "Hah! It'd be better for me an' Velma if we'd never signed them lease papers back in '47!" Velma, leaning on her walker, nodded her agreement. "Wellsir, back then, we never thought they'd get around to drillin'. But now they're here an' we can't do a thing to stop it." He gazed ruefully at his domain, the acres he'd lovingly tended for a lifetime, as if bidding it all farewell.

I tried to offer an idea sure to cheer them up. "Some of these wells are big producers. You might get rich overnight."

Velma hitched forward a step on her walker. "Pah! All the oil money in the world won't buy me a new set o' legs!"

Floyd chimed in. "Ma'am, if it's a gusher, your kids, grandkids, an' great-grandkids'll never want for anything."

She fixed him with a gimlet eye. "We don't have any children."

Harley, Floyd and I slunk away, sheepish, crestfallen, and worried about Art and Velma. The land and the cattle, their children, stood in the path of big oil. I fervently hoped, for their sakes, that the experience might prove beneficial.

Harley gunned the accelerator and the metallic-green Suburban flew down the gravel backroad, the radio blasting Pink Floyd's "Another Brick in the Wall." Our rodman, a Floyd of the un-pink variety, wiped sweat from his brow and shouted from the backseat, loud enough for Heenehan to hear him. "HEY! CRANK UP THE AC!!" I lunged for the dash, adjusted the settings. The air conditioner couldn't go any higher. *Man, it's HOTTER than a MOFO in here!*

Harley, sweating profusely, turned down the volume. I heard Roger Waters' voice fading as he barked, "How can you have any pudding if ya don't eat your meat?" Heenehan stomped the gas pedal, as if he could outrun the staggering heat. "AC's laggard. We'll get the Freon refilled tomorrow."

Suddenly, I noticed that the door panel on the passenger side felt warm. I looked right, saw a wall of flame rising sky-high, the silhouette of an oil derrick in its midst. "LOOK!" I pointed.

Our crew chief pounded the brake pedal with both feet, pulled onto the opposite shoulder from the fire, and eased the Suburban to a shuddering stop. Harley, Floyd and I jumped out of the truck and bounded down the road on foot, toward the disaster, to see if we could help. As we reached the access road, with a cattle guard and gate, I saw men run past us, with fear on their faces. Farther up the access road lay desolation. A man in a tan Stetson hat and a guy in hardhat and coveralls waved at us to stop. The guy in the hardhat hollered, "GO BACK!!!" Harley waved an arm to show we heard him. We halted.

The man in the Stetson jogged toward us. "Where's your VEHICLE? Are y'all OKAY?"

Floyd, Harley, and I nodded in unison. Shocked by the spectacle, Harley stepped toward the Stetson guy, and Floyd and I followed him. "We're surveyors. We staked a well on that acreage not long ago. We were headin' for another well location. Saw the blaze. Slammed on the brakes, parked down the road a piece. We came to help."

The man in the cowboy hat shook his head. He looked stunned, but it seemed talking made him feel steadier. "The area's restricted. When the rig exploded, all hands jumped clear. Nobody dead. But the ground started to give way, swallowed up three trucks and some heavy equipment. There was a pocket of natural gas under there, a big one, and when it blew out it liquefied the surface." He turned to Harley. "You get your truck an' drive as fast as you can. The crust here is unstable. No tellin' what might happen. It just now blew."

Harley nodded, turned and ran for the Suburban, with me and Floyd close on his heels. I looked over my shoulder, saw the man in the Stetson and the one in the hardhat, standing in the road, looking both ways. I figured they might be setting up a road block. Then it struck me they awaited an emergency response team.

The catastrophe had struck the dairy farm belonging to Art and Velma, an oil field accident of apocalyptic proportions. During the months following the blaze, we heard different stories about what caused it. One account I heard was this: Roughneck crews, like any group of workers, have a pecking order, and the new hire is known as the "worm," whose job is to do all the grunt work. The worm on this crew'd been told to fetch a bag of drilling mud, the additives prescribed by a mud engineer to aid the drill bit's penetration of the different strata as the drilling proceeds. The consistency of the additives must match the type of layer the bit is drilling. One additive is used for rock, something different for sand, and so on. On Art and Velma's dairy farm, the worm added the wrong kind of mud, one that was too heavy, resulting in the explosion and fire.

316

After the pocket of natural gas blew, liquid gas seeped out, forming a lake of fire that burned for a year. The industry experts arrived, oil field fire contractors Red Adair and Boots and Coots in particular, but it still took a long time to contain the blaze. From time to time, we'd drive by and see the flames shooting upward into the sky, the charred remains of live oaks silhouetted in the glow. Passing that grim vista, I found myself weighing the environmental consequences of dependence on fossil fuel, and wondered what the world might look like in the future—in the year 2000, for instance, or 2010, or even 2015.

———————

AS THE SUN ROSE HOT AND BRILLIANT OVER THE TREETOPS, harbinger of the scorchfest to follow, I began setting up the tripod alongside a gravel road in Lee County. We'd worked this road the day before, while massive trucks rumbled past, stirring up a screen of dust that seemed to hang in the muggy air for an infinity before settling. *Visibility might be tough, but so am I.* I reached for the theodolite, set it on the tripod and began leveling it up. Perhaps because of the crosshairs in its scope, some guys referred to the theodolite as "the gun." Not me. I thought of it as a telescope...or the zoom lens of a camera; not a weapon, but an enhanced view. I glanced at the ground and saw him lying there on his back, eyes wide open, staring up at the sky.

His body lay only a few yards from where I'd set up. I tiptoed to him—well, tiptoed as quietly as possible in heavy-duty work boots—and leaned down, looking into his enormous, golden eyes. The jet-black pupils homed in on me, very alert. The sharp-edged talons and beak never moved as he continued to meet my gaze. I'd seen pictures of Great Horned Owls, but now I stood in the presence of one. And he obviously needed help.

317

I walked back to where Harley Heenehan sat in the green Suburban, perusing an aerial map and jotting down notes. Floyd stood at the open backdoors of the truck, spray-painting lathes.

"Uhm, Harley."

"Uh-huh." He kept on looking at the map and his notes.

"There's a Great Horned Owl over by the side of the road. He—er, well, maybe she, I can't tell—anyway, the owl is hurt, but it's still alive. I'm pretty sure they're a protected species, or maybe even endangered. Can we take it to a wildlife refuge? I bet there's one in Austin. Or maybe I can make a phone call and get somebody to pick it up."

Harley got out of the truck and walked with me to see the fallen raptor. Floyd followed. Our party chief stared at the owl. "Man, he looks like he's awful weak. Yeah, let's see what we can do." All Benson and Associates crews carried collapsed cardboard boxes in their trucks. Whenever a truck got stuck in the mud, crew members'd lay them out flat under a truck's tires, for traction. And most trucks carried duct tape. After eyeballing the owl's approximate size, we found an appropriate box, un-collapsed it, and reinforced the bottom and side folds with duct tape.

Floyd found an old flannel shirt of his, wadded up in the backseat, and offered it. "We can line the box with it, keep the owl comfortable."

Harley grabbed the shirt. "We can use it to pick him up with."

Together, we gently enveloped the helpless winged predator in the shirt, lifted him, and set him in the box. We stowed all the equipment in the truck, then gingerly set the box containing the owl in the backseat, to ride alongside Floyd. With our current survey situated close to Giddings, we reached the Sam L. office in minutes. After delivering an impassioned speech to Phil Carvey about wild life conservation and the current rate of extinction of species, I culled three hours of unpaid time off. Harley advocated for the

Great Horned Owl, too, volunteering to act as both instrument man and party chief for my three hours MIA.

One of the draftsmen, Randy, spoke up. "I'm finished with my project, just hangin' around, waiting for some new jobs to come in. How about I ride with Marti?" Randy Benson lived in Austin and partied with all of the field crews. He took a lot of ribbing from personnel due to his last name, Benson. Despite being from Waco and definitely not related to the boss, some guys called him "Baby Benson." Popular with everybody, including supervisors, Randy convinced them to let him take the trip. With my draftsman friend's help, I located a wildlife rehabilitation center in Austin and called to inform them we'd be there soon.

Randy and I made the drive in the Pontiac LeMans Jake and I'd purchased after selling the Fury III, the owl's cardboard box anchored in the backseat. "Hey Randy, thanks for helping out with this rescue."

"I mostly wanted an excuse to get outta the office. I've never even heard of a Great Horned Owl."

"Oh. Well, it's good to have a co-pilot, anyway."

When we reached the wildlife refuge, the veterinarian stood waiting. And she was gorgeous! Randy's eyes seem to pop out of his head, but he toned it down. The draftsman's attitude toward wildlife, and Great Horned Owls in particular, did a complete 180. The veterinarian babe's presence transformed Baby Benson into a fervent warrior in the battle for animal rights. The vet confirmed what I'd intuitively known about the owl at first glance. "If you hadn't taken such swift action, this bird would have died today. It's astonishing that he survived until you found him." She picked up a small flashlight, shined it in each of the owl's topaz-colored eyes. The pupils' response to the light revealed he'd suffered a severe concussion. "Where did you find the owl?"

"He was lying on the edge of a gravel road in Lee County, on his back. A lot of big trucks drive that road. Did he get hit?"

"Yes. He might've accidentally flown into the windshield of one of those trucks. He's riddled with parasites, that's why he's so weak. He probably lay there for four days or more."

"I'm so glad I found him. I've never seen an owl close up. I leaned over him and looked into those beautiful eyes."

The vet's face registered mild vexation. "You're lucky you found him today, then. If he hadn't been so weak, he'd have ripped your face off with his beak and talons. Great Horned Owls are raptors."

"Um, yeah. I know." I felt sheepish about getting so close. My fascination had wiped out any thought of self-protection. "So what are his chances? Hey, Doc, is he a he?"

"The owl is a male. Great Horned Owls range in size from about seventeen inches to twenty-four inches long. The females tend to be larger. The smaller proportions—he's around nineteen inches long—show us he's a male. As a veterinarian, I know additional ways to determine gender."

Randy jumped in. "Hey, I'm, uh, VERY concerned about the owl. May I uh, have your card, so I can contact you? Y'know, so you can keep me posted on the owl's status?"

She smiled ever so slightly. "Sure." From a pocket in her smock, she retrieved two business cards, gave one to Randy, the other to me.

The Great Horned Owl recovered fully, and after several weeks of rehabilitation, the refuge center released him into the wild. I have no idea whether Randy Benson ever got a date with the stunning veterinarian. I never asked.

CHAPTER 12
FREEDOM FIGHTERS

THE 1969 COUNTRY SQUIRE STATION WAGON SHUDDERED TO A halt in the gravel parking lot, its luggage rack stacked high with camping equipment, its interior bulging with a hodgepodge of books, clothing, and cookware. A pair of neon pink foam dice dangled from the rearview and a statue of a hula girl swiveled on the dashboard. All of these details piqued my interest, but it was the vehicle's occupants that struck me as compellingly strange. I couldn't quite put my finger on it, but something about these guys definitely inspired the down home cliché, "You ain't from around here, are ya?" And they hadn't even gotten out of the car yet.

The driver, a hippie dude wearing a multi-colored Rasta beret, stumbled out, regained his footing, smiled crookedly, and meandered toward the front office, squinting painfully at the glare from its glass doors. Moments later an ashen-skinned guy with a shaved head vaulted from the shotgun side of the car, his pale blue eyes scanning the parking lot as if inviting challengers. He scowled at me, slapped a hokey straw cowboy hat onto his gleaming ivory scalp, and made an elaborate show of stomping into the building.

"Them boys ain't from around heah." Johnny Landry smiled ever so slightly.

"Heh. Guess they're still hirin'—an' thass good, means they ain't firin'! Right, Johnny?" Mad Dog glanced anxiously at Landry, then began bustling around in the back of their crew's Suburban, arranging flagging, lathes, and fluorescent-orange spray paint cans.

Suddenly Phil Carvey emerged from the office, stood on the steps, waved his arms over his head and called out, "Hey, y'all come over here! Everybody! Move it!" He grinned broadly, tucked his Johnny-Cash-esque black western shirt into his black jeans and shifted his weight from one foot to the other while he watched us gather around the office steps. "Okay, then. This is important. We just hired a coupla guys from Czechoslovakia. They're in there now, finishin' up their paperwork." He gestured over his shoulder with his thumb. "These boys are freedom fighters—they're fugitives from Communism, and we wanna do our part to help 'em out, so I don' wanna hear any jokes about 'Wild an' crazy guys,' alright? Go easy on 'em."

A few guffaws rang out, then withered under Carvey's disapproving glare. One or two of my coworkers looked at the ground, managing to laugh silently. I couldn't blame them for cracking up at our supervisor's fleeting reference to the famous Saturday Night Live sketches starring Steve Martin and Dan Akroyd. The sketches featured the Festrunk brothers—George and Yortuk—from Czechoslovakia, who referred to themselves as, "Wild and crazy guys..." In 1980, America was still deep in the Cold War, and we couldn't help but hold some respect for these guys who'd come so far to get a new start. From the vibe in the parking lot, I felt pretty sure nobody would give the Czech guys too rough a time, especially after Phil Carvey's pep talk.

Phil waved a hand, dismissing us. As crewmembers jumped into trucks and began heading off to work, he strode across the parking lot toward our vehicle. Jake jumped out, nodded to him. Carvey leaned an arm against the Suburban. "I'm puttin' one o' these boys with y'all. His name's Lojza, an' he's kinda thin on his English, needs some practice, the other one talks a blue streak. Marti, you're good with people, help 'im out, okay? Ol' boy'll be out in a minute."

"Sure, Phil. No problem." *Good. We got the hippie dude. That skinhead was hostile.*

And Lojza turned out to be very cool. He smiled a lot and caught on quickly. True, he appeared to speak scarcely a handful of English words, let alone any Texan. But he communicated adequately in spite of the language barrier and took direction amazingly well.

At lunch, we stopped at a barbecue place in Fayette County, on the outskirts of LaGrange, sat down at one of the tables, and ordered some beers. Bird, Jake and I bought Lojza a Bud and some brisket, since we figured he'd be short on cash till payday. The hippie Czech freedom fighter thanked us enthusiastically, then lifted the frosty longneck, pointed to it, smiled and said, "Soup."

Bird guffawed. "Yep, that's your first course. An' just wait till quittin' time. Down at Shorty's, there's a seventeen-course SOUP dinner waitin'!" Bird slapped his knee, chortling. "That's right..." Our rodman took a pull on his longneck.

Lojza laughed hard at that, so we figured he'd picked up the gist of it, or at least the vibe. The rest of the afternoon passed quickly considering the heat wave still raged through Texas like a drunken bully arsonist, bitch-slapping us, then setting us on fire with hundred-degree heat, ninety-nine-percent humidity, and relentless, glaring-hot sun. Lojza took it all in stride, earning our respect. After work, we stopped at Shorty's, a beer joint/cafe in Winchester.

We all liked Shorty, the owner, a wiry cowboy type who seemed to stand barely five feet three inches tall, with his boots on. Shorty let most oil field workers run tabs, and often cashed our paychecks, a benevolence deeply appreciated by one and all. Shorty cracked jokes and kept the rounds coming. And the food didn't suck, either.

At Shorty's, with time to kick back a little, I did my best to engage Lojza in conversation. We used sign language, and drew pictures on napkins for him, but it didn't seem to help all that much. After a few beers, Lojza went out to the Suburban for a moment, then returned carrying a battered army surplus backpack. He sat down at the bar, opened the pack and pulled out a book. It looked like University Press, like a book you'd read in English 102 or American Lit, but with all the text in Czech. Lojza turned to me, pointed to the book, and spoke slowly, in accented English, "The Sun Also Rises." He took a breath. "Ernest Hemingway."

I leaned forward, intrigued. Maybe Lojza could speak more English than Phil Carvey thought he could. Maybe he was merely shy, trying to hold back so he wouldn't sound like, or feel like—an idiot. "Hey! I dig it, Lojza! I've got a copy of that book at home. I mean, in English. Cool! I'll bring it to work tomorrow and you can read them side-by-side. Maybe it'll help." Lojza smiled, nodded his head.

Suddenly it occurred to me that our Czech friend might be acquainted with pop culture: rock music, dope slang, stuff like that. I began quizzing him. "Hey, you like rock n' roll? Like the Rolling Stones?"

Lojza nodded. "Rolling Stones, okay." He made a dismissive gesture with his right hand. Suddenly his face lit up, and he hollered, "Frank Zappa!"

Jake spoke up. "Frank Zappa, yeah. You like Frank Zappa? Like, *Weasels Ripped My Flesh,* or *Joe's Garage,* or what?" He paused for emphasis, looked at our Czech coworker inquisitively, chugged what appeared to be an entire beer, and signaled Shorty for a refill.

Lojza laughed uproariously. "Best is *Veasels Ripped My Flesh.*" His expression grew solemn. Then, "I am Frank Zappa fan! But tell me—vhat is Muffin Man?"

Bird guffawed and slapped Lojza on the back. Jake only smiled and said, "I can't help you with that one, man." I chose not to comment. Jake stood up, jangled the truck keys. "Okay, let's head for the office. We gotta turn in the field notes." Bird, Jake and I threw down some cash to cover our "soups."

On the way back to the office, Bird employed sign language to ask Lojza if he smoked weed. Of course, we knew the answer—he did. And he was no lightweight, either.

That night, after work, I found my copy of Hemingway's novel. I'd borrowed it from my father the last time I'd been home for a visit. The next morning I brought the book to work, found Lojza in the parking lot and slipped it to him. He nodded a thanks, opened his backpack and pulled out his copy. The two books appeared identical. I figured they'd be useful to him in smashing through the language barrier.

When I ducked into the office to pick up the theodolite and distance meter, Phil Carvey stopped me in the hallway. "Marti, 'm gonna send the other Czechoslovakian guy, um, the bald one... Pete's his name—out with your crew today. The hippie one goes with Dave Burrell's crew. We can switch 'em back later on. Got it?"

"Uhh, okay." *Shit. We're gonna miss ol' Lojza. And he'll miss us. Burrell can be cantankerous and bossy.* I grabbed the equipment, carried it out to the parking lot. As I looked around for Jake and Bird, I noticed Lojza'd already been assigned to Dave's crew. *Hmm. Looks like Lojza's got his work cut out for him...*

"Lad-yuh, giddyup, now! Fetch me a armful o' stakes. Chop-chop!" Burrell snaked his head around and spat a stream of Copenhagen into a styrofoam coffee cup, his brow furrowed. Lojza hesitated, only for a moment. "LAAAD-YUH! GIT ME THEM STAKES!" Burrell screamed, not in anger, but as though communicating at top volume might delete whatever block his goat-roper accent might've thrown up against Lojza's lingual comprehension. When the plucky Czech executed Dave's order pronto, it seemed to simultaneously appease and annoy the crew chief, who spat again, vehemently, this time on the gravel parking lot. He muttered, "Fuckin' freedom fighter...Hippie, more like. Goddamit." I managed to catch Lojza's eye, waved, then hurried off.

I spotted our crew's white Chevy Suburban, marched to it, opened the back doors and loaded the Nikon theodolite and Zeiss distance meter inside. Bird'd already loaded up the mirrors and tripods, and now he slid bundles of lathes and stakes into the cargo hold. He looked up from his task, bloodshot eyes radiating the throbbing haze of his customary Jack Daniels hangover, and exhaled pointedly. "We got the other Czechoslovakian dude today...name's Pete. He ain't quit runnin' his mouth since he got here, drivin' me nuts, so I sent 'im to get some nails n' some flaggin'—an' Marti..." Bird's bleary face registered deep disappointment. "Um, I'm pretty sure he's no stoner. You'll see what I mean when he gets back."

Moments later, Pete appeared, walking briskly, rolls of fluorescent orange flagging clenched in one fist, nails gripped tightly in the other. He wore that hokey straw cowboy hat and a plaid western shirt, long sleeves buttoned at the wrists. His near-colorless blue eyes registered surprise, then disbelief as Bird introduced me. "This's Marti, our instrument man, er, instrument person." Bird turned, slammed the back doors shut, sauntered around the left side of the truck and slumped his lanky frame into the backseat. I nodded to Pete, offered a smile.

Pete said nothing, shot me a brooding glance, stalked to the right side backseat door, and boarded the Suburban in a huff. He sat in the backseat next to Bird, arms crossed over his chest, and stared straight ahead, scowling. *Wow. What's got his panties in a wad?* I jumped in the shotgun side of the front seat. Jake sat in the driver's seat, perusing an aerial map for a minute or so, then laid it flat on the Suburban's vinyl-upholstered seat between us. He turned to me and pointed to a heavily wooded area on the map. "We're gonna finish up this job today, then check out tomorrow's. S'right down the road, here."

Jake fired up the Suburban and pulled out of the parking lot. Bird began flipping through a comic book. I cranked up the AC. We drove in silence for a few minutes, then Czechoslovakian Pete spoke up.

"Zis is pipeline crew? I voorked on pipeline soorvey yesterday." I turned, looked at Pete, who appeared to take exaggerated care not to glance in my direction, but fixed his pallid eyes on the back of Jake's head. "Boss?" He lifted a hand to adjust his scraggy cowboy hat and kept staring at the crew chief.

Jake glanced into the rearview mirror to answer, "Nope. We do perimeter surveys n' stake wells."

Pete looked a little crestfallen, then rebounded. He puffed out his chest. "Aha! I vill learn qvickly. I have voorked a lot of different jobs." Pete's pale complexion registered the faintest tinge of observable blood circulation as he warmed to his topic. "In Frankfoort, Germany, I voorked on U.S. Army Air Base, maintaining all types of military vee-HYE-kles." He shifted in his seat, stared around triumphantly. Bird rolled his eyes.

Give him a break. Don't rain on his parade by telling him we pronounce it, "vehicles." I wondered at Pete's vigorous pursuit of Jake's approval. I'd never seen anybody talk this much on his first day out, with the exception of Mad Dog, who, we'd learned later, had ingested some tainted mescaline crystals during his commute to Giddings and had arrived in a semi-psychotic state of agitation.

Pete appeared to be stone cold sober, yet in the way those haunted eyes glinted feverishly beneath the battered, straw hat brim, he appeared to be dancing on the outskirts of Crazytown. *His condition's likely not a temporary one. Hmmm.* I struggled to comprehend how laid-back Lojza could've endured the 1,430.9 mile journey from Los Angeles to Giddings without garroting his travel companion. But my struggle was brief. Instinctively, I knew the formula...Alcohol. Cannabis. Repeat. *Yep. That's how he did it.*

The Czech began talking again. "I need to find U.S. Post Office qvickly, right after voork, to buy stamps. I have letter for lady friend."

"Mmhm." Bird looked sleepy, crossed his arms over his chest. "There's one in Giddings. Right downtown," he mumbled, then closed his eyes.

"My lady friend is lonely vithout me." Pete glanced at Bird, then looked straight ahead at no one in particular, and continued. "I like older vooman. Older vooman is gentler, happier to have man around. My lady friend invited me to move in vith her during first veek of acqvaintance. She has nice house on Holly-VOOD BOO-lay-vard. Older vooman is qviet and knows her place. Not like young vooman." Pete stopped abruptly, then glared at me, as if for emphasis.

What the fuck. I felt an inkling of outrage, a touch of indignation creeping up the back of my neck, then a tingling of the scalp, as I often did when confronting such pathetic displays of bigotry or misogyny. But, I assured myself, this was nothing I couldn't handle. Phil'd asked me to watch out for his Czech "freedom fighters," so I resisted the urge to verbally bitch-slap this guy into a corner on the first offense. I attempted a somewhat neutral stance. "Uh, Pete. Exactly what do you mean by, 'older'? Like, thirty-five?"

The cadaverously pale-skinned immigrant waved a hand dismissively. "Thirty-five is vay too young, vay too young." He leaned forward, looked at Jake, who stared at the road stoically, his face blank. "Older vooman is nice lady, knits me sveaters, alvays cooks vhat I vant her to cook. That's vhy I like older vooman, alvays. I have traveled the voorld, Europe, then Colly-FORN-ya. Older vooman is best for me."

Ookaay...

"Hey now," Jake interjected. "We're comin' up on the property." He gunned the Suburban, sped down the last stretch of gravel road toward the gate, looked in the rearview toward Pete, and jerked a thumb in the Czech's direction. "Pete, you open the gate for us." Our melanin-deficient, newest crew member scurried to the gate, held it open while the Suburban pulled through, closed it and jumped in.

During the next eight hours, Pete demonstrated his "villingness to voork," and his boundless capacity for chatter. Bird rolled his eyes and I stifled my annoyance as Pete rattled on about "older vooman," and how he needed to mail that letter to his "lady friend in Holly-VOOD." We set up all the shots on a creek bank so we could establish the centerline of the stream, which formed a natural border on the perimeter of the ranch. The heat wave and drought had dried up nearly all the water; only a sluggish, murky rivulet remained—just enough moisture to supply an optimum environment for the local insect population, which had exploded with apocalyptic fury.

As I set up and leveled the tripod—halfway down the eroded, fire-ant-infested scree—swarms of mosquitoes buzzed around my head and lit on my forearms and thighs. I didn't swat at them; instead, I'd learned that if you wait till they start biting and then suddenly flex your muscles, it'll annihilate the bloodthirsty little bastards—they drop right off. When applying this pest control technique, you've really gotta focus. Mercifully, this helped me tune out Pete's filibusters on "voomanhood" and "Holly-VOOD BOO-lay-vard."

The heat wave pummeled us mercilessly that summer. By 7:00 a.m., when our workday began, every snake in Texas had already slithered deep into whatever remote cloister of shade still remained and holed up there like a politician under scrutiny from a sex scandal. Water snakes writhed and twisted in the muddy, pathetic remains of stock tanks and creek beds. During that parched, blistering summer, we seldom encountered rattlesnakes.

Previously, greener summers drew them out in the afternoons, and then we'd seen them sunning themselves on the game trails we navigated to reach the property corners. I reckoned that this year's blast furnace must've shriveled even the hardiest pit viper's hide, rendering each rattler a recluse.

Still, despite drought and the hordes of ticks, fire ants, deer-flies, gnats and mosquitoes, the central Texas countryside stunned me with its natural beauty. Stately pecan groves, thick pine forests, rolling hills, and a sky so big and all-encompassing that I couldn't help but glory in my own insignificance: That's the stuff of dreams. When the magnificent sunsets faded into starry, fragrant nights, warm and sweet and sultry, I'd find myself pledging undying love for the Lone Star State.

We caught lunch at a Mexican restaurant on the outskirts of LaGrange, and slogged along the creekside boundary till the bitter end of the job. Our workday ground to a halt at dusk, so we skipped the trip to Shorty's we'd been hoping for, and stopped at a mom n' pop grocery/gas stop between LaGrange and Giddings instead. Jake bought us beers in cans, and the storekeeper slipped a snug-fitting little paper bag around each, to absorb moisture and provide insulation—a practice I found both practical and endearing.

We grabbed our brews, trudged out to the Suburban, and sipped them on the way to the office. For the zillionth time, I breathed a prayer of thanks for the Texas Legislature, whose decree made it legal for us to drive with open containers, and under whose authority the drive-through liquor store existed. Such legal laxity, along with the fact it was just fine to drink at eighteen, rendered the Texican realm a lush and potent Disneyland for alcoholics. At this point, even Pete remained silent, his long sleeves still buttoned over his white T-shirt, his pallor unchanged. The best he could manage was a few staccato outbursts, intermittently jabbering only the names of certain points of interest in "Colly-FORN-ya," specifically "SAHN-ta-MOE-nee-kah BOO-lay-vard," "SUN-set BOO-lay-vard," and the ever-popular "Holly-VOOD BOO-lay-vard."

When we arrived at the office parking lot and started packing the equipment back inside the office, we noticed nearly every other crew rolling in as well. Groups of workers clustered around the steps in back of the office, smoking, drinking beers or sodas, and exchanging good-hearted threats, insults, mockery, and other forms of macho endearment. Brody, a dude from Anaheim, California who'd only been working with us for a couple of weeks, sauntered over to Pete and clapped him on the back. "Hey, uh, Pete, what's up with your lady love? Still robbin' the cradle?" The skinheaded Czech scowled, turned on his heel, and stomped off.

Brody chuckled. "Guy's a fuckin' perve, really gross. But don't sweat it Marti, you're safe. He only goes for the older women."

"Yeah, he wouldn't stop talkin' about it, how he likes 'older vooman.'" I looked down at the gravel, scuffled one of my boots in it. "Like, forty or fifty years old. Said an older 'vooman knows her place.' I didn't know whether to barf or stab him."

Brody laughed. "Forty or fifty's jailbait to Pete. He told me he likes 'em seventy, seventy-five, in their prime. I tell ya, he's practically a necrophiliac. And that skinhead thing he's doin'—I been callin' him, 'Nazi Pete,' an' it's catchin' on. See ya tomorrow, I gotta score some weed and get drunk on Heineken."

"Yeah. See ya, Brody." I turned and headed back to the office, looking out for Jake, and found him scrawling the last few details onto a time sheet.

"Ready to head out, Marti?"

"Oh, hell yes." Jake and I exited the office, jumped in the white Chevy Suburban. "That Pete is a nutbag," I muttered.

"Uh-huh." Jake adjusted the sun visor, turned the key in the ignition, fired up the Suburban and headed for Bastrop. "He ain't quite right. But let's see how it plays out. Maybe he'll drag up, or Phil'l transfer 'im back."

"An' we'll get Lojza."

"Yeah."

"Didja hear the "older vooman" stuff? Weird."

Jake chuckled, nodded. "Yep."

The next morning, Phil put both Pete and Lojza on our crew, which was pretty cool, since we had to start the new job, a perimeter survey involving a fence line that ran through acres of dense brush: yaupon, mesquite, and scrub oak, laced with plenty of poison ivy and wasp nests. On property surveys such as this one, a five-hand crew gave us a clear advantage. Bird set the mirrors for the first shot and gave the Czechs a crash course in the art of brush removal, surveyor-style.

As it turned out, Pete handled a machete pretty well, and so did Lojza. They hacked away at any branch that seemed to block the shots, and we swept along breezily. Both Czechs appeared to have a good sense of timing and pace, and they fell in step with Jake, Bird, and me as we all waded in with blades freshly sharpened, hewing and slashing our way to each consecutive set-up.

By noon, when Jake called for a water break, I counted five wasp stings on my left bicep and a streak of poison ivy laced my right wrist. The sun glowed maliciously, white-hot in the sky, reminding me of how the center of our solar system is nothing more than a nuclear fission reactor. We walked back to the Suburban, huddled around the fluorescent-orange Igloo water dispenser that rode with us to each and every job.

I winced, wiped sweat from my eyes with the back of my left hand, stabbed my machete into the hard-packed soil, and motioned to Bird to drink first. Our rodman's hangover had blown in like a Texas twister. His palsied hands barely managed to wrestle a styrofoam cup from the stack of dozens in a large package in the back of the truck. I held the button down on the Igloo spigot while Bird's gnarled digits clutched the cup and jitterbugged it around beneath the stream of ice water till it filled.

"C'mon Pete, Lojza, get some water," Jake waved a hand at the cooler. The Czechs stepped forward in unison. "We're goin' to lunch after this, but ever'body's gotta drink water first...then beer."

We stood around for a minute, drinking a couple of cups each, not saying much. Except for Pete. "Voorking in Texas is different from Frankfoort, Germany. NO-vhere in the VOORLD have I seen such humidity! Not in Colly-FORN-ya, not in Holly-VOOD, anyvay." He looked at the hard-baked ground at his feet, shook his head slowly. "I am sveating, alvays sveating in this heat!"

"Time for lunch," Jake murmured as he pulled the keys from the pocket of his Levis. "Good thing about this job is, Shorty's isn't far. C'mon, y'all." We tossed our machetes into the Suburban. Bird slammed the back doors and we all jumped in, thankful to be out of the burning sun for a bit.

As we rolled along the dusty back roads of rural Fayette County, I couldn't help noticing—and celebrating, how quiet Pete'd become. He mumbled to himself and looked out the window, never once mentioning his "lady friend." But once we reached Shorty's, and he'd downed a few beers, the pasty skinhead launched into an enthusiastic rant, extolling the praises of "Holly-VOOD BOO-lay-vard," then continuing on down his list of L.A. thoroughfares.

I picked up my beer, sidled between the tables and headed for the jukebox. Since I'd already asked Shorty for a dollar's worth of quarters, I could play four songs. Shorty's jukebox was heavy on country, but he did favor some rock. I selected classics: Patsy Cline's "Crazy," Willie Nelson's "Whiskey River," Elvis Presley's "Jailhouse Rock," and AC/DC's "You Shook Me All Night Long," then moseyed back to our crew's table.

About halfway through Elvis, the food arrived and we took our sandwiches to go. As we headed back to the truck, I tapped Lojza on the shoulder, slowed my pace. He slowed with me. "Hey, uh, Lojza, your uh, friend Pete..." I dropped my hands at my sides, sighed in frustration. *How can I say this?*

Lojza seemed to anticipate my question. "He's veird."

"Yes. He is. Did you guys know each other back home? In Czechoslovakia?"

Lojza burst out laughing, then took a swig of his Bud. "No. In L.A.. Ve shared a ride...to look for jobs."

"Oh." I smiled—reassuringly, I hoped. "That's cool. This is a good job."

Lojza adjusted his Rasta beret and lifted his beer in reply. "Good Soup," he murmured. We picked up our pace and joined the others at the truck.

After work that night, I spent a few minutes hanging out with Lojza in the parking lot sipping beers, and got him talking about his life before Texas. The hippie-styling Czech spoke English with more skill than I'd given him credit for. Apparently he was simply laconic and maybe a tad shy. Lojza explained that he'd earned a degree in fine arts from Charles University in Prague. But since he'd narrowly escaped—with only the clothes on his back—from Soviet-occupied Czechoslovakia, it'd been impossible for him to carry along any proof of his education, so he'd turned to labor jobs in America.

"I ran from police," he said cheerfully, "Got caught selling LSD and Frank Zappa albums."

I threw back my head and laughed. "Wow! Really?" *Fuckin' amazing!*

Lojza nodded, smiled tentatively, glanced at the gravel, scuffled his black combat boots. "I vas selling them at a Rolling Stones concert in Moscow. In the back of the crowd."

Suddenly, I flashed on the first day he worked with us, at Shorty's, when I'd quizzed him on rock n' roll. I'd mentioned the Rolling Stones, for starters. And Lojza'd dismissed them with a wave of his hand, describing them as no more than okay. Then he'd told us he was a Zappa fan, which, in my book, was much cooler anyway.

Pete approached us, and Lojza stopped talking. I figured it must be time to go home, glanced around the parking lot for Jake, waved to him, and turned to leave. "See you, Lojza. Bye, Pete." The Czechs plodded toward the old Country Squire Station Wagon.

On the way back to our apartment, I told Jake about Lojza. "Man, he's got a fine arts degree from Prague. I'm gonna talk to my father about this. I mean, when I was growing up, Dad had friends, professors, who'd escaped from Hungary and other Eastern bloc countries. I bet he'd know some way that Lojza could get help."

As soon as we got home, I went down to the phone booth and called Dad. I filled him in about Lojza's story, but skipped the part about the LSD and Frank Zappa albums. "He's...a political dissident who escaped from Soviet-occupied Czechoslovakia. He's got a degree in fine arts from Prague, and he's working for our company as a gofer. And Dad, I remembered that you had colleagues, political dissidents who'd escaped from behind the Iron Curtain. That one professor—wasn't he from Hungary? He came to our house for dinner."

"Yes. You were just a kid back then. You have an excellent memory."

"Thanks, Dad." It always felt so good, receiving praise of any kind from my father.

"Well, Dear, I'm glad you called me. There is a program for those who seek political asylum in the U.S., especially from Communist countries, and one of the benefits is that those individuals can receive an appropriated degree from one of our universities. Your friend will need to apply for the program, but once he registers he'll be eligible for a variety of benefits."

"Great! I'll tell him tomorrow, at work. Austin's only an hour from Giddings, so he can go to U.T. to ask about it, right?"

"That's right."

"Thanks, Dad. I love you. Bye."

"I love you too. Bye."

———

Next morning, I found Lojza in the parking lot and told him what my father said. "So, Lojza, as soon as you can make it to

Austin, get signed up at University of Texas. They'll get things rollin' for you."

"Good." Lojza beamed. He grabbed my hand, squeezed it. "Thank you, Marti."

We got both Czechs on our crew again, and this time we worked till dusk. On the way home, Lojza sipped his Budweiser in contented silence, blissfully accepting hits from the joint Bird rolled and passed around. Skinhead Pete, demonstrably peeved by the marijuanified atmosphere in the Suburban, shifted restlessly in his seat and muttered into his beer.

Jake pulled the truck into the parking lot and we unloaded the equipment, the last crew to report in. Bird's ride, Skeet, had already taken off, so he needed a way home. Lojza spoke up. "Bird, ride vith us."

"Okay, let's go," Bird half-smiled, then added, "Hey y'all, swing by the Liquor Stop. I'm buyin'!" Jake and I watched as Bird, Lojza and Pete strode eagerly across the parking lot, jumped into the old Country Squire and slammed the doors. Lojza took the wheel, turned the key in the ignition, and we heard the engine sputter feebly, then die. After several attempts to turn it over, Pete jumped out, flashlight in hand, raised the hood and peered in, his pale face registering frustration.

Jake and I joined him. Pete drew a quick breath. "I voorked as mechanic at Frankfoort Airforce Base. Already I know vhat is wrong. It is battery. Ve have been vaiting for chance to buy new vone."

Jake waved a hand toward the Suburban. "I'll give you a jump." Bird looked crestfallen, now that the Liquor Stop was no longer an immediate prospect. Jake and I jogged to the truck. I jumped in the driver's seat and started it, then pulled it up to Lojza and Pete's vehicle. In a few minutes, the Country Squire's engine revved up, and so did Bird's mood.

"How 'bout we make for the Liquor Stop, huh?"

I turned to my boyfriend. "Hey Jake, let's follow these guys, just in case they break down again. We can pick up something to drink, too."

"Alright. But I'm gonna drive, then. Switch with me."

We followed Lojza, Pete and Bird through the Liquor Stop drive-through window, ordered a couple of drinks to go...or, "travelers"—in this case, Jack and water for Jake, a Stoly screwdriver for me, and exchanged greetings with Earl, the store's owner, as he poured our libations into tall plastic cups.

When the Czechs dropped Bird off, they kept their motor idling, probably for fear it'd stall again, but the old car seemed to be running smoothly as they headed out toward Winchester, and then turned down a gravel road toward the Colorado River. The Country Squire stopped along the riverbank.

Jake and I pulled in alongside, parked, jumped out, and walked around to the driver's side window. Lojza sat at the wheel with the window rolled down. "So this is it?" Jake asked, lighting a Camel non-filter and inhaling slowly. Lojza nodded, stepped out of the car and stood, Budweiser in hand, leaning against the driver's side door. Pete got out, walked around to join us. We all stood a minute, listening to the sound of crickets in the drought-ravaged grasses and the river rushing by. Jake finished his cigarette, dropped the butt, crushed it under a booted foot, asked, "So y'all are camping out here? Checks're gonna be big. We get 'em Friday."

"Yeah," I chimed in. "And then you can get into an apartment. Winchester's got some places for rent, but there're lots of cabins outside of Giddings, too. Ask around at work." I hesitated, weirdly reluctant to abandon the Czech freedom fighters to fend for themselves in rural Texas, as if they might get lynched for trespassing, or for being foreigners or something. I shook it off. *What the hell. Lojza's escaped the KGB, he can fend for himself here. And Pete? Crazy granny-fetishist! Anyway they're white—won't even make a blip on the vigilante radar.*

A part of me wanted to engage Lojza in a discussion of Frank Zappa and the quality of LSD behind the Iron Curtain. My curiosity gnawed away at me—I'd always wanted to know whether the scary stuff the nuns taught me about Russia was even remotely accurate. But I shook that off too. "Uhm. Okay, we gotta go now, right Jake?" Jake nodded, headed for the Suburban. I followed.

Over the next few weeks, Pete and Lojza availed themselves of the semi-permanent housing offered to Giddings oilfield workers, and soon after, their widely divergent personalities began to manifest. Lojza took a few days off and made it Austin. After applying at UT, he was accepted into the program my father had recommended, and registered for classes in American Slang and English. Lojza still had to wait a few months before he'd be actually attending, but at least now he had a lifeline to other artists and hipsters through occasional trips to Austin on the weekends. He told me he actually was an artist, a sculptor who dreamed of someday opening his own gallery.

But Pete was a different story. Phil Carvey assigned him to our crew for several more weeks so Bird and I could train him as a rodman. What a drag! As time went on, he lost all inhibition and let his freak flag fly, so to speak. I made a real effort to tolerate the constant jabber about his "older vooman" back home—even though it annoyed the shit out of me. But the wind changed for me when the pallid Balkan began to venture into politics. For a couple of days in a row, he threw out some comments on "...vhat Reagan needs to do about American economy." We all ignored him at first, but one day, while driving back to the job after a brewski-rich lunch, Nazi Pete lived up to his nickname. He sat in the backseat of the Suburban, Budweiser in hand, funky straw hat in his lap, his shiny, bone-white scalp glistening with "sveat," and launched into a diatribe about "za blacks."

"Za trouble vith America is velfare. Too many of za blacks are on velfare and don't vant to voork. Zis is problem with economy in zis country."

"Oh yeah?" My simmering rage began to escalate. I turned around to face him, one arm resting on the vinyl front seatback, and forced a smile. "Tell me more."

My sarcasm seemed to roll off the little skinhead like foam off a mug of Miller draft. *Maybe he doesn't get it...*He jibbered on. "Vell, here is vhat I think vould voork: no more velfare. America must bring back slavery. All blacks can be slaves and zey vill voork, that vay, your country vill save much money."

I half-laughed, half-choked in disbelief. "You gotta be kiddin' me! This is a joke, right?"

Bird lifted his eyes from his comic book. "Hell, yeah, it's a joke."

Pete's watery-blue eyes widened, he leaned forward slightly. "No, is no joking. Blacks on velfare is number vone problem. Slavery is solution."

"Yeah? Like a...final solution, y'mean?" Although I was seething, this pasty dickwad somehow managed to remain impervious to my rage.

"If America vould bring back slavery, Marti, you vould not have to voork anymore. Vomen voorking is not good. Not good for vooman, or for country." Pete leaned forward a little more, his zeal reaching a crescendo, his fish-white complexion tinged with pink splotches. He actually pointed a finger in my direction. "Vooman does not belong in voorkplace! VOOMAN'S JOB IS TO HAVE BABIES FOR STATE!"

"Okay, you little dickhead," I snarled, "Sit back and listen to me. I'm an American, I was born here. We may not be perfect, but we believe in freedom. We abolished slavery a long time ago, an' we don't want it back! Ever! Black Americans fought for freedom and won it over a century ago. And they fought for it again in the 1960s Civil Rights movement. Same thing with American women. In this country, women fought for the vote at the turn of this century, now we're fighting for equal pay and more. Women like me are working, and we have careers because we want 'em, and if we have babies, we do it because we want 'em, and we don't give a fuck what the State wants—and most importantly, WE DON'T GIVE A FUCK what YOU want!!! You got it?"

Pete's pale complexion turned a whiter shade of paler. He sat back, put his hat on his skinhead, crossed his arms over his chest, and turned up his nose like a little schoolgirl. "I am talking to you no more," he sniffed.

"Good. That's good. Because right now, I'm trying to make up my mind which INS office I'm going to contact to turn you in. We got a Neo-Nazi problem here, and I don't think they'd like to hear your 'final solution' shit any more than I do. Keep that in mind next time you wanna discuss current events." I turned back to face the windshield, suddenly reminded that we still kept a gun in the company truck. Delicious fantasies danced through my head: me shooting Nazi Pete's dick off, for starters...But I regained my composure.

The next day, Phil told me Pete'd put in for a transfer to another crew. He went to work with Brody, the guy from California. A few days later, I saw Brody in the parking lot after work. "What'd ya do to Nazi Pete, anyway?" Brody laughed, "Whenever he sees you, he ducks down in the seat, like he's hidin' or scared. I asked him about it, and all he's got to say is, 'I do not vant to talk about Marti. She is like man with breast.'"

I laughed with Brody, glad to know my INS threat had shut that little goose-stepper down, at least temporarily. But I refrained from telling Brody the details.

Lojza moved to Austin, attending U.T. full-time, eking out a living doing portraits of hot college coeds while living in the spare room of a bar and grill on Sixth Street. A few years later, he relocated to New York's SoHo district and opened his own studio. Nazi Pete stuck around Giddings, even though moving to Alabama and joining the Ku Klux Klan might've been more in character for him.

My newfound attorney, Joe Clark, kept in touch with me as the litigation process moved forward. Slowly. For what seemed like an eternity, my hope of contact with Annie seemed limited to short visits at my folks' house. Derek continued his undergraduate studies, and rattled his verbal sabre at me—the one about how he'd now dedicated himself to becoming a lawyer and barring me from ever seeing Annie again. My attorney obtained a change of venue for a hearing, to appeal for visitation rights. He began to prepare me for the moment when I'd take the stand. Derek's representation stalled. I mailed cards, gifts, and letters to my daughter in care of Derek's parents' address. Christmas filled me with sadness, but I managed to convince my ex to let me see Annie briefly on the holiday weekend of 1980. During that attenuated stretch, as the agony of separation lanced through me night and day, a different kind of pain asserted itself. I began experiencing extreme discomfort and swelling in my right leg. As it persisted, I devoted myself to a strict, healthy diet, temporarily abstained from liquor, and ramped up my program of cardio and weightlifting.

Then, a few months later, Joe Clark's efforts won me visitation rights. Derek and his attorney settled out of court. The pain of separation remained, but the joy of knowing I would see Anne Marie over the summer, at my home in Texas, helped me to manage it. The pain in my leg continued to worsen, and it acted crazy, manifesting itself in acute, shooting jabs, and weird zaps that felt like electric shocks—first high, at my hip, then low at the ankle, then anywhere and everywhere, indiscriminately. I kept on working, though, no matter what, continuing through sheer stubbornness.

One day in late spring 1981, at work, my right knee collapsed as I carried the theodolite and tripod uphill. I managed to fall in a way that protected the expensive survey equipment from damage. My very cool supervisor, Don Atwater, told me to take a day off and see a doctor—the equipment was simply too expensive to risk my falling a second time. I found an orthopedic surgeon. He x-rayed my leg and found a fast-growing tumor in my right knee joint, between the tibia and fibula. To my surprise, he sprang into hyper-concerned mode and immediately arranged for surgery. He showed me the x-ray image, pointed out the new growth. I told him I'd like to get a second opinion, even though the pain now felt intense to the point of distraction. "The tumor is the size of a ping pong ball, and it's pressing hard on the nerve. If you'd waited one more day to come in here, you'd have been paralyzed from the knee down." He warned me that, depending on whether the tumor contained malignant tissue, or malignant ganglia attached, risk of amputation was real.

I joked about ordering a peg leg instead of a high-tech prosthesis, and acted cool and confident going into surgery the next day. "Hey Doc, can I have an extra day to shop the antique stores? I'd like to hack one o' those big claw-foot legs off a hardwood dining table. An' how 'bout you write a scrip for a parrot—to go with that peg leg?

In the moments before the general anesthesia kicked in, I took a hard look at my life, taking time to appreciate everything—even the harsh and painful moments—in case, by some freak chance, I might breathe my last on the operating table. When I awoke in the recovery room, I reached for my right calf, and found it still attached. The post-op pain seared through me, but I felt exuberantly grateful to be alive. The seven-hour surgery yielded excellent results: all the tissue proved benign. The surgeon'd sawed the tumor off the bone, and dissected my calf muscle, fiber by fiber, to make sure no malignant ganglia'd grown from the tumor.

I threw myself into physical therapy and made a strong comeback, but even my badass attitude and efforts could not speed up the process enough for the doctor to allow me to go back to work. He ordered me to stay home and continue physical therapy for a few months. This arrangement enabled me to spend the summer with Annie. Jake and I now lived in a house with a big yard, near the town of Bastrop. What a sweet summer, in 1981. Yes, I still experienced painful grief and loss when the time came for me to return my daughter to the Midwest. But now, I drank from a wellspring of hope—continued contact, protected by written, legally enforceable contract. Yet sadly, during the first few days of missing Annie and despite the fact I'd quit for months, I drank from a frosty bottle of Stoly to ease my pain. And again I returned to work, burying my anguish in physical labor. The company promoted me to party chief, so I now led my own crew.

The day before Halloween, 1981, I'd been out in Flatonia, Texas, picking psilocybin mushrooms with my friend Ken, a mud engineer from a little town near Milwaukee. Ken loved Halloween, horror movies, and ghost stories. Resting at my place after an intense morning of shroom-hunting, Ken regaled me with stories of a gibbering madman who'd terrorized his Wisconsin burg back in the Sixties. According to the local myth in Ken's hometown, the raving lunatic's relatives kept him chained up in the attic of their ramshackle farmhouse. However, he'd occasionally break free of his shackles and run naked through the town dump, howling at the moon.

Ken, grinning lazily, sucked in a monster hit from his glass bong and swore his hyperbole was gospel truth. "It can happen in any town. There's prob'ly a guy like that right here in Bastrop, runnin' naked through the pines, right this minute. Or he could be standing outside your door right this minute, listening." That said, he guffawed, carefully exhaling to avoid choking on pot smoke. Like all cannabis connoisseurs who spin yarns while smoking, when pressed, Ken conveniently failed to recall the guy's name or the address of the family homestead.

"Yeah, right." I'd quit smoking weed when I'd had the knee surgery, but in order to be polite, I inhaled a hit and passed it back.

I willfully ignored the madman-of-the-town-dump story. I wrote it off as being the same type of claptrap as the one about the guy that waterskied into a nest of water moccasins and got bit to death. That tale was popular in Texas...and every person telling the story always claimed to be the cousin of the dude that met that ghastly, watery, venomous end. If the snakebit water-skier did exist, he had gazillions of cousins.

Like all of my local friends and coworkers, I was hip enough to know that Bastrop County yielded many a fine harvest of Killer Green Bud. Sure, Texas cops were jack-booted fanatics when it came to fighting the war on drugs, but pot-growers in Bastrop County's piney woods held a powerful ace tucked up their collective sleeve.

Rich deposits of iron ore gave the local soil its reddish hue, and this unusually high iron content caused the pine trees to grow a particular shade of green, a tone indistinguishable from that of the high quality marijuana being cultivated beneath the canopy, a condition which rendered aerial and infrared efforts useless. Knowing this helped many a pot grower to sleep better at night, dreaming of a bountiful harvest.

Roughly two weeks later, when I first heard the helicopters overhead, I thought another oil rig had blown up. I set down my frosty glass of beer, vacated the kitchen, and meandered toward the bedroom of our little A-frame house, where Jake and I kept a small television atop the dresser. I switched on the power button and fumbled around, hunting for coverage of an oil well explosion on a local news channel, when I heard the phone. I ran to it, picked up on the second ring and mumbled, "H'lo?"

The caller, Jim Hollister, hippie mechanic and renowned local weed aficionado, rasped excitedly, "Hey, Marti! Y'hear the helicopters? There's a major, major weed bust goin' down over here by my place! Turn on Channel 4 News and see my interview with reporters from the scene. Gotta go, I'm getting hoarse from callin' everybody!"

"Got it." I whipped back into the bedroom, switched to Channel 4, and stood transfixed, watching the scene unfold. A pretty blond newscaster stood in the piney woods. Late autumn evening sun illuminated the Channel 4 news chopper in the background, and I strained to discern the hustlings and bustlings of uniformed personnel further back, beyond the helicopter.

The reporter spoke somberly into her microphone. "This is Stacey Kent, live at the scene of a phenomenal marijuana bust, deep in the pine forest of Bastrop County. An anonymous tip led local police to the scene. Apparently this is an organized effort by a number of offenders—two of whom were seen running from the area have so far evaded police. At this point, officials are unclear as to how much marijuana has been seized, but they assure me it is substantial."

The camera then cut to a small group of what looked to be locals. I recognized Jim among them. The camera zoomed in on perky reporter Stacey as she leaned toward Hollister, waving the microphone in his general direction. "This is Jim Hollister, a local resident. Mr. Hollister, your land adjoins that of the perpetrators. How did you feel when you learned that a gang of highly organized criminals had been growing marijuana right in your backyard, so to speak?"

Now the camera panned Hollister as he took a deep breath. "I'm shocked and appalled," he began. The pert correspondent batted her eyes and gave Jim an encouraging nod. The hippie mechanic continued. "Yeah, and horrified that an egregious crime occurred in my neighborhood! I'm a registered voter, and I say—Hollister looked straight into the camera—THIS BUST IS A CRIME! Marijuana should be immediately and totally legali—"

Abruptly, the broadcast cut off for a nanosecond, then returned with an aerial shot of the piney woods and a voice-over from Stacey Kent: "More at eleven."

I grabbed the phone and dialed Jim Hollister. "Wow, Jim, ya knocked it outta the park! You spoke out for legalization of marijuana!"

Silence on his end, then, "Thanks, but the truth is I'm bummed. Thanks to censorship, I spoke out for 'legali—' of marijuana. Fuck! I delivered a soliloquy—it was truly inspired, and they CUT IT. Bastards! If CNN had picked it up, this could've been a turning point for Texas NORML."

"Man, that sucks. But any halfway intelligent viewer's gonna read between the lines. They'll know what you said, and it's fantastic that you got as much airtime as you did! What if they'd interviewed one of those asshats in the Wranglers? The ones dipping Skoal, wearing belt buckles with their names engraved on 'em? That woulda been a horror show! Dude, like I said, you stepped up to the plate, and you knocked it outta the park!"

Hollister sighed, then chuckled softly. "Well, I guess it was okay." I heard the flick of a lighter and deep inhalation of smoke. He spoke while holding in the hit. "The grower guy is a genius, whoever he is. All that time I thought the land was vacant." He paused to exhale, coughed, then continued, "I never knew anything was goin' on. Had I been aware, I could've stopped over with a six-pack, y'know, made friends with them. The way the cops were crawling all over the scene, the operation musta been extremely sophisticated—lots of employees around the clock, security systems, everything. And the coolest part of it is, the plants were giant! I mean, giant sinsemilla TREES! It's like Jack and the Beanstalk!! A fairytale come true! Imagine!"

"You're kidding me? Really? Did you see them?"

"Yeah, but from real far away. They looked like trees, I'm tellin' ya. Trees with green bud tops! HUGE kola tops!! And so close to harvest—musta been superb resin crystals on 'em. What a loss to the community..." Hollister's voice registered such sorrow I feared he was actually weeping.

"Jim, I'm working tomorrow. Gotta get going. But let's keep in touch. Did you tell Suzie?"

"Of course I did! Her place borders mine on the other side. She wasn't home, neither was Trigger Jim, and it's a good thing, really."

"Right. Well, I'll see her at work tomorrow, I hope. Thanks for the call, Jim."

I filled Jake in on the news. We watched the eleven o'clock broadcast for more specifics on the bust. Channel 4 News gave it only brief coverage, but word among stoners was that the cops'd listed a University of Texas botany professor as a prime suspect. The newscasters mentioned, "...an extensive, sophisticated, possibly experimental operation," whatever that might mean, and promised, "...more as the story develops."

That night, I giggled myself to sleep, envisioning massive bud trees in the forest. *Amazing. Like a Jules Verne fantasy! A gargantuan crop, right here in Bastrop! Hey, that rhymes...Weed enough to bake the masses...*

At work the next day, I talked to Suzie in the parking lot. She'd only heard about the bust from Hollister. Apparently she and her boyfriend Trigger Jim had split when they first heard helicopters, managing to escape out the gravel road to Hwy. 71 before all the cop cars came screeching in. Anticipating being suspected due to their coincidental proximity, they'd spent the night with friends. Besides, Trigger Jim'd been holding.

After work, Jake and I stopped by a bar in Bastrop, where we ran into Ken and a coworker of ours, Emilio. Emilio told us his brother Gustavo worked at the Bastrop town dump. Gustavo'd gotten the heads-up from the Sheriff's office that cops planned to use chainsaws to fell the giant bud trees, then haul all the weed to the dump.

Emilio, Suzie, Jake and I worked very long hours back then, but thanks to Emilio's brother Gustavo, we learned that local sheriffs executed their plan the next day, with local newspaper reporters in attendance. Redneck cops posed for photos next to the huge sinsemilla trees. Real Jack and the Beanstalk stuff.

After deputies sawed down the forest of green bud trees, they brought in a logging truck and stacked the fallen giant cannabis, trunks and tops included, right onto the flatbed. They secured the payload in place with straps, chains, and ropes. I'm told they threw tarps over the gargantuan crop in hopes of concealing it from the public as they trucked it down Hwy. 71 on the way to the dump. Word on the street was that in an attempt at discreet and clandestine disposal of the goods, the sheriffs decided to send out the logging truck alone, without the high profile, red-light-flashing, law enforcement vehicle escort.

Unfortunately for the cops, things didn't go exactly as planned. The transport took place during late afternoon around 5:00 p.m., in brisk traffic. When the logging truck accelerated on a slight rise, the wind picked up and began riffling back the tarp, revealing their confiscated cargo to flabbergasted commuters, breaking loose buds and scattering them to the four winds.

Football-sized kolas blew onto windshields, leaving fragments stuck to the glass, thanks to the high resin content. A few uptight motorists reacted with annoyance, but most seemed to be overjoyed at this unexpected windfall, manna from heaven. Good-natured chaos ruled as drivers braked, pulled onto the shoulder, and jumped out of their vehicles to snatch up monstrous chunks of flying green bud, lending new meaning to the term, "rush hour." Magically, the whole thing went down quickly and smoothly, devoid of collisions or consequences.

The driver of the logging truck must have seen what was happening but chose to speed on up the highway to the dump. I'm not clear on every detail. I only learned what Ken had told me. He'd left work early that day and had been following the truck at a cautious distance in hopes of getting a glimpse of the crop. He got much, much more than a glimpse.

Ken dropped by our house to show off his prizes. "Look at this, will ya?" Ken crowed, pulling a tennis-ball-sized chunk of green bud out of his backpack and waving it wildly. "And that's only a tiny taste!" His eyes sparkled as he grabbed a pineapple-sized kola out of his pack. "This is a score, but the big haul is up at the dump, and we gotta get over there before they burn it! Gustavo, y'know, he works there. And Gustavo saw the cops dig a pit, throw all the giant bud into it, and splatter it with diesel fuel. He thought they were gonna torch it right then and there, but they didn't. And Gustavo heard one of the cops saying they'll be back in the morning to torch the whole load!"

Ken took a deep breath, then continued. "So here's what—Gustavo can't salvage any of it, it'd be too obvious. He had to act like he didn't even give a fuck about any of it so he won't be implicated. He slipped Emilio an extra key to the front gate. But Emilio's gonna go up to the dump around midnight and open the gate. He invited us to come along and see if we can get whatever's not been soaked with diesel. You guys in?" Jake and I looked at each other. I shook my head. No way could I go along on that operation, even though it did seem exciting. I couldn't risk getting arrested. Even if Annie was gone till next summer, I was still a mom, with responsibilities that filled me with happiness.

"I gotta work early in the morning, so I'd better pass."

Jake nodded. "Thanks for the invite, man. And good luck."

The following night, after Jake and I got home from work, Ken stopped by our place, a bong and a chunk of a giant kola in his backpack. He fired up the pipe, took a deep hit, held it, exhaled. A jubilant raconteur, he zestfully recounted his adventure. "Okay, so we geared up for our mission. Once we'd parked our vehicles in various places, far away from the scene, we met at midnight in front of the dump and sneaked through the gate." He hit the bong one more time, set it down, and obviously stoned now, rapturously began waxing poetic. "The cool night air felt sweet as a lover's caress. A full moon illuminated the landscape. We made our way to the pit, climbed among the cannabis tree branches, black trash bags in hand, and scooped up what bud we could salvage." He took a sip from a Heineken we'd brought him, continued his tale. "The plan was to work quickly, salvage as much as possible, sprint for the gate, then scatter in all directions to reduce chances of arrest." He leaned forward, lowered his voice to a near-whisper. "We swung our trash bags over our shoulders and rushed for the gate. My heart'd been slammin' in my chest the whole night. Paranoia set in and my adrenalin level surged." Ken leaned back on the couch, shook his head in disbelief, and dissolved into a paroxysm of giggles. "Man, I know it was the adrenalin and, uh, yeah, total paranoia, but all of a sudden I heard a rustling in the piney woods. I froze. And for a fraction of a second, out of the corner of my eye, I coulda sworn I saw him."

I leaned forward. "Saw who?"

Ken guffawed, slapped his thigh. "HIM, man! The naked lunatic dude, from my hometown in Wisconsin. The one that runs through the dump, howlin' at the moon. Remember? I told ya about him, the night before Halloween, after we got done picking shrooms." He burst out in giggles again. "My knees started knockin' and I damn near screamed." He laughed silently, his shoulders shaking. "I was so freaked out, I couldn't even run—had to SCURRY!" He gulped the Heineken, set it on the coffee table. "I looked over my shoulder, but he was gone—Aaww, hell, I know he wasn't real. But when I got back to my house, safe and sound, you know what I did?" He didn't wait for an answer from us, didn't need one. "I stashed my weed haul, ran out into my front yard, and howled at the moon."

He guffawed again, picked up his bong, inhaled another hit of the historic, Jack-in-the-beanstalk-giant weed.

While writing this book, I took a trip to Bastrop, researched old newspaper archives, found pictures of the bust, and talked with some of the residents. The giant weed is famed among locals who lived there in those days, a legend, in a way. And in my opinion, a legend far more scintillating than that of a lunatic howling at the moon.

CHAPTER 13

OIL FIELD TRASH AND PROUD OF IT

Over a span of several years, the Lone Star State, and the oil patch in particular, favored me with prosperity, education—the kind you can't access in books, and confidence—a brash, badass assurance acquired by emerging unscathed from daily encounters with violent men, venomous snakes, and tests of endurance. I will forever thank Texas—its wild, rowdy weather extremes and its resilient, eccentric native citizens—for teaching me how to adapt, survive, and discover my inner strength by thinking for myself. Oil field life taught me that it's not whether you're up or down on your luck that matters, but how steady is your resolve, will, and focus. Hope dies hard in the oil patch, and when I arrived in Texas, hope was damn near all I carried with me.

Surveying taught me about point of departure, closure, and every stop in between. Today, if I look at my life as a line through time and space, with birth as the point of departure, and death closing the loop, then at each point in between, I do what I learned operating a theodolite. At regular intervals along the line, I check the backsight, where I've come from, then home in on the foresight, where I'm headed next. On the frigid, windy day when I stepped up to the tripod, peered through the scope, and turned my first set of angles, I began to think of life that way. It's a strong philosophy for staying focused and moving toward goals.

I've dodged bullets and worked with explosives. I've stood off rattlesnakes, water moccasins, copperheads, and even a coral snake; been bit by every kind of multi-legged crawling thing, attacked by fire ants, scorpions, and every winged harpy in the insect world. I've witnessed one oil rig fire at close range and several more from a distance. I've worked waaay out in the woods, day after day, as the sole female among males of questionable moral character and unquestionable ability to do harm. Some of these experiences taught me how not to show fear. Others showed me how to sideline hindrances and push forward to the goal. All of them schooled me in honing my sense of humor, and never taking myself too seriously for my own good.

All those earned skills and learned lessons came in handy when I stumbled into the world of standup comedy. Texas graced me with genuine friends. From the first night I met Billy and Terri in Chicago—genuine allies—I learned how to get back up after getting knocked down, and to be proactive: to make things happen, rather than passively reacting to what happens in life. Billy and Terri served as role models for me. Both worked on the North Slope, on the Alaskan Pipeline. Billy, along with his friend Randy, started an international quality control company, from nothing—and they employed any of their friends who possessed the needed skills to work in that industry. Terri, one of the first women to work on the Alaskan Pipeline, showed me that I could excel in a man's job. Over the years, I met with this newfound family of friends on a regular basis, usually for a party or celebration.

As I saw it, my most important role and function at these gatherings was to be funny, to make my friends—and everyone else within earshot—laugh. Looking back on it now, I recall how I'd arrive in character, with attitude and a chosen shtick. I'd work the room, cap on others' comments, do punchlines, callbacks, all of that. My performance wasn't conscious at the time—it was instinctive, intuitive.

I called it, "party gear," and thought of it as a part of my brain I could slip into and go with the flow. I also did this working at Sam L. sometimes, depending on the situation. Most of the time, work demanded a badass attitude, for security purposes.

One night, as I slid into party gear, Terri urged me to try standup comedy. "Marti, you're like a female Lenny Bruce. Listen, I've seen live standup in comedy clubs in New York, Chicago, even L.A. and I'm telling you, you've got it—something real. You missed your calling."

At that, a faint whisper in my brainstem signaled the awakening of my childhood dream—*there's still time to be a comedian!!!* But I knocked it out cold with a rant. "A female Lenny Bruce! Are you fucking kidding me? Lenny Bruce overdosed—died shooting up on a toilet seat in some sleazy hellhole apartment or something like that. And look at Freddy Prinze—blew his brains out. It's gotta be depressing, man. And those guys MADE IT BIG. What about the ones that never make it? What happens to THEM? No thanks, I'll stick with staking oil wells for billionaire wildcatters." My objections stemmed from something deeper. My oilfield work represented a bridge to visitation with my daughter once a year. And I still planned to launch another legal effort—to obtain joint custody rights. I missed Annie all year long between visits. And in my mind, standup comic meant starving artist.

I stuck with my work. And then, in late 1982, close to the holidays, the bottom dropped out of the oil business for me. Since '81, the Giddings Gravy Train's engine barely chugged along, now it began wheezing to a halt. Benson and Associates had been laying workers off for quite some time; only a handful of crews remained. Even though I knew it was coming, as one of the early hires, kind of a charter member at Benson, I felt only a mild jolt of shock when I discovered I was second in line for the axe. First in line, one step ahead of me, was Vic, a Mexican guy who labored on a pipeline crew to support six kids and a wife south of the border.

I felt confident I could segue into another line of work after Benson and Associates. In fact, I'd been talking with an old tool pusher about hiring on as a roughneck. And I'd made a trip to Houston to apply for a job with Sperry Sun. Vic took it hard, his family depended on him. So I talked home office into letting me switch with Vic, in hopes he might hang on a little longer.

The company laid me off, I registered for unemployment, and joined Jake in searching for work. As luck would have it, my Houston friend Billy Castor threw a big party right around the time I cut myself loose from Benson. Jake decided to stay and do carpenter work for a neighbor, but I drove to Houston to hang out with my surrogate family of Texican friends. No better way to usher in a new chapter in my life, right? Terri flew in from New York. The party lasted three full days, due to a high level of cocaine consumption among certain houseguests. On Saturday night, as I shifted into comedy mode, Terri announced, "We're going to a comedy club, Marti! Let's see if you can ignite your new career."

I took a swig of Stella Artois. "What the fuck, let's go."

Terri and I piled into our friend Neil's BMW sedan, along with Billy, Randy, and Randy's girlfriend Shanna. Neil's roommate Barclay, a guy from New York with a passion for LSD, The Grateful Dead, and Twinkies, jumped in, too. Neil worked at a marketing firm, a really conservative corporation, so he doubled down on crazy weekend party behavior in an attempt to mitigate the stressors his necktie-and-blazer workweek imposed on him. Neil handed Barclay his car keys. "Go ahead, Brother. You drive. I'm too jittery from all that blow." Barclay grabbed the keys, started the engine.

"Hey Y'all—Wait for me!" A pretty redhead, Danielle, ran toward the car. Barclay let the engine idle till she squeezed in.

First we cruised in search of an improv club Neil'd heard about, but never found it. Danielle guided us to another club, The Comedy Workshop, on Shepherd Drive, in the vicinity of posh River Oaks.

We bailed out of the car, strolled into the club, and seated ourselves near the front. At first glance, the place didn't impress. A smattering of audience members occupied the tiny theater space, sipping wine and highballs and listening politely as a parade of mostly despondent performers took the stage one after the other. Our posse, fresh from the house party and hopped up on coke, made a collective effort to laugh long and raucously at all the comics' jokes, hoping that in so doing, we'd encourage them to be funnier. I even hollered, "Yeee-haaaw!" and "Whoooooooo!" a few times, thinking it might ramp up the energy, a viable strategy if you're at a rock concert. Later I learned that in the world of live comedy, yee-haws and whoooos tend to be interpreted as heckles or catcalls. But what the fuck—in that moment, I hadn't the faintest inkling of comedy etiquette. I was hell on wheels, oil field trash and proud of it.

Our efforts—and especially mine, though well-intended—didn't produce the desired effect. The comics seemed agitated now, a few seemed highly skittish. When a petite chick with closely cropped blonde hair took the mic, Terri whispered, "Finally, a woman. I hope she's good!"

The chick comic stood onstage, her face and body visibly tense, reciting her lines as though she couldn't wait to get it over with. Suddenly it dawned on me: we're not helping out, we're intimidating them. I listened carefully as she wrapped up her set, then applauded as she exited the stage. The next comic did a long bit based in homophobia. He lisped out a very poor impression of a drag queen, used the character to do a string of what comics call "dick jokes." The gay-hating stuff pissed me off. When I'd first moved to Houston, I'd hung out with drag queens and shared an apartment with two gay friends. I leaned in, whispered to Terri. "This guy is an asshole. Now I wanna go up there. I'm damn sure I can do better than that fuckwad with my mouth duct-taped shut. Hey Terri, ya think this club has an amateur night?"

Terri grinned. "See? You're a natural! It's in your blood. C'mon, let's talk to the bartender and find out who's in charge. I'll bet you can get onstage. They need some zip in their line-up."

After watching comics performing live, an electric jolt of excitement shot through me at the prospect of trying to do it myself. I shoved away my Stoly screwdriver, stood up. "Okay. Let's do this." I strode to the bar, Terri beside me. We asked the bartender who to talk with about getting up onstage. He pointed to a closed door.

"That's the green room. Go in and ask to talk to the artistic director." The bartender returned his attention to washing glasses and pouring drinks. *ARTISTIC director?? How can the barkeep utter those two words without rolling his eyes?*

We entered the green room. A couple of skinny, morose-looking dudes paced back and forth, another leaned against the wall, eyes downcast, a tormented vibe emanating from him. The pacers stopped moving and stared at us. I spoke up. "Hey, which one of you is the...uh, artistic director?"

The guy with the anguished aura pushed away from the wall, exited the room in a snit, and set the two skeletal neurotics in motion once again. I looked at Terri. She shrugged. The door opened and the haunted-soul-comic stood in the doorway, pointed an accusatory finger at me and Terri. "There they are." Sullen, he slouched past, leaned against the back wall, arms crossed over his chest, and stared at the floor.

A dark-haired man entered the green room on the heels of the afflicted one. He patted his hair, a fussy mannerism. His heavy-lidded eyes swept over me, then Terri, then back to me again. I got the impression he longed to look down his nose at me—and if only I'd been six inches shorter, he could have tried. He tilted his head. "Yes? You asked to see me?"

Terri cut in. "My friend is very funny. We'd like to know where to sign up on the list. To get onstage."

The artistic director's face registered surprise followed by chagrin. He exhaled and made a tsk-tsk sound, simultaneously, his face
reddening for a moment, then going pale. "There IS no list." He
turned to me. "You CAN'T get onstage."

I placed a hand on my hip. "Why not?"

Terri took a step toward him. "Yeah, doesn't this club have an
open mic night? What kind of comedy club is this, anyway?"

He took a step back, waved a hand in my direction. "I'm doing
you a favor. If you make an attempt at standup, you'll regret it."

Suddenly, I realized that the dark-haired guy, designated shepherd of the depressed comics, might be intimidated by me. I felt
annoyance, mixed with pity and a touch of amusement. I took a
step toward him. "If I, uh, make an attempt at standup, I'll regret
it? And what do you mean by that, exactly?"

"First of all, women aren't funny." His eyes raked over me. "And
good-looking women can NEVER be funny."

"Hmmm." I laughed and stared back at him.

Terri snorted in derision. "Oh yeah? What about Goldie Hawn?"

He lifted his chin. "She's an actress, not a comic." He sniffed.
"She started out as a dancer." He patted his hair again, turned to
Terri, glared at her.

I tapped him on the shoulder. He spun around to face me, a
hint of alarm in his eyes. "Well, Joan Rivers does standup. And how
about Phyllis Diller?"

He raised his eyebrows, crossed his arms over his chest. "They
were from another era."

Terri and I exchanged glances. I suppressed my "Fuck you" re-
flex, decided to take another run at it. As I leaned in, I saw a glint of
terror flashing in his eyes. I took a half-step back, slapped on what I
hoped was a warm and winning smile. "Okay, Sir, help me out here.
So, there's no list to sign up, and women aren't funny. What about
the chick in your line-up tonight? How did she get up there?"

He threw up his hands in an over-dramatic show of exasperation. "My job as artistic director comes with responsibilities. I've spent enough time talking." He spun on his heel, headed for the door, then stopped and turned our way. "There is an open mic night. Ask the manager for details. And please! This is the green room, for comics ONLY." He huffed out of the room.

Terri and I stifled a laugh, exited the green room, headed back to our table. Barclay raised an eyebrow. "How'd it go? You gonna get up there, Marti?"

"Nah. The 'artistic director' says no. What a neurotic asshole. Let's get the hell outta Dodge." We left a healthy tip for the wait staff, then cleared out. I never even bothered to ask the manager about open mic night. After all, I lived in the Austin area, not Houston. Back home after the party weekend, I still waited for news from the different oil industry jobs I'd applied for. 1982 morphed into 1983. I settled for short-term work, serving drinks at a fancy restaurant near the Texas State Capitol—something to tide me over. Patrons of the establishment and coworkers started asking me if I did standup. Grocery store clerks asked me similar questions in the checkout line. All of this surprised and even annoyed me a bit, since I wasn't trying for laughs.

I was feeling pretty down and out at the time, full of sarcasm and a slow-simmering frustration with waiting tables again after years in the oil field. On a weekday lunch shift at work, I served a Tanqueray martini to a woman close to my age, and a Johnny Walker Black on the rocks to her male companion. She asked me a question and I tossed off a comment. They both laughed out loud, and the woman said, "Hey, you're funny. Are you a standup comic?"

I smiled in spite of myself. "No, but people keep asking me that. In fact, I have a friend who's been hard at work for years, trying to convince me to get onstage."

The woman chuckled. "Well, you oughta listen to your friend. They just opened a comedy club at 15th and Lavaca. It's called the Comedy Workshop. Check it out."

"Really? Right here in Austin? Y'know...I'm gonna do that."

Six months later, in August 1983, after my summer visitation with Annie ended, I finally stopped by the Comedy Workshop. Jake'd been interested in overseas work, and now applied for surveying jobs in the Middle East. I would've competed for the same opportunity, but the country he'd be shipping out for didn't allow American women to work as laborers. I'd interviewed for a really cool job with a directional drilling project in the jungles of Colombia, but decided against it. If I'd hired on with that expedition, I'd be the only woman in the encampment, sharing a communal shower with three hundred males over a six-month period. Sure, I could've rigged up a shower for myself in the jungle, using a fifty-gallon drum of rainwater—but decided it wasn't worth it. Jake and I were drifting apart. He wanted to have a child, and I knew I couldn't bear to do that. I'd vowed never to replace my daughter, wanted to focus all my love on Annie alone.

I strolled into the comedy club on a Wednesday night, took a seat in the back, and watched the comics. One guy impressed me, he did a lot of different characters and voices. That night, the audience response to most of the comedians seemed subdued. I talked with one of the comics, who told me that people living in Austin, a hotspot for music, at first didn't know how to react to the standup comics. "They're used to listening to music, and applauding at the end." I suspected this might be rationalization, wondered if this guy'd ever seen live music in Austin. Back then, I'd been a part of the audience during a variety of concerts, at the Armadillo, at Austin City Limits, at Club Foot, and a host of other music spots in town. Austin music audience members screamed, whistled, howled, and otherwise expressed appreciation before, during, and after performances.

After the show, I learned that the Comedy Workshop was an extension of the club I'd visited in Houston, and that this Austin location offered an open mic on Monday nights. Intrigued, I stopped by the club the next Monday. I watched the local comics, two of them women, performing. They all struck me as developing comics, putting together their acts. I began to think maybe I could come up with five minutes. I noticed the artistic director from the Houston club, advising the comics after they finished their sets. I introduced myself. He either didn't remember me, or did a good job of pretending he didn't. He told me some stuff about comedy writing, mainly that things are funnier in threes. And he told me how the comic's set is comprised of bits. He explained how bits are arranged in order, and how you need a segue to move to a new topic without losing the audience's concentration. The guy expounded on how every punchline needs a good setup. The setup provides the audience with any information they need. I figured maybe he wasn't a total asshole after all. At the time, he impressed me as being a competent comedian.

That night, I went home and put together some material for my debut five minutes. Throughout the week, I memorized my bits and timed myself. On Friday and Saturday, I hung out at the club, watching comics. Jake didn't want to come with me, probably figured—or hoped—that comedy was a fleeting distraction. I didn't care. Comedy now enthralled me. Monday found me down at the Comedy Workshop, waiting for my set. Tom, the manager, warned me not to go over my time limit. "When you see the light, wrap it up and get off the stage."

When I stepped up to the microphone stand, I left the mic in place, mainly because I'd never used a mic before and didn't want to fuck it up. The stage lights shone really bright, so I couldn't see the individual audience members' faces. *Good thing I memorized this.* I opened with some bits about working in the oil field. To my surprise, the stuff killed! The crowd laughed—at the right places. Hearing those laughs intoxicated me, thrilled me. Amazed, I kept going till I saw the light, then wrapped it up to resounding applause. Standup provided me with a rush beyond anything I'd ever experienced. I remembered how, even as a kid, I'd dreamed of being a comedian.

The artistic director and the owners of the club attended the open mic that night. I stuck around for the entire show, and when the lights came on, hung out with the Austin comics I'd seen the week before. Johnny Torrez, one of the local comics, pulled out a set of dice, and taught me how to shoot craps. I rolled sevens first time, then elevens. Johnny grinned, chortled. "You're lucky."

"I feel lucky."

The artistic director came over. "Good work, you guys." He turned to me. "You did really well for your first time onstage."

"Thanks."

"But I was talking with the owners, and we're trying to figure out how we're going to dress you."

"Whaddya mean?" I'd worn a tank top with lace around the neckline and arms, a pair of khaki shorts, and sandals. The tank top, my favorite, I bought at a Stevie Ray Vaughan concert.

"You can't wear clothing like that. The fact you did well—it was obviously a fluke. Women need to wear clothes that tone down their sexuality. You're a fucking statue—a blonde piece of ass up there. You gotta cover yourself. Buy some men's shirts and some pleated slacks."

"Whaaat?" I looked to my new friend, Johnny Torrez. He shrugged, held up his hands.

"I'm just starting out. Nothing for the record." He sauntered off toward the bar.

"Oookay. I'll wear something different next week." My thirst for a shot at standup success clouded my judgment. I listened to everything that the artistic director, Keith Dixon, said.

Next Monday, I wore a black and white shirt and a pair of black slacks. The purchase had been compulsory, required for a job waiting tables. I'd worked it for one day, then quit because I hated the dress code that required me to don shitty clothes like that. I looked like a busboy, but since I'd done so well the week before, I arrogantly and foolishly assumed I'd kill again, no matter what I wore. Another dumbass move I made was that I wrote an entirely new five minutes, on different topics. And—I bombed! The silence from the audience became a palpable thing, a beast gnawing at my soul. Determined to finish, I powered on through the new set, then exited when I saw the light. The manager, Tom, marched toward me as I stepped offstage. "Marti! You were ramblin', man! What happened to your other material?"

"Uh, oh, I, uh. I thought I'd try some new ideas."

"Lose the new stuff. You gotta work that first five that got all those laughs. Work it and PERFECT it."

"Yeah, right...Sorry, Tom." I skulked out of the club, headed for my little pickup truck, drove home. I felt as if not only one audience, but the whole world had rejected me. But by the time I reached my front door, I realized I couldn't wait to get onstage again.

My standup journey began. I bombed for months before discovering how to consistently connect with an audience. At first, I listened to every bit of ignorance, disguised as sage advice, that the other comics threw at me. Not my peers in Austin, but the headliners that came from Houston to work the weekends. Some of those guys told me I was "too strong for a woman." My original stage persona had been my true self: badass, high-energy, funny, unabashedly female. With those weirdly manly-type clothes, I didn't even feel like myself, and my material didn't work. One headliner from Houston told me I was talking about all the wrong things, in his opinion. "Female comics need to talk about how they can't get laid, can't get a date. You need to say stuff like, 'I'm so ugly, I'm so fat, I can't get laid.' Then the audience will relate."

I stared at him. "The audience wouldn't relate, because that's not real for me. Comedy is truth." I smiled at him. "Now, you—YOU can DO that kinda stuff." His mouth hung open. I turned and left him standing there, slack-jawed.

I started driving to Houston and Austin both, in order to catch the open mic in each city. My work dropped to part-time so I could pull it off. Brett Butler was one of the comics performing in the open mic in Houston, and I related to her. Bill Hicks, a guy about eighteen or nineteen years old, headlined both clubs. Hicks' fluidity and brilliance onstage blew everybody away. Everyone stood in awe of Bill's genius.

I quit wearing the baggy clothes, returned to my own personal style, started harvesting laughs again. The artistic director voiced his disapproval. "Marti, you're really scary. You remind me of a guy that used to do comedy here. Now he's gone. Banned from the club. His name was Sam Kinison, and he did all kinds of offensive material. He moved to L.A.."

For a few months, I thought I'd figured out a way to ingratiate myself with some of the comics in Houston, and with Dixon the artistic director, who held a position of power in that he decided who got a set, and the duration of that set. My friend Ken'd begun dealing cocaine after the layoffs cut his mud engineer job. I scored coke from Ken and sold it back to some of the Houston crowd, with no markup. In spite of my pharmaceutical favors, the guy continued to comment on my supposed similarity to banished troublemaker Sam Kinison.

I decided to quit supplying. Dixon had asked me to bring a gram of coke to the Austin club that night, but I showed up empty-handed and signed my name on the list anyway. He refused to let me onstage. Cornering me in the green room, he sputtered, "Where's the coke?" A few other comics heard him. I felt my heart beating faster. All my pent-up frustration began rising. Volcanic rage. I'd been putting up with his controlling, power-trippy, passive aggressive form of sexual harassment for what seemed like eons. Now this!

I stared him down. "There isn't any."

A rat-like gleam entered his eyes. "Oh yeah? No coke, huh? Well, what did you come here for, to spread joy? You'd better make yourself useful if you wanna get on. No coke? What ELSE can you do for me, then?" He spat the words, loud enough for anyone in the green room to hear. Sneering, brandishing his glass of burgundy, he leered.

Time slowed to a crawl. My hand drew back, then began its arc toward his face. Nanoseconds before contact, I reminded myself to ease up, or I'd break his jaw. When it connected, the sound of that slap was symphonic, immensely satisfying. A blood-red, hand-shaped mark appeared on the right side of his head. Instinctively, I lifted the glass of wine from his frozen grasp and splashed its contents onto his face, staining his camel-hair Perry Ellis blazer and slacks.

As I turned and walked slowly out of the green room, I heard him screaming, "YOU'RE THROUGH IN SHOW BUSINESS! I'LL MAKE SURE YOU NEVER GET ON A STAGE AGAIN!! EVER!!!" I never looked back.

Now banned from both of the Comedy Workshops, I rustled up stage time elsewhere, a process that helped me to strengthen my confidence and skills. On Sixth Street, I worked the breaks for the bands at one of the jazz clubs. I got steady laughs, and the musicians appreciated the opportunity to smoke joints while I performed. And at Esther's Follies, I did standup during the intermissions between shows, for fifty bucks per weekend. I even found a North Austin Mexican restaurant that let me work the lobby while people waited to be seated. Halfway into a twenty-minute set, a black-clad waiter would step into the lobby, calling out something like, "Rodriguez, party of six!" and thirty percent of my audience would disappear into the dining room. Undaunted, I'd continue to pound out my material, and keep the laughs coming from the remaining diners.

In spite of being shunned by the Comedy Workshop, I kept in touch with Johnny Torrez and other comics from Austin. Arthur Cicchese and Sam Cox, managers at the Austin Comedy Workshop, were cool guys, hip actors from L.A., and friends of mine as well. So I knew that Jay Leno, the highest paid nightclub comic at the time, and a frequent guest on both the Tonight Show with Johnny Carson and the Late Show with David Letterman, was coming to Austin. All of us newbie comics awaited Leno's advent with breathless anticipation. Word was that Bill Hicks would open for Leno. And even more exciting news from upper-level management: Leno would be doing a standup comedy class for all the beginning comics—only fifty bucks to attend.

Hearing all of this, I felt like Cinderella without a fairy godmother or even a pumpkin. The ban could not prevent me from attending Leno's shows as a citizen, but my banned status barred me from Leno's class. I planned on paying the cover charge and three-drink minimum for as long as my cash held out. On the opening night of Leno's first week in Austin, I stopped by the Driskill Hotel for a drink with my cousin Janet before heading to the comedy club. I sipped water, Janet ordered a glass of Chardonnay. Doing standup taught me not to drink before or during a performance—alcohol insulated me, kept me from connecting with the crowd. Tonight, I needed to be laser-sharp while observing the famous Jay Leno, so I could learn as much as humanly possible.

My cousin lifted her glass, then gently set it down. She leaned forward, murmuring, "Jay Leno walked in and sat down, and he's got this gorgeous woman with him."

I froze. "Really? That must be his wife, Mavis. The comics in Houston say she travels with him."

"She's got terrific hair. C'mon, let's move closer to them." Janet, a hairdresser, worked at a hip salon in Austin, and almost had enough money saved to open her own business.

"Oh fuck no. I can't do that."

"Why not? C'mon, don't tell me you're scared."

I dropped to a whisper. "Fuck you, Cousin!" She dissolved into paroxysms of silent laughter, her shoulders shaking ever so slightly. We gathered our drinks and paper cocktail napkins, crossed the room, and settled in at the table opposite the Lenos. Janet leaned across the narrow aisle and smiled at Mavis.

"Your hair is gorgeous! I'm a hairdresser, and I was wondering—who does it for you?"

Mavis smiled. A genuine, warm smile. "Oh, thank you. I get it done in West Hollywood."

Mavis and Janet exchanged a few pleasantries about hair. My cousin didn't waste a moment. "I'm Janet. This is my cousin, Marti." She pointed at me. "She used to work in the oil field, but now she's a comedian."

I blurted out everything at once. "Mr. Leno, uh, Jay. I am a comedian, new to it. But I gotta tell you, I can't attend your comedy class for beginners. I've got the fifty bucks, so I could pay to get in. But, I, uh. I'm banned from the Comedy Workshop." I felt my face tensing up. "But that's not gonna stop me from coming to your shows! If I pay cover charge and three-drink minimum, they'll have to let me in. And I'm gonna be there every night this week, so I can watch and learn. I know you're one of the best."

Jay and Mavis sat silent. *Oh my gosh, now what've I done?* Jay sat up straighter in his chair, leaned back, smiled sarcastically. "What's this about FIFTY BUCKS? When they asked me to talk with beginning comics, I said, 'Yeah, sure.'" He waved a hand in the air. "I do that in every town. But what kind of a JERK would I be, chargin' FIFTY BUCKS to guys that're just startin' out?"

Tom, the manager, along with one of the bartenders, now entered the room and proceeded to Leno's table. Leno turned to face them, sarcastic smile intact. "Hey, what's this I hear about FIFTY BUCKS for a comedy class? I gotta talk to my agent about this! I don't recall any FIFTY BUCK COMEDY CLASS in the contract. Do you, Honey?"

Mavis smiled, set down her glass. "No. Definitely not."

Tom looked very uncomfortable. It clearly had not been his idea to charge money. The decision must've come from Houston.

Jay turned to me and Janet, waved a hand in our direction, then fixed his gaze on Tom. "Marti and Janet here, they're our guests tonight. Got it?" Tom and the bartender nodded. "Okay, let's go." He and Mavis stood. Jay addressed me and my cousin again. "You heading over there now?"

I stood. "Yep. Right behind ya."

Janet stood, waved to Jay and Mavis. "See you there!"

When we reached the club on the corner of 15th and Lavaca, the line stretched all the way around the block and beyond. I pulled into a parking space a few blocks away, and Janet and I hurried up to the front door. Jay and Mavis stood just inside. Jay leaned out, extended a hand. "Hey Marti! Janet! C'mon in. What are you drinking? Same as at the hotel? I'll get your drinks for you. You can sit in the green room with me and Mavis." He and Mavis headed for the green room and we followed, unimpeded. Apparently, the ban had been lifted temporarily, courtesy of Jay and Mavis Leno.

That night Jay did two shows. For the first, Mavis and Jay sat in the audience, watching the resident emcee warm up the crowd, then Bill Hicks' featured spot. Seeing this, I learned that even at the top of your game, you need to know the line-up, see the effect the comics preceding you have on the audience: their attitude and their material. For Jay's set, I stood at the back of the room, where I could get an overview of the crowd response. Leno took the stage, delivered a blistering hot, rapid-fire, smart, real, and incredibly strong show. I saw people laugh so hard they literally fell off their chairs. Some audience members cried and laughed at the same time. Bold and edgy, Jay touched on all the topics comics back then were scared to hit, and every single bit killed. Until Leno, I'd only seen the headliners from Houston, and they talked about the difference between men and women, the difference between dogs and cats, stuff like that. Some of them did material at the expense of others: gays, women, handicapped people, street people. Jay's stuff blew all of that hack shit away. And listening to him, I laughed and felt good. Never mean-spirited, his material impressed me—sarcastic, lightning-quick, wickedly funny.

As Jay and Mavis' guests, I hung out with them in the green room between shows that first night, and every other night that week. I learned a lot of things about comedy, and life in general, from them. After Jay's first show, my cousin and I sat in the green room, alone with the Lenos. Jay and Mavis asked me why I'd been banned from the club. I felt my fists clench involuntarily, and my breathing speeded up. I told them the whole thing, didn't try to sugar-coat it. I figured they'd find out anyway.

Besides confessing that I slapped the guy, and that I'd previously supplied coke to him and some others, I told them the stuff that still lingered in my mind, creating conflict and self-doubt. How the artistic director and some of the Texas headliners told me women couldn't be funny unless they wore baggy-ass, frumpy clothes and talked about how they couldn't get laid. I also told them how these guys said I was too good-looking, too tall, too strong, too brash, too loud, and blah, blah, blah. "And on top of all that, the artistic director told me I should get onstage and talk about how my voice wasn't feminine enough, and how guys like women with higher, softer voices. Hey, they CAN'T be right about all of that, can they?"

Mavis dispelled all of their bullshit with a wave of her hand. "Marti, a lot of guys get into standup in the hope of attracting women—those guys can't get laid, and they can't play guitar, so they do comedy, hoping there'll be groupies. When they see a woman like you come on the scene, they're threatened. You're strong, so they try to stifle you. Having a lower voice is good in standup—it carries, everybody can hear you. Being tall helps, too. The women who are petite and have naturally quiet voices have to work harder to be more authoritative. You've got all kinds of things going for you." She leaned forward. "Consider moving to California; there are a lot of women doing standup there. New York, too."

Jay leaned back in his chair, his sarcastic smile returning. "Texas is not the hub of the entertainment industry. Move to L.A., you belong there." His smile widened. "You're banned here, anyway, right?"

At that, I shared a laugh with Jay and Mavis. "Yeah. But I'm getting stage time here in spite of the ban. I play the breaks for jazz bands, and do other gigs. I'm gettin' paid, too." I looked at Jay, then Mavis. "I WILL make the move to California. I'll have to save up for it. But I'm gonna visit L.A. as soon as possible—for a couple of days at least—to check out the scene, see what level I need to reach in order to compete."

Jay and Mavis nodded. Jay looked at his watch. "Time to go to work." He stood up, walked out to the stage, and gave the standing-room-only crowd a stellar performance. *THIS is how you do standup.* I watched part of his second show that night, but went back to the green room to talk to Mavis. A professional comedy writer before she met Jay, Mavis was brilliant, funny, and down to earth. When she talked to me, I felt instilled with confidence. The insights she shared validated my comedic instincts, and my talent.

Mavis went on to tell me some very important things about comedy. "Marti, nice guys make it in this business. All the great comedians are approachable and friendly. Audiences pick up on phoniness and can read a comic's character. Don Rickles does insult comedy, but he's the nicest guy in the world. That's how he can pull it off. The crowd reads his true personality beyond the stage persona."

Mavis and Jay never did cocaine or any other drugs. On rare occasions Mavis sipped a glass of wine, Jay never drank at all. This fact both surprised and impressed me. Since my first time using drugs at fifteen years old, I'd taken it for granted that all people in show business did loads of drugs and alcohol, partied all the time—like rock stars.

Attending Leno's comedy session turned out to be the crowning glory of a life-changing week. Jay met with all of us beginners in the green room, during the afternoon when the vacant club presented no distractions or interruptions. Even Bill Hicks showed up—at first. He walked out early, though, which surprised me at the time, but looking back now, I understand it. Hicks never listened to any other comedy voice but his own, and that must've been a big part of his genius.

Leno's generosity toward other comics is legendary, and with good reason. Jay taught us the inside stuff, the essence of comedy. I remember all of us on our feet, listening to Jay. Leno stood, too—after all, the subject of our focus was standup. "Stage time is everything," Jay said, "Every night, you get onstage. Your skill in standup is in direct correlation to the amount of stage time you have." Johnny Torrez and I stood shoulder to shoulder, comrades in comedy, drinking it in as Jay continued. "And when you're not doing comedy, you should be watching comedy. Watching live is where you learn the most, but if you can't get to a club, then watch it on TV. And hang out with other comics." Torrez and I looked at each other, nodded. We'd already been doing that. So far, so good.

Leno taught us the importance of rhythm and cadence. "Every comedian has his or her own rhythm. When you're startin' out, you don't know what yours is, you're still working to find it. It's okay to adopt some other comic's rhythm—temporarily!" He gave a self-deprecating chuckle. "My role model was George Carlin. I listened to his comedy albums over and over. And when I started putting together my first stuff, it was in Carlin's rhythm. First few times I got up onstage, I'd be repeating some of my favorite Carlin stuff in my head before I went on, to put me in that cadence." He paused a moment. "I didn't get up there and do Carlin's act. I just got his rhythm going in my head first, then put my words to it. I did that for a while, till I found MY rhythm."

He looked around the room. "You don't have to raise your hand to ask a question. We're hangin' out."

Scott, a Comedy Workshop regular and a full-time student at U.T., spoke up. "What about punchlines?"

Leno nodded. "Yeah, so the punchline is the payoff. Stand strong and deliver that punch. Even if you're pacing back and forth during your setup, stop and take your stance to do the punchline. It's like martial arts. Make the most of your payoff. Get it?"

I nodded, Johnny said, "Um-hmm." I heard others responding in the affirmative.

I chimed in. "What about writing material?"

Jay smiled. "I don't actually write it—I generate it, though. Everybody's different. Some guys do write it all down on paper. I tried that at first, but after I wrote it down, it wasn't funny to me anymore. So I write down a key word, a list of key words." I totally related to this. I'd experienced the same thing, but had felt like I should be writing some kind of script. Now I felt lighter, freer.

Leno kept on going, pouring out helpful strategies. "A lot of my best stuff comes from things I say when I'm hangin' out with friends, especially comedians. When you're hangin' out, you might say something that gets a laugh. You're not trying out material, though, you're relaxed, having a good time. If you say something in that situation and it gets a reaction, you might be able to build that into a bit. If I say something and it gets a laugh, makes me laugh, I take it onstage that night. I go up there in front of an audience, and say it exactly the way I said it to my friends. And if it still gets a laugh with the audience, I know I've got something. And I go home and build on it, keep taking it onstage, and adding. The next part of the process is trimming it down. I've got a bit about this car of mine, a 1957 Buick Roadmaster."

A chain of "Uhm-hmms" rippled around the room. That bit killed, we'd all seen it in his act that week.

"The Buick Roadmaster bit started with one line, and I kept adding to it till it was about twenty minutes long. After I trimmed it down to the strongest lines, it ended up being around five minutes."

Johnny cleared his throat. "So, we hear a lot about stealing. What about that?"

Leno looked around the room. "Write faster than they can steal. That's the best thing you can do to protect your material. And write stuff from your own life. That way, if somebody does steal your material, it won't work as well for them." Gratitude welled up in me as I listened to Jay Leno share valuable, practical truths—without grandiosity, fear, or negativity. It struck me that comedy might be more than a craft, it could be a way of living, a credo, a philosophy. And I liked that idea.

All of the insights Leno revealed to us that afternoon were specific, and clearly stated. He didn't waste our time with the vague generalities that some of the headliners often passed off as advice, like, "Be yourself," or "Be lovable." What the fuck do adages like that mean, anyway? I began to question the competency of any performer who couldn't hand down something useful. I came away from that session armed with field-tested tools from a comedy legend, my new comedy role model—Jay Leno. I began putting his advice to work, generating new material. I devoted myself to living, breathing, and even sleeping standup. After Jay and Mavis left town,

I stayed in touch with them. I asked Mavis if I could write a letter in care of their agent when I moved to Los Angeles. Her answer floored me. "Call us any time. We're in the phone book under 'J. Leno.' It's not a very common name, we might be the only one listed."

In the wake of Leno's blockbuster week at the Austin Comedy Workshop, the club begun booking a cavalcade of nationally headlining comics: Elayne Boosler, Vic Dunlop, Mark Schiff, Kevin Nealon, Emo Phillips, Judy Tenutta, Ritch Shydner, Bob Saget, Rick Overton, Alex Valdez, Robert Schimmel, and others. Houston prodigy Bill Hicks, now an Austin sensation, returned again and again. And eventually, thanks to Jay and Mavis' approval, the Austin club lifted the ban against me, restoring all the privileges of being a club regular: a preferential spot in the Monday night open mic line-up, and the opportunity to stand at the back of the club, observing the performances of rising standup stars and comedy legends in the making.

Elayne Boosler, one of the top standup comics in the U.S., came to the Austin Workshop shortly after the Lenos left. A brilliant writer and performer, she blew us all away. As with Leno, people stood in line for blocks to see Elayne Boosler. Boosler dressed stylishly, delivering laser-sharp lines that instigated apoplectic fits of laughter every ten seconds or so. She sustained that level for her entire set, over an hour. Gorgeous and magnanimous, Elayne used material that connected with women and men alike. Watching her genius and skill, I set new goals for myself as a comedian. She exploded all the stereotypes those Houston comics clung to regarding women in comedy, and embodied many of the best aspects of standup.

Ritch Shydner, a favorite at the club, never failed to do a killer show, every night, every time. A spontaneous performer and a prolific writer, Shydner's energy onstage kept any crowd on the edge of their seats. Year round at the Austin Comedy Workshop, Sam Cox and Arthur Cicchese deftly executed crowd control, politely but firmly removing hecklers and hostile drunks from the equation, without disturbing the rest of the audience or the flow of the comics' acts.

During a Friday night second show, while Ritch bantered with the audience, improvising and harvesting wave after wave of laughter, a muscly, tequila-soddened dude sitting toward the rear left-hand side of the room, nearest the exit, began hurling insults at the top of his lungs. Shydner zinged him with comebacks that reaped a whirlwind of even louder laughs. Arthur and Sam moved in, extracted the burly heckler, and escorted him from the club.

Ten minutes later, the heckler somehow sneaked back into the club, appearing out of nowhere, zigzagging through the tables till he reached the foot of the stage—and pulled a knife on Ritch. Shydner never broke stride, somehow kept the snappy comments coming, but moved into a fighting stance. Anyone could see he now prepared himself to disarm the assailant. In the same instant, Arthur Cicchese tackled the knife-wielding guy, grappled with him. The heckler dropped the knife, Arthur dragged him away, Ritch threw out a punchline, and the audience returned to a blissful, laughing state, as though the aborted knife incident'd been part of the show.

Vic Dunlop hit Austin like a hurricane. Both onstage and off, Vic blew the roof off the place. Both Torrez and I gravitated toward him; he mentored us, made us feel included, even competent as comedians. We felt the same way about Alex Valdez. A hilarious comic, both Latino and blind, Alex killed night after night in Austin. He broke down barriers in so many ways. Valdez was the first comedian with a disability to earn national recognition. Both Vic and Alex taught us so many things about the craft, the attitude, and the life that standup comedy encompasses. Rick Overton, a master of improvisation and standup, rocked the house like nobody's business. Each time he rolled into Austin, audiences absolutely loved him.

A month or so after the Lenos departed Austin, I scraped together enough money to buy a roundtrip plane ticket to Los Angeles. I had enough cash left over to cover a night or two at some fleabag motel in Hollywood, if I ate only one cheap meal a day. I reckoned I could walk down to the Comedy Store and the Improv each night, to hang out. Arthur Cicchese heard about my plans and helped me out by vouching for me with a couple of his L.A. friends who lived in West Hollywood. Thanks to the generous hospitality of two different people Arthur knew, I couch-surfed, stretching my funds so I could stay several nights in the City of the Angels. One of my hosts, Sue, worked at a big talent agency and lived a couple of blocks from the Improv. My other host, Jack, lived within a half mile of the Comedy Store.

Jack, an actor and a mensch, picked me up at Los Angeles International Airport, LAX, in his car. I paid my way by purchasing gasoline, and some groceries to stock the refrigerator in his apartment. That first night, I walked down to the Comedy Store at 8433 Sunset Boulevard. I paid my cover, entered the Main Room, and sat down in the back, where comics like to sit, to see the show. I soon figured out that most of the comics loitered in the hallway. At one point, I chatted with a couple of guys, told them I came from Texas. An hour or so later, a stout little guy with long, dark blond hair clambered down the aisle, sat next to me. He leaned in, spoke in a hoarse whisper. "Hey, I heard you're a standup and you're from Texas."

"That's right."

"Ever been to the Comedy Workshop in Houston?"

"Yeah."

"Ever met a guy there named Keith Dixon?"

A lightning strike of terror hit me, my pulse accelerated. I could hear the artistic director's voice in my head, screaming: "I'LL MAKE SURE YOU NEVER GET ON A STAGE AGAIN!!" I wondered if his influence reached as far as Hollywood. I braced myself for the worst, then decided to put all my cards on the table.

I turned, looked the chunky, long-haired comic in the eye. "I gotta be honest with you, man. Keith Dixon, uh...he won't have anything good to say about me. He—well, he banned me from the club."

The comic's face split into a grin. He lunged toward me, his throaty rasp increasing slightly in volume. "Hey, what didja do to 'im? C'mon, WHADIDJA DO?"

I exhaled softly. "I uh, I slapped him."

The comic grinned even wider, thrust out his hand, gripping mine in one of those Sixties-style, stick-it-to-the-Man handshakes. "RIGHT ON!!! I broke his leg in three places! Fuck that little weasel. I'm Sam Kinison."

Now it was my turn to grin. "Good to meet you. I'm Marti Mac-Gibbon." *Sam Kinison. This is the guy the artistic director compared me with on the many occasions when he said I was scary. Fuck YEAH!*

In that moment, Jay Leno's advice popped into my head. "Texas is not the hub of the entertainment world." All of the pieces began to fall into place, and I saw that the world of standup was both an island and an ocean, limited and vastly expansive. I knew I'd find my way. As I continued to hang out at the two premiere Hollywood comedy clubs that week, I saw Richard Belzer, Billy Crystal, Arsenio Hall, Diane Nichols, and Richard Lewis. One of my favorites at the Comedy Store was Paul Mooney. Sam Kinison hadn't made it big yet, but I saw him one night at the Comedy Store that week, and I thought he could be a star. Years later, my prediction proved accurate.

On one of my last nights in Hollywood, I saw Ritch Shydner in the lobby of the Improv. We talked for a moment. Just then, a glamorously dressed blonde woman approached, greeted Shydner, then addressed me. "I love your look. Do you want to be on TV?" I stood silent a moment, in shock.

Shydner, generous to fellow comedians in the same way that Leno is, spoke up. He introduced me to the woman, a talent manager. "Marti's a standup comic. She's got ten minutes of material."

I regained my cool. "That's right, I've got a solid ten minutes. I'm from Texas, but I'll be moving here soon." The manager, Marilyn, set me up with an audition the next day, an open opportunity known as a cattle call, at NBC. I had no idea what the project involved, but figured it'd be an interesting experience. Strangely, I kept getting callbacks and moving through the process. People at the network told me they needed a tough-talking, sassy blonde in the repertoire of characters. I ended up in the finals. The process took much longer than a week, and taught me some things about the entertainment business. One is that you should never take yourself too seriously. I had to rearrange my plane fare and secure an extra few days off from my current employer, the Stephen F. Austin Hotel, where I worked as a cocktail server.

On the final day of auditions, I left the line of actresses to find the women's restroom. Returning, I took the wrong turn and headed down one of the nondescript hallways. Pretty soon, I figured I might be lost, so when a dark-haired guy passed me in the hall, I decided to ask him for directions. I slapped on my winningest smile and slathered on a little bit of Texas-good-ol-girl attitude. "Scuse me, I don't know my way around—see, I'm from Texas, and I've never been here before."

The guy stopped, laughed. "Texas? What're you doing here?" He continued to walk down the hallway, so I walked with him, figured it'd be better to do that than get shot for trespassing at a television network headquarters.

"I got invited to a big audition, a cattle call. Now mind you, in Texas, a cattle call is whooole different thing."

The dark-haired guy laughed again, harder. He turned a corner, and I followed. He pointed ahead of us, down this new corridor. "All the auditions are in this area, up ahead." We walked in silence a moment. He turned to look at me. "By the way, what's your name? And what do you do, back there in Texas?"

"It's Marti. I used to work in the oil field—set off explosives at one job, and staked oil wells for a surveying outfit after that. Now I'm doin' standup comedy. That's why I came here for a few days, to check out the scene. Then I got roped into this cattle call, and yee-haw, here I am, four days later."

The dark-haired guy chuckled. "Well, work that Texas stuff. It's like being ethnic."

"Really? Okay, then! But enough about me, Buddy, let's talk about you. You work here?"

He laughed again, looked at the floor, then back at me. "Yeah, I work here."

"You do? Well, that's cool! What do you do?"

Still laughing, he said, "I'm a producer. I produce."

"Well, what shows do you produce?"

The guy stopped stock still, nearly doubled over with laughter, looked at me, regained his composure. He waved a hand at a series of doors, on both sides of the hallway. A sign on the first door read, "Diff'rent Strokes," on another, "Gimme a Break!" The sign on the third door read, "Facts of Life."

"You mind tellin' me your name?"

He threw back his head and laughed. "It's Alan. Alan Blankenstein."

Back then, I didn't watch television shows—only Carson and Letterman, so I had no idea whether these productions were successful. But I figured since he was such a nice guy, I'd better say something. "Well, I gotta be honest with you, Mr. Blankenstein. I don't watch TV, but when I get back to Texas, I'm gonna watch alla these shows. And I'm gonna watch for your name in the credits, and I'm gonna tell all my friends, "I know that man, Alan Blankenstein. I know a producer." I stuck out my hand and he shook it, still laughing.

"I'd better get back to that audition. Thanks for the directions." I headed off. Later, while standing in line for the final decision to be announced, I saw Mr. Blankenstein from far off, down the hall, with a couple of guys walking alongside him, pushing carts with equipment. He waved. I waved back.

He waved both arms over his head, laughing, and called out, "Give 'em what fer, Marti! Good luck!"

I waved again, looked around, noticed the other women in line staring at me. A few hours later, they announced the name of the one chosen for the job. The rest of us congratulated her and began walking out of the cavernous building toward the exit. One woman I'd stood in line with throughout the final two days caught up to me in the hallway. "Wow! I thought you had it in the bag when I saw you talking with Fred Silverman."

"Who's Fred Silverman?"

Her mouth stood open. She blinked. "Fred Silverman, he runs NBC, owns Metromedia?" She exhaled sharply. "He used to run ABC and CBS, too. He's huge in show business. He was shouting out your name and wishing you good luck."

"Oh. He told me his name was Alan Blankenstein. I don't watch TV, so I had no idea who he was. I met him in the hallway, coming back from the women's restroom."

She shot me a look like she wanted to punch me in the face. But the look melted into one of pity. "Well, you're going home to Kansas, anyway. Right?"

"Texas. Yes."

We walked together out the front doors, both of us silent, contemplating how we almost made it. Later, I felt lucky. The show we'd competed for was called, "Thicke of the Night," a late-night talk show hosted by Canadian talk show host Alan Thicke. The show was one of the historic bombs of its day. Silverman later was quoted in the New York Times, saying it "was probably the nadir of my career."

On my final day in Tinseltown, I picked up the phone book at Jack's place, found the Lenos' number in the book, and called. Mavis picked up, and I told her I'd been in town on a visit, had even auditioned for a TV show.

"Marti, that's terrific, congratulations! We just got back in town. Jay's working at the Improv tonight, you should go down there and say hi."

That night, I walked down to the famous club on Melrose. After Jay's set, I talked with him for a minute, related the same news I'd shared with Mavis. "I want you to know that I'm serious. I gotta catch a plane outta here in the morning, but I'll be here soon."

He grinned. "Whaddya need a plane outta here for, Marti? You belong here."

When I got back to Austin, I watched all three of the shows Alan Blankenstein/Fred Silverman told me he produced. And I found out he'd put many historic TV shows on the air. No wonder the guy laughed so hard! Back then, in Los Angeles, especially in the entertainment business, he probably never laid eyes on anyone that didn't know who he was.

Now even more determined to migrate to L.A. in pursuit of a standup career, I doubled down on writing and performing. My efforts yielded results—I began to develop a local following, people that came to open mic nights to catch my set in the "showcase" part of the line-up. One night, after a really good set, Sam Cox took me aside. "There's a friend of yours at the door. He wants to talk to you."

I made my way to the doorway, where my friend and former supervisor at Benson, Don Atwater, stood tall, in Stetson hat and dress cowboy boots, smiling like the sun itself. "Hey, I watched you up there. You're real good, Marti!"

I felt a rush of pride, mixed with happiness at seeing a true friend. My oil patch years formed a deep bond for me, both with the State of Texas and the friends with whom I shared the work and wealth. "Thanks. Been workin' at it."

Don Atwater's eyes gleamed, he smiled beatifically. "Y'know that well I invested in with Ben Kramer and Tom Stills?" I nodded. Kramer and Stills were also cool supervisors at Benson, but not as cool as Atwater. I knew they'd all gone in on a wild card, a shallow well in Tennessee. Don continued, grinning broadly. "Well, we got a hit!" He pointed to his dress boots. They looked extra shiny in the light of the neon-lit buildings along the street. "The oil from the gusher's still on my boots."

"Congratulations, Don! This is fantastic!!"

We stood together, savoring the crazy rush that news of a big oil strike can give. I looked up at Don, clapped him on the shoulder. "Oil Field Trash and Proud of it." We laughed, but I knew it to be true. And today, I still feel some of that pride, running strong and deep within me.

CHAPTER 14

FORTUNE FAVORS THE BOLD, AND OTHER SAGE ADVICE

JAY LENO'S SECOND VISIT TO THE AUSTIN COMEDY WORKSHOP triggered a wave of anticipation among both local comedy fans and local comedians. Word around the club was that this time, Keith Dixon would be coming from Houston to be Leno's opening act. At first, I worried that the ban against me might be reinstated, but then I got a grip. To my relief, when I arrived at the Comedy Workshop, no ban presented itself. I hung out at the back, with the other comics, watching and learning, as usual. On Wednesday morning, I called the Driskill hotel and left a message for Mavis. She called me back an hour or so later, suggested we meet for lunch. "That guy, the one who banned you, is working with Jay this week, so I wasn't surprised you didn't stop by the green room."

"Aw, well, I am a little bit worried he might slap the ban on me again."

"We talked with him last night. He went out of his way to bring up your name in conversation. Jay invited him to go out to get dinner after the show, and he leaned forward—real heavy vibe—said, 'Okay, but I feel it's only right to caution you. There is a woman who used to do the open mics in this club, and I've heard she now waits tables somewhere in Austin. She's violent, dangerous. She might even be mentally ill. Her name is Marti MacGibbon.'" I felt like I'd been punched in the sternum. Mavis continued. "Right away, I realized this must be the guy. And I said, 'Oh, we know Marti! She's a working comic now.' And Jay jumped in, too. Said something like, 'Marti? Yeah, she was in L.A. not long ago, I ran into her at the Improv.'"

Their generosity and kindness stunned me. "Thank you for doing that!"

Mavis chuckled. "The look on his face...Anyway, your name didn't come up a second time."

I laughed. "That's so cool. Thank you again."

She waved away my thanks. "Everything we said was the truth."

Friday night, after the first show, while the audience members sauntered out of the club and the staff hurried to set up before the second show's audience filed in, the artistic director saw me standing, leaning against a wall. He marched over to me. "So, what are YOU doing here?" A herd of snarky retorts stampeded through my consciousness, jostling for position, for the chance to administer a verbal shredding. But I took a deep breath, and maintained silence. At that moment, Leno appeared.

"Hey Marti! D'you know if there's a Popeye's Fried Chicken near the club?"

"Yeah."

"Can you drive me over there and get me back in time for the second show?"

"Yep. I can do that."

Leno waved an arm in the direction of the exit. "Okay Marti, let's go."

I pushed off the wall, stepped around the artistic director, and hurried to catch up with Jay. Outside the club, I reached into my purse, pulled out my keys, and pointed down the street. "I'm parked over there."

"Marti, you're gonna run into guys like that all the way up the ladder in show business. No matter what happens, all you really gotta do is stand your ground and work on your act. You stand your ground, and eventually these guys will have to come to you and apologize. And then, just be nice. In show business, be nice to people. And be funny."

I nodded, feeling wealthy by virtue of hearing such sage advice. All of a sudden, I recalled Jay Leno's being a collector of fancy cars, and owner of several motorcycles. I felt my face tensing up, knowing that I'd agreed to drive him to Popeye's in my bashed-in, decrepit, Mazda Sundowner pickup truck, a hopeless La Bamba. *Fuck it. Too late to turn back.* I stopped walking when we reached my vehicle. Leno never batted an eye, jumped in the passenger side. I slid behind the wheel, turned the key in the ignition, furtively whispering a prayer to the comedy gods, hoping against hope that tonight, the truck would perform like a normal vehicle. The engine coughed once, then turned over, and I angled it into traffic.

So far, so good. Then, to my dismay, the little truck began shuddering and backfiring—as usual. I turned up the radio, hoping it might cover the tortured sounds of the engine. Now on the cusp of purchasing a new ride, I wondered if this one would bring any trade-in value at all. Or would they charge me a fee to abandon it on their lot? I gently pressed the gas pedal, and the truck accelerated slightly. I fixed my eyes on the road ahead, doggedly determined to complete the roundtrip to and from the fried chicken joint. A moment later, the truck backfired again. Leno reached out and killed the radio, turned to look at me. "Marti, you've, uh, got some mechanical issues here."

It struck me that the famous comedian might not feel safe riding with me. I figured he'd rather call the cops, or a taxi at this point. "Aw, Jay, I'm sorry about the backfiring, it does this all the time. I promise you, it'll get us to Popeye's and back in time for the show." I felt shame creeping in. *I never should've done this.*

"Hey Marti, I was a mechanic for Mercedes Benz. I'm pretty sure I can help you out. Pull over and park for a minute, lemme take a look."

I eased the spasming truck off the road, turned off the engine. Leno stepped out of the passenger side. I got out, too, stood alongside while Jay set to work. He looked under the hood. Then, to my amazement, he removed his fancy suit jacket. That article of clothing, I figured, easily cost more than my little truck did the day it rolled off the showroom floor. He loosened his tie and rolled up his sleeves. Then Jay Leno turned his upscale jacket inside out, laid it on the pavement beneath my pickup truck, and slid under the vehicle to do repairs.

The entire episode elapsed in minutes. "Hey! Marti! Got any tools in your truck?" I passed him the paltry assortment of socket wrenches, pliers, screwdrivers and other crap I carried behind the seat. "Hey Marti, I gotta show you something. C'mere." I leaned down. He thrust a hand out from under the truck, and in it, I could see a battered auto part. "This is your problem, the fuel filter. You need to replace this part as soon as you can. It's clogged, but I can do a temporary fix. I'm gonna clean it out." He put the part to his lips, blew on it to clear the obstruction, then reattached it. "Okay, we're good to go."

I stepped back, awestruck, walked around to the driver's side. Leno slid out from under the truck, stood, picked up his suit jacket, shook it a few times, turned it right-side out, and put it back on. In minutes, we reached Popeye's Fried Chicken, Leno placed his order, and they filled it. On the way back to the comedy club, the little Mazda hummed along. No more backfiring, no more shuddering. "When my truck started acting up, Jay, I kinda panicked. Like you'd call the cops, or a cab. I wouldn't blame you. Y'know, I've almost got enough money saved to buy a new car."

Leno looked out at the night and the road ahead, politely ignoring the three-inch-long crack in the windshield on the passenger side. "Marti, you're making a mistake that a lot of comics make startin' out. You don't give people enough credit. What kind of a guy would I be if I bailed out of your vehicle, took off in a taxi, and left you on the roadside? I know how to fix cars, so of course I'm gonna help out. You gotta realize that other people see the same things you do, and they pick up on the truth about what's really going on. Like that guy Keith, back at the club."

"The artistic director."

"Yeah, him. He can't hurt you if you stand your ground. And you gotta understand that people can talk to him for five minutes, and talk to you for five minutes, and they'll know what's really going on. Most people are exactly as smart, kind, generous, and honest to you as you are to them. You gotta keep that in mind all the time. That's why a lot of comics miss the mark, they underestimate their audience. Never underestimate your audience. And don't underestimate yourself."

I pulled up to the front door of the club, and Leno got out. I watched as he disappeared through the entrance. I parked my truck, opened the glovebox, grabbed a ballpoint pen and a crumpled receipt. I smoothed out the receipt, and on the back of it, jotted down a note, reminding myself to buy a new fuel filter at the auto parts store. Next day, I bought the new part and got the truck fixed. Soon after, I traded the truck in on a new car, a maroon Datsun Sentra. Today, when I look back on the night Leno fixed my pickup truck, I remember the words of Mavis Leno: "Nice guys make it in this business." She was so right. Jay made it all the way to the top. He deserved his twenty-two years hosting the Tonight Show, and all of his other successes.

Now that I'd made an iron-clad decision to move to California, I began finalizing my plans. My recurring dreams, having receded for well over a year, hit me with one brief but vicious salvo. My 1984 summer visitation would be coming up soon—if Annie's father gave consent. The visitation contract stipulated that I send a written request each year to Derek, attesting to the fact that I could provide an adequate temporary home for her. Each year, my ex had taken his time replying to my appeal, stretching out the suspense, finally deigning to give his permission at the very last minute. Now, in '84, the excruciating pain of waiting reached a new apex. Fresh off the road from a week at Jokers in Oklahoma City, the serial-killer dream troubled me. But the second dream, the one with me, my daughter, and the shark, shook me to the core. I woke up sweating, gasping for breath. Reluctant to risk a replay of the nightmares, I sat up, fixed myself some espresso, and waited till the Comedy Workshop, my second home, opened.

At the Club, I confided in Arthur Cicchese. Arthur hailed from Boston originally, but'd spent years in California. Like Johnny Torrez, Arthur knew a few things about the world of gambling, and he was lucky. He'd picked the right horse at Santa Anita and, with the cash from that big win, he'd bought a brand new, shiny, fast car and traveled to Texas in style. Arthur'd once told me his nickname in Los Angeles was Strong Boy, then he'd laughed in his self-effacing way. Arthur listened as I poured out my story—the heartbreak over my daughter, my struggle, all of it. "And Arthur...my ex is gonna be a lawyer soon. He told me he's dedicating himself to making sure I'll never see my daughter again." I straightened my shoulders, steeling myself. "Sometimes I wake up in the night and the pain of separation is almost overwhelming." I looked at Arthur. "And the older I get, the worse it gets."

Suddenly the bottled-up grief surged, overcame my fierce resistance. Wracked with sobs, I felt shame over crying in front of anyone, especially a friend in the comedy biz. Arthur put his arm around my shoulder. "Marti, you don't have to cry alone." I tried to pull myself together, but failed. Arthur said, "Go ahead, you can cry on my shoulder. For a while, anyway—I've got a liquor shipment coming in." I burst out laughing, relieved to change gears. I wiped my face with my hand. He looked me in the eye. "You've got FRIENDS here. Always remember that. Hey, y'know that bridge in your dream, the one where you see your friends standing there? That sounds like the Bay Bridge. It's longer than the Golden Gate Bridge. And you'll beat the shark, man, no doubt about it."

"You think so?"

"Yeah, I do. California's full of sharks. Especially land sharks—they come out in the daytime." We both laughed. Arthur warmed to his topic. "In California, surfers get out there with sharks in the water every day. They do it because they love to surf, it's their life. Like standup, Marti. You do that every day, while millions of people would never try it even once; it's scary, like surfing with sharks. But you can win. You've got a plan. That's good. Lemme give you a tip about California, and especially Hollywood." I nodded. "In California, every guy you meet is an actor, no matter what. Keep your eyes open for scams and cons. And stick with comedians, people you know. Find people you can trust."

"Thank you, Arthur. Don't tell anybody I cried in front of you, okay? I'm supposed to be a badass chick comic."

He dragged a finger across the left side of his chest in an "X" pattern. "Cross my heart and hope to die. Your secret is safe with me." He looked at me and smiled, and the sky opened up for me, because I knew for sure I could trust him. I walked out of the club armed with some kickass advice, reaffirmed in the knowledge that in comedy, I had friends. Eventually, my ex-husband granted the summer visitation.

By now, I'd managed to jump onto the comedy club merry-go-round. Vic Dunlop helped me out by recommending me to the guy who booked the Jokers club in Oklahoma City. I drove up there and did a guest set one night, after getting the okay from Kevin Nealon, the club's headliner that week. My set rocked, and they booked me. With that cred under my belt, I called Chris DiPetta, the guy who booked the Punchline in Atlanta and a number of other clubs. "I'm gonna be coming through Atlanta next week. Can I get a guest spot?"

"Tuesday's audition night. C'mon by around seven-thirty."

"Perfect, thanks!" I drove to Atlanta from Austin, stopping to nap in rest areas. I got into town on Tuesday evening, stopped in a gas station restroom, put on my fancy stage clothes, and hit the Punchline. My guest set passed the audition, and he booked me for the club in Birmingham. I kept doing that with comedy clubs whenever possible, following leads from headliners who came through the Austin Comedy Workshop. I soon booked weeks in Phoenix, Pasadena, San Antonio, Louisville, Lexington, and one-nighters in Houston, Tulsa, Bakersfield, and Bloomington, Indiana. And in the midst of it all, the Austin Comedy Workshop hired me for a paid week, an honor bestowed upon regulars that ascend to "pro comic" level.

On the way back from Atlanta, I stopped in Nashville at Zanies. Thanks to a recommendation from another Austin regular, I connected with one of his Nashville friends, Josh Crewe, a cool musician, and his girlfriend Lana, who taught ballet at Vanderbilt University. They let me couch-surf at their place overnight. At Zanies, I introduced myself to one of the club's owners and asked him for a guest set.

"Leno's here, and Sinbad's opening for him. We're not allowing any guest sets this week, sorry."

"Hey, that's alright. I gotta get back home to Austin anyway."

"Austin? Hey, that's cool. One of the investors in this club lived there awhile. He worked in the oil business."

"No kidding? I worked in the oil field! In fact, one of my supervisors, Tom Stills, invested in an oil well with two other supervisors—right here in Tennessee, near Gatlinburg. They struck oil, too. Small world, isn't it?"

The club owner's face lit up. "Oh man, you're KIDDING me! Tom Stills is the partner in this club. Too bad he's outta town right now. Hey, that oil well helped to make this place happen."

I stood up, shook the man's hand. "When Tom Stills gets back to town, tell him that Marti MacGibbon, from Benson and Associates, says hi." I smiled.

The club owner offered to pay all expenses for me and my friends to see one of the shows that night. This time, Mavis wasn't traveling with Jay, so I didn't want to hang out. I told Leno that I now had begun to book comedy clubs, here and there. That night, I also talked shop with Sinbad, the opening act. On the way back to Texas, I skipped stopping in Memphis, kept driving till I got home. Back then, comedy clubs popped up in every city, even small towns. With tenacity and grit, an opening act could stay booked most of the year. The road offered an opportunity to hone an act, try out new material, and get ready for the big time in New York or Los Angeles.

Even though I'd booked a lot of work, I still needed my part-time job serving drinks at the newly-renovated Stephen F. Austin Hotel, a magnificent historic place. Most days, a jazz singer played piano, doing covers of Billie Holiday and Sarah Vaughan—she rocked. One weekday afternoon, before the singer arrived, a guy strolled in, one hand gripping a carrying case. He seated himself at the bar. I noticed how carefully he set the case down beside him, then gave the bartender his drink order. My section was empty, the shift'd only begun a few minutes before. As I approached him, he flashed me a friendly smile, so I felt it'd be cool to ask, "Hey, is that a musical instrument?"

"Yeah. Blues harmonica."

"Cool, I love blues. You playing in town this week?" Austin in the 1980s served as a Mecca for classic blues, jazz, punk rock, new wave, rockabilly, R & B, country, Zydeco, blue grass, southern rock, hard rock, metal—an entire array of styles.

"I'm here to meet a friend, another harp player." The bartender brought his drink, set it down on the bar. "My name's Jerry Portnoy. I played blues harp for Muddy Waters for the past six years. Now I'm playing with the Legendary Blues Band." I nodded slowly. I knew that Blues legend Muddy Waters had died the previous year, April 30th, 1983. The harp player smiled. "What's your name?"

"I'm Marti MacGibbon, and I'm a standup comic. This is my day job." I felt sheepish at my compulsion to explain the day job.

"Oh yeah? Standup, huh? Jay Leno opened for us once. He did great."

"Leno's the best. He's kind of a mentor to a lot of us here at the local comedy club. He advised me to move to L.A., and I'm gonna move there real soon."

Jerry Portnoy's face, for a moment, seemed to register concern. "Well, if you're sure that's your plan, I'd like to pass on a few things I've learned along the way."

"Sure!"

"I've seen guys in the music business, chasing their dream, heading for L.A. or New York, and they lose their heads—they get caught up in the race for money and fame. Don't be like that, Marti." He sipped his drink, set it down. "Here's what. Love your art first, and dedicate yourself to upholding it in its purest form. Know what I mean?"

"Yeah, I think I do." I began to think about the very best of the live comedy I'd seen—the fucking beauty of it. And my best standup sets flashed before my eyes, the moments when I'd been in the zone, now crystallized in my consciousness. I lived for those moments. Those pure moments of...the art.

"You can't go wrong if you love your art. You'll keep getting better and better, and the money, the recognition, maybe even fame—they'll follow. And when your break comes, and you vault to the top, you'll take your art with you. That's important. I played in Muddy Waters' band, and I've seen the Rolling Stones, big stars like that, come up and ask if they can jam with us. They asked permission, because Muddy was a master of the art of the blues." He leaned forward, reached for his drink, took a sip, pushed it away. "During my years with Muddy Waters, I've also seen big stars, guys that got to the top, got there by accident, almost, and with those guys, you know and THEY know, they chased the fame and forgot about the art. They've got no STAYING power without the art. And they gotta catch up on the art."

I nodded. "I see what y'mean. If I focus on the art form, I'll have...honor. No matter whether I make it big, or not."

Jerry nodded, half-smiled. "Yeah. The art is the equalizer. Muddy loved the blues, his art form. He recognized it in others, always had time and energy to commit to upholding the art, and to passing it on to others, encouraging others. That way, the art lives on; it's something greater than any one artist's individual success or failure. Sometimes, our tour bus would roll into a city, park in front of a music hall, and there'd be a guy lyin' in the gutter, lookin' half-dead. People'd be walking by, and you'd see a couple of them step over the guy, like he was trash. And then we'd all start getting off the bus. Muddy'd come along, and he'd stop and lean down, tap the guy on the shoulder and call him by name, invite that guy from the gutter to jam with us. Muddy'd buy him dinner, get him cleaned up, and afterward, when we'd jam, the guy'd play like a virtuoso. He was down on his luck, all the way in the gutter, but his art never abandoned him and neither did Muddy. Because the art lives on, through us." Portnoy paused.

"Hey, keep going, okay? Please. All of this is—valuable." I checked myself, didn't want to act all weird and beg him to keep going. But the things he said fascinated me.

"Like I said, Muddy Waters was a master. From city to city, young guys just starting out would ask him specific questions, about technique, things like that. And I never saw him shut a guy out. He always took time to sit with them, share the secrets and the treasures of the art."

"Yes! I've seen that in comedy, too." I thought about Leno, how he took time with comics starting out, in city after city. And I remembered the generosity he and Mavis showed toward me.

"He took the time, because he loved the art. As a true master, he could afford to be generous. And that, my friend, is how you can recognize the masters of your art. Never hesitate to step up, ask questions, seek wisdom from those who've attained the higher places. The ones that arrived there with their art within them will never hesitate to share the best of their insights and their knowledge with you. If they act all stuck up and pretentious, they are exactly that: pretenders. And they have nothing to teach you." He turned slightly on the barstool. "Okay, that's it. Wait, I've got one more thing."

"Yes?"

"Believe in yourself. And never give up."

I grabbed Jerry Portnoy's hand, shook it. "Thank you."

"No problem." Jerry turned toward the entrance, waved at a guy coming through the doorway. Portnoy turned back to me. "There's the man I came to see." As his friend drew nearer, I recognized Kim Wilson, the lead singer and blues harp player for the Fabulous Thunderbirds. Jerry politely introduced me to Kim, then paid his tab and picked up his harmonica case. Jerry looked at Wilson. "You ready?"

Kim nodded. "Yeah. Always."

The two musicians strode toward the door. Right before he exited, Jerry turned, called out to me. "Good luck in California, Marti!"

As my 1984 summer visitation with Annie drew to a close, I prepared to depart for the West Coast. At the last minute, I decided that since Los Angeles was such a huge city, I might do better adapting to California in smaller San Francisco. I didn't know anybody there at all, but thanks to the fierce and fabulous gay men in my life, I found a way. One of my best friends, Michael, connected me with his friend, Dennis Mooney, who lived at the Russian River, north of San Francisco. I figured my journey would begin in Northern California out of necessity. But as soon as possible, I'd make my way south. I'd heard reassuring things about the San Francisco comedy scene and its legendary hotspots like The Holy City Zoo, a renowned developmental club frequented by Robin Williams.

Fortune favors the bold. I spent one night at Dennis Mooney's, and on the morning of the next day, with a copy of the San Francisco Chronicle's ad section in hand, I set out in search of an apartment for rent. I rented the first one I saw; the fully furnished guest cottage of a gorgeous house in Stinson Beach, in Marin County, just north of the Golden Gate Bridge, for five hundred dollars a month. Perfect! Stunned by the beauty of the Bay Area, and flabbergasted by the fog and Mount Tamalpais, I drove haltingly and over-cautiously, arriving late for my appointment with the landlord. But the pace in beach towns is a little easier than in the city, so I walked away with the lease and the keys. My new home occupied a coveted spot on the private beach.

Within a few days of my first visit to the bar at the Sand Dollar Restaurant, I signed up for the Stinson Beach Volunteer Fire Department. At the time, a big fire raged, up on Bolinas Ridge, threatening to swoop down on the town of Stinson Beach. I overheard some of the locals talking about it. So far, the only volunteer firefighters in the community had been males. Females functioned as paramedics, but didn't go out on the fires. I told the fire captain how I'd worked in the oil field, and he decided to give me a chance. The entry exam included driving a hook-and-ladder truck around the town, backing it into the fire house garage, and parking it. I passed, and became the first woman volunteer firefighter in Stinson Beach.

A couple of days later, I started doing sets around San Francisco, wherever they'd let me onstage. Almost immediately, I received some very good press. A popular columnist in the San Francisco Chronicle, Herb Caen, mentioned me in his column, with a quote from my set, after I appeared at a jazz club downtown. I began working the comedy showcase at Miramar Beach Club in Half Moon Bay. I landed a SAG agent, and started going out on auditions in the City. I booked a couple of those jobs, too. Now I found myself on the way to getting a Screen Actors Guild card. My luck seemed to spike.

In Marin County, I met some of the best people I've ever known. On my first day in town, I met Bob and Tony Weiler, two brothers from New York, who introduced me to their circle of friends. Bob and Tony knew how to sling East Coast sarcasm in the Golden State, without wounding anyone, a rare skill. Those guys and their friends helped me to get acclimated to California.

Within my first week of residency at Stinson Beach, I fought my first fire. I was lounging on the beach under a sunny sky, liberally applying Bain de Soleil to my skin, when the fire alarm sounded. I jumped up, grabbed my towel, and raced for my little house. Inside, I pulled a T-shirt and jeans over my bikini, put my hair up in a baseball cap, and grabbed the nearest pair of shoes—brand new, white Keds sneakers.

I reached the Stinson Beach Fire Station in less than a minute, and they assigned me to a crew riding in the tank truck. Winds had carried sparks down Mount Tam, igniting the madrone, chaparral, and manzanita. Now the slope angling down toward our town was in flames. Farther up, on the ridge, I could see the bigger fire. As we drew closer, the smoke filled my nostrils, and the air I breathed nearly scorched my lungs and sinuses. Suddenly, I caught a whiff of singed hair, and realized the shafts of silky white fuzz on my arms must've caught fire. "Hey! I'm sorry, this is my first fire. I was on the beach when the alarm went off, so I didn't have time to shower off the suntan oil." I felt silly, but fuck! How did I know? My training sessions were scheduled for the next week.

One of the firefighters tossed me a remnant of a terry cloth towel. "Here, wipe the oil off with this." I did as he said, grateful for a means of reducing my flammability.

The guy riding next to me gave me an old, long-sleeved shirt to wear. "It's okay, it's your first time out. You didn't know."

Those Stinson Beach firefighters proved totally badass. They parked the truck and hooked up a high-pressure hose. I saw guys strapping smaller, portable water tanks with attached hoses, onto their backs and marching into the fire, seemingly fearless. One guy, Todd, only had one arm, but he strapped that tank on and dominated. I hadn't yet been trained to handle the hose or wear a tank on my back, so they gave me a Pulaski, a tool that combines an axe and an adze, and set me to work chopping back brush to create a firebreak. Swinging an axe felt like swinging a machete, so I held my own.

After the blaze abated, my fellow firefighters showed me how to use the adze end of the tool to dig out the roots of the manzanita, madrone, and other vegetation. Manzanita is very dense and burns at an extremely high temperature for long periods of time, so the roots can stay hot enough to reignite the fire if they're not dealt with. I walked up and down the slope, digging up the roots of burned-out stumps, extinguishing any sparks that flared up. At one point, I plunged the adze-end of my Pulaski into a stump, and flames leapt up at me. The earth under my feet grew so hot that the rubber soles of my Keds began to melt. I promised myself that the next time I heard the fire alarm, I'd take time to find my work boots.

After that first fire, I attended two classes with the Stinson firefighters. One commenced at dawn, and we learned how to put out an electrical fire. The hands-on training involved setting fire to the ruins of a house on the seaside, then completely extinguishing the flames. I learned how to hold and aim the high-pressure hose. The second class, held in the early afternoon, demonstrated the correct way to load an injured person onto a stretcher, and how to properly load the stretcher into a harness for airlift via chopper.

I fell madly in love with the Pacific Ocean and Stinson Beach. But my love affair with Stinson ended when my landlord, a retired zoology professor from the University of California at Berkeley, died suddenly during a weekend vacation in Vancouver with his wife. His stricken spouse put the beach house, and the little guest cottage where I lived, on the real estate market. I searched in vain for a room or house to rent in Stinson Beach or nearby Bolinas, found all rentals occupied long-term. With Christmas approaching, and two weeks left to occupy my house at Stinson Beach, I drove my Sentra down the coast to L.A., and rented a room at the Tropicana Motel, 8585 Santa Monica Boulevard, for a week. The Tropicana, a funky favorite lodging of working rock bands and comedians, offered a rate of twenty-nine dollars and seventy-five cents a day, if you stayed for a week. At one point, singer and musician Tom Waits had taken up residency at the Trop for nearly three years. Arthur Cicchese had tipped me off to the rates, and the legend, of the Tropicana.

I strolled into the Improv wearing Calvin Klein Jeans, a red sweater, and my San Francisco Forty-Niners jacket, scanning the crowd for familiar faces. Suddenly I recognized Kevin Rooney, a favorite headliner at the Austin Comedy Workshop, and a friend of Jay and Mavis. Rooney stood talking with several others I didn't know. "Hey, Kevin!" I waved at him. Always a nice guy, he smiled and waved back. I headed for the bar, to get a drink.

Then I heard a man's voice call out, "Kevin!" in an exaggerated falsetto, mocking. I turned, saw the mimic was Robin Williams, standing beside Kevin Rooney. At first, I hadn't even noticed him. Smiling, confident, I walked straight over to the group of comedians gathered around Kevin. I figured the guys that didn't know me must've thought I was a groupie or fan. Standup comedy today is a heavily male-dominated field, but back then the ratio of men to women was even higher.

"Hey Kevin, how's it goin'?"

Kevin Rooney threw me a lifeline. "Hey, Marti." He turned to Robin Williams. "Haven't you met Marti? She's a standup comic, from Texas. She used to work in the oil field." He continued to introduce me around the circle. All of them seemed to be taken aback, especially Robin Williams. The way I figured it, my tall stature and oil field background possibly made me seem too badass. Or too butch.

I slapped on a smile. "Nice to meet you. Good to see you again, Kevin." I turned, strode to the bar, ordered a club soda. I knew that since Belushi died, working comics didn't drink on the job. And, as I learned from Leno, hanging out in a comedy club is part of the work.

"Excuse me, did you really work in the oil field?" I looked to my right, saw a smiling, well-dressed man. One of the guys talking to Kevin, I realized. For some reason, I couldn't remember his name, but felt sure he'd be a standup.

"Yeah, in Giddings, Texas. A big oil boom known as the Austin Chalk. I staked oil wells. On another job, I set off explosives for a seismic outfit, north of Houston. I didn't work on the oil rigs, though."

The guy smiled. "So, how'd you get into standup?"

"When the bottom dropped out of the oil business, I kinda stumbled into it." I laughed. "Almost literally stumbled. See, right before oil prices took a dive, my knee collapsed at work, and when I went to the doctor, they found this bone tumor in my knee joint. They rushed me into surgery. It was a fast-growing tumor, and the doc said if I hadn't come in when I did, I'd have been paralyzed from the knee down."

"Whoa! Was it cancerous?"

"No. Benign. But they found some pre-malignant tissue. Kinda woke me up to how fragile life can be. I saw a Chinese doctor last year, friend of a friend kinda thing. She recommended some Chinese herbs. I quit eating meat for months, too. According to Chinese medicine, that's got something to do with your life force."

We started talking about alternative medicine, and new theories about what might cause cancer. This guy was really nice, and as we conversed, I got the idea that he might know somebody currently fighting cancer. The subject seemed really important to him. I felt concerned for him. We began talking about positive mental attitude, and how it can affect the immune system. Robin Williams walked up beside us. I recognized Steven Wright standing there with him. Robin tapped me on the shoulder. I turned. He waved a hand toward the guy beside me. "Since you're a standup comic, I want you to know that this is THE man for the Tonight Show. He gave me my break."

The guy shut down for a second, so I figured he might actually be somebody important. Strangely, I felt annoyed at these comics for interrupting the spontaneity of our conversation. "I appreciate you guys lookin' out for me, but we're engaging in a serious conversation right now. Also, I just moved to California—I'm not ready for the Tonight Show yet!" I stopped, looked back and forth between Williams and Wright, then gazed directly into the face of the supposed guy from the Tonight Show. "And besides, how do I know you're not a motor home salesman from Nebraska, tryin' to get laid in this town?"

The guy from the Tonight Show burst out laughing. The bartender, a beautiful woman with long black hair, narrowed her eyes at the guy, in mock outrage. "Are you trying to use that old Tonight Show line again?"

The guy threw back his head and laughed some more. I turned to face him. "Hey, I'm gonna give you some up-to-the-minute dating tips, things they don't teach ya in the motor home school back in Nebraska. Get yourself one o' those little gold spoons, and wear it on a chain around your neck. That'll draw the chicks in." The guy kept on laughing. He reached for his card, tried to give it to me. I looked at the card. It said something like, "Jim McCawley, Talent Coordinator, The Tonight Show."

I gently pushed the card back toward him. "Let's just talk, I told you I'm not ready. Jim McCawley. Is that a Scottish name?"

"Yes, in fact, the tie I'm wearing is in my family's tartan plaid."

"My name is Marti MacGibbon, is that Scottish enough? My father's middle name is Duncan. Scottish with a bullet."

We shared a laugh. I liked Jim McCawley. We stood and talked for a long time, laughing a lot. Guys I didn't recognize, or only faintly recognized, sidled up to me—"Marti! Hi!"—and acted like long lost pals, trying to elbow their way to Mr. McCawley. I almost felt sorry for the guy—comics harassing him, trying to impress him all the time. Finally, I accepted his card and headed for the door.

As I drew near the threshold, Jim McCawley shouted after me, "Marti! Call me!"

Two days later, I picked up the phone in my room at the Tropicana, and called Mr. McCawley. His secretary answered. I asked to talk with him. "Who's calling, please?" I stated my name. Moments later, I heard Jim's voice.

"Marti, it's great to hear from you. I want you to come down to the Tonight Show. You can hang out backstage, and see how it works. Then, if you're up for it, I can get you onstage for a set at the Comedy and Magic Club in Hermosa Beach. I'd like to see you do a set."

"Okay. I'll need the addresses."

They filmed the Tonight Show in the afternoon, in front of a live audience, then broadcast it in the late night slot. I sat backstage in the green room, with Michael Keaton and Paul Rodriguez. After the show, Jim McCawley introduced me to Doc Severinson and Ed McMahon. McCawley asked me if I wanted to meet Johnny Carson. Across the room, Johnny stood talking animatedly to a cluster of adoring onlookers. I told Jim I didn't want to make a fuss. To this day, I can't figure out why I turned shy like that. Maybe it was because, when I was in junior high school, I had a big crush on Johnny Carson.

I left the studio and headed for Hermosa Beach. The Comedy and Magic Club was then, and is now, a premiere comedy club. During my ten-minute guest set, the laughs kept coming. As I exited amidst a round of powerful applause from the capacity audience, Gary Shandling stepped up to congratulate me. "Hey, great set! You weren't nearly as nervous as I was the first time I auditioned for Jim McCawley."

"Thank you. Do you think Mr. McCawley liked my set?"

"Yeah, he liked it. I was sitting beside him. He was laughing really hard. He's sitting in the back, having dinner. Go talk to him! I'm telling ya, you did great!!"

I walked to the back of the club to join McCawley. He told me he loved my material, my attitude, everything. "Marti, I want to put you on the show next week. You can sit on the couch and talk to Johnny about the oil field. You'll do your first appearance as a character, then perform later. That's what Bette Midler did, and she became a big star. You're the kind of character—natural, effortless—that people study in acting school for years to learn how to create onscreen."

"Thank you for the opportunity, but I want to wait till I'm ready, till I can go on the show and perform my material. Being a standup comic is an art, and when I get my break, I'll need to be ready for the road, right? I'm thinking long-term." I remembered what Jerry Portnoy told me, about how the art lives on through us, and how Leno told me not to underestimate myself.

Jim McCawley looked me in the eye. "Okay. Move down here to L.A. full-time, and we can groom you for your first Tonight Show appearance, Thursday December 5th, 1985. Can you do that?"

I smiled. "Yes! I can do that. Thank you!!" I stood up, walked out of the club, got into my car, and headed back to the Tropicana. Looking out at the big-city-bright-lights view of Los Angeles through the windshield of my Sentra, I felt ecstatic, entered a near-dreamlike state. *A year from now, I'll be in a very different place than I am today—a place I can't even imagine.* I dared to hope that when I did my Tonight Show and hit it big, maybe my ex would grant me joint custody rights. But even if he didn't, I'd have lots of money to spend on my daughter, and I could set up a trust fund for her, she'd never want for anything. I would leave her a legacy. And my art would live on.

As I reached Santa Monica Boulevard, and saw the Tropicana Motel looming up ahead, I thought about my childhood dreams of becoming a standup comic. My life journey between those dreams and this one had been riddled with potholes, wrong turns, and missed exits. But now my future opened up like a multi-lane superhighway; smooth, straight and bright. And I'd be focused on standing my ground—fierce, funny, and female.

THINGS I LEARNED DOING STANDUP THAT CAN HELP YOU MEET ANY CHALLENGE

HERE'S SOMETHING I LEARNED FROM YEARS OF PERFORMING standup in clubs, colleges, auditoriums, and a federal penitentiary: Standup is a metaphor for life. It's tough, thrilling, often painful, often fun, always rewarding. And in standup, as in life, there are myriad things that are completely beyond your control. You learn by trial and error, and discover how to think on your feet, making the best choices you can under pressure. And when—not if—you fail, you get back up onstage as soon as possible, knowing that the process will ultimately bring you success.

Okay, even though I think everyone would benefit from trying standup at least once in life, I realize that most people don't want to do it and never will. And that's perfectly cool. After all, somebody's got to sit in the audience and laugh, heckle, or get offended and walk out, right? But the biggest lessons I learned in my ten thousand hours or so of professional standup experience can help you to meet any challenge or obstacle in life.

Employ some or all of these techniques and principles and see where they take you. Here they are:

Stand Up. Respect yourself, take a position, stand up for what you believe in. When you know who you are and you like yourself, you can approach life's challenges with confidence. Build your character by taking on difficult projects and associating with people who are smarter, better, stronger and faster than you are. Never be afraid to present yourself as you are. Never underestimate yourself. Be honest, and have a point of view. Be bold. "Fortune sides with he who dares."—Virgil

Have Fun. This is a fantastic motivation for doing anything! If you're having fun and you're committed to your position, passionate about your process, no barrier can stand in your way—you'll be invincible. It may take some time to win, but if you keep re-energizing your sense of fun and passion, you will conquer.

Be Prepared. Timing is important, in standup and in life. Take time to prepare yourself well for any challenge or event. Stay healthy physically so you live in a state of strength and well-being. Work out at a gym and build your stamina. Study and research an upcoming project, and take time to plan carefully. After that, you can let yourself go with the flow. Learn to love rehearsal and preparation. Then you can be spontaneous, knowing you have structure and discipline to fall back on.

Never Take Yourself Too Seriously. Remember that life, like standup, is about the audience, i.e., everybody else. You'll always do best if you allow yourself to let go of self-centeredness and self-preservation. Toss your ego and its expectations out the window and focus on bringing your performance. Get out of your head and into the moment. Once you're in the moment, stay there, so you can think on your feet with precision.

Never Hang Back, Always Move Forward. Be Proactive. Audiences respond to confidence and like-ability. When you're onstage, always move toward the audience. Be ready to make friends, and don't anticipate adversaries. Optimism always pays off, and when you expect good things to happen, they are more likely to happen. Retreat is not an option. Radiate self-assurance, give yourself an inner pep talk, and muster your enthusiasm. Your energy will be contagious and others will go with your vibe.

Respect Others. Respect, but don't fear others. Never underestimate your audience, or your friends, family, associates or competitors. Refrain from taking anybody, or anything for granted. Start out your day with a moment of appreciation for the people you work with. Recognize and acknowledge the accomplishments of others and know that you are part of a greater reality.

Be Yourself. Let go of the urge to downplay who you are, or to overcompensate for any real or imagined flaw or weakness. Recognize that in the white hot truth, the reality of universal thought and consciousness, no one is above you, and no one is below you. You never have to try to impress anybody, or intimidate anybody, or play any games. Standup strips away everything but what's funny. Life strips away everything but what's real. So why feel like you've got to bullshit anybody or anything? You are enough, right now, as you are, and if you continue the brave work, you will continue to become more, and greater, exponentially. Trust in that, build your tenacity, and continue on your path, no matter the challenges.

Finally, remember that life, like comedy, is tough but fun. Focus too much on the tough and you break down. Focus on the fun and you win out. So have fun, be strong, and keep working it.

Marti MacGibbon doing standup, present day.

AUTHOR'S NOTE

IN A RAMSHACKLE BAR IN FLATONIA, TEXAS, A GRIZZLED OLD redneck swiveled on his barstool, sipping Shiner Bock and regarding me balefully. I avoided focusing on his glass eye as he rumbled, "'Dwell on the past an' y' lose one eye, fergit the past an' y' lose both.' That's an ol' Russian proverb, an' it's dead right." He tossed that zinger my way, then scowled as if daring me to dispute it. The old coot had a point. I gave a curt nod of agreement and bought him another round.

Personally, I refuse to dwell in the past, but know the value of remembering it. Look back, learn, and whenever possible, laugh— that's my motto. My memories aren't all sweet, but they're not boring, either. I was one of the first female laborers in the Texas Oil Patch. I worked in the historic oil boom known as the Austin Chalk from 1979 to 1983, and during those years I witnessed raging oil field fires, rigs exploding, and wild javelina striking terror in the hearts of stalwart, redneck, macho dudes.

I experienced bullets whizzing past my head and a few knock-down, drag-out fights. I bitch-slapped a whiny, racist misogynist co-worker, fended off sexual harassment—believe it or not, it was not yet illegal back then—developed expert technical skills, and advanced in my career due to my consistently superior job performance. All of this took place at a time when the gender war raged like a hurricane surging through the Gulf of Mexico.

The final section of this book segues into the arena of standup comedy. In 1983 I morphed from oil field worker to standup comic, clawing my way up through another male-dominated field to obtain a scheduled appearance on The Tonight Show with Johnny Carson.

I want to chronicle this period in my life, in part because I think it's important to record women's empowerment at a time when a lot of people seem to want females jettisoned back to the Eisenhower era. And that would be suck-tastic for men and women alike.

When I began seeking work in the oil field, I was reeling from the negative impact of a horrendous divorce—lost everything—and was struggling to muster my inner strength and find my purpose in life. Having survived sexual abuse and assault, I teetered on the brink of man-hating. But after working side by side with men in one of the last bastions of male supremacy, I came to recognize that men and women share the same fears, weaknesses, strengths, and motivations, and that we are all adrift in the same boat, so to speak.

Initially, I feared that working with men in a male-dominated field might render me less feminine, somehow, but during my years as "Oil Field Trash," I came to appreciate the best attributes of both male and female. I discovered more deeply what it means to be a woman. And I cultivated some of the most admirable male attributes within myself. I believe that this experience has given me a unique outlook on life and enabled me to relate to both men and women on a deeper, more comfortable level.

The Texas oil field taught me what it means to be badass: tough, unswerving, and willing to take risks. I believe that my experience working with, and keeping up with the Billy Bobs and Jimmy Joes of the world has been surprisingly enlightening—and a lot easier than I thought it would be.

Once I made my bones in the Texas Good Ol' Boy Mafia by demonstrating that chicks can kick ass, my supervisors hired a few more women. I'd smashed through gender barricades, oblivious to the uptight, stodgy old white men who ran the show in those days.

I believe this memoir is important and timely, because positive change is something to be celebrated, cherished, and always remembered. Tremendous social advances have taken place in America between 1980 and today. Back then, racism, sexism, homophobia, and xenophobia ran roughshod.

Things got a helluva lot better. As I write these words, Barack Obama, the first black President of the United States, has served two terms in office. And although we've yet to see a female chief executive, Hillary Clinton is the Democratic presidential nominee, and women consistently win elections to high positions in government. In 1980 these realities were only fantasies. But the price of liberty is eternal vigilance, if I may borrow an old white man's words, and these victories over bigotry must not be taken for granted or they will vanish like Lone Star beer down a drunken cowboy's gullet.

October 27, 2016

411

Marti MacGibbon, CADC-II, ACRPS, CAPMS, is a humorous inspirational speaker, a nationally award-winning author, and an expert on trauma resolution and addiction. She holds five professional certifications in her specialized field.

Few speakers have a personal comeback story as powerful and inspirational as Marti's. A popular keynote speaker who inspires, entertains, and empowers listeners, she's been interviewed in Investor's Business Daily and Entrepreneur, on ABC-TV, CBS-TV, FOX-TV and numerous radio stations.

As a national advocate for human trafficking victims and survivors, Ms. MacGibbon has shared her expertise at the White House and the State Department.

She is recipient of the IAIC Lifetime Recovery Advocate Award, for outstanding accomplishments in support of recovery and reducing the stigma surrounding addiction, mental illness, homelessness and human trafficking.

She has performed at the world famous Comedy Store and Improv in Hollywood, and has traveled the U.S. as a professional standup comic.

Marti married her true love, Chris Fitzhugh, and lives with him in California.